DECEPTIVE DISTINCTIONS

Deceptive Distinctions

Sex, Gender, and the Social Order

CYNTHIA FUCHS EPSTEIN

YALE UNIVERSITY PRESS
NEW HAVEN AND LONDON
&
RUSSELL SAGE FOUNDATION
NEW YORK

Published with assistance from the foundation established in memory of Calvin Chapin of the Class of
1788, Yale College.

Designed by Sally Harris
and set in Times Roman type and printed in the
United States of America by Vail-Ballou Press,
Binghamton, New York.

Library of Congress Cataloging-in-Publication Data

Epstein, Cynthia Fuchs.
    Deceptive distinctions : sex, gender, and the social
order / Cynthia Fuchs Epstein.
        p.   cm.
    Bibliography: p.
    Includes index.
    ISBN 0–300–04175–6 (alk. paper)
    1. Sex role—United States.   2. Sex differences
(Psychology)   3. Social structure—United
States.   4. Sexism—United States.
I. Title.
HQ1075.5.U6E67   1988
305.3—dc19   88–5717
                        CIP

The paper in this book meets the guidelines for permanence and durability of the Committee on Production
Guidelines for Book Longevity of the Council on Library Resources.

10   9   8   7   6   5   4   3   2   1

To those who provided the inspiration and support for this inquiry:

Margaret Olivia Sage

Colleagues at the Russell Sage Foundation, 1982–1988

Howard and Alex

WITHDRAWN

Since the world is so full of a number of things, . . . we must categorize and simplify in order to comprehend. But the reduction of complexity entails a great danger, since the line between enlightening epitome and vulgarized distortion is so fine.

Dichotomy is the usual pathway to vulgarization.

—Stephen Jay Gould, 1984a

In no country has such constant care been taken as in America to trace two clearly distinct lines of action for the two sexes, and to make them keep pace with the other, but in two pathways which are always different.

—Alexis de Tocqueville, 1835–40

Yet we as observers should know that the way sexuality and particularly rituals surrounding sex are used can tell us something not so much about sex per se as about the society.

—Mary Douglas, 1975

Contents

Preface

When Marshall Robinson, then president of the Russell Sage Foundation, invited me to write a book on the scholarship of gender research for the foundation's anniversary series, I was both elated and dismayed. I was delighted by the intellectual company: Charles Tilly, Otis Dudley Duncan, Lawrence Friedman, and Morton Hunt. But I was not sure I could adequately review the burgeoning research on gender. On the other hand, I knew I could bring the experience and overview of twenty years of research and study to the task.

As a relatively early explorer in the contemporary investigation of sex and gender roles, I was eager to take on the project because I had become concerned about certain theoretical frameworks in the social sciences and within the women's movement. In the face of an accumulating body of scholarship showing gender differences to be "social constructions" embedded in social structures and many so-called basic differences between men and women to be ephemeral, these frameworks assumed a "separatist" condition and conceived gender differences as inevitable and even desirable—a stance that seemed to me off course as well as inaccurate. My own theoretical works on these issues were obscured in the case studies that illustrated them. I published other articles expressing my point of view almost haphazardly in journals of merit but poor visibility. Here was my chance to speak my mind.

Unlike the other volumes in the series, this book, because of the nature of its subject, could not be written without a grand sweep of data and without crossing disciplinary boundaries. Arguments and critiques of theory and research on gender jump over disciplinary lines, making comparison difficult and forcing the "specialists" to be eclectic. Like all grand sweeps, this one focuses on certain areas of inquiry and bodies of research while passing others by. I could not analyze the sociological literature alone. I had to deal with sociobiology, because it has had a resurgence as an explanatory model for behavior and social organization. And I had to treat aspects of anthropology and psychology because the debates in these fields affect sociological explanation as well.

It was never my intention to write an encyclopedic work, and I have not done so. The proliferation of books and articles on gender issues over the past two decades has been dazzling. We know more about how social forces create gender distinctions than ever before, although those writers who believe gender distinction to be inborn dismiss much of this knowledge. Now, as before, gender research is replete with ideological overlays, reflecting the values of the scholar and of the social group.

I have aimed for objectivity in assessing the research, but I acknowledge a bias for equality. I believe my bias fits the evidence. Not all will agree. I hoped for comprehensiveness but have had to make do with selectivity and emphasis. Some of that selectivity was intentional, but I am also aware that I have not covered every base and have not mentioned every important work. I have not even covered every topic that could reasonably be included in such a work. Two such omissions stand out. First, I have not detailed the debates among various camps of feminist scholars: liberal feminists, socialist feminists, Marxist feminists, and so on. These have been reviewed ably by others (for example, Hester Eisenstein, 1983). In addition, I made the decision to consider many issues raised by these scholars in the course of discussing their place in social science analysis without attributing sectarian labels. Second, I have not emphasized issues of sexuality and sexual preference. Although some would argue that these are necessary for an analysis of gender distinctions, I believe they are only a piece of the story and are subsumed under the more general discussions of categorization and social arrangements of the sexes. Since I am not prepared to put forth a complete case for this view in this volume, I shall leave it at that, stating my intellectual bias, but also keeping an open mind.

I am aware that there may be several audiences for this book, including those who are suspicious of my claims and those who come to the work friendly but might leave it antagonized. I have made many judgments about many scholars' work, praising some and criticizing others. I have challenged the work of some whom I do not know and whose work I do not respect and of some whom I do know and whose work I do respect. I hope all these writers recognize that inquiry into problem topics is not a personal matter but an intellectual one.

I also have concern about a wider audience. When I began to do research and to write about problems of women, I was working in an atmosphere where equality of women and men in all social roles was prized and integration was a goal. Today, the notion of equal abilities and treatment of men and women is under attack, and even many feminists do not support the integration of men's and women's domains. Descriptions and prescriptions flow into each other in this world of scholarship. The political is not easily separable from the intellectual, even for those who feel that they ought to be—and of course may believe they are the same thing!

What looked like an emerging consensus in the mid-1970s that it was wrong to assign position and privilege automatically on the basis of ascribed characteristics has now become polarized around a number of axes. Scholars argue about the appropriate roles for women in every sphere of life, and some argue for entirely separate spheres. There are arguments about the role of the scholar, whether it is to describe and interpret or merely to accept methodologies and language used in the past.

In this book, I emphasize the role of people and institutions as active agents in setting goals and policy. Although the focus rests heavily on actions that create distinctions by which women have been disproportionately disadvantaged, the acknowledgments that follow indicate how the goals of institutions and the intentions of leaders and other participants in them can provide the best kind of environment for open inquiry.

Although I cannot name them all, many people have contributed to this work, and their contributions have been diverse. The genesis of the idea was Marshall Robinson's and grew out of the important effort of the Russell Sage Foundation to support a research program on Gender and Institutions. Robinson, then president of Russell Sage, and Peter de Janosi, vice president, provided the most facilitating environment a scholar could ask for through residency over the past six years at the foundation. They were also staunch advocates of the project and offered personal encouragement throughout. The support has continued under the presidency of Eric Wanner. A former officer of the foundation, Alida Brill, an architect of the Gender and Institutions program, also encouraged my efforts and facilitated the project. Her wide circle and knowledge were of great value to me as I cast my net across the social science community asking for wisdom, and, wearing her other hat, as a political scientist, she served as a good colleague in reviewing my work on political behavior. Harold Proshansky, president of the Graduate Center of the City University of New York, and the members of the sociology department there made it possible for me to maintain my residency at Russell Sage for an extended period of time; I appreciate their affirmation and support. At the foundation, the lunchtime and hallway conversations created the best kind of informal milieu contributing to evaluation of ideas and a new perspective.

I have also been fortunate to have had a short but very productive residency at the Virginia Center for the Creative Arts at Sweet Briar, Virginia, in 1984. A good portion of the first draft of this manuscript was accomplished there during a month uninterrupted by any obligation or responsibility save the task at hand. My thanks go to William Smart, director of the center, for this gift of time, resources, and peace.

The contribution of Claire Rappoport, who served as my research assistant for four years, was inestimable. Her training as an anthropologist, her ability to ferret out obscure works, and her talent at synthesis made her an integral part of the enterprise. Beyond that, she was an ever-willing and thoughtful colleague.

Two able assistants also created neat and organized manuscripts and a neat and ordered life at the foundation. Madge Spitaleri did so in the early days of the work. For the past three years, Dorrie Ackerman helped craft the manuscript with understanding and intelligence and offered crucial assistance of many other kinds.

A number of other generous people served as able readers and critics of particular chapters, including Orville Brim, Jr., Barbara Farah, Ruth Bader Ginsburg, William J. Goode, Patricia Gurin, Carol Jacklin, Kent Jennings, Alice Kessler-Harris, Mirra Komarovsky, Carol Tavris, David Tyack, and Elizabeth Hansot. Three anonymous referees also offered cogent and constructive commentary. I was inspired too by the long and thoughtful letters I received from a number of scholars in response to my request for guidance in identifying topics to be considered for this book. Among them were Helen Austin, Mariam Chamberlain, Cynthia Chertos, Lenore Davidoff, Bonnie Thornton Dill, Myra Dinnerstein, Beverly Guy-Sheftall, Lilli Hornig, Joan Huber, Carol Nagy Jacklin, Barbara Laslett, Laurie Lein, Marjorie Lightman, Elaine Marks, Gloria Orenstein, Phyllis Palmer, Letitia Anne Peplau, Bernice Sandler, Joan Scott, Barrie Thorne, and Irene Tinker.

But one name must stand out above all others in the honing of this book. Robert K. Merton took on the task of editing this volume, as he has the work of other Russell Sage scholars and several generations of social scientists scattered through the land. Merton's contributions to social science are well recorded in his published work. Myriads of students have also learned and applied the perspectives of his unpublished work, passed on in the oral tradition. Perhaps fewer know of his incredible gifts as an untiring and inspired editor. His challenge of the unfounded conclusion, the empty phrase, the uncovering of the writer's "tic"—in language and substance—is an experience to be enjoyed even as it causes some painful reexamination. I have been saved from many failings by Merton's critical eye.

My thanks for an expert final round of editing also go to Gladys Topkis, my editor at Yale University Press, and to Cecile Watters. Stuart Snyder and Letitia Rowe ably assisted in the search for information their keen observations demanded.

I also wish to acknowledge the ongoing editorial help and constant encouragement of Howard Epstein. An equal partner in all enterprises, he reinforces my belief that equity is not only manageable but a most pleasurable way to order life. My son, Alex, also provided encouragement, somewhat harsher and less tolerant of procrastination. The occasional criticism he offered was usually right on target.

Thus, I have benefited from the generous assistance and talent of many in my immediate and extended world. Of course, the deficiencies that remain are my own.

DECEPTIVE DISTINCTIONS

CHAPTER 1

Introduction:
Sex and the Social Order

This book was begun with the aim of reporting and assessing the recent surge in scholarship on gender in the social sciences, most particularly in sociology. It has since become more than that. Immersion in this vast sea of research materials and investigation of the social context in which they were created have produced a perspective that orders the book and makes its own claims.

Research on gender over the past fifteen years has been oriented toward rectifying the exclusion or misrepresentation of women as subjects in previous research. Much past research that claimed to be valid for all people was conceived and executed from an androcentric perspective and must therefore be reconsidered. Sociology, like political science, economics, philosophy, and psychology, has been blind or biased in its vision of women for decades. The roles of women were neglected or misrepresented in all these disciplines. Assessments of human behavior could be described most charitably as incomplete and often wrong.

When the study of work and behavior was limited to men, we were given only partial knowledge of the worlds of politics, the economy, and religion. With research thus limited in scope, even the family, regarded as "women's sphere," was misrepresented and misevaluated because of inattention to *male* participation. Other men's roles too were stereotyped and misrepresented, although the consequences probably were less costly for men as a group than for women. Thus, insights into human nature were skewed by the tendency to perceive separate spheres and separate characteristics and qualities for men and for women. Much of the "research" conducted within these models served to rationalize and justify inequality, and even helped create it.

It has not been possible to learn much about women or men, much less

1

the society, from the myopic views offered by most social philosophers and the social scientists who continue in their tradition. Indeed, the most searing critique a radical and feminist challenge has produced questions the very organization and value structure of science and the knowledge-seeking and creating industry.

Neglect or misinterpretation of women by the social sciences and the attendant damage done to women and the various disciplines themselves go far back in social thought. Respected scientists and philosophers made women the victims of incorrect assessments of their natures, psyches, or "proper place." In *Women in Western Political Thought* (1979), Susan Moller Okin describes how the suppression of women's rights has been legitimized since the Golden Age of Athens, despite social philosophers' arguments for the rights of individuals in general. Thinkers from Aristotle and Rousseau to Talcott Parsons and Erik Erikson in our day have argued that women not only differ from men but are not as equipped mentally and physically to function in the spheres of society in which men predominate, such as the sciences and the creative arts. Curiously, confidence in women's ability to perform "male" tasks such as governing or decision making, clearly expressed by Plato and by John Stuart Mill, has received less attention than these philosophers' other ideas. By some ironic twist of logic in the evolution of ideas, "might" has made "right." The intellectual gatekeepers have reinforced the ideas that supported the established hierarchy and retained the power to define, a power women have been unsuccessful in attaining up to the present. Even among those who argued for a value-free social science, many have allowed prejudice to blind them to the bias in their own experiments and observations.

It is sometimes difficult to identify the ideological implications of perspectives in social science and to understand why a particular viewpoint gains currency or persists at a given time. Why do certain ideas survive and others die? What makes the time right for the acceptance of some ideas and not others, and what can we say about who controls the flow of ideas?

Through the sociology of knowledge and science we have learned something about the diffusion of ideas, the ways in which they are adopted by the culture as well as by elite and scientific networks, and also about resistance to discovery and new ideas, even among scientists. Some believe that the truth will win out and that reason guides thought, that enlightenment is a function of a modern outlook which all will achieve in time. Yet reason is not a modern commodity, nor is intellectual intransigence an attribute only of primitive life.

In the competition of ideas, the rule of reason has not had many successful advocates where women are concerned. The quality of an idea is supposed to take precedence over majority rule in science, but one wonders whether the number of advocates influences the survival of an idea. Among modern philosophers, John Stuart Mill (1869) stands out as a supporter of the equality of women and as one who understood the causes of their observably different behavior and presumed different nature.[1] Mill recognized what most modern social scientists missed until the 1970s—and some still miss: how biases prevent the formulation of objective descriptions of women's behavior and motivations. He questioned the stereotypes of women and pointed out how the same behavior was at times labeled differently when demonstrated by a man than when enacted by a woman. "All [women] who infringe on any of the prerogatives which man thinks proper to reserve to himself," he wrote, "are called masculine, and other names intended to convey disapprobation" (Mill, 1824: 526). He thus inquired why what was considered meritorious in a man was considered a failing in a woman, so that, for example, independence was prized in a man, but helplessness of body and mind in a woman. Yet, according to Mill, such prized behavior in women was taken as evidence that they were innately and irremediably inferior in ability to men (Okin, 1979).[2]

Mill discounted the notion that characteristics attributed to women, such as unselfishness and restraint, were fundamental to their "nature." He explained women's tendency to be dependent or passive, for example, not as the manifestation of a female trait but as the consequence of circumstances that encouraged women to act and feel dependent.[3] Instead of focusing on social conditions and situations that may have affected wom-

---

1. Mill collaborated with Harriet Taylor (who became his wife) for more than twenty years. He wrote his major statement on the equality of women, "The Subjection of Women," in 1861—three years after she died. But, as Alice Rossi points out (1970), it is doubtful that the essay would have been written had it not been for the role Harriet Taylor played in his personal and intellectual life. The ideas formulated in the essay were discussed during the two decades of intimacy and intellectual collaboration between the two, and Mill freely acknowledged her influence. He also credited "some important ideas" to Helen Taylor, Harriet Taylor Mill's daughter by a previous marriage (Rossi, 1973). As Rossi further points out, Mill was probably also affected by the thinking on sex equality in the two main social circles within which they moved, the Unitarian radicals and the philosophic radicals. Both Harriet Martineau and Mary Wollstonecraft were Unitarian intellectuals who had written proposals for women's education.

2. This process was later defined by Robert K. Merton as a "damned if you do, damned if you don't" mechanism by which "in-group virtues become out-group vices"—used by members of in-groups such as white Protestant men to maintain their advantage over out-groups such as blacks and Jews (Merton, 1957).

3. In Mill's words, "even the least contestable of the differences that now exist, are such as may very well have been produced merely by circumstances, without any difference of rational capacity" (1869:11).

en's behavior, some social scientists well into the mid-twentieth century still echoed Rousseau's claim that women have a kind of intellect different from and inferior to that of men and lack the capacity for abstract reasoning and creativity.[4] "Reason in women is a practical reason, which enables them easily to discover how to arrive at a given conclusion, but which does not enable them to reach the conclusion themselves; . . . the search for abstract and speculative truths, for principles, for axioms in science, everything that involves the generalization of ideas, is not within a woman's province" (Rousseau [1762], in Okin, 1979: 131). The human capital school of economic thought today explains the disproportionate employment of women as clerical workers and unpaid housekeepers as being due to women's interests and preferences rather than to factors in social organization that keep women from opportunity tracks and limit their access to a broad range of employment.

Not only have the traits and characteristics of women been conceptualized so as to rationalize their state of subordination, but many recent studies in the social sciences have ignored them altogether. Some analysts see this omission as a problem integral to the organization of the social sciences (A. Rossi, 1973), as we shall discuss later. Others have noted the distorted vision created by existing models in science (Lewontin, Rose, and Kamin, 1984). There is no doubt, however, that general cultural bias, which has defined women's realms and behavior as relatively uninteresting or insignificant compared to those of men, has also defined them as less important to scientists as objects of research attention. Scientists, after all, wish to study the important problems of life and to determine the causes of important phenomena. Since women have been defined by the culture as not being engaged in important activities, or as being merely reactive to policies and viewpoints set by men rather than expressing their own ideas, study of them has ranked low in most disciplines.

For a very long time, then, scientists have not contributed much to the understanding of social reality with regard to gender distinctions. Too many of them have accepted the vision of reality that prevailed in the cultures in which they lived. They have tended to find support and justification for gender distinctions and inequality rather than to locate the sources of these distinctions and understand their dynamics. In this sense, scientists have also been active agents perpetuating distinctions based on mainstream cultural viewpoints.

4. These perspectives have been criticized from many sources, one of which is the "dialectics of biology group," whose work has come to notice recently in their attacks on biological determinism, sexism, and racism in the sciences (described in Lewontin, Rose, and Kamin, 1984). Members of this group dispute the arguments of the sociobiologists, who hold that differences between social groups such as blacks and women are established by brain size or hormones.

Even intellectual divisions, locating men's and women's spheres and identifying masculine and feminine traits, have been accepted by scientists directly from the general culture. As Pierre Bourdieu has pointed out, "The division of reality is a serious struggle." Some people create divisions according to their point of view. The divisions people create also locate them in social space. But there are also contests between points of view. The ensuing "struggles over social reality," a classification struggle, is a political struggle in that it is a contest to decide what will become the legitimate vision of the world institutionalized in social structure.[5] Only with shifts in power, the entry of women into the scientific establishment, and their political mobilization have women been able to challenge the mainstream models promulgated in the institutions of society, including science.

This book, then, is an inquiry into the sociology of knowledge and, as such, is both a critique of the scientific analysis of gender distinctions and an evaluation of what science has contributed to progress in understanding. It aims to identify the work that has put women back into the analysis of society. It reviews attempts to correct impaired perspectives on women and their nature, including the notion that they are a breed apart from men. It also attempts to place these efforts in the larger scientific, social, and political context. Finally, it reviews certain aspects of the critique of the sciences offered today and points to issues in gender studies that provide the opportunity to reanalyze ongoing paradigms in the sciences.

The book also offers a theoretical orientation to the understanding of gender distinctions, one that underscores the interaction of culture and social structure in creating and maintaining these (and other) distinctions. This orientation emphasizes the investments people and institutions have in the social arrangement of men and women and the conscious and intentional quality of the decisions and behavior that perpetuate it; it also explores the more amorphous processes by which conceptual and actual boundaries are formed.

What Is Gender and Why Study It?

Ten years ago this book would have been labeled a study of sex differences and similarities. Today scholars use the word *sex* to refer to attri-

---

5. These quotes are taken from a lecture given by Pierre Bourdieu at the Graduate Center of the City University of New York on April 21, 1987. The perspectives are spelled out in his books: *Outline of a Theory of Practice* (1972. London, New York, and Melbourne: Cambridge University Press, 1977), and *Distinctions: A Social Critique of the Judgment of Taste* (1979. Cambridge, Mass.: Harvard University Press, 1984).

butes of men and women created by their biological characteristics and *gender* to refer to the distinctive qualities of men and women (or masculinity and femininity) that are culturally created (Oakley, 1972). This is how these concepts will be used in this book.

In the context of today's thinking and research on sex and gender differences and similarities, however, even the choice of concept entails an intellectual commitment. Not all people nor all scientists believe that biological and social differences can be separated. Some believe that they are intertwined, and others that the social is an outgrowth of the biological. This is not merely a matter of disciplinary boundaries. Some social scientists lean toward biological explanations, and some biologists regard biologically deterministic paradigms as wrong, as we shall see in chapter 3.

The study of gender is remedial not only in that it attempts to add women to studies that have been done of men. The study of women and their relations with men is also necessary in order to reconsider stereotypes about men and the ways in which social systems work. It raises questions about the ways in which we think about the social order and hierarchy. It has also raised anew the age-old issue of biological determinism.

From one point of view the analysis of gender is as large as the world. Gender distinctions are basic to the social order in all societies. Like age, gender orders society and is ordered by it. Only by some social arrangement (ordering) between the sexes can societies reproduce, and certainly a concern for reproduction constrains the way in which social groups regard the sexes. Nevertheless, some societies place more emphasis on ordering the sexes than others, although none ignores it.

All societies provide an explanation for the distinctions between the sexes, and because biologically based sexual dimorphism is a simple, visible basis of differentiation, it tends to be used as a major rationale. No respected scholar argues that sexual or other biological factors are not relevant to human behavior, but, as Stephen Jay Gould (1984b) warns, the problem is how to distinguish between biological determinism, a theory of limits, and biology viewed as a range of capacities, a theory of "biological potentiality." We must also ask why men and women are classified in the social order in ways unrelated to their biological differences and biological functioning—that is, by their intellectual, moral, and emotional makeup. We also should identify the ways in which only the female sex is identified in terms of biology while members of the male sex are regarded as social beings.

Social scientists, like social philosophers before them, have contemplated the ordering of society based on sex and have either explained it as organic and necessary to life or questioned it as a creation of human society subject to chance, convenience, self-interest of the powerful, or aesthetic complementarity. And social scientists, like social philosophers, have been biased and blinded because of the difficulty of considering models different from those they experience directly as actors in a particular social order, learning a heritage of scientifically "acceptable" work that taints their analytic ability.

Social scientists are motivated not only by questions of pure science—learning about the social order and how it is created and maintained—but also by questions of ideology. Many are dissatisfied with explanations of the social order which assert that what exists is rooted in biology and neither can nor should be changed. They have asked age-old questions, such as whether human nature is responsible for inequality and injustice.

We have not come far toward achieving consensus on how to define a human being and ascertaining the limits and possibilities of human nature. Some theologians argue that humans have souls and are born evil or good. Scientists believe that people have egos or selves. They disagree about how much arrives with the body at birth and how much is created or modified by individual decisions or social exposure. Scientists know that the brain is necessary for intellectual functioning and that people's ability to think may be impaired by disease or damage to the brain. But they do not know (although some speculate) whether the brain creates attitudes like love or tolerance with the stimulation of social exchange. The arrangements of our chromosomes and cells are also considered agents of human nature. We have no evidence to establish that criminals (or kind people or con artists) are born, although some scientists, from Cesare Lombroso, founder of the school of criminal anthropology in the late nineteenth century (S. Gould, 1981), to the criminal cytogeneticists of the 1970s (Lewontin et al., 1984), maintain they are (see Jacobs et al., 1970; Pyeritz et al., 1977). We believe we know that some people are born more quick-witted than others, but it remains difficult to measure the impact of environment on intelligence. According to the speculation of some sociobiologists, such as Barash (1979), E. O. Wilson (1978), and Dawkins (1976), genetic inheritance accounts for any number of social traits, from nurturance to aggression, dominance to submission, altruism to selfishness. Investigation of these connections has often rationalized the position of the privileged, many of whom are convinced that their place in the world is appropriate to their capacity and that others are made of different and lesser stuff. Thus analytic distinctions that define people by type or characteristic inevitably create classes or categories in which one group is regarded as superior to another. Some scientists argue that not all such distinctions are invidious, but they would be hard put to locate many that are not.

Different visions of human nature have abounded throughout history. Most have not stood the test of logic and scientific inquiry. Assumptions about the essential natures of men and women have also been integrated into the common culture, philosophic thought, and social institutions.

The social sciences, like the church and the polity, have searched for a logic underlying the distinctiveness of or similarities among people. The church has asked, "Are we not all God's children?" Statesmen have asked, "Are we not all created equal?" And social scientists have asked, "What is the source of human diversity and inequality?" The way the question is asked has had serious effects on the inferences drawn from the inquiry. Some questions heighten differences, others focus on similarities, as we shall see. The questions have also at times resulted in different agendas. Churches and governments have had interests in promulgating one perspective or another, and the policies they have set have affected scientific inquiry. This has occurred at many levels, from the location of the university in the church in medieval times to the offering of patronage and grants to some kinds of inquiry and not others. Within these institutions, distinction-making agendas have been set in an attempt to define social reality. Some of these clearly have had the intent to control; others have resulted from historical patterns of control which created a social reality leading to the "objective" distinctions that reflect this "reality" (Bourdieu, 1977). Thus, sometimes it is the fit between categorization and function that is reported, although the fit may have been intentionally created long ago, the causal policies may be long forgotten, and the categorization may be unrelated to function or any other facet of reality.

Thus, visions of human nature have sometimes been consonant with reality, but at other times they have been believed although they were quite contrary to experience. Certainly, powerful people have the authority to impose their version of reality more effectively than those who have no resources to command attention. But as people's and groups' fortunes rise and fall, and circumstances permit or conceal reality testing, visions of reality also change.

Because men in the church and in governments as far back as we can recall have held greater resources than have women, it is their version of human nature that has been most evident. Furthermore, their version has been adopted by most women as well as men. And first and foremost in this spectrum of beliefs has been the insistence on the basic and pervasive difference between men and women—that reproductive differences should be the main basis for the classification of all traits.

Thus, most models of women have been inconsistent with models of Man, the generic category. And, not surprisingly, models of women have been as misinformed as the historic conceptions of human nature. Further, there is a discrepancy between models of women and the more general models of mankind—for example, the competitive animal Hobbes depicted as characteristic of Man in nature. And models of women's nature have been more readily accepted and less subject to critical review through the ages.

It is distressing to learn that many scientists make judgments about the nature of men and women without much more systematic evidence than the philosophers of the past, who, after all, had little scientific information available and were constrained by theological doctrine and popular belief. Of course, a commitment to the scientific method is relatively recent among students of human nature. By scientific method I mean nothing more than a commitment to consider any evidence that emerges, even though it may prove the theory wrong (Popper [1935] 1959). "Commonsense" experience was the test of theories of the past, and as common sense usually is based on limited experience, many theories of human nature ultimately have turned out to be wrong when tested adequately.

If large-scale theories of human nature have had poor empirical confirmation, theories about women's nature have had even less. I believe there are compelling reasons for this. First, it is difficult for members of any social order to question their own order and not regard it as necessary for the continued functioning of social life. Second, social structure makes some kinds of thinking and knowing easier than others.[6] Third, because gender distinctions are a basic element in the creation of the social order— and because those distinctions are typically stratified, with men at higher ranks—men have a stake in justifying and continuing the status quo. Challenges to a social order do not typically come from those who benefit from its arrangements. As Mary Douglas (1984) notes, "A . . . social order generates its pattern of values, commits the hearts of its members, and creates a myopia which certainly seems to be inevitable." Science is not immune to this, and scientists' "thoughts are held in the grip of social

---

6. Mary Douglas (1984) points out how the social organization of the Nuer tribe helps individuals remember as many as eleven generations of their ancestors. She suggests that such learning is motivated by the Nuers' need to prove kin links to the right ancestor to obtain the cattle they require in order to marry.

order.'' Whether consciously or unconsciously, from the time gender distinctions were made, and from the time they were made invidious, the social order generated a system of thought that legitimated gender inequality. Agents of the social order, people with a stake in it and people persuaded by them, are the insiders.

The powerful are the gatekeepers of ideas (to use Lewis Coser's term), the owners of intellectual production, who can affix and have affixed values to distinctions between men and women. In those cases where distinctions would not exist without intervention, they can create distinctions through coercion and other obvious forms of enforcement or through the more subtle use of such mechanisms as the self-fulfilling prophecy (Merton, 1957), by which people are pressured, persuaded, and directed to behave according to the expectations of others.

Sociobiologists, like social philosophers, churchmen, and others before them, argue that the division of labor by sex is a biological rather than a social response. But if this were so, sex-role assignments would not have to be coercive. Social groups do not depend on instincts or physiology to enforce social arrangements because they cannot reliably do so. Societies make it the responsibility of people from certain groups to be responsible for such social needs as food, shelter, child care, and leadership. Nowhere do they depend on ''nature'' to get the jobs done. The range of work that men and women do in each society is stipulated by that society, and few individuals are permitted to choose outside the approved range. These assignments are justified on the basis of ideologies and popular cultural opinions that maintain the assignments are just and the arrangement is good (or that, if not, little can be done about it). Such ideologies and popular views, in other words, suppose that a fit exists between job and worker—a fit that makes sense. This argument relies on the maintenance of gender differences and usually on hierarchical categories. Thus, division according to sex is reinforced by requirements that men and women dress differently, learn different skills, and engage in different forms of activity—and violators are severely punished.

The literal binding of women's feet or constraint of their minds by law and social custom, however, is only part of the process by which the gender division of human beings perpetuates a two-class system. The hierarchy is kept in place more subtly by the insistence that people behave as society's opinion molders say they should. Gender distinctions are made on the basis of ideal types (or archetypes), in Max Weber's sense. They may correspond to a piece of reality or they may be a proposal or a plan for reality. They often mask a fundamental similarity in personalities, behavior, and competence. Values have always played a part in the sifting and sorting of ideas. Men individually and collectively have had an interest in justifying the second-class status of women until recently. Although there have been notable exceptions, men with resources have used them to bar alternative views. Furthermore, women, individually and collectively, have often been persuaded or pressured to accept these views.

A preference for dichotomous thinking in many (if not most) social groups facilitates the dissemination of such ideas. This model, as Simone de Beauvoir (1949) has written, casts men as the norm and women as the "other," possessing traits opposite to those attributed to men.

How can we explain the acceptance of theories that so deviate from reality?

Categorization and the Social Order

Consider the kind of analysis that focuses on distinctions between the sexes. Human reason makes it possible to make categories of discrete things and events in nature and in social life. Developing concepts that group things and events is economical and practical. But, as we know, people often treat concepts as real even though in fact they are only representations of real things. Since humans also make value judgments, they organize and create categories and often reorganize them according to these perceptions and interpretations.

Usually the organizing principles individuals use have a basis in logic and refer to empirical reality. Thus persons of all cultures usually categorize as the same or similar things that look alike or are alike in function. Tangible things like apples and grapes, trees and plants, are relatively easy to group, but people also create concepts for categorizing intangibles, such as friends and political groups. In both cases, they sometimes bend logic and deny empirical reality. For example, in some societies people define food we know to be nutritious as taboo and therefore inedible; in some societies harmful acts, such as scarification during puberty rites, or clitoridectomies, are declared to be desirable and necessary. In others, dead men are declared the fathers of children delivered by their widows more than nine months after the men's death.

Categories also may be based on only one or a few of the attributes of the discrete items being grouped. Thus a person may be part of a category by virtue of one attribute, such as age, but not on the basis of another, such as ethnicity. All men are brothers by one logic, but by another they

are all competitors for rank and resources. Particulars are denied or overlooked in each categorization. To believe that all men are brothers, one
must overlook their differences; to believe they are competitors, one must
ignore their similarities and common interests. The extent to which people
attribute qualities and capacities to the two sexes is an example of how the
concepts ''male'' and ''female'' cause the sorting and skewing of perceptions of reality by a focus on differences rather than similarities. Often
these distinctions are based on very slim evidence.

The Social Order Creates ''Nature''

Yet interpretation has a certain power to make categorization real. As we
can make friends into enemies by insisting that their friendly overtures are
attempts to colonize or co-opt us, and as we can cause the young to behave
immaturely by denying them the power to act on decisions, so societies
make men and women different by giving them different education and
work and by denying that when they do the same jobs they are doing them
the same way or by holding that when they accomplish the same goals
they have not done so. And, as some peoples insist against all evidence
that they are civilized but others are barbarians, so men (and women) have
long insisted that the other sex is more or less civilized, human, competent, and so on.

A full investigation of the social, cultural, and psychological reasons
for humans' conceptualization of dichotomous distinctions—good/bad, dark/
light, and of course, masculine/feminine—and the fact that values are usually given to categories that could be logically regarded as neutral (soft/
hard; tall/short) is beyond the scope of this book. But it is important to
note that many cultural and social investments are made to reinforce the
continuity of this kind of thinking. Since polar sex distinctions (what is
female is not male and vice versa) belong to the class of dichotomous
distinctions, it is useful to step back for a moment to consider the general
functions of such distinctions.

First, it is important to note that the preference for dichotomous categorization exists. It may be that such thinking is more economical, rewarding, seductive, or just easier in that mutually exclusive categories are
parsimonious and even aesthetic.[7] Of course, ambiguities may capture the

7. Of course, the duality of self and other has always been recognized. It can be found in
tribal and ''primitive'' cosmologies in the form of their ancient mythologies. Often it serves to
explain or label phenomena that are different, foreign, or otherwise inexplicable in terms that are
understandable—that is, that bear relation to one's own existence.

imagination of poets and create literature, but the ambiguity created by a transsexual person or a homosexual or even by the use of gutter language by an English Ph.D. is difficult to tolerate for most people, who find comfort in consistency and punish those who deviate from its practice. Closure, as well as clarity, seems paramount in the reinforcement process toward mutually exclusive categorization.

But even to attribute the tendency to dichotomize to such needs and propensities is plainly unsatisfactory, since social groups do not leave role assignments and ideological foundations to chance. Closure is not merely a logical extension of human nature but is insisted upon and enforced by a structure of prescribed dogmas and rules which compel belief. Certainly both Western and Eastern philosophic[8] and religious[9] systems provide ideological foundations for these beliefs and so do scientific modes of thought. One could argue in a Durkheimian mode (Durkheim, 1915) that societies have self-maintenance mechanisms and that distinctions based on polarities such as heaven and hell, sacred and profane, good and bad—perhaps even male and female—serve these functions.

Anthropologists have contributed much to these discussions. Ortner (1974) has explored the possibility that the female-male contrast is a metaphoric transformation of an allegedly universal nature-culture contrast (MacCormack and Strathern, 1980). Lévi-Strauss attributes the transition from nature to culture to the capacity to distinguish between "us" (as a kin category) and "other," leading to the creation of rules in favor of exogamous marriage and against incest. Thus he maintains that we can achieve a Rousseauian social contract, giving up the state of nature for reciprocating non-kin ties. Unlike most of the other basic requirements for individual survival, procreation, which is necessary to maintain society as a whole, demands paired opposites, male and female. In an extension of this observation, Lévi-Strauss has claimed that the foundation of social structure is the human capacity to build a perception of the world by perceiving opposites or contrasts (1978: 22–23). For Lévi-Straussian structuralists this tendency toward contrasts is unconscious, much as any power struggle may be unconscious. Yet elsewhere Lévi-Strauss (1969: xxix, cited in MacCormack and Strathern, 1980) does suggest that the nature-culture contrast is a creation of culture.

A number of writers have examined the nature/culture distinction in

8. In Western philosophic thinking this traces to both Pythagoras's concept that all things are composed of contraries and Plato's notion that any object is composed of the tangible object as well as the perfect conception of that object. In analytic thought, polarity is rooted in the dictum that every statement has a corollary—its negation.
9. Certainly Pauline Christianity.

various societies and analyzed its ideological consequences for women, since women are usually associated with nature and men with culture. The latter usually implies control or superiority over nature, but this distinction is by no means universal, for it depends on each society's particular characterization of nature as, for instance, wild or orderly. The philosophes of the eighteenth century, especially Diderot, entangled mechanistic physiological theory with social and moral considerations. These writers, rejecting the corrupt mores of French society, saw a return to nature as a move toward freedom. Their view of women, although correspondingly positive, was essentially conservative; women's role in civic and social reform was to become better mothers, and Rousseau urged the importance of breastfeeding to that end. Under whatever auspices, the association of women with nature and therefore, by anatomical analogy, with child care has long provided an excuse for excluding them from the political realm.

Anatomical sex characteristics, such as the physiological correlates of age, provide a framework to which cultures can attach a broad range of social differences that in fact have little to do with anatomy. But gender differences are only one aspect of the larger scheme of conceptual ordering based on dichotomous distinctions. Not only have such polarities become part of the common culture; they have been integrated into systems of scientific thought supposedly designed to be free of illogical distinctions.

Some feminist academics, notably in France, argue that science constitutes a masculine mode of thought, reflecting the order of the "outside" structures of system and hierarchy. Defining "reason" and "logic" according to masculine/feminine opposites, such critics merely repeat what men, whose thinking they deplore, have traditionally propounded. This has, alas, affected some modes of feminist scholarship in the United States and Europe which, like the biased research of the past, focus on the small differences between the genders rather than on the large similarities found in human behavior and therefore conclude that men and women are essentially different.

This error has led to two faulty assumptions. First is the assertion that feminine/masculine distinctions in addition to the biological reproductive apparatus have an empirical reality, and second, that the distinctions are also ranked. Most dichotomous conceptual pairs are linked to qualitative distinctions—for instance, good is better than bad, and beautiful better than ugly; thus male is better than female or, among feminists who think in terms of polarities, female is better than male.

An insistence that gender differences are rooted in the most basic nature of men and women still colors the work of respected scholars in such disciplines as economics, sociology, psychology, and the hybrid field of sociobiology.

In subsequent chapters, we will see how dichotomous distinctions may rationalize and provide the basis for social arrangements in such institutions as work (chapter 7), politics (8) and the family (9). Chapter 10 looks at how symbolic distinctions compel gender distinctions or obscure similarities.

It is no surprise that dichotomous models are an ideological weapon and survive challenge because it it easier to propose a dichotomy than to explicate the complexities that make it invalid. Changing historical circumstances and even social survival needs in a world threatened by conflict require different peoples to become ever more dependent on one another. Such conditions demand that leaders and intellectuals possess the ability to appreciate complexity and ambiguity, to reason in terms of ranges and dimensions of theory rather than discrete qualities. One might argue: as technological progress makes people more and more dependent on science, it is science whose rational rigor provides the tools to reject the vast number of oversimplified dichotomies.[10]

Dichotomous thinking has been integrated into scientific thought along with other models that have feedback effect on political and social ideology. But this book could not have been written unless science, for all its inadequacies, left room for challengers and we did find out, initially from dissenters and eventually from the establishment, what Robert K. Merton (1984a) has observed: that "what everyone knows to be true often turns out not to be true at all."

Today scholars are asking questions about the social arrangements of the sexes, in part because powerful changes in the behavior of men and women and the decay or violation of old rules have called the traditional conceptions and models into question. The overwhelming evidence created by the past decade of research on gender supports the theory that gender differentiation—as distinct, of course, from sexual differentiation—is best explained as a social construction rooted in hierarchy, not in biology or in internalization, either through early experiences, as described by psychoanalysts, or through socialization, as described by psychologists and sociologists. Not that these processes have no effect. Rather,

10. I am grateful to Alexander Epstein for this point.

the accumulating evidence suggests that the wide variations in behavior in all societies'through history are due primarily to social construction and that the division of the world by sex is an ideal construct.

Much of the research reported in this book points to the continuous work that must be done in society to differentiate the sexes and to perpetuate inequality between them. This effort, as the research documents, must be made on both the micro and the macro level, by separating the sexes physically and making distinctions between them symbolically and conceptually and thus intruding in the relationship they might otherwise have if there were no rules (or different rules) of conduct and no mechanisms of enforcement emphasizing the differences between them.

This book investigates in chapter 2 the ways in which ideas—culture or ideology—have infiltrated the studies and methods of social scientists and how the selection of certain research methods has resulted in findings that give us a distorted view of the ''truth'' about the division of society by sex. Chapter 3 is a critique of the explanations of biological determinists, who attribute psychological and social characteristics of men and women to physiological causes.

I consider changing and unchanging perspectives regarding women's and men's cognitive and emotional capacities in chapter 4. Chapter 5 offers through a sociological framework an analysis of the division of society by sex, and outlines general principles and processes of social organization based on a cultural structural analysis. Chapter 6 focuses on processes of social control by the state and through social policies in other institutions.

Greater detail regarding the analysis of several major institutions is supplied in the following chapters: the workplace and the stratification system (chapter 7), the political system (chapter 8), and the family (chapter 9). Chapter 10 looks at the way symbolic segregation compels gender distinctions or obscures similarities in everyday behavior, in verbal and nonverbal behavior, in social custom, and in manners.

The conclusion offers a tentative theory to explain the perpetuation of gender distinctions and its consequence, gender inequality, in society.

CHAPTER 2

A Question of Method: The Sociology of the Scientific Analysis of Sex and Gender

Institutionalized Biases in the Social Sciences

S cientific analysis of gender distinctions has removed the old blinders from scholars but given them new ones. Before we scan the vast literature on gender issues, an appraisal of outlooks and critiques is in order. The most virulent charge by feminist scholars against mainstream social scientists has been one of bias. But that seems too general a term. Bias on gender issues in the social sciences stems not only from ideological and epistemological perspectives about the nature of the division of society by sex but also from the analytical problems and social structures of the social sciences themselves. There are the biases linked to prejudices against women and cultural notions emphasizing differences between the sexes and also the biases built into perspectives and models in science, which have their own values and sets of assumptions. These are not easily separated. We shall, however, review some of the debates and evaluate the merits of the respective arguments, as well as locate those endemic problems that come from the scientific establishment itself.

Male Bias: Neglect and Distortion

Scholars in the feminist community have criticized the social sciences for their neglect of women as objects and subjects of research and for distortion of the data about them. In fact, today there is some agreement about this failing, both among feminist scholars and among many of the male scientists who were their target. Many agree that it is necessary to put the missing women back into the analyses of social life in which they have been relatively invisible. There is considerable debate, however, about the further claim by some scholars that the modes of analysis and inquiry of science are a product of a "male perspective," that they do not reflect or take into account a "female perspective," and that there can be no objective, gender-free analysis—a claim that I believe is also contaminated by bias.

One of the early critiques of male bias came from the psychologist Naomi Weisstein (1971: 70), who attacked male psychologists for acting unscientifically and neglecting or misrepresenting women in their research. Psychology "has nothing to say about what women are really like, what they need and what they know, essentially because they [psychologists] do not know," she wrote.

Through the 1970s and more recently, other scholars maintained that "feminist scholarship is at cross-purposes with traditional social science" (Nebraska Feminist Collective, 1983; see also D. Smith, 1974, 1977; Shields, 1975; Bernard, 1973; Keller, 1982, 1985) and that positivist knowledge produced by the scientific establishment is uniquely male because it is an extension of male personality and interests. Stacey and Thorne (1984) summarize the critique of scholars who have articulated this position: Evelyn Fox Keller (1982, 1983), Dorothy Smith (1978, 1979), and Nancy Hartsock (1983). These writers have "theorized complex relationships between masculine standpoints and interests and the structure of [positivist] knowledge." They argue that "the sexual division of labor and male dominance produce fundamental differences in the lives and experiences of women and men, with important consequences for knowledge." Stacey and Thorne (1984: 309) assert that the male character infects scientific perspectives: "rationality divorced from feelings, and sharp separation between the knower and the known—an objectifying stance basic to positivist social science—may be founded in structures of gender. This stance is characteristic of a rigidly autonomous personality that, for reasons of social organization and family structure, is more often found among men than women."

Writing on bias in sociology more than a decade ago (Epstein, 1974), I expressed the belief that there was nothing intrinsically limiting—or male— about the various paradigms and methods in the sciences which prevent the attainment of knowledge about gender issues. Although I am now convinced that there are limitations, I do not believe that they can be pegged to intrinsically different "male" and "female" modes of thinking. I do not believe that there is or can be or should be a "male science" or a "female science" any more than I believe in a Jewish science or an Aryan science, a black or a white science. Writing in 1974, I pointed out "that to the extent that the profession's work has been male oriented (a matter of interests, not ability) it has been skewed and is therefore wrong; the same would have resulted from work done from a 'female' perspective. That sociology had no right to its claims of scientific objectivity had been heard from other quarters long before the criticism of the women's movement, but the feminist critique identified the bias of gender whereas the others were more concerned with what they believed to be political bias." Moreover, not only "feminist" scholarship had been produced by women scholars working in conventional paradigms, including Marxist, structural-analysis, role-theory, and sociology-of-knowledge approaches (Bernard, 1964; Komarovsky, 1971; Rossi, 1964; Epstein, 1970a),[1] but analyses that today would be regarded as having a feminist perspective were published by male sociologists as well. In fact, among the contributions by social scientists in the past that laid some of the groundwork for today's perspective, the works of male sociologists Everett Hughes (1945) and William J. Goode (1963) stand out in the attention they give to locating the social sources of women's inequality in all societies. More recently, Erving Goffman (1977) has studied the "arrangement between the sexes" and the creation of gender distinctions.

Many of the new feminist scholars have brought vision and criticism to their disciplines, resulting in corrections and additions to the work in their fields. But it would be difficult to note anything particularly "female" about the techniques women have been said to offer, such as affiliative, qualitative, and intuitive approaches. For one thing, men have made claims to these also as part of the entire repertoire of methods and models. For another, no evidence indicates any differences between men and women in styles of thought. Of course, Marxists and blacks had raised specific questions in the 1960s in reaction to their perceived neglect or misinterpretation. They did so not only for mainstream paradigms but for Marxist theory as well: What is missing from contemporary models? Which groups are ignored? How has analysis of the whole society become distorted as a result (Epstein, 1984a)?

A fruitful distinction might be made between feminist and "female," or good and bad science, in that science is ultimately either objective or not. In this I am in agreement with certain feminist scholars. Haraway (1983a: 3), for example, argues that "feminist epistemology, history, and

1. An important example is Margaret Mead, a student and later a colleague of Franz Boas, who of course was one of the first anthropologists to be concerned with sex roles. Alice Rossi's classic "Equality between the Sexes: An Immodest Proposal" (1964) is another example of critical analysis by a mainstream-trained sociologist of how women's roles were regarded, as is my 1970 book, *Woman's Place*.

philosophy of science are in basic tension with their academic sources and also challenge neighboring political theory and practice, for example, Marxism.'' She asserts that ''there can be, rooted in the historical activity and struggles of women, a specifically feminist theory of how people know the world, a more adequate and less distorted scientific knowledge and practice for everybody.''

This perspective, however, differs radically from one offered by Evelyn Fox Keller (1983), who argues that the ''sciences are deeply gendered; they are perceived as properly male activity and they produce knowledge and procedures for relating to the world that are inherently masculine.'' The values of domination (instrumentality) and separation (objectivity) are built into Western sciences, she claims in offering her psychoanalytic view. According to this theory, early childhood experiences of boys with their mothers create ego insecurity, which results in males' ''escalating dialectics of domination, dividing the world into walled cities to ward off their terror of and longing for fusion with the female, and producing girls with fluid boundaries of self who might be capable of practicing a very different kind of science'' (Keller, in Haraway, 1983a). Like some other critics, I find such psychoanalytic accounts of science and scholarship profoundly unconvincing and agree with Haraway (1983a) that there is a ''comprehensive, seductive 'just so story' '' quality to these analyses. They tend to posit universal (although separate) experiences for all boys and all girls in infancy, which they claim have unvarying but differentiated impacts on adult life. I have not seen any tests of this theory. As some men become artists and others boxers, some mystics and some accountants, so women, too, may develop various ways of thinking.

It should be noted, however, that psychoanalytic theories are prominent in feminist thought (see Dinnerstein, 1977; Chodorow, 1978; Horney [1924] 1967). In the Harding and Hintikka (1983) collection of essays investigating scientific epistemology, a third of the contributions depend on object-relation theories for an understanding of the social production of gender and its consequences (Haraway, 1983a). These theories, like all psychoanalytic theories, are untestable. Although they may account for certain patterns of reaction, it is doubtful that a single pattern can be said to apply universally. For example, they do not account for the feminist critical perspectives of some male scholars, who, according to psychoanalytic reasoning, have a different experience in the family in infancy and early childhood, and therefore should be unable to be feminists. Another criticism of this cluster of feminist scholars is that feminist research ought to concentrate on ''experience'' or ''everyday life'' rather than social structure, which is too removed from both women's daily lives and from the way women think. Stanley and Wise (1983) believe that ethnomethodology and symbolic interaction are consonant with women's bent for understanding lived experience, and Dorothy Smith asserts that sociology must start from specific, historically grounded experience and build to a structural analysis from there (1974; cited in Chodorow, 1985).

These theories and proposals for a particular women's methodology have the same flaws as many of the perspectives feminists have deplored. They imply that all women are essentially similar in psyche and behavior and that all men essentially think and behave alike, regardless of race, historical period, class, education, occupation, or marital status.

Some of the most penetrating attacks on bias in the sciences (including bias about sex and gender) have come from male scientists with training in genetics, neurobiology, psychology, geology, and the philosophy of science. In several books and a number of articles (S. Gould, 1981; Lewontin et al., 1984; Kamin, 1976; Kitcher, 1985) and in reviews of books, these "critical scientists" (as they call themselves)[2] have criticized models of human nature that they feel have rationalized inequalities of status, wealth, and power between classes, genders, and races in Western society.

It is true, however, that because most men have ignored important questions concerning the division of labor between the sexes or went about their investigations in ways now found to be biased, women—long "outsiders" in their disciplines—have created most of the scholarship in this field. "Segregation can make for asymmetrical sensitivities across the divide" (Merton, 1972).

Although the new field of sex roles (later, gender studies) opened up in the social sciences and the humanities in the 1970s, this was not a time of "normal science." The process of "organized skepticism," which Merton (1957) held is generated by the norms of the scientific community, was exercised by peripheral dissidents and led to recognition of both manifest and latent biases in theory and method. In the past two decades (not

2. The worldwide radical movements dating from the 1960s have produced literatures on social relations, science, and epistemology: for example, *Science for the People* in the United States and *Radical Science Journal* in England. Haraway (1983b) credits Thomas Kuhn's *Structure of Scientific Revolutions* (1962), a work not identified with the political Left, with providing frameworks and methods for understanding the thesis of the radical social construction of scientific knowledge, including approaches rooted in inner biases of anthropology, history, sociology, and philosophy. See also Knorr-Cetina and Mulkay, 1983. Of course, the vision of science as rooted in culture and social structure hardly began with Kuhn. For one example in sociology, Robert K. Merton's work begun in the 1930s moved into the systematic analysis of the sociology of science.

unlike the time of Galileo), strongly held assumptions have been challenged, with both challengers and challenged grinding political axes. Scientific knowledge about the traditional division between the sexes calls into question the present ordering of the world and the distribution of its punishments and rewards. As the clerics who fought Galileo were concerned that their church might fall if not supported by an androcentric model of the universe, so powerful modern gatekeepers resist views that social organization is the product of social construction rather than nature.

The organized revolt against invidious distinctions created by the division of society in terms of sex raised complaints within the sciences that the models used to explain that division were inadequate or culturally laden. The questioning of these assumptions came very late in the development of the social sciences.

Although a focus on the analysis of sex differences (and similarities) was part of the social science agenda prior to the 1960s, inquiry was partially confined to a few studies done by small numbers of scientists in areas such as personality and child development. Furthermore, women were not studied in certain spheres such as politics or the workplace (and substantial numbers of women in the social sciences became discontented with this situation), and men were not studied in other spheres such as the family (although most did not object to the omission).

Social scientists seemed to have been "inoculated against understanding," wrote Erving Goffman in 1977. "More even than in the matter of social class, these students simply acted like everyone else, blindly supporting in their personal conduct exactly what some at least should have been studying. As usual in recent years, we have had to rely on the discontented to remind us of our subject matter" (Goffman, 1977: 301).

Sex differences and the salience of sex status in functionally inappropriate settings (Merton, in Epstein, 1970a) became a subject of serious study only in the late 1960s and 1970s. The studies of "sex roles," as then conceptualized, were primarily studies of women. This resulted partly from the remedial intent of feminist scholars who aimed at putting women "back into" the study of "mankind" (Epstein, 1973a) and ending the biased perspectives that tainted research.

In an article entitled "Paradigms and Politics" (1984a), I proposed that political conflict had been responsible for spurring the development of knowledge in several areas. Certainly the women's movement that began in the 1960s had by the early 1970s alerted academic women that something was amiss with existing paradigms and research. The conflict generated by the women's movement, beginning with the formation of the

National Organization for Women in 1966, created pressure for a new and different evaluation of women. In the course of seeking equal rights in employment and in the law, women social and physical scientists reviewed and challenged the basic assumptions regarding women's competence in intellectual matters and their presumed personality traits which underlay the inequities they faced. By 1973 there were some seventy women's caucuses and organized women's groups in occupational associations as diverse as the American Bar Association, the Association of Cell Biologists, and the American Sociological and Psychological associations (Epstein, 1973a). The scientific groups among them challenged the formal organizations of the scientific establishment as a prelude to contesting the body of presumed scientific knowledge about women. Unlike the men of the scientific community who believed it to be an open meritocracy, women scientists who faced discriminatory exclusion were aware that it was not. In order to develop and correct knowledge about women and society, and to have their findings accepted and integrated into the body of knowledge, it was important for women scientists (and feminist male scholars) to be part of the formal scientific community.

It is necessary to distinguish "male" bias from the general cultural perspective emphasizing different attributes for the sexes which is embedded in science as in other institutions. Certainly many male scientists tried to exclude women from the scientific community because they were prejudiced. They sought to legitimate this exclusion by insisting that women lacked the capacity or ambition to be productive scientists. But this type of personal bias ought to be distinguished from the bias that was a product of the peculiar structure of scientific procedures and the reward system in the sciences, identified by Carolyn Wood Sherif (1979) in a critique of mainstream psychologists' study of gender. Some feminists faulted the "objective" positivist analysis in science, which they claimed excluded women because they had a subjective relation to the world not captured in a method that objectified social relations. I must admit I am not altogether clear about this reasoning, but I certainly do not believe it was "objectivity" that impaired the work of male scientists studying women in the cases disputed by Dorothy Smith (1979). Rather, I believe the work suffered from the subjectivity of biased, largely male, scientists.

Consider the difference between willful intent and mindless acceptance of popular views. That there was a deliberate effort to keep women out of the universities and, for those who were admitted, to deny them equal access to fellowships and research assistantships is attested to by a considerable body of evidence. Some gatekeepers evidently believed that women were less competent and less likely to return the investment that would be made in them. Some preferred the "male club" ambience of an academy free of women for various reasons, including the enhancement of male status and its protection from a potential class of competitors.[3]

Women were not regarded as a focus of interesting research, even by many women scientists, until the last decade. Although some women scientists were aware of the impact of bias upon their own careers and those of other women, many remained aloof from the study of women and some forswore identification as "feminists."[4] Scholars centered in the women's movement defined the inequality of women as a "social problem" (Epstein, 1976b: 416), developing courses on the subject and contributing chapters to introductory texts.[5]

Social scientists did not perceive a "natural" flow of research questions on gender issues; rather, these questions were raised by the political agenda of the women's movement, which insisted, through caucuses and women's groups in professional associations, that gender was a subject worthy of serious attention. One outcome was that sex roles or gender studies were focused almost exclusively on women, without comparable attention to men.[6]

In the end a body of work on gender had developed. Perspectives relevant to a feminist analysis of society were introduced in the early and mid-1970s by a number of scholars (Epstein, 1970a, 1971a, 1974; Bart, 1971; Bernard, 1973; McCormack, 1975; D. Smith, 1974), some of them unaware of the others' contributions.[7] In time, special issues of journals and books were devoted to the question of bias in various disciplines.[8]

    3. See Reskin and Hartmann, 1986; Epstein, 1970a, 1970b, 1981b; Rossi, *Academic Women on the Move* (New York: Russell Sage Foundation, 1973). See also the ongoing documentation by the Project on the Status and Education of Women of the Association of American Colleges, in its publication *On Campus with Women,* edited by Bernice Sandler since 1971.
    4. As an example, the geneticist Barbara McClintock wrote to a friend on being elected to the National Academy of Sciences in 1944 (the third woman ever to be so named): ". . . concerning the National Academy. I must admit I was stunned. Jews, women and Negroes are accustomed to discrimination. I am not a feminist, but I am always gratified when illogical barriers are broken" (cited in S. Gould, 1984a).
    5. Textbooks on social problems began to include chapters on sex roles or gender inequality only in the 1970s. One such was Merton and Nisbet's *Contemporary Social Problems* (1976), which included my chapter on sex roles in its fourth edition (Epstein, 1976c).
    6. Arlene K. Daniels's review of sociological feminist writing in Millman and Kanter (1975) shows that most of this research has been done by women scholars and is focused entirely on women.
    7. Articles on these subjects tended to be published in journals out of the mainstream and often were known only to particular networks of sociologists.
    8. Among them are Victoria Schuck and Judy Corder Tully, eds., "A Symposium: Masculine Blinders in the Social Sciences," *Social Science Quarterly* 55, no. 3 (December 1974); Sherman and Beck, eds., *Prism of Sex,* 1979; Millman and Kanter, eds., *Another Voice,* 1975; Elizabeth

Yet there has hardly been a clean sweep of wrong-mindedness and wrong methodology. Research and researchers are still prey to personal biases and the institutionalized biases lodged in the disciplines. Furthermore, as pointed out earlier, two feminist perspectives compete today to explain the sex division of society.[9] One model—a dichotomous one—holds that there are basic differences between the sexes. Catherine Stimpson (1983) calls this the "maximalist" perspective. Some of its proponents believe the differences are biologically determined; others believe they are a product of social conditioning (typically set early in life) or lodged in the differing psyches of the sexes by the psychoanalytic processes that create identity; still others believe the causes of the differences are a mixture of both factors. These scholars typically believe that differences are deeply rooted and result in different approaches to the world, in some cases creating a distinctive "culture" of women. Such differences, they think, benefit society and ought to be recognized and rewarded.

The other model (which some call "minimalist" insists that the two sexes are essentially similar and that the differences linked to sexual functions are not related to psychological traits or social roles. This perspective suggests that most gender differences are not as deeply rooted or immutable as has been believed, that they are relatively superficial, and that they are socially constructed (and elaborated in the culture through myths, law, and folkways) and kept in place by the way each sex is positioned in the social structure. This perspective is critical of the notion of a separate women's culture and of the idea that women's psyches or values are different from men's. This view ascribes observed differences in behavior to a social control system that prescribes and proscribes specific behaviors for women and men. As noted in the introduction to this book, the research I find convincing tends to support this perspective.

Bias in the Models, Methods, and Structure of Science

The 1960s and 1970s were a time of critical analysis of the vaunted objectivity of the sciences. Out of this analysis came the realization that cultural biases may be built into the perspectives and models of science itself. Other biases stem from scientists' positions in the social structure,

Langland and Walter Gove, eds., *Soundings: An Interdisciplinary Journal* 64, no. 4 (Winter 1981); and review essays by discipline in *Signs: Journal of Women in Culture and Society;* Dale Spender, ed., *Men's Studies Modified: The Impact of Feminism on the Academic Disciplines,* 1981; and Rayna Reiter, ed., *Toward an Anthropology of Women,* 1975.

9. Hester Eisenstein (1983) has succinctly reviewed this debate in her book *Contemporary Feminist Thought.*

which have an effect on the questions they consider most worthy of attention.[10] Yet, this set of revelations or rediscoveries of the way perception is selectively ordered in science moved some observers to reject one set of biases only to accept another.

An often cited article by Edwin Ardiner (1972: 136) suggests that "those trained in ethnography evidently have a bias toward the kind of model that men are ready to provide (or to concur in), rather than toward any which a woman might provide." He asserts, without evidence to support his claim, that women have a different model of society based on a different cosmology, and thus they live in a different world than men do.[11] This reasoning could easily be used to support the view that women's so-called different quality of mind makes them poor candidates for scientific posts.

The route to objectivity is beset with obstacles. The values of scientists are embedded in their quest in many ways: in the initial choice of the problems to be studied, the selection of hypotheses, the selection of methodological tools, and the choice of modes of interpretation. Even while social scientists struggle to be value-free—that is, to be objective—the very fact that they use one means rather than another in the search for the "truth" limits them to abstracting from one reality while neglecting another. As the philosopher of literature Kenneth Burke (1935: 70) observed, "A way of seeing is also a way of not seeing—a focus upon object A involves a neglect of object B."

Values, as Max Weber noted long ago, fundamentally determine a scientist's choice of problems for investigation and affect science as an institution. In medicine, for example, certain diseases (such as AIDS) or problems (such as infertility) have become a focus of concentration partially because of public attention and concern. In the social sciences, the perspectives and methodologies in common use have in the past resulted in the serious neglect of the study of women's participation in social life, or have been inappropriate to such study, resulting in distorted findings.

The subject matter of the social sciences and the physical sciences as well, some sociologists of science argue, has always been rooted in the cultural milieu from which it emerged and which it serves. Yet, methods and technologies have been developed to help the social scientist to rise above his or her cultural embeddedness.

10. This was not an original view in the 1960s and 1970s, however. In 1952 Bernard Barber had pointed to scientists' own resistances to discoveries that came from persons trained in disciplines other than theirs. For example, a chemist might not be receptive to a contribution to chemistry made by a biologist.

11. The claims of Carol Gilligan (1982) that women have a different moral structure might be interpreted quite differently depending on whether the observer was oriented toward finding differences or similarities between the sexes.

It has been argued that certain spheres of scientific inquiry are less free of social context than others. It is easier for the physical scientist than for the social scientist to be value-free. And in the social sciences, it is easier for the investigator to be value-free when studying certain problems rather than others (for example, how often people move their residences rather than how they change their political beliefs). It might be argued that the most bias occurs in the scientific investigation of problems that seem most ordinary in life because even scientists bring to their studies folk knowledge that needs to be set aside.

But certain critics argue that the problems of bias in science are rooted in its basic epistemology. Stacey and Thorne (1984) have claimed that there are ways in which the basic epistemology of a discipline may affect its congeniality or resistance to "feminist rethinking." They point out that the new scholarship has made most headway in anthropology, literature, and history because these fields have strong traditions of interpretive understanding in contrast to sociology, psychology, political science, and economics, where there has been more resistance to "feminist transformation" because of these fields' positivist epistemology. The lines cannot be so clearly drawn, however. Outstanding contributions to feminist theory have been made in sociology, and resistance to it has been exhibited in literature and history. But there is merit to the argument that lines of thinking that are more contextually oriented produce a greater receptivity to alternative models than those phrased in abstract, universal terms.

Some scholars trace bias in the scientific establishment to philosophic origins—for example, "the standard methodology" of reductionist reasoning that has ruled orthodox science ever since Descartes (S. Gould, 1984a). Others prefer to start with Aristotle. Judith Stiehm (1983), for example, suggests that Aristotle's "functional" model of society and the family, and woman's place within it not as an independent individual but only as a wife and mother, is a basis for modern theory and practice in political science. Lynda Lange (1983) has pointed out that Aristotle's thesis of the alleged inferiority of women formed the basis of his analysis of biological functioning, an analysis that has carried over to contemporary discussions.

Models in Science

The cultural models of women's nature, created by theologians and philosophers, have had their impact on scientists. Various scholars have identified the ways in which these perspectives were made a part of the scientific writings and experiments of their day. Carolyn Iltis (1978) has shown that mid-seventeenth-century natural philosophers incorporated the tradition of male superiority in their analysis of natural order and reproduction. And Lewontin, Rose, and Kamin (1984), in a pointed attack on scientific methodology with ramifications for research on gender, have offered an analysis of the development of dualistic models in science. Derived from Cartesian analysis and its attendant mechanical view of human nature, these models embody some pseudoscientific views that continue today to bias the science of gender, race, and class.

The theory of evolution, for example, became a justification for the social order of bourgeois society and for the inequality of certain social groups. The belief in an organic hierarchy proved fertile ground both for scientific theories about biological division refurbished within the Darwinian evolutionary framework and for the construction of a model for society. Leonore Davidoff's (1979) study of social divisions in the nineteenth century examines a worldview that divided society between masculine and feminine, working class and middle (upper) class, and urban and rural, as well as the physical and the moral. Descartes's body/soul distinction was translated into imagery in which certain groups were seen to be closer to nature than the rational adult middle-class man who dominated educated opinion. These groups included not only women, children, and servants and other elements in the working class but also natives in the colonies and by extension, all nonwhites. Within this framework, sexuality—particularly male sexuality, Davidoff points out—became the focus of a fear of disorder and of a continuing battle to tame natural forces.

The most highly regarded forebears of modern sociological thought—Marx, Durkheim, and Weber—were probably affected by these cultural viewpoints. For example, Davidoff points out that Max Weber considered sexuality a nonsocial, even an antisocial force, "the drive that most firmly binds man to the animal level. . . . Rational ascetic alertness, self-control and methodical planning of life are threatened the most by the peculiar irrationality of the sexual act, which is ultimately and uniquely insusceptible to rational organization" (Weber [1922] 1968: 603–04). But for the most part, sexuality was not a subject Weber emphasized in his work. He posited a model of social action based on rationality. He, and later Talcott Parsons, tended to see emotions as irrational when located in the world of occupations and public life. For Parsons, emotions were normal in women's sphere—the private sphere or the world of the family or religion. Because emotions were not regarded as *normatively* appropriate for the public world—a sphere of "affective neutrality," to use Parson's concept—they were denied behaviorally and omitted from study of the important questions related to the public world.[12]

Davidoff (1979) links the separation of male and female domains that occurred under industrial capitalism to the changing view of men's and women's positions in the cosmos and their relation to nature. One might argue that this combination was hardly typical of the Victorian period alone, but the case provides convincing evidence of how gender distinctions have been constructed and emphasized as part of other boundary-creating and -maintaining elements of society. Davidoff also alerts us to the way a focus on physicality can be used to degrade certain social groups. Here again, the "women are closer to nature" theme is part of a larger value scheme in which peripheral groups are associated with their supposed physiological nature (the presumed special propensity of blacks for rhythm, for example). Many of these groups are regarded as more brutal and/or more sensual, or physical, and are assigned tasks appropriate to their social standing, such as domestic labor and child care. Davidoff points out that it is not the tasks themselves that degrade but their definition as degrading by the powerful, who can assign such labels to people who have no control over their fates. The Victorian model of society as organic had consequences for the attitudes and behavior of Victorian standard setters in many institutions. According to this model, society was able to operate as a system because of its hierarchical ordering by interdependent parts. The adult middle-class (or aristocratic) man representing the governing group was seen as head of the social system as well as of his household, which was society in miniature. Middle-class women represented the emotions, the heart, or sometimes the soul, seat of morality and tenderness. Women performed their household functions as keepers of the hearth; here we find a body-house connection that figured widely in the Victorian worldview. Working-class women (and men) dealt with the physical necessities and became associated with them.

Anthropologists today such as Sanday (1981) and Ortner (1974) point out that even current inquiry is affected by an ideological heritage that views women as more connected to and directed by their biology than are men. In chapter 1, I raised the issue of tying women's lot, more than men's, to physical determinants. That "women are to nature as men are to culture" is the focus of a debate in anthropology attempting to explain

12. Although Georg Simmel wrote about the emotions as a subject of sociological analysis and Robert M. MacIver and Robert K. Merton in the 1940s each made a case for the "sociology of emotions," it remained for scholars focusing on gender—Arlie Hochschild (1975, 1979, 1983), in particular—to create a sociology of emotions. Today it is not confined to gender issues and has been developed by Shott (1979) and Kemper (1981).

why folk wisdom creates a presumed relationship between women's hormones, their reproductive apparatus (and the related processes of menstruation and menopause), and their social and political roles and psychological states of mind. Although many perspectives linking human social
arrangements with physical factors have been dismissed as naive, other
such perspectives continue to be considered appropriate to the study of
gender relations. As social science researchers have moved toward analyses showing only negligible sex differences in many spheres, the theoretical suggestions of a new crop of sociobiologists once again propose
the primacy of biological factors in attempting to explain the nature of
men and women (E. Wilson, 1975a, 1978; Barash, 1977).

The boundary distinctions of a class system justified by "scientific
models" of distinctive parts hierarchically ordered or separable are also
applied to gender. Is this model appropriate for understanding "human
nature"?[13]

Lewontin, Rose, and Kamin (1984) argue that the scientific persepec-
tive that attempts to derive the properties of wholes from intrinsic properties of parts—properties that exist separate from and before the parts are
assembled into complex structures—is reductionist science and therefore
poor science. It is characteristic of reductionism, for example, to assign
relative weights to different partial causes and to attempt to assess the
importance of each cause by holding all others constant while varying a
single factor. Their argument seems particularly convincing in the analysis
of social relations (I cannot evaluate it for the physical sciences). It is
generally more useful to the social scientists to see abstract properties of
parts not in isolation from their associations as wholes but as arising out

13. One may ask whether it is even useful in the study of physical science. Of course the
answer must be both yes and no. Stephen Jay Gould (1984a: 6), in his review of Evelyn Fox
Keller's biography of Barbara McClintock (1983), points out McClintock's special facility for
seeing the whole picture in her analysis of genetic transformation. As he wrote, "McClintock
does not follow the style of logical and sequential thinking often taken as a canonical mode of
reasoning in science; she works by a kind of global, intuitive insight. It is a common procedure
for some people, though perhaps rare (and certainly not generally appreciated in science). It is
neither mystical nor, in another vulgar misrepresentation, feminine as opposed to masculine in
character.

"The experimental sciences (like molecular biology) generally work with the simplest organisms and try consciously to avoid the individuality of any particular creature. They concentrate
instead on repeatable properties of large groups (so that a clone of bacteria becomes the analogue
of a population of atoms with no individuality by definition).

"This style has had remarkable triumphs in the history of biology, though I believe that it has
now reached definite limits in the attempt to understand genetic systems and their complex interactions with the developing forms of organisms. . . .

"Biology is a unity, and we will not solve Aristotle's dilemma of morphogenesis, the origin
and development of organic form, until we marry the distinctive styles of natural history and
reductionist experiment."

of their associations. According to this view, which Lewontin, Rose, and Kamin term dialectical, the properties of parts and whole codetermine each other. This approach, of course, is difficult to accomplish, but it has the advantage, for the social sciences at least, of taking into account the history of the organism and its relationship to its environment. The approach, they assert, would also free the investigator from the dualisms of hereditary/environment, nature/nurture, and perhaps (in the context of this analysis) male/female.

This sounds like a plea for the analysis of elements as parts of a system, hardly alien to the social or physical sciences. Yet systemic analysis has been attacked for being static by critical social scientists for decades,[14] although it can provide insight into interactions and multiple consequences and a focus on process rather than static states.

Structure of the Social Sciences

Alice Rossi (1973) has suggested that the omission of women from social science investigation stemmed from general analytical problems and the structure of the social sciences themselves. Commenting on the lack of serious attention given Simone de Beauvoir's analysis of the place of women in society when *The Second Sex* appeared in the 1950s, Rossi suggests that de Beauvoir's eclectic interdisciplinary approach was at odds with what she characterized as the narrow specialization of the social sciences at that time. Rossi observed:

> Such human characteristics as age and sex play havoc with the specialization that had the academic disciplines in its grip during the 1940s and 1950s with the result that researchers often simply confined their attention to one particular age group and dropped women from their research altogether. Thus a typical sample of subjects in psychology or sociology for more than a decade consisted of young college-age males. . . . In academic circles the very strength that flowed from its [*The Second Sex*'s] broad synthesizing framework was criticized as a weakness; since no one, the view went, could be a specialist in so many areas, the work was therefore suspect. (1973: 673)

There were, of course, exceptions to the pattern Rossi noted, but her critique identified important sources of neglect and selective perception of women's place in the social structure.

14. Merton's rebuttal (1957) fell on deaf ears, a phenomenon that Merton, Barber (1952), and many others have probed in analyses of social receptivity to discovery.

Carolyn Wood Sherif's analysis (1979) of the bias in psychology further explored the problems. As Naomi Weisstein (1971) posed it, psychology "constructed" the female. Sherif examined mainstream psychological perspectives which attributed women's lower status in society and their personal problems to certain psychological qualities, such as docility, passivity, emotionality, and so on, that made both appear to be inevitable. In 1963 both Betty Friedan in *The Feminine Mystique* and Sherif pointed out that orthodox methods of studying and interpreting sex differences were capable of delivering only mischievous and misleading trivia. As Sherif observed in a public symposium:

> Apart from the hoary sex-differences tradition (euphemistically called the "study of individual differences"), psychologists' treatment of the sexes contained several brands of psychoanalytic thought and a growing accumulation of research on socialization to "sex-appropriate behaviors," which was actually the old sex-difference model mixed with psychoanalytic notions and served [up] in a new disguise. (Sherif, 1964: 93–94)

Sherif, like Rossi (and Bernard, 1973), locates one of the sources of bias in the social structure of the social sciences, focusing particularly on the structure of psychology. It was the quest to make psychology as close in model and method to the physical sciences that resulted in deflecting psychologists from following through on the findings of some early practitioners.

The problem of bias in psychological research was enunciated early in the discipline's history. As Sherif (1979) notes, E. G. Boring, in his *History of Experimental Psychology* (1950), pointed out that there are limits to scientific advance which stem from (among other restraints such as ignorance) "habits of thought that pertain to the culture of any region and period." This "zeitgeist" of particular laboratories was repeatedly found to affect results of the same or similar studies, whether the problems concerned issues of thought, learning, or the accumulating research on sex differences. In his history, Boring thought he had successfully dismissed the basis for arguments of deep-rooted sex differences in psychology when he assessed the results of Francis Galton's psychological assessments of 9,337 persons at the 1884 International Health Exhibition: "No important generalization as regards human individual differences appeared, however, unless we should note Galton's erroneous conclusion that women tend in all their capacities to be inferior to men" (Boring, 1950: 487).

Many scholars have tried to understand why one set of ideas gains currency in social and scientific life while others go unheeded. "Is there a natural selection of ideas?'' Gregory Bateson asked in his philosophically provocative book, *Steps toward an Ecology of Mind* (1975). We know that social philosophers of the 1700s and 1800s such as John Stuart Mill and Mary Wollstonecraft asked important questions challenging assumptions about the sexes, questions that would not become part of the research agenda until the 1970s and 1980s.

The ideas of social philosophers are in some sense more constrained by the tenor of their times than the ideas of scientists ought to be. Historians and sociologists of science have documented how scientists also face constraints, particularly when they are forging new ground or are themselves not part of the scientific establishment (Barber, 1952; Merton, 1957; Kuhn, 1962). Sherif (1979) also recounted how some psychologists working in the early 1900s attempted to reveal the sex bias in psychology but were ignored (see also R. Rosenberg, 1982). Among these were Helen Thompson Wooley, who critically exposed the bias in sex-difference research in 1903 and 1910 in two works published by an establishment journal, the *Psychological Bulletin* (1910), and the University of Chicago Press (1903). Leta S. Hollingworth and Mary Calkins (who later became president of the American Psychological Association) wrote against the hypothesis that women's intellectual capacities varied less than men's.

Answering the question of why sexist bias in psychology, recognized early in the century, continued to the present, Sherif (1979) located the answer in the discipline itself. In her view, practitioners in each of the subspecialties in psychology sought to improve their status by adopting the theories, perspectives, and methodologies regarded as "highest"— that is, most like the physical sciences—taking the laboratory as the purest setting in which to study human behavior. The laboratory setting removed behavior from its social context, and thus psychologists seldom looked for or found evidence of historical, cultural, or structural factors in explaining behavior. In the campaign to isolate "variables" that could be measured and designated as independent or dependent in a causal line, the language of applied mathematics and statistics could be seen also to affect research. Sherif argues that a person's sex has usually been considered an "independent variable," that is, a variable which one looks to for causality, because it is believed that attributes of people's sex statuses are known. She suggests it is not at all clear which way causation takes place when analyzing "sex" as a variable. The result of this is "utter confusion in almost all discussion of the variable 'sex' or of sex differences" (1979: 101), as we will explore in another section of this chapter.

Sherif also raises another important objection to the adoption of the "hard" and "soft" analogy in psychology and the other social sciences.[15] It is the physical sciences that are called "hard" sciences and therefore are regarded as intellectually tougher than the social sciences, which are labeled as "soft." Thus these adjectives have been used by some scientists to dismiss the work of others. Since in the past these opponents usually have been male scientists in different camps, she points out that it is misleading to suggest that "hard" also implies men's perspectives and "soft" implies female perspectives. Further, "hard" versus "soft" name-calling is usually heard when issues of "scientific" versus "humanistic" psychology are discussed. Psychologists' self-anointment as hard researchers is an implied critique of those who do not accept their orthodoxies.

Of course, the quest for a hard science approach has affected all the social sciences in their attempt to prove themselves as "scientific" as the physical sciences, and it does entail a propensity for reductionism. This reductionism is applied and believed notably when the issues regarding gender differences are considered and also in the course of explaining racial differences.

The Reward System in Science

The reward system in the sciences has also affected the choice of scientific study, often to the detriment of studies of gender differences. The value perspectives rooted in the social control system of the sciences and in the culture of science are manifested in the designation of important and prestigious subject matter. Gender difference was never regarded as a "hot" field of social science—that is to say, a field characterized by a huge rate of significant discoveries, one with an inordinate amount of highly consequential ideas and findings.[16]

It is commonly observed that the more abstract a problem is, the more prestige it is given as a social science topic. And the more prestigious the subject, the more prestigious the study. Thus the study of elites and professions has been of interest to social researchers from the 1950s to the present day. It was not considered a wise career choice for women sociologists to choose research topics dealing with gender studies or the family

15. In a parody of this terminology, the sociologist Pauline Bart (1974) substituted the terms *wet* and *dry* to characterize research methods. These terms, however, were "censored" so that in print they appeared as *hard* and *soft*.
16. See Merton (1973: 331) for a discussion of hot and cold fields in science.

until the 1980s because this was not considered a path to professional success (and still is not regarded as the wisest move). Discussions among women social scientists in the new organizations such as Sociologists for Women in Society (sws) indicated that it was hard to get such research funded or interest professors in supervising dissertations in this field. Funds are now more available and dissertations have proliferated, but some bias remains. One example of this bias is in the labeling of certain research as "women's studies"—a field apart, not worthy of integration in mainstream analysis of social institutions. But when male sociologists have studied occupations such as law, printing, or mining, they have not been criticized for studying "men."

Even today, male gatekeepers complain that women sociologists are "narrow" if they specialize in occupations in which women predominate; their work is labeled "women's studies" rather than part of the sociology of occupations.[17] It is not surprising, then, that the science community, which presumably (according to Merton, 1973) provides for the socially organized assessment of scientific work, was inattentive to the problem of sex differences, yet to be defined as a social problem and not to be defined as an important issue in the social sciences.

Furthermore, science does not always operate as a system of "institutionalized vigilance." Not only has it been inattentive to the study of gender issues and women, but when findings of the few studies done on these subjects were reported they were not recognized or rewarded. Much of the social scientific treatment of gender has exemplified the fact that "the operation of the gatekeeper role affects contemporary science in every respect" (Merton and Zuckerman, 1972).

Prejudice remains about the worth of research focused on gender. Although there is no doubt that such research is regarded with greater interest than in the past, repeated observation suggests that there is less career payoff for people who choose to work in this area than for those who deal with other topics. Important consequences flow from this situation. It means that knowledge generated in this area of study is viewed from a different angle of vision than that generated by people more wedded to traditional paradigms. Thus, this knowledge is less likely to be incorporated into the mainstream of disciplinary data.

Leon Festinger et al. (1948) and Coleman et al. (1977) pointed out a relationship between the spread of information and the degree of integra-

17. Although this book could be regarded as an inquiry into the "sociology of knowledge," I suspect that it will be considered primarily an inquiry into "women's studies" by book distributors and other classifiers of sociological knowledge.

tion in a group. Although information in a field is typically exchanged among people who work in that area, research findings and analyses on women seem particularly ghettoized. Ironically, although women scholars writing on women have recently achieved notice, and some are respected members of the scientific community with posts in professional associations, it is my impression that much of their work is not well known; few male scholars feel it necessary to keep up with it. With the possible exception of anthropology, gender-oriented research has not had as much impact in social sciences as its content and scientific significance merit. Courses on sex roles and gender abound, but few courses on sociological theory or methodology include this literature.

Modes of Interpretation and Conceptualization

Problems of method also bear on the field of gender studies. Method means interpretation as well as technique: they are important aspects of the same thing. Interpretation comes before objective measurement in selecting items to be measured as well as in analyzing the results of inquiry.

A book on changes in sex typing and social roles between 1971 and 1976 by two masters of method, Duncan and Duncan (1978), reported no revolution in sex roles in the American social structure. Such trivial items as "Are dusting, shoveling walks, washing the car, and making beds male or female tasks?" were used to assess change. No wonder the authors' methods revealed little change. In a review of this book (Epstein, 1980) I suggested that questions based on expectations about work life might have been better indicators of change, considering the revolution (if subtle) (R. Smith, 1979) in women's participation in the work force in the past decade.

No matter how sophisticated the research technique, the choice of items to be measured and the interpretation of measurement may be guided by personal or social politics or by simple flights of fancy. Duncan and Duncan found that more women than men think there might be a new depression like the one in the 1930s and do not have "faith in the economists [scientists] who say they know how to avert economic disaster." The authors deduce from this and such other indicators as the expectation of nuclear war with the Russians in the next twenty-five years that women are fearful of recession and that they suffer "anomie" or "collective sadness"; a "mix of diffidence, disengagement, and pessimism . . . distinguishes the answers of women," according to "one of us, at least," write the Duncans, in one of many characterizations of *women* as an inclusive category. Methodologists often tend to report the tails of distributional curves and not their centers.

Sex as a Variable

Furthermore, the context-free approach common in experiments and surveys in the social sciences has contributed to our ignorance about gender when sex is identified as the independent variable. As we saw earlier, it is to independent variables that one looks for causality, Carolyn Wood Sherif (1979) has warned, despite textbook cautions to the contrary. In using sex as a variable in studies, social scientists often make the mistake of surmising that sex *causes* certain behavior (such as voting for a Democrat or a Republican) merely because two variables (sex and voting) are found in association with each other. Although every beginning graduate student is warned against confusing correlation with causality, the line of reasoning that focuses on sex as an independent variable explaining behavior is grounded in a conceptual-methodological bias. The assumption that the sex of a person is responsible for behavior creates a dichotomous perspective that obscures similarities in behavior that may be characteristic of the majority of a sample. This bias makes it more difficult to locate intervening variables, which may be more responsible for behavioral differences than is sex. Lazarsfeld and Rosenberg (1955) alerted us to this methodological wisdom years ago. Survey results that showed a "gender gap" in voting, for example, led people to believe that men and women tend to have substantially different political behavior, when in fact the "gap" expressed differences of only several percentage points and reflected the behavior of single women and not those who were married, as we shall see in chapter 8. Reports of sex differences tend to gloss over the size of difference. The titles of the articles that report findings convey the impression of mutually exclusive categories rather than overlap. Thus, results tend to be perceived as based on attributes that are innate or set early in life. Using sex as a variable, therefore, generates invidious comparison and reinforces splintered thinking that recasts the world into male and female categories.

As is discussed in chapter 1, differentiating categories tend to shape the conclusions of the search. Data categories impose boundaries that do not reflect unclear distinctions. Studies that report black-white differences in testing, for example, do not differentiate between blacks of pure African heritage and those who have one white parent and therefore a number of white ancestors. For convenience, all people with *any* discernibly black relative become "black" and part of a "scientifically sorted" category. In fact, race is a socially created category that has been accepted by the scientific community. Similarly, when we choose to differentiate people as male and female on the basis of their genitalia, we ought to be aware that this, too, is a socially created category that may or may not be relevant to the inquiry, depending on the problem being considered.

In the study of gender issues as in other inquiries, we may have to depend on our good sense to determine whether statistical significance corresponds with social significance. *Not* thinking according to sex-defined boundaries, given the enormous cultural emphasis on them, may be one of the most important contributions scientific objectivity can offer. Recasting our thinking to assume that no differences exist unless it can be proved that they do would be useful but is a hardly probable course of action at this point in history.

Problems of Time Specificity

The preference for quantitative studies in the social sciences in the past has also placed "an emphasis on states and rates—or statics and snapshots," as Rosabeth Kanter (1977b) commented in her critical analysis of studies on work and the family for the Russell Sage Foundation. This diagnosis applies to much of the work in gender studies. Kanter pointed out that much survey research tends to seek associations between variables measured at only one point in time and often based on self-reports, with the nature of the intervening links left to speculation rather than to measurement or observation. Studies of women's aspirations, for example, often use high school or college student populations. Although this is clearly a time when anxiety about one's future is high and normative answers are especially likely to be given (for girls, this would entail being modest about one's aspirations), generalizations about women are commonly made from such studies.[18] Research among adult women and men in the work world might better indicate how aspiration is enhanced or modified by

18. As a case in point, the famous study by Matina Horner (1972) on women's "fear of success" was based on a sample of Michigan college students but was reported as an attribute of women in general. Many studies that report sex differences in general based on small samples may be found in the journal *Sex Roles*.

actual opportunity structures. Although his conclusions on sex roles, as we have seen, were flawed by his choice of trivial items as indicators of change, Duncan (1968: 694) was sage in warning social researchers against using "class" and similar concepts in such a way that they represent little more than the "imposition of more or less arbitrary intervals" on a scale of a status variable. Kanter cites Duncan's warning that "an incredible amount of paper and ink has been wasted in presenting factitious solutions for the artificial problem of where 'class boundaries' really belong." If there is a problem in identifying the overlap between social classes, there surely is a problem in identifying the overlap between behaviors identified as "masculine" and "feminine."

"Modes of Interpretation"

The Similarities-Differences Focus

Other problems of method bearing on gender studies are characteristic of science as an institution. One has to do with the need to produce "findings." The scientific culture defines a significant finding as one that reports something new or different from previous findings.

The failure adequately to report similarities between males and females because it is the differences that are regarded as "findings" is a consequence of the pressure exerted on scientists to produce findings. An orientation toward finding differences may lead to a different interpretation from an orientation geared to the assumption of similarities or little or no difference. Maccoby and Jacklin (1974: 4) point out that the major problem in studies of sex differences lies in the failure to report findings of no difference. They indicate a tendency for isolated positive findings to sweep through the literature, while findings of no difference, or even later findings showing the opposite results, are ignored. Positive findings are reprinted in books of readings, cited in textbooks, and used to buttress theories about the nature of the development of sex typing.

They also note that it is almost always impossible for observers to be blind to the sex of subjects. Stereotypes about the kind of behavior to be expected from the two sexes run very deep, and even when sex differences are incidental to the main focus of a study, observers tend to be biased. This bias may take the form of sometimes "seeing" stereotypic behavior where it does not exist and is compounded by the use of rating scales that force the observation into a stereotypical context (Maccoby and Jacklin 1974: 7).[19]

Any classification scheme can be arranged so that differences or similarities are highlighted in analysis. To some extent the outcome of any inquiry is contingent on the categories the scientist chooses to study. Clusters and regularity of like things encourage looking only at the clusters. The irregular and deviant cases are put aside for the purpose of analysis, permitting generalizations and hypotheses that are based on incomplete data but are then considered "facts." Often the deviant cases are forgotten. Leaving women out of studies because they were deviant cases meant that scientists learned little about the mechanisms and processes that functioned to exclude them. To ignore those women who showed "male" strength or intellectual interest meant that the range of all women's capacities was believed to be limited and circumscribed.

Of course, in the social sciences, unlike the physical sciences, a "wrong" interpretation does not lead just to misunderstanding; it may also lead to a further outcome *created by* the wrong interpretation. So, for example, if we misjudge the time one needs to get out of the way of a falling rock, the rock will nevertheless hit us on the head exactly as foreseen by the laws of physics; but if we misjudge a woman's talent, we can indeed create incapacity by withholding instruction or vocational opportunities from her. Robert Merton (1957) has identified this phenomenon as "the self-fulfilling prophecy." The implications of this concept, which has entered the general culture, have not been sufficiently taken up by the scientific community, and the concept is used mainly to explain individual rather than group behavior. It could be a powerful analytical tool, particularly if paired with the notion of selective perception (also used primarily to explain individual rather than group behavior). To illustrate this process we can note how defining women as passive or unassertive has had the consequence of limiting their employment in such occupations as sales and law. Acceptance of the definition by employers and by many women themselves has caused women to retreat from such occupations because they "knew" they were not likely to advance in them. Although some women do succeed, their cases are not considered to be *evidence* proving that there are no basic inadequacies. This selective perception of women's capacities results in the self-fulfilling prophecy of their being clustered in "women's jobs," occupations not regarded as requiring "male traits."

There is, in scientific inquiry, always a tension between the search for

19. Masculinity-femininity scales (such as Bem's) are the worst of these forced-choice biases, followed by the interest and preference tests given to men and women by schools and industry.

laws of nature—the quest for universals—and hence for similarities and the quest for distinctive categories, for boundaries that create analytic entities. Social scientists differ from physical scientists in that people often have an emotional investment in the categories of analysis they create with regard to a range of issues; that is, many people care that differences rather than similarities are or will be found. For example, studies in social science usually group people by race (an analytic term) and label them as white, black, or yellow. Although the concepts are identified by color categories, actual color variations serve as poor indicators. Many "white" people are darker than many "black" people. Politicians and societies have created rules that also are only loosely congruent with indicators of color. Thus, to this very day in Louisiana, a person with one thirty-second share of "Negro" blood is regarded as black and is subjected to a "black" set of experiences. Some scientists, aping southern mores, have measured the intelligence of persons designated as "black" and have decided that their average IQ is different from that of persons classified as "white." Indeed, no one has measured IQ by sensitive gradations of hue. Who are the black people we measure, or the white? Usually populations accessible to the researcher. And even if a random sample of this cohort is taken, it has already been arbitrarily selected.

This same process has been utilized in considering the issue of class. Social scientists, beginning with Marx, have divided clusters of people by wealth or education and have come up with class designations. Certainly this has informed us about the effect of having or not having money and good nutrition, but it also creates boundaries and assumptions that may or may not be valid for particular social analyses.

Ideological Components of Concepts and Classification Systems

The concepts chosen by social scientists both reflect and create a larger worldview—a culture. Although we do not normally think of such scientific concepts as "force" and "energy" as ideological when they are applied to physical processes, scientific concepts applied to human behavior often take on an evaluative dimension. For example, "energy" is often viewed as a "good" quality of a social group, whereas "force" is "bad." No one cares if a nontoxic chemical is "unstable," but many care if a group is "unstable."

Concepts used in classification schemes vary in their ideological loading. "Group" and "individual" are less ideological in their consequences than are "race" and "sex." Even to think about human groups as races is to assume a biological distinctiveness in sets of humans; similarly, to think of humans as divided into two sexes focuses on a set of biological distinctions.

Erika Apfelbaum (1978) argues that dominant groups create disparity between themselves and others. Highlighting the distinctiveness and inferiority of "others" justifies the dominant group's control and limitation of their rights and privileges and the dependency of the subordinate group. As dissymmetry, real or apparent, is differentiated, it becomes (or gives the illusion of having become) insurmountable and irreversible. The disparity that results from the workings of power is also the necessary condition for the maintenance of power because it justifies and reinforces that power. A linear model is inadequate to describe this process; a circular or feedback model is needed. That is why developmental, socialization, and biological models are inadequate.

Biased concepts and method have been seen as continuities in science arising from its philosophic origins or its unique structure and reward system. I have pointed to the impact of cultural bias and personal prejudice on research dealing with women. But this analysis would be incomplete if I did not also focus on the direct association between contemporary political ideology and scientific analysis.

Science and Politics

Reductionism and its manifestation in the old nature-nurture argument, long thought to have retreated in favor of a more sensible perspective that acknowledges the interaction between culture and biology, has reappeared with a particularly virulent connection to political stances. Politics encouraged some new looks at the nation's scientific agenda in the past two decades and was responsible for generating reassessment of old mythologies and stereotypes. But politics is interwoven with the scientific agenda of groups that found those traditional perspectives appealing. Fundamentalist Christians, for example, find creationism a more congenial perspective on human development than evolution. Such groups also favor "scientific" perspectives that suggest that subordinate roles for women are natural in human life. There do seem to be different political consequences for different scientific frameworks. Clearly, one agenda seeks to establish that humans are basically equal and another, that they are basically unequal. Theoretically these two positions pose legitimate inquiries, and those of us who are convinced that the evidence indicates more equality than is apparent must rigorously scrutinize our own motivations.

Those who espouse inequality are particularly suspect. First, it is curious that researchers who maintain that there are basic (that is, biological) inequalities between groups almost never find that their own group is the inferior one. Second, the claims of some scientists (particularly sociobiologists) that rules and laws created by society to ensure equality go against "nature" are statements of ideology, not of actuality. For example, some analysts believe that when women move toward greater equality in the political and social spheres, scientific authority can usually be found to suggest that they are moving "unnaturally" away from their biologically determined roles.

Although the same scientific findings can be used to argue different sides of social issues, the work of scientists who speculate beyond their data must be assessed with particular care. The campaign to prevent ratification of the Equal Rights Amendment to the U.S. Constitution made extensive use of the claims of sociobiologists that male supremacy is immutable. At the peak of the struggle for the amendment, prominence was given to the view of E. O. Wilson of Harvard, who assured his readers that "even in the most free and equalitarian of future societies, men are likely to play a disproportionate role in political life, business and science" (Wilson, 1975b, cited in Lewontin et al., 1984: 20). Wilson's views have also been used by the National Front in Britain and the Nouvelle Droite in France to support the argument that racism and anti-Semitism cannot be eliminated because "territoriality, tribalism and xenophobia are part of the human genetic constitution, having been built into it by millions of years of evolution" (Lewontin et al., 1984: 27).

Not only is this kind of speculation suspect for its support of gender and racial inequality and for its extension of findings from animal studies to human social behavior, but critics assert that the biological determinists' entire scheme is faulty. They have been held to be unfair to animals in their analysis of animal communities as they are to human beings in their analysis of human communities.

The sociobiologists' work is said to be impaired by their minuscule samples, uncontrolled experiments, and unsupported speculations. Why, ask the critics, do biological determinists use the concepts of nature and nurture as separate sources of behavior when developmental genetics long ago showed them to be inseparable?

As part of this discussion about bias in method, theory, and orientation I would like to bring up a question that Robert Lynd (1939) raised so engagingly a generation ago: "Knowledge for what?" Scientists engaged in the production of basic knowledge cannot turn their backs on the meaning of that knowledge to society. I am not speaking here in the sense of the use of knowledge to do good or evil; that is a moral question. I am referring, rather, to the responsibility of scientists to be cautious about the interpretation of their knowledge.

Much of the bias in social science reporting of gender issues comes from scientists' inability to capture the social context or their tendency to regard it as unnecessary to their inquiry—in a sense, their disdain for it. Some of this comes from the triumph of methodomania over common sense. In the rush to exhibit findings, many scientists manage to miss the point of the inquiry. For example, why do scientists who study childhood gender differences often suggest that findings of behavioral or attitudinal differences between boys and girls are sufficient to explain inequalities of their situations in later life? Most often, findings of difference are used to justify men's dominant positions and women's subordinate ones. To illustrate, a finding that a greater proportion of boys than girls exhibit aggressive behavior at early ages is used to explain men's assumption of leadership roles. Yet scientists do not similarly suppose that women ought to become preachers and politicians because as girls they usually outperform boys in tests demonstrating verbal ability. Thus, scientists' bias in locating childhood factors for adult performance leads them to selectively highlight the cases supporting stereotypes and underrecognize the cases that might refute them. Such bias also undercuts observation and reporting of nonfindings.

The demonstration of difference at one point in time may not, after all, be significant for establishing competence at a later period. For example, in spite of girls' demonstration of greater average skill on verbal ability tests in childhood, there is no question that ultimately both males and females acquire language, speak it, and use it with comparable facility. If scientists took a broad view, they might more often reach the conclusion that many differences found early in life may be negligible or unrelated to the assumption of later social roles. They might also search for a wider range of factors affecting the distribution of adult roles.

Furthermore, reporting the findings of small studies with specialized samples as if they are representative of all men and women may be regarded as evidence of irresponsible scientific behavior. I have pointed out elsewhere (Epstein, 1984b) that the same social scientists who pride themselves on appreciating the fine distinctions between wines of neighboring vineyards in France ("A Château Margaux is described as silken, delicate, and perfumed; St. Julien as having the best equilibrium, finesse, and a rounded quality'')[20] feel comfortable in describing the entire female sex in terms of such undifferentiated qualities as ''caring'' or ''nurturing'' or ''good at detail.''

The same insistence on differences that pervades most cultures colors the work of respected scholars in all disciplines and is to be found as well in the work of distinguished feminist scholars. These scholars' works are proof that the most recent word is not necessarily the best word[21] on any subject.

20. I am grateful to oenophile Peter Hellman (personal communication) for this analysis.
21. To paraphrase one of Robert K. Merton's recent observations (1984a).

CHAPTER 3

The Bio-Social Debate

Is Biology Destiny?

A decade ago, in spite of the then-meager reservoir of studies on women, there would have been no need to consider biological factors and evolutionary theory in a book about the sociological study of gender. But old questions about the primacy of nature or nurture have been raised anew in an attempt to explain many aspects of human social organization, including the roles of women and men in the family, the economy, and the polity. Challenges have been raised in some cases on the basis of new research or new conceptions and interpretations of data by anthropologists, biologists, primatologists, psychologists, sociologists, and practitioners of the new discipline of sociobiology.

There is no consensus among scholars, men or women, in any of these disciplines on the relative impact of culture or biology; their disagreements are basic as well as nuanced. This chapter will consider some of the relevant issues that have been raised and will offer a critical evaluation of them.

One of the most prominent paradigms to emerge in the past few years is the sociobiological. Attributed in large part to the Harvard entomologist E. O. Wilson (1975a, 1978), this view defines sociobiology as "the systematic study of the biological basis of all social behavior" (Wilson, 1975a: 4) and holds that "sociology and the other social sciences, as well as the humanities, are the last branches of biology waiting to be included in the Modern Synthesis." Sociobiologists base "insights" about the relationship between the evolutionary process and human behavior on observations of animal behavior. This perspective stands in a long tradition of attempts to discern the elements of human nature and social organization in the behavior of nonhuman animals (Kitcher, 1985). Much of this sociobiologically oriented thinking uses as its organizing paradigm Darwin's theory of evolution, a model that provides the framework for all the biological sciences. Evolutionary theory hypothesizes about the parallel development of the human species and African apes from some primate ancestor and offers the paradigm that, within a given species, individuals who possess traits most adaptive in the species' environment are likely to stay alive until they can reproduce and pass on the genes to a new generation. Thus the natural environment "selects" individuals with these adaptive traits.

Wilson's work and that of his disciples is, as Tavris and Wade (1984) have put it, "Darwin with a twist." They maintain that whereas Darwin speculated that within a given species, the best-adapted individuals are the most likely to reproduce, Wilson has extrapolated from the species to the individual and from physical characteristics to psychological ones. Thus, sociobiologists believe that nature has bred into humans the *desire* to pass on their genes and that much, and possibly most, behavior is motivated by this innate impulse to see their genetic code survive (Wilson, 1975a, 1978). Men and women follow reproductive strategies that maximize the continuity of their "lines."

According to this perspective, the genetic code has affected the brains, the hormones, and thus the behavior of men and women whose interrelationships and place in the social order reflect the "selection" of evolutionary focus. Male dominance is seen as an evolutionary response in the maximizing strategy of men to procreate with as many females as possible to ensure continuity of the male line, and women's passivity as a strategy that maximizes the survival of offspring of the female line. For example, Wilson has written, "Polygyny and sexual differences in temperament can be predicted by a straightforward deduction from the general theory of evolution" (1978: 138).

The argument that men and women are motivated differently in their reproductive strategies is believed to account for their different placement in the division of labor and in the social hierarchy. A recurrent suggestion in this work is that, like some primate groups, human ancestors clustered together in small bands, defended by "dominant" males prepared to act with violence (Wilson, 1975a: 553–55; Barash, 1979: 188–89). Dominant males are likely to be the fathers or other close relatives of the weaker individuals they defend (Wilson, 1975a). On the basis of this review of the behavior of baboons and rhesus, macaque, and vervet monkeys as well as some other animals, the sociobiologists regard human male dominance as ordained by nature. Male dominance in the political and economic spheres is the extension of an "inevitability of patriarchy," according to Steven Goldberg, a sociologist who has popularized the sociobiological perspective.

Actually, some sociobiologists distrust the idea that the theory of evolution offers any direct insight into human nature (Kitcher, 1985), but those whose analysis extends to inequality between human males and females, explaining that there are genetic constraints on gender roles, have received the most attention and are those particularly referred to in this chapter. They are, in addition to Wilson, Richard Alexander (1979), Robert Trivers (1971, 1972, 1974), Richard Dawkins (1976), David Barash (1977, 1979), Pierre van den Berghe (1979), and Napoleon Chagnon (1979).

The sociobiologists challenge the contentions of sociologists who explain much human behavior as a result of culture and social learning—not that sociologists and other social scientists dismiss the importance of biology. Of course, biological factors create differences between men and women and "cause" certain kinds of behavior. Reproduction is a biological process, and body structure, determined by one's genes, creates opportunities for some people to perform better or worse in activities such as basketball or crawling through small spaces.

But the broader claims of sociobiologists assert many more links between social behavior and genetic makeup. Much of this speculation is based on studies of the social life of animals which, in their natural habitat, manifest patterns of behavior seemingly analogous to that of humans. "Sociobiology has two faces," according to Philip Kitcher (1985), a philosopher of science at the University of Minnesota who has reanalyzed the studies offered as evidence by the "Wilson school." In *Vaulting Ambition*, Kitcher notes: "One looks toward the social behavior of non-human animals. The eyes are carefully focused, the lips pursed judiciously. Utterances are made only with caution. The other face is almost hidden. . . . With great excitement, pronouncements about human nature blare forth" (1985: 435). He and other critics of the sociobiology that "blares forth" about human nature—such as Haraway (1983b), Fausto-Sterling (1985), S. Gould (1981), Bleier (1978, 1985), and Lewontin, Rose, and Kamin (1984)—are wary of the anthropomorphism and speculative conclusions offered. As Kitcher puts it, the implications of their assumptions "are grave," for their view "fosters the idea that class structures are socially inevitable, that aggressive impulses toward strangers are part of our evolutionary heritage, that there are ineradicable differences between the sexes that doom women's hopes for genuine equality.'' Kitcher maintains that one face of sociobiology has produced ''interesting results about the social lives of insects, birds and mammals,'' but he believes that the building of ''grand conclusions about ourselves is premature and dangerous'' (1985: 435).

Adultery, rape, incest, racism, altruism, the family unit, xenophobia, dominance, and mate selection are some of the behaviors that sociobiologists suggest have roots in humans' animal heritage. For example, on the basis of his observations of ground squirrels, who tend to treat their biological siblings in a ''nicer'' way than peers reared with them but not of their litter, David Barash (1979) argues that ''genes help themselves by being nice to themselves'' (p. 153) and that ''the principles of kin-selected altruism'' favor genes promoting antagonisms toward those who look different; thus, evolution may ''incline us to a degree of racial bigotry'' (p. 154). ''Rape'' observed in the behavior of mallard ducks is another example of the use of analogy. Barash explains the rape of women by men as a reproductively adaptive trait of men who do not have access to women. Observing scorpion flies, Thornhill (1980; Thornhill and Thornhill, 1983) hypothesizes that men rape when they are unable to compete for the resources and status necessary to attract and reproduce successfully with desirable mates.[1]

The sociobiological perspective that human behavior stems from rational reproductive strategies is also found in the work of women primatologists who have attempted to explain human behavior by referring to their studies of primates. Sara Blaffer Hrdy's observations on langurs (Asian leaf-eating monkeys) led her to what some regard as a feminist perspective; her *Langurs of Abu: Female and Male Strategies of Reproduction* (1977) claims to be the first book to analyze the behavior of wild primates from the standpoint of both sexes, showing female langurs' contribution to troop organization as well as males'. But Hrdy, who worked with Irven DeVore, Robert Trivers, and E. O. Wilson, also accepts the model that the social grouping of primates is *one* possible result of the strategies of individual reproducers to maximize their genetic fitness. In the 1970s, the reported infanticide practiced by male langurs was held to be a key to issues of domestic violence, cooperation in the family, and parenting

---

1. Critics of this theory point out that a considerable number of rapes are performed on women far beyond the age of reproduction by men who have wives and by men against other men (in prison and other all-male communities) who obviously cannot reproduce.

(Haraway, 1983b). Infanticide was seen as a reproductive strategy of langur males, a strategy not employed by the females, whose reproductive interests were regarded as different from those of the males. There was considerable discussion about whether langur males actually killed the babies of their competitors and, if they did, whether the act was pathological or normal. Hrdy argued that infanticide was key evidence of male dominance. Other primatologists, however, such as Phyllis Jay Dolhinow and her students believed that the same phenomenon was not an important indicator of the struggle for male dominance but was a manifestation of stress (Haraway, 1983b). Dolhinow's emphasis was on the role of females in maintaining a troop's stability.

An evolutionary biological perspective that raises speculations about human nature is an area of emphasis among scientists disposed to search for biological underpinnings of human behavior. They also study biochemical changes during physical growth, the effects of glandular secretions, and the effects of chemicals, speculating on the consequences both to the mind and to social behavior. Biological or biologically linked processes such as natural selection, hormones, brain size and shape, circadian rhythms, the biological clock that sets developmental stages in the life cycle have all been proposed as basic factors determining human social structures and processes. The discussion is broader than the analysis of the linkage of physiological and behavioral features it extends into grand theories of social order. But while sociobiologists argue that underlying physiological states determine human personality, sex-role behavior, and social action, other social scientists stress the primacy of culture or social experience, pointing to the diversity of behavior and social organization among humans and the effect of social learning in changing the life course.

The issues involved in the debate are the extent to which biology explains human behavior and whether any animal behavior provides clues to the origin and perpetuation of human social organization. At one extreme on the continuum are the sociobiologists of the Wilson school. In the center are other biologists (including some other sociobiologists) who are far more moderate in their claims or who do not explain patterns of social organization as being due to biological factors or who question whether human social organization can be understood by observing the habits of other animals. At the other end are biologists who acknowledge a strong effect of social experience on the human body and on the environment and thus on the evolutionary process. Most social scientists tend to be at this end of the continuum, with a few exceptions (van den Berghe, Goldberg).

But the extremes are not polar opposites. The behaviorist B. F. Skinner believes that biology plays a part in determining human behavior but feels that humans are enormously malleable and subject to social conditioning. And even E. O. Wilson has conceded that environment may alter a person's behavior from the course set by genetic predisposition.

Because the debate focuses on politically charged issues such as the social and juridical inequality of women, the arguments on both sides extend to the consequences of holding such views. Sociobiologists have not, for example, claimed that humans are what they eat, although eating is a biological necessity. (They do claim, however, that a preference for meat has guided the establishment of such social institutions as the nuclear family.)[2] Today biologically deterministic explanations of gender behavior compete with social explanations of a wide array of social phenomena. As we have seen, biological explanations have been used to support inequality between the sexes, as they have been used to support inequality between the races and other dominant and subordinate groups.[3]

There are no clear-cut camps, although various positions have been taken. But most of the evidence and critical analyses do make a convincing argument for resisting simplistic biological explanations and models of "man" that indicate an evolutionary and genetic basis for the hierarchy affixed to sex status. This is not only because the political perspective of many sociobiologists—justifying male dominance and social hierarchy— is objectionable to the egalitarian-minded but also because the argument is said to rest on dubious, inappropriate, highly selective, and flawed data,

2. The argument is implied in many of the papers that constitute the volume *Man the Hunter* edited by Lee and DeVore (1968). In it, Steward (1968) points out that "hunting . . . gives men a distinctive and important subsistence role and was presumably the principal factor that created the nuclear family" (p. 331). Although men "depend primarily on the more stable and abundant food sources (vegetables   ), they are nevertheless willing to devote considerable energy to the less reliable and more highly valued food sources such as medium and large mammals. . . . Life would be boring indeed without the excitement of meat feasts" (Lee, 1968: 41). Furthermore, Washburn and Lancaster (1968) point out that "men enjoy hunting. . . . Part of the motivation for hunting is the immediate pleasure it gives the hunter" (p. 299). They suggest that in the division of labor, because men hunt (women are less mobile) and share the meat from the hunt, certain adaptations occur that make the process run smoothly. The nuclear family reduces competition between the men for women (each woman becomes dependent on one man). The incest taboo prevents premature assumption of adult roles for men as fathers (which brother-sister sexual relations might precipitate). This leads to exogamy and other adaptations in the family structure to ensure equal sex ratios.

3. "Biology has always been used as a curse against women. From Darwin to Desmond Morris, from Freud to Robin Fox, from animal behaviorists who consider themselves open minded but 'realistic' to the sober professors of ethology, the message has rarely changed: men are biologically suited to their life of power, pleasure, privilege, and women must accept subordination, sacrifice, and submission" (Naomi Weisstein, 1982: 41).

oversimplification in logic, and inappropriate inferences by use of analogy.[4]

Brain Function and Differentiation

Size, shape, and lateralization of the brain have been used to explain intellectual differences between women and men, blacks and whites, and Asians and Europeans.

Nineteenth-century anatomists and anthropologists attempted to link brain size to intelligence. They claimed that the smaller size of female brains accounted for differences in intellect between women and men; a similar argument was used to explain differences between blacks and whites. The obsession with brain size continued into the twentieth century. The inaccuracy of these views and the faulty evidence on which they are based have been exposed in a detailed reevaluation by the paleontologist and historian of science Stephen J. Gould in his book *The Mismeasure of Man* (1981).

Today, the work of Norman Geschwind (1972, 1974, 1979) on differences between women and men in left and right hemispheric dominance has received a great deal of attention and is regarded by many social and natural scientists as establishing a cause of perceived sexual differences in orientation and capacities.[5] He believes that the male brain is more lateralized (that is, each half works independently) and women's are less lateralized (the two halves interact more than do those of men). Thus, it is argued, men can do different types of things simultaneously, whereas women can do only one thing at a time without confusion. Investigators have also claimed that a connection exists between brain lateralization and sex differences in verbal and spatial abilities, mathematical ability, cognitive style, and reproductive function (Holloway and de Lacoste-Utamsing, 1982).[6] Critics, including many brain researchers, dispute these views as unsupported by evidence and completely speculative (see Marian Lowe, 1983b,

4. Many scientists have made the case in great detail. In addition to those already cited, see Tanner and Zihlman (1976), Hubbard and Lowe (1979), Hubbard, Henefin, and Fried (1979), Sayers (1982), Haraway (1983b), Lewontin, Rose, and Kamin (1984), and Bleier (1984).

5. An anonymous reviewer for a journal to which I submitted a paper on the consequences of dichotomous thinking about gender (my presidential address to the Eastern Sociological Society, March 1984) wrote a long critique insisting that I consider Geschwind's work rather than social-structural variables as the explanation for gender distinctions in social roles.

6. According to these authors, the data suggest a sex difference in the shape and surface of an area of the posterior section of the brain—the corpus callosum. Animal studies have suggested that this area of the brain is involved in the interhemispheric transfer of visual information.

for a review and Fausto-Sterling, 1985, for an analysis of the history and dispute about brain lateralization research).[7]

Animal studies indicate differences between male and female brains in cell nucleus size in specific areas of the brain, and in axonal growth (a nerve cell process that generally conducts impulses away from the brain) and dendritic growth (the branched part of nerve cells that carry impulses toward the cell bodies that make up the brain), both of which are hormonally sensitive during the early years and later in life (Gorski, 1979, in Baker, 1980: 96). Geschwind and his colleagues suggest that the fetal brain interacts with hormones such as testosterone, which slows the growth of the left hemisphere relative to the right. Data from animal experiments show that part of the right cerebral cortex of the rat is thicker in males, while the corresponding part of the left hemisphere is thicker in females. These differences can be modified by experimentally changing the hormonal balance of the animals in infancy. Critics state, however, that there are major problems with this work and the conclusions drawn from it. One is that much of the evidence is based on animal studies and, in humans, on the medical case records of aphasia associated with unilateral brain damage (Thompson, 1984).

One researcher concedes that although "it is relatively parsimonious to assume that biological facts in nonhuman species are probably also true for humans, there are no human data in these areas of research" (Baker, 1980). This inevitably leads one to ask, does such parsimony lead scientists to the right conclusions? In their book *Not in Our Genes* (1984), Lewontin, Kamin, and Rose point out that although nerve cells—the basic units that make up the brain—are virtually identical in organisms as diverse as sea slugs and humans, the number of cells, their arrangement and interconnections, differ dramatically. Humans have between ten billion and a hundred billion cells, compared with tens or hundreds of thousands in mollusks' brains. Further, in organisms with less complex brains, most of the neural pathways are laid down—genetically specified—to form rather rigid and preprogrammed connections. This invariance gives these organisms a comparatively fixed and limited behavioral repertoire.

In contrast, the human infant is born with relatively few of its pathways already committed. Studies of brain electrical activity also provide evidence that brain lateralization can be affected by environment and behavior and is by no means a fixed or "wired-in" aspect of brain functioning

---

7. Carol Tavris has told me that there is now disagreement between Holloway and de Lacoste-Utamsing about the conclusions one may draw from their research, with de Lacoste-Utamsing taking a more conservative view on the implications for sex differences.

(Lowe, 1983b). Furthermore, Lewontin, Kamin, and Rose note that homologies of structure between species do not mean homologies of function. Locating emotions and behavioral capacities in various parts of the body has been the sport of biological determinism since the days of phrenology. *Not in Our Genes* outlines some of the functions and qualities believed to stem from brain structures. For example, the linguistic skills of the left hemisphere are paralleled by spatial skills in the right; the left hemisphere is cognitive and the right sphere is affective; the left is linear, digital, and active while the right is nonlinear, analogic, and contemplative; "the left is Western, the right Eastern." One prominent Catholic neurophysiologist has placed the seat of the soul in the left hemisphere. To this list of speculative differences are now added sex differences. If men have better spatial perceptual abilities and women better linguistic skills, these scientists reason, one might anticipate that men would be more "right-hemispheric," and women more "left-hemispheric." Yet men are said to be cognitive (left-hemispheric) and women affective (said to be a right-hemispheric function).

Even some feminist writers have adapted the lateralization argument, but they interpret its meaning somewhat differently. One strand of feminist writing, like the male biological determinists, contends that there are essential differences between men and women in the ways in which they think and feel, but claims superiority or special competence for females. Gina (as quoted by Lewontin et al., 1984: 147) argues that women should welcome "the intuitive and emotional strengths given by their right hemisphere, in opposition to the over-cognitive, left-hemisphere-dominated, masculine nature." The sociologist Alice Rossi (1984) has suggested that women may be more adept at nurturing infants because of biological factors. In her 1982 presidential address to the American Sociological Association she argued that "women have a head start in easier reading of an infant's facial expressions, smoothness of body motions, greater ease in handling a tiny creature with tactile gentleness." By contrast, "men have tendencies more congenial to interaction with an older child, with whom rough and tumble physical play, physical coordination, teaching of object manipulation, are easier and more congenial." She notes that these are general tendencies but that "there is, however, a good deal of evidence in animal and human research to support the view that sex hormones and sex differentiation in neurological organization of the brain contribute to these differences" (Rossi, 1984: 13).[8]

8. Rossi, however, claims that gender differences in certain abilities such as spatial visualization and mathematical ability are not immutable. Instead, she proposes that such deficiencies may

Brain lateralization theories have now found adherents among other groups seeking to maximize their distinctiveness. Clyde Haberman (1984) writes of a Japanese physician, Tadanobu Tsunoda, who has described how the Japanese brain functions differently from other brains. According to Tsunoda, the Japanese process natural sounds such as the wind in the left hemisphere of the brain while all other peoples use the right hemisphere.[9] I have not read any commentary by American sociobiologists on this phenomenon, but it had broad appeal in Japan. Haberman reports that the book was a best-seller and that many Japanese still accept its basic premise. It is illustrative of the compelling appeal of simplistic biological explanations, especially those that support cultural stereotypes.

Respected biologists acknowledge that although the evidence for hemispheric differentiation and specialization of function is among the most intriguing of the past decade's developments in human neuroscience, its relationship to individual differences in behavior is unclear. The cultural anthropologist Richard Thompson has warned that the "weight of modern evidence argues against rigid dichotomies in the interpretation of hemispheric functions—particularly the shopworn verbal/nonverbal distinction—and in favor of continuities, differences in degree rather than in kind" (1984: 98). Thompson declares that there is an "irresistible human urge, to which science is not immune, to erect grand explanatory edifices on limited and often contradictory evidence." He expresses concern that some anthropologists are being seduced by the findings of "split-brain" researchers because they offer simple answers to perplexing questions about relationships between culture and cognition. The dichotomous distinctions that are the frameworks of these views, he suggests, "pose substantial impediments to our thinking" and divert us from recognizing that "the brain's normal mode of functioning is *unity,* not dichotomy." As Springer and Deutsch (1981) put it, a sort of "dichotomania" seems to have us in its grip when we talk about the brain. We search for and see differences rather than integration in cerebral functioning.

Studies of lateralization have been of interest and utility to those studying the impact of impairment to parts of the brain because of strokes and other damage and, of course, to those studying the brain's general func-

---

have to be treated by means directed to their biological genesis—for example, dealing with math anxiety in girls by biofeedback training.

9. More curiously, Haberman (1984: 16) argues that everyone except the Japanese processes music in the right hemisphere. "Somehow they rely on the right half only for Western musical instruments. Japanese instruments go to the left. The doctor concluded, among other things, that the Japanese brain simply was not equipped for foreign languages and that Japanese debilitate themselves by even trying to learn them."

tioning. But even the leading "split-brain" researcher, neurobiologist Roger Sperry, commented in his Nobel laureate address: "The left-right dichotomy . . . is an idea with which it is very easy to run wild" (1982: 1224).

The psychologist Carol Tavris reports that the argument that hemispheric differences account for different abilities in women and men is rapidly becoming dated among brain researchers (personal communication). The objections of the scientists noted above are reinforced by reviews of research literature that indicate a lack of data to support the relationship between brain lateralization and behavioral differences of the sexes (for an overview, see Fausto-Sterling, 1985).

Sex Hormones

Neuroendocrinological differentiation between the sexes is also interpreted as a cause of the existing social order, and particularly of patriarchy. "Attempts to create society where males are not in dominant positions must fail," argues the sociologist Steven Goldberg (1974), who has promoted the sociobiological explanation of human behavior. Goldberg claims that this is so because of "the inexorable pull of sexual and familial biological forces which eventually overcome the initial thrust of nationalistic, religious, ideological or psychological forces that had made possible the temporary implementation of Utopian ideas" (1974: 36). Domination by men thus is ensured in groups and in pairs with women and children. Biologists such as David Barash (1979: 189), who reason that male domination is inexorable and that "the exclusion of women from major policy roles is an international, species-wide phenomenon," argue that genes may produce differences in behavior or ability by programming the activities of the sex hormones, which create noticeable distinctions between the sexes during fetal development and at puberty (Tavris and Wade, 1984). The "male" hormone, testosterone, is said to affect the fetal brain at a particular phase of development, predisposing boys to greater physical activity and more aggressive behavior than girls and accounting for males' higher social ranking (a process also true for nonhuman primates).

The biologist Anne Fausto-Sterling (1985) explains, however, that although it is clear that hormones play a part in developing sex characteristics, it is not at all clear that they play a role in creating social behavior, even nurturing or sexual behavior; high testosterone levels may not cause aggression or low levels reduce aggression. For example, studies of male sex offenders who have been chemically castrated conclude that "the procedure is not particularly effective." Marion Lowe (1983b) also notes that in humans no correlations have been found between levels of testosterone and social rank or aggression. Further, although hormones are produced by gene-initiated processes, they are subject to changes in the social environment, such as exercise and stress. For example, Fausto-Sterling (1985) points out that "elevated testosterone levels may, in fact, result from aggressive behavior."

Hormonal differences between men and women have long been identified. Since experimenters tend to use the findings of animal studies to support their claims that male hormones produce dominance, it should also be noted that scientists have found evidence for the effect of environment on hormones (Hoffman, 1982). In experiments with monkeys, Barchas (1984) and Rose, Gordon, and Bernstein (1972) have shown that social position can alter hormonal ratios. Monkeys whose hierarchical positions have shifted because of the removal of the dominant member of the group manifest a change in their testosterone levels.

The question relevant to the genders in society is the meaning of differences in hormonal levels. Lewontin, Rose, and Kamin report that for Goldberg, there is an unbroken line between androgen binding sites in the brain, rough and tumble play in infants, and the male domination of state, industry and the nuclear family. Wilson is more cautious. We can go against it if we wish, he maintains, but only at the cost of some efficiency. (Lewontin et al., 1984: 154). If the hormone testosterone is supposed to make men aggressive and thus fit for public office, "female" hormones and the cycles attached to them are seen as a detriment to women's participation in public life. Edgar Berman, medical adviser to the late Hubert Humphrey, warned against women's participation in public affairs because of their "raging hormones,"[10] and more recently UN ambassador Jeane Kirkpatrick reported that some White House critics resisted her appointment because of her female "temperament" ("Sexism Is Alive," 1984). No similar hormonal barriers to decision-making posts have been seen to exist for men. Curiously, men have been excused from infidelity by the popular culture as the victims of "male menopause," and by sociobiologists who see such behavior as an evolutionary response.

The link between hormones and menstruation has been widely viewed in the common culture as an explanation for women's emotional behavior

10. Berman later published a book, *The Compleat Chauvinist* (1982), in which he provided "biological evidence" for his views that menopausal women might create havoc if they were in public office. Chapter titles from his book: "The Brain That's Tame Lies Mainly in the Dame," "Testosterone, Hormone of Champions," and "Meno: The Pause that Depresses" (Tavris and Wade, 1984). See also E. R. Ramey (1973), "Sex Hormones and Executive Ability."

and as somehow related to their intellectual competence or incompetence. A "scientific" basis has been claimed for this folk-culture view by some psychologists, psychoanalysts, and physiologists. For example, one of the most widely cited proponents of this view, Katherina Dalton (1964), claimed that her studies established that women's crimes and test scores could be correlated with their menstrual cycle. But the biologist Joan Hoffman (1982) suggests, in her review of literature on biorhythms in humans, that the degree to which hormone changes affect moods and behavior varies from person to person and even from month to month in some individuals. Furthermore, women have much lower rates of crime and accident compared to men, whether these rates are associated with menstrual periods or not. Periodic fluctuations in hormone levels of women because of the menstruation cycle have been associated with mood changes and physical complaints. But the superstitions that surround menstruation and the difficulty of conducting unbiased studies have made resolution of the matter problematic.

Although physical discomfort is experienced by some women, evidence of hostility, depression, and anxiety associated with the cycle is contradictory. The psychologist Mary Parlee (1973, 1982) has attacked findings for the existence of a "premenstrual syndrome" because of faulty methodology and unfounded interpretations. Her own research shows fluctuations in women's moods, but they differ from those reported in other studies. Golub's work (1975) shows no differences in test performance over the course of the menstrual cycle, and Persky (1974) has found no changes in mood across the cycles of a sample of women. Several studies show that some of the distress reported by women results from their own beliefs and expectations. In one such study by Burke, Burnett, and Levenstein (1978), men and women filled out a questionnaire asking about their physical and emotional symptoms that day. Those women who knew the study concerned menstruation reported more stress if they were in the premenstrual phase of their cycles. But those who did not know the purpose of the study did not differ overall from men.

Claims for the existence of premenstrual syndrome, however, have now spread to the courts—attorneys of women indicted for murder have even attempted to use Dalton's work as a defense. So too, a new industry of drugs and psychological therapies for women suffering the emotional effects of premenstrual syndrome has recently arisen. Of course, some women do experience menstrual pain (dysmenorrhea) that is related to physical causes and can be treated.

In reality a wide range of behavior is exhibited in daily life by each sex. This variety is not easily explained by sociobiologists, who see dominance and passivity as the distinctive characteristics of men and women, respectively. But many men are passive and many women are aggressive.[11] There are few data, however, on the relationship between hormones and behavior derived from experiments with or observations of humans. Moreover, the human studies that have been made usually focus on individuals suffering from abnormal genetic or hormonal syndromes (Baker, 1980). Although many scientists have issued warnings about inferring human behavior from that of animals, much of Steven Goldberg's analysis (1974), like that of other sociobiologists, rests on studies of animals that are convenient to use in the laboratory, such as rats and mice whose "aggression" levels, sexuality, and nurturing behavior are manipulated by injection and castration. Of course, animal experiments can yield important insights into the functioning of the body, and we depend on them in the development of many medical and surgical techniques used to help humans. But medical professionals know it would be foolish to confine their experimentation to animals before applying new techniques to larger numbers of humans, and probably most sociobiologists would object to using a new drug that had been tested only on rats and mice. In any event, animals genetically and functionally closer to humans vary in their linkage between hormonal levels and behavior, and they differ from rats and mice.

Not only do some scientists use animal analogies to make inferences about human behavior; they use human behavior to make inferences about animal behavior. Thus, they speak of "gang-rape" among mallard ducks, "harem-keeping" by baboons, and "prostitution" in hummingbirds and sometimes mention these activities in turn to explain the "naturalness" of such acts in the human species (Lewontin et al., 1984: 158).

Some correctives to anthropomorphic models of male dominance, female passivity and nurturance, and male disdain have been found in new studies over a range of animal groups. Many of them show evidence for female dominance, autonomy, and power; for male nurturance and cooperation; and for monogamous behavior as well as promiscuity in both males and females. They also indicate that the selection of the specific animal group can yield different conclusions when collecting or considering biological evidence to support or dispute the "natural" basis for some human pattern.

11. There is also a male climacteric, which entails gradual reduction in the production of testosterone over the years as part of the aging process (Bahr, 1976; Flint, 1982).

Evolution and Anthropological Studies

Many sociobiologists of the Wilson school have been committed to a model
of inequity as a product of the natural order; they argue that male domination (patriarchy) is the most adaptive form of society, one that confers
an advantage on individuals who operate according to its precepts. Thus
E. O. Wilson (1975a, 1978), Tiger (1969), Fox (1971), and Goldberg
(1974) maintain that the near-universality of male dominance arose because of the long period of dependence of the human infant and the early
modes of obtaining food—hunting and gathering. Male-based cooperation
was expressed through dominance relations. Men guarded the band and
thus ensured its survival. There was pressure on men to perfect hunting
skills and on women to stay home and mind the children. Each sex developed cognitive abilities attached to these activities. A socially imposed
hierarchical division of labor between the sexes gradually became genetically fixed (Tavris and Wade, 1984; Fausto-Sterling, 1985; Kitcher, 1985;
Lewontin et al., 1984).

Anthropological accounts can help test this theory because they provide
cross-cultural and intracultural analyses from small-scale nonliterate societies to large complex societies. Those anthropologists who have compared only modern societies to ascertain the sources of human traits and
social arrangements are limited by the fact that these societies related to
one another by philosophy, economy, and even political systems. As a
result, some forms of social organization appear to be universal. But even
these comparisons indicate a wide variety of social forms and much variation between the sexes and among individuals, groups, and races. Certain
questions about social organization—such as "Is the family universal?"
"Is the sexual division of labor universal?" "Is hierarchy characteristic
of all human societies?"—can be answered only with the help of anthropologists who consider a wider range of societies than do other social
scientists, and who also interpret the material evidence of prior human
societies and, in the case of physical anthropologists, of past and present
"close relative" primate societies.

To this end, too, nonliterate cultures have been explored to provide
clues about what we can expect of our own societies. Margaret Mead
(1935) first made popular the notion that societies could vary considerably
in the ways their members exhibited sex-role behavior, thus suggesting
the extent to which sex roles were socially created rather than biologically

dictated.[12] Although this opened the discussion, it was still some time before anthropologists, who, like other social scientists, have been affected by the methodological problems and biases spelled out in chapter 2, engaged in a broad rethinking of past models and methods. In any case, even carefully designed observations of nonliterate societies must be kept in perspective. Most of these societies are groups of fewer than one hundred individuals (Dahlberg, 1981). Nevertheless, whatever the limitations of analyses in describing the origins of human society, hunting and gathering societies exist in which women are not subordinate to men.

In recent years, anthropologists have reevaluated the perspective of man the hunter, which long served as the principal model of the origins of human society (Haraway, 1983b; Dahlberg, 1981). Posed as complementary to this model, or in some cases contradictory of it, the model of woman the gatherer, which emerged in the 1970s, suggested new insights into what early human society might have been like and what the sources of present social organization and the evolutionary development of the human species might have been. A further refinement of models, viewing both men and women as both hunters and gatherers, has provided yet another perspective on the division of labor.

The man the hunter model has long been a source of speculation about the development of human intelligence and male dominance. Using this paradigm, primatologists and anthropologists such as Washburn and DeVore (1961) and Morris (1967) reasoned that hunting, a male activity, was a creative turning point in human evolution; that it required intelligence to stalk game and to make hunting and other tools. It also required social bonding of men and the use of language to cooperate in the hunt (Tiger, 1969), to develop tools for killing and cutting up the prey, and to distribute the meat. According to Washburn and Lancaster (1968: 293), "In a very real sense our intellect, interests, emotions and basic social life—all are evolutionary products of the success of the hunting adaptation." [13] Women, the breeders of children, fed and protected by the men, were relatively passive associates in this process. As Stephen Gould (1984b) has put it, the myth of "man the hunter" and "woman as nothing in particular" was created. Genetic and social selection for these attributes created society and human nature as we know it today, and a division of

12. Although her field work supporting these views has been questioned (Freedman, 1983), I do not believe the criticism has undermined her conclusions and general principles. See also Brady (1983); Turnbull (1983); R. Levy (1983); Marcus (1983).

13. Yet Donna Haraway (1981) points out that Washburn opposed sociobiology "for ruining social science by biologizing," in a later essay in Gregory, Silvers, and Sutch, eds., *Sociobiology and Human Nature* (1979).

labor based on sex became genetically fixed. Analysis of this model has come to have an importance beyond its usefulness in explaining the course of human history. The notion of male bonding as a product of evolution has been used frequently to justify discrimination against women in professional and business activity, in clubs, and in sports. Furthermore, bonding has been considered a process that prepares men but not women to engage in corporate life and public affairs. Thus the question arises: what merit is there to the model and the explanations derived from it?

Dahlberg (1981), among others, suggests that the account can be considered only a "just-so story" in the light of new scholarship. Beginning in the 1960s, research on primates, and on hunter-gatherer societies, and archaeological and fossil records have made the story obsolete.[14] For example, the paleoanthropological myth of man the hunter was deflated when Robert Ardrey's "killer ape," the presumed australopithecine forbear of humans, turned out to be predominantly vegetarian (S. Gould, 1984b). Ardrey (1963, 1966) had hypothesized that unique among primates, men alone "killed for a living" and committed murder for reasons other than survival; he explained concepts of human society, such as male privilege and private property, as deriving from this behavior. Lee and DeVore (1968), editors of *Man the Hunter*, did not depend on a view of man as a killer, however, and showed that gathering was an important part of the foraging way of life for nonliterate groups and probably for early humans. Further, new evidence indicated that both women and men gathered food for the group. In this analysis, however, women were hardly seen as social movers. Their contributions to society were conceptualized only in their roles as childbearers and mates.

A greater challenge to the man the hunter model came from Sally Linton (1971), who attacked the validity of theories of evolution that excluded or diminished women's contributions to human culture and society.[15] From the fact that women contribute most of the diet in contemporary hunting-gathering societies, she hypothesizes that small-game hunting practiced by both sexes probably preceded large-game hunting by men, and that females as well as males probably devised tools for their hunting and gathering and some sort of sling or net to carry babies. The collaboration and cooperation of women were probably as important to the development of culture as those of men, according to this view. Nonhuman

14. The analysis of part of this section is based primarily on Frances Dahlberg's collection of studies, *Woman the Gatherer* (1981), and her introductory essay in that volume.

15. Sally Linton's article, "Woman the Gatherer: Male Bias in Anthropology," is reprinted under the name Sally Slocum in R. Reiter, ed., *Toward an Anthropology of Women* (1975).

primate behavior was also used to provide clues to the most likely path of hominid evolution in support of the man the hunter thesis by indicating that a humanlike dominance system was to be found among our ape relatives. Like the maligned australopithecine, other primate groups were slandered or extolled according to selective human bias and the evidence sought.

"Soon after the advent of modern primate studies in the early 1960s," Erik Eckholm (1984), a science writer for the *New York Times,* wrote in a review of primate studies, "many scientists believed that they had discovered the key to primate social systems when they described hierarchies of aggressive males competing for the right to mate with seemingly passive females, whose roles appeared limited to the bearing of young." And the primatologist Sara Blaffer Hrdy was quoted as saying, "It was as if scientists had projected onto primates a mirror image of the social structure of an American corporation or university." The historian of science Donna Haraway (1938b: 182) points out that Washburn, in collaboration with his student Irven DeVore, framed "the first development of the baboon comparative model for interpreting hominid evolution from the viewpoint of man-the-hunter." Their grant proposal to the National Science Foundation in 1961 cited the relevance of baboon social behavior studies to human psychology and psychiatry.[16]

New data on nonhuman primates, however, have changed perspectives on male dominance, hierarchy, and aggression in primate societies, and today, other interpretations have been advanced. Male baboons, for example, have been observed to be very aggressive and to form alliances with other males, and these observations had been used to "prove" that it is natural for men to be aggressive and to bond with other men in social clubs. The choice of baboons, however, has been questioned as an appropriate model for human behavior. McGrew (1981) and others have pointed out that it is more useful to study chimpanzees than baboons because they are probably the primate closest to human beings. Their brains are generally similar to humans' except for size; they have cognitive capacities for symbolic communication (Linden, 1974) and self-recognition, and therefore possess a rudimentary concept of self (Gallup, 1977); they make tools (as opposed to simply using tools) for feeding, grooming, and investigation, and nests for sleeping; and they share food. Although these findings about chimpanzees had been reported in the past, it was not until the 1970s

16. Haraway (1983b: 182) explains that DeVore and Washburn were the principal investigators of this National Science Foundation study (entitled "Analysis of Primate Behavior"), although the grant supported others' work as well.

that scientists discounted the insights claimed by primatologists who based their research on other species and urged the use of the chimpanzee model for insights into human social organization.[17] This model offered, for example, different perspectives on male and female behavior. New data show that male chimpanzees keep closer emotional attachments to their siblings than females do, but not with their offspring (Eckholm, 1984). Females frequently initiate mating, and with a number of partners (Tanner and Zihlman, 1976).

Even the utility of studying the chimpanzee is questioned, however, for the chimpanzee, like all other nonhuman primates alive today, is not now and never has been a forebear of early or modern Homo sapiens. As McGrew states:

> We are neither descended nor ascended from apes in the form that we know them today. The African apes are the other living primates with which we last shared common ancestry, and the two families, Pongidae and Hominidae, have been separated for millions of years. Just how many millions of years were involved remains a matter of controversy, but whether it has been five or thirty million years the differences are acute. Our hominid predecessors are, however, extinct and chimpanzees are (just) extant. The best that we can do to reconstruct our prehistoric heritage is to infer the capacities and characteristics of the long-lost ancestral hominid from the accessible apes. (1981: 37)

Probably the most dangerous practice in the use of models and experiments to explain human nature is the selective use of data. New techniques of observation have shown how any species' behavior may be misrepresented if the researcher studies behavior only in special circumstances— of animals in zoos and cages, of humans in conditions of opportunity or repression. Whatever the utility of studying primates to learn more about human nature, McGrew and other primatologists warn that only recently have they been getting a correct account of authentic animal behavior. ''We've learned more about primate behavior in the last ten years than in the previous ten centuries,'' Alison Jolly, a primatologist, told the *New York Times* (Eckholm, 1984). Observations reported in earlier investigations have been discovered to be biased. Recent field studies of chimpanzees, gorillas, and numerous Old World monkeys have led many scientists to reconsider theories of an evolutionary or genetic basis for some forms of social order and hierarchy.

17. Much of this work is due to technological developments in DNA analysis showing that humans and apes exhibit only a 1 percent difference in DNA ordering (Rensberger, 1984: 95).

Consider the proposed biological basis for female nurturance and male indifference or male dominance and defense of the troop, derived from observation of other primate groups. For example, male rhesus monkeys in the wild show little interest in newborn infants and may behave viciously if an infant gets too near (although in the laboratory, when paired with orphaned infants, male rhesus monkeys become protective [Mitchell et al., 1974]). But male owl monkeys and marmosets often carry infants, giving them to females only for nursing (Weisstein, 1982; Tavris and Wade, 1984). Among baboons, male dominance is clear, but female dominance is typical of all the social lemurs studied (Hrdy, 1981), and gibbons manifest no sex difference in dominance (Tavris and Wade, 1984). Female prosimians push males away from food sources and hit them on the head when they get cranky (Jolly, 1966). Furthermore, females may exhibit a collective dominance by banding together to deal with males who are monopolizing a food source (Lancaster, 1973).

When one looks at a span of animal groups, one finds that among species that tend toward monogamy (including some prosimians such as the indri, gibbon, and siamang), both males and females tend to stay with a mate, but among those that are promiscuous (so to speak), such as the chimpanzee, females as well as males may copulate with as many males as they have energy and time for, even when they are not in estrus and even when they are already pregnant (Lancaster, 1984). As Tavris and Wade (1984) have pointed out, this calls into question the sociobiologist's claim that men have evolved toward promiscuity and women toward fidelity because these are their best gene-continuity strategies. Quite the contrary pattern ought to be typical of human society if chimpanzees, our closest relations, are a true model of human behavior.

The view that in all animal species males initiate sex (because of their "aggressive" nature) is contradicted by observations that females play an active role in courtship. In humans themselves, studies by Masters and Johnson (1966, 1970) have shown that initiation of sexual behavior by women is a widespread practice.

Although a good proportion of the new knowledge about primates is from research done by women,[18] including those who call themselves both feminists and sociobiologists,[19] their findings do not lead to similar interpretations. Some, like Hrdy (1977) and Ripley (1980), agree with the men

18. About 30 percent of the American Society of Primatologists are women, and about 16 percent are in an anthropological institutional division, according to Haraway (1983b).

19. Haraway (1983b) calls them "daughters of Washburn"— a prominent advocate of the man the hunter thesis and the mentor of some primatologists.

who were their mentors and who are their current colleagues that males and females may have different reproductive strategies. Others claim that this is farfetched even in the aggregate (Dolhinow, 1972; Bogess, 1979). But among the primatologists doing work in the field there is general agreement, as is summed up by one of them, Jane Lancaster: "It is virtually impossible to generalize about what [all] male primates do or how female primates act" (cited in Eckholm, 1984). For each species, sex roles have been shaped differently according to its evolutionary history and ecological setting.

The new studies of primates and nonliterate human groups have been instructive in changing the definition of man from one emphasizing single attributes (such as "man the toolmaker") to one entailing more complex combinations of social, cultural, and physical qualities. New techniques for analyzing archaeological sites and assessing the kinds of artifacts likely to be found in them forced reevaluation of theses pinpointing hunting and aggression as the main characteristics defining the human condition (Tanner and Zihlman, 1976). Artifacts likely to decay, such as straw baskets and wooden implements, had not been considered in the analysis of toolmaking, only the stones and flints that survived—thus skewing the picture of early man's and woman's activities. New studies also suggest that early tools were used not for hunting large animals but for gathering plants and hunting small burrowing animals.

It would be misleading, however, to say there is a growing consensus about "origins." Anthropologists still do not agree in their speculations on prehistory. But in most of the revised models, women join men as shapers of the species. For example, the anthropologist Nancy Tanner (1981) argues that mothers and the young, learning and gathering in an environment of growing cognitive efficiency, were the central actors in evolution. Anthropologists also vary in their views about the reproductive strategies of men and women. McGrew (1981) supports a very ancient sexual division of labor accompanied by male bonding as the basis of living groups, and Zihlman (1981) believes that the behavioral flexibility of humans precluded a rigid division of labor by sex.

Prominent among revised views of evolution is a shift in attention to female mate choice, a change from the view that it is men who choose mates. With the importance of dominance and aggression at question, the cartoon model of men with clubs dragging women into caves gives way to an image of men and women sharing grooming and food. This model coincides with the emphasis on sharing in the study of human evolution. Food sharing doubtless would have been beneficial to early hominids and need not have been based on hunting. Zihlman (1981) and McGrew (1981) suggest that sharing of gathered food could have been established before hunting because such food was abundant and predictable and required less expenditure of energy. The division of labor by sex is also challenged by anthropological analysis, including theories of man the defender and man the hunter. Defense against animal predators, according to current specu- lation, was the task not of males only but of both sexes. These probably were "rare, noisy displays, and throwing objects as a last resort" would do the job, as is common today among the !Kung bushmen and also chim- panzees (Tanner and Zihlman, 1976).

One suggestion (explained in Friedl, 1975) for the origin of the division of labor in which men are hunters is that the relative immobility of early hominid mothers burdened with infants may have encouraged a spe- cialization in range between the sexes. Unburdened males could travel farther, and when hunting was established it was males who traveled long distances after large game. (This fits with contemporary views of the geo- graphical constraints on women in their career preferences and opportu- nities because of their child-care roles.) The model of man as a long- distance hunter probably derives from observations of the prevalence of males practicing spear and bow-and-arrow hunting in today's foraging societies. But modern hunting-and-gathering societies vary with regard to the division of work. In some, men, women, and children forage together, and the men occasionally hunt. In others, women may join men in the hunt although the men may do the killing; in yet others, the sexes are highly segregated; and in a fourth type, the men provide large game, vir- tually the only source of food (Friedl, 1975: 19). In these four types, relations between men and women range from egalitarian to supremely male-dominated.

Relying on modern foraging societies for insights into the life of early hominids must be done with caution. Modern tribal societies probably do not preserve the patterns of early humans any more than do Western urban communities. We have no way of knowing whether their social relations reflect those of people who lived a hundred millennia ago (Goode, 1982b). But, as Dahlberg (1981) points out, anthropologists studying foraging so- cieties today have seen a diversity that provides evidence of the error of some sociobiological speculation. For example, they have noted the wide- spread practice of collective hunting in a variety of ways: with nets, as done by the Mbuti, with fire and noise, or with exploitation of riverbanks and other natural features. Collective hunting involves both men and women and sometimes children and is unrelated to differences in physical size or geographic range. These observations have suggested an expanded woman the hunter model arising from the study of tribes such as the Agta that do not exhibit a division of labor in food production and do not assign hunting exclusively to men (Estioko-Griffin and Griffin, 1981). Both male and female Agta can choose to be hunters when their stamina and ability make it worthwhile and cease when they lose strength. Women do not become hunters only as replacements for absent men, as is the case in some other tribes, or only in cooperation with men, but also independently.

The new anthropological literature has also provided revised views of the differential status of women. In the search for universals, women's work in food production has become an important issue in discussions of the status of women. Eleanor Leacock (1978) proposes that equality was probably the original mode and that it persisted well into early horticulture, when hunting and gathering were replaced with domestication of plants and animals. Following a Marxist interpretation, she maintains that inequality arose with private property and the alienation of the worker from the ownership and control of the means of production. She argues that in most foraging societies private property is minimal; all have access to the means of production. Connie Sutton (as cited in Weisstein, 1982) dates the subjugation of women to the development of the state. Tanner and Zihlman (1976) suggest that

> whenever women's troubles started, hunter-gatherers are of utmost importance to the understanding of our genetic legacy. They indicate that male dominance is not in the genes. It is not something we inherited in becoming human, along with a big brain. It emerged afterward and is a cultural legacy. Indeed, a new model of natural selection suggests that variability and flexibility of humans was a quality that made them survive and thus it is no surprise to find the multiplicity of social patterns that we do.

Research focused on women and children does not support the legend of man the hunter or woman the gatherer but leads to a more complex story of integrated labor. With men and women interdependent, women should not have had low status. The collection of essays edited by Dahlberg (1981) includes the work of Estioko-Griffin and Griffin, who claim that the equality of Agta women rests on their contribution to the food supply. Agta women also make decisions concerning themselves in marriage, divorce, and childbearing, their daily activities, and the distribution of the food they hunt, fish, trade for, and collect. But contribution to the food supply is no guarantee of equality. In Peggy Sanday's study (1974) of twelve societies in which female status ranged from very high to nonexistent, she found that females enjoyed most equality when they contributed just about the same amount as men to the food supply—neither very little nor the major portion. The organization of work is also important, according to Tavris and Wade (1984). When the sexes are mutually dependent and work cooperatively, as in husband-wife teams, there is more respect between the sexes than when work is organized along sex-segregated lines (Poewe, 1980; Schlegel, 1977).

It stands to reason that men or women may be at a disadvantage when they go to live with the family of their spouse far from their own family and friends. Most nonliterate societies are patrilocal: the woman goes to live with her husband's family, which requires her to make an adjustment to a new setting without the support of her own kin. But on this point, too, there is disagreement. Kaberry (1970: 180) argues that residence in the husband's band in hunter-gatherer societies does not put woman at a disadvantage in participation in its political, juridical, or religious activities. But it seems illogical to me that residence is not important in creating power differences.

In all hunter-gatherer tribes, however, size and mobility can offset the limits imposed by residence patterns. Dahlberg points out that in their small living groups, the Agta, Mbuti, Australian Aborigines, and Chipewyan resemble other foragers, of whom two-thirds live in groups of fewer than one hundred persons. In all these tribes decisions are usually made within the immediate group. Few foraging groups have a political structure beyond the local one, for with so few members it may be difficult to maintain hierarchy. Not only are living groups small, but their size and membership change throughout the year in response to changing seasons, ceremonial demands, and personal preferences. This flux regulates social relations in the absence of political structure. The formation of male peer groups, which are crucial to making women as a category subordinate to men, may be precluded when there is a shift in the ages of men in the group or a drop in membership (Draper, in Dahlberg, 1981). In the matter of mobility, its presence increases women's independence, and its absence increases their dependence. Boulding (1976) notes that mobility is usually liberating for women because few goods are carried and their housekeeping burdens are light. Mobility also reinforces interdependence among all the members of the group.

The analyses of hunter-gatherer tribes, whatever their limitations in describing the origins of human society, demonstrate the variety of ways in which both women's and men's roles are broader and less rigid than traditional stereotypes. The Agta and Mbuti are clearly equalitarian, proving that hunting and gathering societies exist in which women are not (or not very, writes Dahlberg in an aside) subordinate to men. Anthropologists who study them claim that women have a separate but equal status at this level of development. Yet the status of women in foraging societies is not always unambiguously high. Along with the "joyous pygmies," writes Dahlberg, one finds the "wife-beating" Australian Aborigines. Berndt (1981) finds consensus that Aboriginal women are the breadwinners, yet do not possess the equalitarian autonomy that Leacock hypothesizes they should have. If women contribute to the food supply and have the authority to make decisions affecting their lives, why should they be less valued than men?

Another hypothesis traces women's lower status to motherhood. But the evidence from forager societies indicates that childbearing and child care do not necessarily restrict women. In these societies many women put their work first and adjust child care to work needs, and they limit the number of children they will have by a variety of techniques. Thus this body of studies does not support the idea that women are valued less than men because of the restrictions of maternity or because of their lesser economic contributions. Neither does it support the necessity for hierarchy in all social organization. In the realms of ritual activity and symbolic values, the evidence shows flexibility and diversity and interdependent cooperation between the sexes. Furthermore, humans, unlike animals, have a particular kind of intellect and language that permits learning and communication, which can alter the environment and change the rules for survival.

Certainly, biology can provide the potential for certain kinds of social behavior and it can restrict as well. Today, scientists are finding that certain kinds of mental illness as well as physical illness may be caused by physiological factors, perhaps genetically determined. As genetic heritage may cause disability, so it may cause ability. That this is so for individuals seems clear. When we move to the group level, however, we need to exercise more caution. Some groups are disproportionately afflicted by genetically produced maladies, such as sickle-cell anemia and Tay-Sachs disease; we do not know whether some groups disproportionately inherit genetically produced abilities or other traits. But women do not belong to distinctive groups. They live with men. Women and men differ genetically with respect to the development of sexual characteristics, but they share gene characteristics for eye and hair color and basic intelligence. Are some emotional and cognitive attributes disproportionately inherited or developed by men and women? In this inquiry, as in others we have specified, how we view the problem, the questions we ask, and the categories we choose to compare will have a great deal to do with our findings. So far, as I will indicate in the chapter to follow, social factors can account for most of the variation seen between men and women.

By any system of accounting, what people and social groups make of themselves with their collective imagination far exceeds what raw physiology might indicate; in "nature" our bodies give us the capacities to do more than most of us actually try to do. Of course, a failure of imagination, fear, and discouragement also limit what we can be.

Social evolution, a process measured in millennia, can be speeded up or altered by humans. Cultural and technological change can influence the impact of a group's biological heritage. Even those most devoted to iden tifying our biological roots recognize how our physiology may be manipulated or the consequences of its structure altered through technology and the control of fertility. We have limited our reproductive potential through fertility control, and we have expanded our biological potential—as Alfred Krober (1952) and Ralph Linton (1945) remarked forty years ago, and as Marshall McLuhan reminded us in a flurry of media attention in 1964— by extending our feet with cars and bicycles, our land-rootedness with airplanes, our eyes with microscopes, telescopes, and eyeglasses. We use oxygen to breathe better and aspirin to ease our pain. Opinion structured by ideology suggests that it is unwise or even sacrilegious to tinker with some of these processes—by insisting on equality of the sexes or using birth control, for example—but not others—using glasses, automobiles, or aspirin. Of course, there would be no birth without wombs or sight without eyes or intelligence without brains. But humans can decide to have twenty children or none, to be myopic or to see far into other galaxies, to become informed or to burn books. As humans are ordered by nature, so too do they order it.

CHAPTER 4

It's All in the Mind:
Personality and Social Structure

P hrases such as "just like a woman" or "he's not a *real* man" are common enough in the popular culture. They allude to intellectual abilities, emotions, and personality traits, such as aggressiveness, passivity, verbal facility, analytic ability—traits believed to be character-istic of one sex or the other. They are often identified as "feminine" or "masculine," and it is believed that women and men possess them (a descriptive notion) or should possess them (a normative idea) according to their gender. Those who deviate from the accepted conventions may be regarded as abnormal or lacking in judgment or taste.

Every culture has its views about male and female traits as about the traits of all subgroups within the society. People everywhere tend to as-sociate physical differences with mental differences. Those who look dif-ferent because of skin, eye, or hair color, or shape of nose are assumed to have a different mentality. Sometimes even superficial differences in ap-pearance such as dress are believed to be a manifestation of the person within.

Like assumptions about the attributes of blacks (that they are more sex-ually or musically proficient than whites) or Jews (that they are overly ambitious, avaricious, cunning, or smart) or women (that they are less sexual, more emotional, more practical, less creative then men), what "everyone" believes, or even observes, may not be so at all.[1] Social scientists have long been engaged in trying to learn the extent to which men and women or persons from these other groups actually do possess distinctive cognitive and emotional traits. As we have seen in chapter 2,

1. For a recent discussion of the protean nature of stereotypes and their place in scientific discourse as well as common views of them, see Gilman (1985). His discussion reviews the often contradictory attributes assigned to certain groups (for example, Jews are wretched and sickly, but tough), and in particular, views of sexuality, madness, and degeneracy.

this research has been scrutinized for bias, and some long-held notions regarding basic differences between the sexes have been questioned (Maccoby and Jacklin, 1974; Sherman, 1971).

The discussion of male and female psychological differences is further complicated because questions about how and if men and women develop along different cognitive and emotional paths are usually linked to more general speculations about human development. Various theories of development still compete. Among them, the nature-nurture and continuity-discontinuity debates continue, and stage, learning, and life-span views all have their advocates. These theories try to provide a way of thinking about a variety of questions: Are dispositions to think and act part of the organism, ready to develop along a prescribed set of stages? Do people learn them early? Are all humans similarly endowed, or can only some develop certain traits and others not? What causes differences in talent, mood, loving or caring, creativity, aspiration, and the host of other attributes that characterize individuals?

Today there are competing views about the relative merits of the various models of development. Not all have been assessed by rigorous testing, and critics have questioned the procedures by which they have been evaluated. There is growing agreement, however, among many psychologists and social psychologists that human development occurs through the interplay of biological inheritance and social experience. Most believe that some combination of early and later experience is important in determining what kind of person a man or woman is apt to become. But social scientists do not agree on the relative weight of early versus later experiences, especially with regard to qualities believed to be at the core of a person's psyche—the essential self.

How scholars stand on these issues is important to the way they think about gender, although there are no consistent connections. Psychologists with a psychoanalytic perspective derived from Freud have tended to believe that the sex of an infant determines its relationship to its mother and father and that the parent-child relationship is crucial in creating lifetime identities, with males and females developing personalities characteristic of their sex. According to this model, women's personality constellation is characterized by passivity, vanity, masochism, and jealousy,[2] and women are believed to share a contempt for other women that men also feel (Freud,

2. Freud himself, however, did not believe that women and men had personalities that were polar opposites, but rather that there was overlap between the sexes. "Every individual," he wrote, "displays a mixture of the character traits belonging to his own and to the opposite sex" (1905: 219–20n). (This quote and that in note 3 are identified by Tavris and Wade [1984].)

1924).[3] Many Freudians believe that personality is established early and is unlikely to change significantly later in life. Developmental psychology is based on the work of the psychologist Jean Piaget, whose most significant contributions were made in the 1920s and 1930s, and the psychoanalyst Erik Erikson, who followed in the 1940s and 1950s. Both men set the foundation for their disciples to think in terms of set stages of development in emotional and cognitive functioning. Piaget showed that children's ability to reason and their understanding of the physical and social world change in predictable ways as they mature, and Erikson specified distinctively female and male orientations in their course of development.

Sociologists and social psychologists have followed paths originally set out by Marx and Durkheim, focusing on the role of social factors such as social class, education, and religion in determining how people think and behave. But even among sociologists there has been disagreement between those who believe that external social factors shape personality and those who think that there is nonetheless an inner core of personality that is resistant to change. Although most tend to emphasize how social situations and circumstances determine the ways in which men and women manifest different attitudes and behavior, some of *these* (such as Chodorow and Rossi) also believe that early experiences are the most important, whereas others (such as Brim, Wheeler, Kohn, Schooler) are alert to personality change even during adulthood.

But many psychologists and sociologists, as we shall see, have questioned speculations about how the personality becomes organized, whether personality traits exist, and how stable they are, and the prospect of social scientists' ascertaining with any confidence whether women and men differ substantially in personality and cognitive abilities.

Most social scientists, however, come to the study of personality and intellectual functioning believing that men and women are good at different tasks and that there is some fit between their capacities, their emotions, and their activities. These attitudes have important consequences for the way women are treated and their views of themselves. Distinctions in personality between the sexes are said to determine the choices they make among alternatives in social life and to cause them to follow particular sequences in the course of their lives. Traits, preferences, and place in the life cycle, according to many theorists, create predispositions for men and

3. "After a woman has become aware of the wound to her narcissism [realizing she lacks a penis] she develops, like a scar, a sense of inferiority. . . . she begins to share the contempt felt by men for a sex which is the lesser in so important a respect" (Freud, 1924: 253).

women to work for wages or for no pay in the family, and to work at one thing rather than another in the paid labor force. Personality traits are believed to create patterns of motivation and commitment that are different for men and women, especially in ways that affect choice and progress in their careers and the material rewards they will receive. Women's distinctive traits are said to make mothering a different kind of commitment than fathering. Interestingly, theories of this type, maintaining that the biological and social inheritance of women and men predisposes them to different values and objectives, are accepted by a diverse array of scholars, encompassing social scientists in the mainstream, feminists, Marxists, neo- and old "liberals," as well as sociobiologists and right-wing fundamentalists.

The notions that people have distinct and unchanging personalities and a consistent personality structure (Bloom, 1964; Lerner, 1986), that they go through "predictable" stages or crises that they must resolve (or fail to resolve) (Erikson, 1959), and that they are reared and socialized to have these personalities have had considerable repercussions on explanations of the different life chances and experiences of men and women.

Several avenues of research have been responsible for opening these models to scrutiny and suggesting other models for the different life sequences followed by men and women. One is the analysis of the concept of personality, its components, its unity, and its development, whether set early or unfolded in cycles through the life course. Another is the reevaluation of the processes of socialization, the ways in which social norms and values are internalized. Finally, there is the impact of situations and circumstance on personality, on motivation and aspiration, and on other personal qualities.

Of course, many variables go into the formation of a "personality" (Murray and Kluckhohn, 1950), and there are many theories to describe the process. Thousands of books and papers have been written on the subject, so one cannot review them all. But some of these explanations are particularly relevant to the question of gender differences in personality and their relationship to social roles. Personality traits are often believed to exist in combination with intellectual traits. Therefore such traits as sociability, empathy, emotionality, dependence, susceptibility to influence, self-esteem and confidence, nurturance, aggressiveness, self-assertion, isolation, and the urge to master, as well as verbal ability and abstract reasoning, are regarded as clustering in particular ways for men and women (Rossi, 1980).

Traits and Personality: The Debates

Socialization implies that people acquire traits through internalization and that the way traits are organized creates an identifiable personality. But there has been serious debate in the last decade about how much credence ought to be given to this conception. Behavior is seen as an indicator of underlying mental and emotional traits (Murray and Kluckhohn, 1950). But psychologists who have focused on the study of personality have usually recognized the complexity of understanding or typifying personalities. Over the past decade, some scholars have been critical of social scientists who tend to reify the concept of "trait" and the specific qualities that are believed to compose a personality.

Carolyn Wood Sherif, for example, has asked, "How do we know what a personality trait is, and how do we know what a personality is?" She suggests that personality is measured by tests developed by social scientists who think they know what it is, and she notes the hazards of this route: "The score on a test or the level of task performance is taken as indication that the person *is* intelligent, or aggressive, or submissive, or anxious, or *has* this or that motive. By verbal magic, a specific set of actions in a specific research situation is transformed into the label for something that the person has, is, or possesses as a trait" (1979: 115).

Presumably traits should cluster so that a total personality with coherence emerges. We often observe coherence. A man who demonstrates cutthroat tendencies in business might also steal the girlfriend of his partner. On the other hand, he might not. There are widely accepted stereotypes that men demonstrate clusters of traits such as self-protection, self-expansion, taking charge, and assertiveness and that in women are found clusters of traits such as docility, sweetness, caring, and a sense of being at one with others.

The study of personality is an example of scholarship that is an expression of stereotyped views. This includes the work of some feminist scholars, of whom Carol Gilligan (1982) stands out today as an advocate of the view that women and men have different orientations and perspectives toward nurturance, morality, and justice. Gilligan claims, for example, that boys have selves "defined through separation" and that girls have selves "delineated through connection" (p. 35). She further asserts that women feel "a responsibility to discern and alleviate the 'real and recognizable trouble' of this world," whereas men's moral imperative "appears rather as an injunction to respect the rights of others'' (p. 100).[4] Gilligan does not state that these distinctions are biologically determined, although she suggests that they are deeply rooted. Her delineation of differences between the sexes has been enthusiastically received by many feminists, who regard her characterization of women's ''caring'' morality as a positive orientation to behavior.

Gilligan's work and its reception raise a number of questions—most of them asked many times before. More than a decade ago, Carlson (1971) assumed that women tend toward ''communion,'' defined as contact, openness, union, and cooperation, and that men tend toward ''agency,'' defined as tendencies toward separation, isolation, an urge to master, and repression of feeling and impulse. The conclusions of these psychologists does raise large questions. Do women have distinctly different clusters of traits? If they do, are they evidence of deeply rooted and persisting personality differences or of skin-deep role playing (with sometimes profound human consequences)? What kind of evidence is persuasive in answering these questions?

Many inventories of sex differences in intellect and personality have been assembled in past years. In 1968 Josef E. Garai and Amram Scheinfield cited 474 studies in their monograph ''Sex Differences in Mental and Behavioral Traits,'' which, as Tavris and Wade (1984) point out, reported findings that conform to popular stereotypes. For example, Garai and Scheinfield concluded that females are generally found to have greater social needs than males and that males are superior to females in abstract reasoning and conceptualizing—which explains ''the outstanding achievements of men in science, philosophy, and the construction of theories.'' Garai and Scheinfield, however, did not explain how they chose their studies or evaluate the quality of the procedures used in them. Research on sex differences before the 1970s was, as we have seen, often contaminated by bias.

The feminist scholar Arlie Hochschild (1973), in a review of research on sex roles, reported on studies showing that the sexes differed in the ways they think (Maccoby, 1966), perceive (Bieri et al., 1958), aspire (Horner, 1968; Turner, 1964), experience anxiety (Sinicle, 1956), daydream (Singer, 1968), and play competitive games (Uesugi and Viachke, 1963). Her overview of this research concluded that very young girls exceed boys in verbal ability but do as well in counting, spatial ability, and analytic tasks, and that young girls do better on certain measures of crea-

4. See Kerber et al. (1986) for a discussion of Gilligan's work in a special symposium in *Signs* 11, no. 2 (Winter 1986): 304–33.

tivity but not on others. But on virtually every measure, the studies found
that boys sooner or later do better (Maccoby, 1966; Freeman, 1970; Suter,
1971).

Some of these studies have been reviewed and criticized and their validity questioned because of the findings of new studies and critical reviews
of the body of knowledge in the field. As a case in point, we shall explore
the research on aggression in some detail. Aggression has been identified
as a "trait" found to occur among males more than females (Maccoby
and Jacklin, 1974). It is an important attribute to examine because it is
supposed to account for the domination of men in the power structure of
society and in their relations with women. Yet the very term *aggression*
refers to a loose collection of behaviors and attitudes often unrelated to
one another, as a review by Brinkerhoff and Booth (1984) points out.
Predation, initiative, competition, dominance, territorial behavior, and
hostility are among the ideals incorporated into studies of aggression.

A comprehensive review of hundreds of experimental studies on adult
female and male aggression by Frodi, Macaulay, and Thome (1977) notes
the methodological and logical perils that lurk in research on sex differences in aggression. Among these they report that a majority of the 72
studies they reviewed that involved a measure of some form of aggressive
behavior in adults concluded that males are more aggressive than females.
Yet 61 percent of these studies did not show the expected higher male
than female aggressiveness under all conditions. Men clearly took the lead
in physical aggression without anger, but this is only one indicator of
aggression among others such as verbal abuse and taking over leadership
in a group. Because bias on the part of aggression researchers has led them
to assume that all males are more aggressive than females, they have rarely
felt constrained to explain variations among indicators. Reviews of these
studies also revealed that many are not as comparative as they claim to
be—many that label men as aggressive use only male subjects. When
Frodi, Macaulay, and Thome examined 314 experimental studies of various kinds of aggression reported between 1967 and 1974, they found that
54 percent included as subjects men only, 24 percent both sexes, and 8
percent women only; 14 percent did not specify the sex of the subject or
analyze sex differences. In a survey by McKenna and Kessler (1974; cited
by Frodi et al., 1977) of more than 80 general theoretical discussions of
human aggression in books and journals up to 1974, they found that only
a handful assessed the magnitude of the differences detected between men
and women and questioned whether they were large enough to warrant
characterizing women as less aggressive than men. Eagly (1987), using

the technique of meta-analysis for a more recent review of sex differences in aggression, concludes that aggressive and nonaggressive behaviors are tied to social roles. In some, such as the military, men are required to exert aggressive behavior, but in others, such as medicine, they are discouraged from such behavior. The magnitude of differences in adults was found to vary with situational factors and perceived consequences of the behavior.

Aggression studies have been further challenged on the ground that a difference in theoretical starting points leads to the creation of very different experimental situations, often with unrecognizable and uncontrollable factors that may produce varying results. Studies using hypothetical behavior—designed to yield aggression as a personality trait—have shown that males *report* greater physical aggression than actually takes place (Frodi et al., 1977). Many of these studies have been taken to prove the existence of greater aggression in males, when in actuality the data may be merely reflections of internalized sex stereotypes. As Frodi and her associates point out:

Studies that do not involve angered subjects or (known) specific, live targets, but that are concerned with the general expression of hostile or aggressive attitudes or with uncovering individual personality traits, seem to produce the sex difference that the sex-role stereotype would predict—that is, men display more overt or explicit aggression than do women, in response to hypothetical or requests for self-report. However, in approval of violence, appreciation of hostile humor, and willingness to admit hostile feelings, sex differences do not always appear. (1977: 641)

Frodi's encyclopedic review also assays various categories of studies, published for the most part between 1966 and 1973, of perception, learning, and memory; intellectual abilities and cognitive styles; achievement motivation and self-concept; activity level and emotionality; social approach-avoidance and power relationships.

On the basis of their evaluation of the empirical literature, Maccoby and Jacklin (1974) concluded that many beliefs about sex differences are unfounded, a few are supported, and several reverse common belief. Among the unfounded ones are those that report that girls are more "social" and more suggestible, have lower self-esteem, and excel over boys at repetitive tasks; that boys are more analytical; that girls are more affected by heredity and boys by environment; that girls are less motivated than boys toward achievement; and that girls are more auditorially oriented and boys are more visually oriented. They report equivocal evidence with regard to tactile sensitivity, fear, timidity, anxiety, competitiveness, dominance, compliance, nurturance, and "maternal behaviors." But in their estimation certain sex differences *do* hold up—that girls excel in verbal ability and boys in quantitative ability, and that boys are more aggressive.

Certainly, Maccoby and Jacklin showed that many popular stereotypes are *not* supported by any research. They also analyzed studies to match data with interpretation and found inconsistencies. But the conclusions of their effort, no matter how comforting or dismaying to believers or nonbelievers in sex differences, have been criticized by some psychologists because of the problems the critics say are inherent in most if not all studies of sex differences (Block, 1976; Sherman, 1975). They question the merit of using the kind of studies produced by psychologists to determine sex differences and similarities. Maccoby and Jacklin simply collected all studies on "sex differences" based on "any differences observable between groups defined as male and female regardless of the source of the difference" and tallied the pro and con findings regardless of their assessment of the studies' methodological merits.

The validity of the entire enterprise is questioned by Sherman (1975), since "research involving human males and females necessarily fails to control or randomize relevant factors: therefore few, if any, scientifically valid conclusions can firmly be made about psychological differences attributable to the *sex* of the subjects." Eagly (1983) has called into question the results of laboratory studies of sex differences that make claims to control for status differences. Eagly points out that laboratory experiments often yield specious findings because they do not account for the influence of expectations created in the real world about the relative rank of men and women. She suggests that it is foolish for researchers to expect subjects to suspend belief about what they know to be real differences in power (for example) in the world outside the lab because of the equalitarian assignments made within it. Interpreting her studies of influence, in which small differences were found between males and females, she suggests that these are not due to different traits of each sex but to assumptions about or attributions of traits, emanating from social structural factors, such as the existing distributions of women and men in social roles.

Other objections to studies revealing sex differences or similarities relate to the use of limited cohorts of subjects and generalizing from them to all men and women. Deaux (1984), for example, objects to extending findings on individual differences, when they are often small, to entire social categories.

Sherman has a further objection to the sex-difference studies on which

Maccoby and Jacklin based their analysis. For the most part, these studies draw conclusions from research on early childhood which are then applied to males and females generally. Block (1976) also objects to the use of child subjects and hypothesizes that sex differences would seem more differentiated if they were based on samples of adults; alternatively some sex differences found in children disappear in adults.

Other criticisms of the literature on sex differences center on the fact that sample sizes often are small and studies with widely discrepant samples are compared. Furthermore, sex differences account for only a small percentage of the variance.[5] As Maccoby and Jacklin (1974) and, more recently, Deaux (1984) and Eagly (1983) point out, sex has not been a consistently powerful predictor. When sex differences are found, the determinants of the behavior are likely not to have been identified.

How can an effort to summarize findings of studies on sex differences be valuable if the research on which it is based is impaired to begin with? Consider the research used by Gilligan to support her assertion that women speak and think in "a different voice" from men's. The primary research on which Gilligan's book rests is a study of twenty-nine women confronting a decision about whether or not to have an abortion. No study of a comparable dilemma faced by men is offered in this work.[6] To this "evidence" is added the results of an experimental study of eight boys' and eight girls' responses to a classic dilemma, in which a man must decide whether or not to steal a drug needed by his dying wife. Gilligan's interpretation of the accounts by the eight boys and eight girls of the "right" thing to do supports her view that girls are more "caring" than boys, but my reading of these accounts indicates no such conclusions. I find considerable variation among the girls' reflections on this problem as I read the protocols in her book, for example. Furthermore, in a forum assessing Gilligan's work, Catherine Greeno and Eleanor Maccoby (1986) assert that Gilligan has attacked a straw man. The central theme of her book is an attempt to dispute Lawrence Kohlberg's finding that women's moral reasoning is less mature than that of men. In a comprehensive review paper, Lawrence Walker (1984) considers sixty-one studies in which the Kohlberg paradigm is used to score moral reasoning for subjects of both

5. In Eagly and Carli's review of social influence, sex differences accounted for 1 percent of the variance (1981); in J. S. Hyde's recent assessment of the aggression literature, there was a median variance estimate of 5 percent (1982). These and other examples are reported in Deaux (1984).

6. Zella Luria (1986) also points out that twenty-nine women considering abortions in Boston may provide an important example of decision making, but they cannot provide data on how men and women differ in such thinking.

sexes; there is no trend of males scoring higher than females on Kohlberg's scales. Among adults, the large majority of comparisons reveal no
sex differences. Greeno and Maccoby conclude on the basis of this study
and other research that women have a different *reputation* for altruism and
empathy than do men, but that whether the reputation is deserved is another question.

The notion that men and women differ significantly in their perception
of themselves in relation to others has also been challenged by Carol Stack
(1986) on the basis of her research on black migrants who have returned
to the rural South. Stack reports that the poor black men and women of
her study converge in the ways in which they relate to others and in their
"vocabulary of rights, morality and the social good" (1986: 323). Thus,
even if Gilligan's view of sex differences in morality were correct for
middle-class white men and women, it does not hold for other cultural
groups.

The Gilligan research also failed to take into account other broader inquiries into the psychology of morality. For one thing, she did not study
actual behavior and actual decisions. For another, she did not incorporate
the work of psychologists who study morality from another angle of vision. For example, Bibb Latane and John Darley's 1970 book *The Unresponsive Bystander* deals with a fundamental question in morality: whether
individuals will involve themselves in other people's troubles and help
them out when they see assistance is needed. The investigators showed
that it is not "general" morality that determines whether or not a person
will help another in trouble but the conditions of the situation—whether
others are watching, for example.

Jacklin, Maccoby, and their associates (1984) are trying to produce a
model research project on sex differences that will not be subject to many
of the objections expressed about the studies they evaluated and tallied in
preparation for *The Psychology of Sex Differences* (1974). This longitudinal research with a group of 275 children, using biological indicators as
well as psychological measures, has been conducted over a ten-year period and continues; thus it meets the criterion of longitudinal perspective
and avoids a "snapshot" view of difference. In the course of their research, which tracks the development of the children from birth to the first
grade, they have examined hormone concentrations in both sexes from
birth, studied behavior and temperament, and observed parents' treatment
of the children. Not claiming generalizability to all males and females,
the report of the first stage of their inquiry concludes that little boys and
girls are more alike than has been generally assumed. "The similarities in

little boys and girls are far more significant than their differences," they report. Furthermore, they did not find a relationship between sex hormones and sex-stereotypical behavior.

But they did find a few differences. For example, a slightly larger number of girls than of boys show a tendency toward timidity, and a somewhat larger proportion of boys show a greater readiness for arousal to anger and aggression. But these differences and others are overshadowed by a wide overlapping of distributions between the two sexes. Sex differences, like differences in height, are found at both ends of the scale, Jacklin explains, but most people fall in the middle, where males and females share a common range. Variation *within* the sexes is more important, in any case, than the difference between them. This analysis musters no convincing proof to support the contention that sex differences are tied to inborn or ingrained qualities of character and intellect. There are other issues in the analysis of personality that have been revealed through the analysis of gender distinctions.

Complexity of personality traits is important to consider. Men and women do not have *one* trait such as timidity or aggression; they have many. As Tavris and Wade (1984) point out, when sex differences appear in research they are usually linked to specific situations and conditions. The differences may be real enough (that is to say, statistically significant), but they do not become molded into entirely consistent personality traits. Different roles evoke different "personality" characteristics in people. The work of Veroff (1983), Gurin (1985), and others (Mischel, 1984; Cantor and Kihlstrom, 1983) has shown it is theoretically impossible to isolate a stable personality factor out of context.

Role theory in sociology has been criticized by some feminist scholars on the ground that it encourages researchers to think in stereotypes. Role theory, however, can help explain how "female" and "male" roles create not only behavior but "personality." Analyses of personality traits do not typically focus on the multidimensionality of people's personalities and the normative prescriptions of attitudes attached to social roles.

Capacity and Achievement Attribution Theory

Most theories of gender, regardless of the discipline, deal either directly or indirectly with role differentiation. Psychologists focus on the attributes that both men and women feel are appropriate and particular to each gender, an approach called attribution theory. Broverman and her colleagues

(1972; Rosenkrantz et al., 1968; as discussed in Deaux, 1976) have identified in a series of studies two distinct clusters of traits that distinguish
men from women. The first set clusters around competency and in the
case of males includes independence, competitiveness, objectivity, dominance, activeness, logicality, and ambitiousness, and self-confidence. The
opposites of these traits are regarded as female and include dependence,
noncompetitiveness, and subjectivity. The second set clusters about expressive qualities. Women are typically seen as tactful, gentle, and aware
of the feelings of others, whereas men are viewed as blunt, rough, unaware of others, and unable to express their feelings. Often men and women
who do not exhibit these expected traits are thought to be homosexuals,
thus negating their given-gender association.

These stereotypes reflect cultural values as well. Broverman and her
colleagues (1972) as well as others have found that higher values are assigned to the competency (male-associated) cluster than to the expressive
(female-associated) cluster (Broverman et al., 1972; McKee and Sheriffs,
1956; MacBrayer, 1960). This, of course, has serious consequences for
the value placed on men's and women's activities.

One criticism of attribution theorists is that they leave the individual
"lost in thought" with no machinery to link thought with action (Snyder
et al., 1977: 657). Thus, it is important to discuss the role of stereotypes
as a linking mechanism. Perception of a person's sex or race is often
noticed first in social interaction and "can gain high priority for channel-
ing subsequent information processing and even social interaction" (Snyder et al., 1977: 657). Stereotypes create a self-fulfilling prophecy (Merton, 1948) in that others' behavior is mediated by the expectation created
by the stereotype.

In sociology, Berger, Zelditch, Cohen, and others have tested this process, which they call status-expectancy theory. Their experimental work
links stereotpyes with behavior, showing how discrimination results from
the expectations people have of others who belong to groups believed to
possess certain traits. Both this theory and attribution theory explain the
workings of stereotypes in modifying the behavior of a person and the
other with whom he or she may interact. This has important implications
because many judgments are made on an intuitive or "first impression"
basis in such situations as meetings, interviews, or candidacy for public
office. What is happening in these situations is that judgments based on
stereotyped behaviors or physical attributes supply the information used
in the evaluation of the person in question.

Attribution theory has been useful in debunking myths about the capabilities of both men and women. Changes in behavior can also undermine the evidence for ongoing myths. An important change occurs as women realize their full potential. For example, the cultural myth that women are not as capable as men in professional jobs has been successfully challenged in the fields of law (Epstein, 1970a, 1981b), medicine (Lorber, 1984), and the military (Stiehm, 1981). A similar perception regarding women's performance in craft jobs has also been debunked (Walshok, 1981).

Studies by Berger, Cohen, and Zelditch (1966, 1972) and those reviewed by Moss and Susman (1980) and Kaufman and Richardson (1982) show that behavior consistent with what is expected is usually attributed to a characteristic of the actor, and behavior that departs from what is expected is attributed to a peculiarity of circumstance or other temporary causal factor. Since success is not expected for women as it is for men, any success they might achieve is thought to be the result of a special situation rather than ability or skill. Analyzing differences in the attribution of internal and external causes by performers themselves, Feather (1969) found that women displayed a greater tendency to use external attributions than did men in explaining their behavior.

Deaux and Emswiller (1974) made an analogous argument for the evaluation of performance by males and females of tasks in which expectations are sex-linked. They tested whether performance on a sex-consistent task would be more readily attributed to internal factors such as ability, and whether performance on a sex-inconsistent task would be more often attributed to external factors such as chance. Their findings gave clear indications that equivalent performance by males and females is not explained by the same attributions. Men were seen as more skillful, independent of the task, than were women, and performance on "male" tasks was seen as superior by the subjects. These results illustrate the popular conception that men's accomplishments are better than women's.

Deaux (1976) showed that for a wide range of tasks, the success of men and the failure of women, both more expected, tended to be attributed to ability or lack of it. In contrast, the failure of men and the success of women, being less expected, tended to be attributed to effort or luck. These trends appear in attributions for both one's own performance and that of others. M. Zuckerman (1979), reviewing the literature on unexpected performance outcomes, found a preponderance of evidence consistent with the principle that unexpected task outcomes in both females and males are attributed less to ability and more to luck.

Specific Attribute Studies: The Achievement Motive

Sex differences in the "motive to achieve" became the subject of social-scientific and popular interest in the early 1970s. In a classic study, Matina Horner (1970) reported the finding that women did not respond as men did on achievement-motivation tests. She argued that women, unlike men, have a motive to avoid success. Because they learn that achievement is considered aggressive, they worry that they will be seen as masculine should they be successful. Horner tested the theory by asking undergraduate women to respond to a hypothetical story about a young woman who rises to the top of her medical school class. Young male undergraduates were asked to respond to a similar story about a young man. Horner found that 65 percent of the young women gave negative accounts about Anne, the medical student, but that 90 percent of the men characterized John as an unequivocal success.

The first response to this study was that its results explained women's failure to achieve at the same level as men. But as the study was replicated, other researchers (Tresemer, 1977; Condry and Dyer, 1976; Shaver, 1976; Levine and Crumrine, 1975) found that men also fear success and that "fear of success" may not actually keep anyone from striving. Horner herself found that women who had demonstrated a high level of fear of success as students were successfully working in professional careers ten years later (personal communication).

In another analysis of achievement in women, Kaufman and Richardson argued that looking to success orientation as a "motive" or a personality trait was misleading. They wrote that there was a "tacit assumption that the motive was pervasive and enduring, leaving incentive and expectancy secondary in the analysis. Moreover, few had questioned whether it was truly a motive that had been tapped as opposed to a gender-role stereotype or a socially scripted defense mechanism to cope with achievement-related situations" (1982: 58).

Attribution theory has looked primarily at people's subjective interpretations of the causes for success rather than at the conditions that reinforce gender-related perceptions. It is through this process that the cultural myths play an important role. Both "fear of success" and other attributes singled out in attribution-theory studies rely on the assumption that early socialization experiences set personality according to a limited gender-role script. These theories assume that people internalize appropriate characteristics for their sex which remain with them through life (Epstein, 1976a; Brim, 1966; Kaufman and Richardson, 1982). An alternative mode regards individual achievement as a process rather than as established, fixed, and limited in its alternatives over time. Many models of achievement assume that goals set early by young girls and adolescents persist and thus influence their later decisions. But Kaufman and Richardson propose that as we examine

> the social context in which achievement-related scripts are learned, we shift the focus from gender-related passivity, dependence and fear to dynamic historical and economic forces that open and close achievement opportunities. As we turn attention to such macro issues as cultural dictates and economics, we stress that changes in these areas are as complex and variously determined as are the motives of individual actors in experimental research. (1982: 61)

In a 1986 assessment of gender differences in achievement, Brim (unpublished) maintained that "both men and women in general have equal interest in achievement and both equally face the need to resolve on an event-by-event and day-to-day basis their aspirations with their actual attainments in their particular and current fields of interest." He reminds us that even when they focus their endeavors in different spheres (such as career or family) they still engage in achievement-oriented behavior. Rearing a family, for example, may be evaluated as a success or a failure. Of course, in American society, "achievement' is usually regarded as confined to activity in the occupational world. In my observations it has seemed much more fruitful to regard achievement aspirations in all spheres as dependent on context, as Richardson and Kaufman suggest.

A Sociology of Emotions

A new "sociology of the emotions," developed by Arlie Hochschild (1975), examines how "feeling rules" in the culture prescribe the kinds of emotions that go with certain social roles. She points out that not only do social organizations specify what these feelings ought to be and techniques for enforcing them, but also that people do "emotion work" on themselves to create the appropriate feelings. Hochschild's research (1983) on the training of airline flight attendants (formerly an all-female occupation, then described by the term *stewardess*) provides an example of an institutional attempt to mold the personalities of young women to conform to the culture created by the airline industry. Thus, rules for "niceness," "sweetness," and other qualities are outlined in the training (airlines evidently do not count on women to be naturally nice or sweet). Hochschild (1979) also observed that college men and women work on themselves to "fall in love" with appropriate partners, or work at falling out of love with rejecting or unfortunate partners.

Emotion-norms have been identified in other aspects of social life. Studying achievement and job satisfaction, Joseph Veroff and his associates found that the meaning of work and achievement differed for men studied in 1957 and again in 1976 (Veroff et al., 1981). He reasoned that normative expectations had changed in the two decades. By 1976, the norms led people to believe that they *should* derive a sense of personal accomplishment from work, a change from the prior period. Thus, the expression of job satisfaction may have had a different meaning and content to a highly motivated person in the two eras.

The women lawyers I studied in the 1960s gave responses to questions about their ambitions that were reflections of cultural norms. Many of the hardest workers denied that they had high aspirations or wished to earn a high income; in the 1960s it was considered "unwomanly" to concede such attitudes. In interviewing some of these women ten years later (or in learning about their career changes through newspaper reports), I found many had organized strategies to become judges and to attain other prestigious positions (Epstein, 1968, 1981a).

The awareness of social scientists that individuals report feelings and "traits" normatively prescribed as appropriate for their sex or group is not completely new. Evans-Pritchard (1940) explored how the Nuer people learned the ways in which they should express grief at funerals—not just to express feelings of grief, but to create grief should it not be felt. Merton and his colleagues (1957) studied "anticipatory socialization" among medical students and others, showing that people were likely to take on currently the attributes and attitudes attached to social statuses that they expected to hold in the future. This process was seen to be an important phase in the socialization experience, although it was not clearly identified as self-socialization and the person's active role in the process was not clearly delineated. Other studies have incorporated the process of anticipatory socialization, but as far as I know only Hochschild has related it to the ways in which women are directed to experience and manifest "feminine" feelings (such as niceness) and men to feel "masculine" feelings (such as assertiveness).

"Self-selection" into the job market and up the success ladder on the basis of personality characteristics is a concept that has informed research and supported an industry of testers (industrial psychologists) who provide corporations with examinations purporting to determine whether an applicant's personality will fit a particular job. The self-selection model, of course, has some merit, but it does not tap external pressures on people to exhibit the behavior or feel the emotions dictated by social context.

The most dramatic recent research on the question of the malleability of personality and its social causation is the path-breaking work of Kohn and Schooler (1973, 1978, 1982) and their associates. They were the first to use a national sample of men to study the relationship between work and personality. In a design that enabled them to ascertain the causal relationship between personality (as assessed in inventories) and job characteristics, they found that "jobs affected the man, more than the man affected the job." Although Veblen suggested sixty years ago that the social setting affected the person and Merton explored the interaction between bureaucratic settings and bureaucratic personality forty-five years ago, the psychological-testing industry was geared to a model predicated on the notion that personality affected the way a person adapted to work rather than a model suggesting that the work might create alterations in personality. Kohn and Schooler examined the ranking of individual measures of job commitment and satisfaction, anxiety, self-esteem, intellectual flexibility, and moral perspective and found them to be affected by such structural variables as complexity, pace, pressures, and routinization. The complexity of the job was especially important in affecting all facets of the men's psychological functioning and was directly related to their self-esteem. High job complexity makes for high self-esteem because a man's job "confronts him with demands he must try to meet," these scholars reported, corroborating Merton's observation. The average woman, they noted, has less chance to rise to the occasion than the average man.

In the next phase of their research, Kohn, Schooler, and their associates, Joanne Miller and Karen Miller (see Miller et al., 1979), studied women and, as one might suppose, found that their personalities also were affected by their work. Women who could work at their own pace, make decisions, and otherwise exercise autonomy tended to be intellectually active, flexible, and not authoritarian. But women with boring, routine jobs had the opposite traits and also scored low in self-esteem. Job conditions affected women's personality, regardless of their reasons for working, their education, the number of children they had, and even whether they wanted to be working or not.

These large-scale studies confirmed what other researchers as well as lay people had found in other settings: *people can change*. Moreover, social circumstances can change the individual's personality or an unchanging social environment can reinforce personality attributes acquired earlier. Some scholars have been instructed by their observations of people who went through the social movements of the 1960s. Many of us learned through our research on blacks and women that people changed psychologically and socially as their opportunities and options changed (Deaux, 1984; Crowley et al., 1973; Levitan et al., 1971; Epstein, 1973b, 1974, 1981b). Studies reported that women who moved into business and professional careers felt more powerful than previously, and their ambitions seemed to escalate. The change could not have been predicted from their past histories; it is unlikely that their socialization had been different from that of older siblings who made more conventional life choices. It seemed clear that people could and did change as the social settings in which they lived changed (Epstein, 1982). Gurin and Brim (1984) also showed that adults change feelings about the self when events and situations are psychologically compelling. Their studies and others found changes in the self-concepts of members of minorities toward greater competence when they were involved in political action (Gurin and Brim, 1984; Caplan, 1970; Gurin et al., 1978).

As Brim (1976) has pointed out, there are "hundreds of investigations which substantiate personality change in adulthood in reactions to situations, in attitudes, in reference groups," although "most current research and theory assume that the experiences of infancy and early childhood have a lasting effect on adult behavior and personality" (Brim and Kagan, 1980: 1).[7]

Views of enduring psychological consistency not only are held by many psychologists (Moss and Susman, 1980) but may be consonant with general cultural values. Kagan believes "the fact that the intellectual community believes in stability and continuity in development" makes it "permissive regarding the validity of the supporting facts, and eager for any evidence that maintains the belief." He attributes these intellectual commitments to a "faith in connectedness" characteristic of scholars in

7. Lowell Kelly (1955), in his presidential address to the American Psychological Association, expressed the belief that personality is one issue on which there appears to be unanimity among the diverse psychological theories represented in the profession. He observed, "Whether one is an extreme hereditarian, an environmentalist, a constitutionalist, or an orthodox psychoanalyst, he is not likely to anticipate major changes in personality after the first few years of life" (cited in Moss and Susman, 1980: 531). In the years since Kelly's statement, there has been considerable controversy over this view. However, Brim and Kagan (1980) and others (Mischel, 1969; Nesselroade and Baltes, 1974) believe it is a persistent belief. Patricia Gurin (personal communication) feels that the consistency view is in eclipse.

the Western world (1980: 44). A different "angle of vision" and observations led other prominent scientists to conclusions that resulted in a
model of change—for example, in the studies done by Kagan and also by
Orville Brim, Jr., in the 1960s (Kagan and Moss, 1962; Brim, 1966; see
also Brim and Kagan, 1980). A dramatic example was Kagan's reports on
his research in Guatemala (brought together in a book in 1984), which
indicated that personality was *not* set indelibly early in life. The Mayan
Indians, he reported, swaddle their infants in pieces of cloth and leave
them suspended in hammocks in the darkness of their homes for many
hours a day. According to the psychological perspectives of the day, such
treatment should result in withdrawn, passive behavior in these children
later in life. Yet at ten years of age, Kagan reported, there were many
personality types among them. These differences, he said, could be explained by the social positions assigned to the children in the village and
their other experiences.

In his review of Kagan's book, Daniel Goleman (1984) pointed out that
the conclusions contest treasured beliefs held in America—that a certain
set of essential experiences in children's home life allows them to grow
into happy and healthy adults, that the temperament of the infant fore-
shadows the character of the child, that the child's personality foreshad-
ows the adult's, that the child's psychological traits are shaped by what
happens between parent and child (including the notion that a mother's
love for her infant is necessary for the child's future mental health), and
that what happens in a prior stage of development shapes those to follow.

Kagan describes several studies showing that the evidence does not support a strong connection from phase to phase. One of the best known of
these is the New York Longitudinal Study (see Thomas et al., 1963; Thomas
and Chess, 1977) in which more than a hundred men and women have
been interviewed every few years since early infancy. When those who
had been referred to a child guidance clinic because of childhood distur-
bance were assessed as adults, there were in most cases no lingering signs
of the problems for which they had been referred.

Thus, although Kagan's research centers on children, in formulating his
theoretical conclusions he is attentive to work done on samples of adults.
Criticisms of research interpretations made by other scientists who have
based their analyses of adults on studies of children have been written only
in the last decade. Russo (1978) points out that most of the literature on
developmental psychology stops at adolescence "and is replete with non-
developmental, fragmented and methodologically questionable studies."
In noting the consequences of theories of consistency, she points out that

"they are not limited to research on women, but have a particularly det-rimental effect on them" because they reinforce stereotyped views of women's inadequacies. Actually they also are of dubious merit in en-lightening us about male characteristics through the life course.

Life-Span and Life-Course Theories of Development

Social scientists interested in adult development have created a field var-iously named life course (by sociologists), life span (by psychologists), and life cycle by others. Scholars in this field have considered and moved beyond the views expressed by "stage theorists" such as Erikson, Piaget, and Kohlberg. According to Rossi (1980), sociologists using this ap-proach focus on "pathways through the age-differentiated structure in the major role domains of life . . . and search for social patterns in the timing, duration, spacing, and order of life events." Life-span psychologists, by contrast, are apt to be more "interested in individual development, and to focus on psychological qualities like ego strength, interiority, time per-spective, rigidity, and achievement striving" (p. 78). Psychologists, how-ever, have done most of their work on developmental patterns of adults.

Two models have emerged, characterized as "normative-crisis" and "timing of events." The crisis model stems from Erik Erikson's devel-opment theory—the notion of a patterned sequence of stages, each with appropriate physical, emotional, and cognitive tasks to be accomplished (1959). The model grew out of work with children but was expanded to include early adulthood and the middle years. Those who built on Erik-son's theories incorporated the idea of crisis linked to the transitions be-tween stages of life as a normal part of adult development. George Vail-lant (1977) and Daniel Levinson and his colleagues (1978) suggest that the middle-years period is one of crisis and self-reevaluation. Focusing on men's lives, Vaillant dates the period of reevaluation at age forty, "give or take as much as a decade"; Levinson claims that it does not occur before thirty-eight or later than forty-three. In both studies, men are said to define work as their first priority until middle age, when they shift to a greater investment in family and private life. Most men in their twenties, according to Levinson's study, are not capable of "a highly loving, sex-ually free and emotionally intimate relationship." It is not until the reso-lution of their mid-life crisis that they can change and balance their work life with warmth and intimacy with another person. Levinson's theory of mid-life crisis, in particular, reaching a broad audience as a best-seller, was attractive to the public. He reported (personal communication) that men wept at his lectures, recognizing themselves in his case material and theory. The "predictable stage and crisis" model of life also has appeal. Psychologists and psychiatrists as well as popular writers have written books on this theme, including Gail Sheehy's *Passages: Predictable Crises of Adult Life* (1977), Srully Blotnick's *The Corporate Steeplechase: Predictable Crises in a Business Career* (1984), and Roger Gould's *Transformations: Growth and Change in Adult Life* (1978).

Many questions have been raised about the methodology and model used by Levinson and other "predictable crisis" researchers. Critics such as Brim (1985) find that the conclusions are not obvious from the relatively few cases, nonrepresentative in nature, on which they are based. The narratives of men's lives gathered by Levinson, like the interpretation of narratives collected by Gilligan in her study of ethical dilemmas, do not support their conclusions.

Bernice Neugarten (1968, 1976, 1979), whose longitudinal studies of development began in the 1950s, rejects the developmental crisis model in favor of a psychology of timing. This model is set not by mere chronological markers (such as a crisis occurring between ages thirty-eight and forty-three) but by changes in individuals' bodies, careers, or families. Mid-life, she points out, occurs at different points to different people. Rossi (1980) criticizes developmental models, whether called "life span" or "developmental crisis," or whether tied to biological stages or social stages. First, she points out that most of their data were provided by respondents who grew up in the same distinctive historical period, thus forming a cohort born between the early 1920s and the 1930s. Therefore most studies of middle age are based on people who were born or spent their childhoods during the depression; many of the men in the sample participated in World War II or the Korean War. Unlike their "fathers' experience of job loss and talent underutilization, today's middle-aged men have achieved well beyond their earliest aspirations . . . in an era of easy promotions" (1980: 14). "The profile of the mid-life man . . . may strike a future developmental researcher as one of men 'burned out' at a premature age, rather than a reflection of a 'normal' developmental process all men go through" (p. 15). The women represent a cohort that pioneered the settlement of suburbia in the post–World War II period, attracted to the larger homes, which affluence made possible, with well-known results: more domesticity, more isolation from kin, and larger family size.

The development pattern that appears typical of contemporary middle-aged men reflects their common experience of working within a bureaucratic organization in an industrial economy, Rossi has observed. She notes that Neugarten also reports that middle-aged men in the 1960s "perceive a close relationship between life-line and career-line" (1980: 16). Thus, "no invariant developmental pattern has been confirmed by such studies . . . for the close correspondence between age and career stage may flow from the opportunities and pressure unique to the American economy at a particular stage of development." Rossi concludes, "It may be the case, in very general terms, that the 'timing of events' model of adult development [described by Neugarten] emerged in a period of social history—the 1950s and 1960s—more stable and with a more expectable life cycle than ever before or since" (p. 16).

Rossi's critique of the timing-of-events research extends to its lack of concern with physiological variables. This focus in her own work has elicited considerable debate.[8] In this work she characterizes gender differences using Bakan's concepts of agency and communion (1966) but substituting "affiliation" for "communion" in her subsequent analysis. The emphasis in agency is on separation, isolation, the urge to master, and repression of feeling and impulse, whereas the concept of communion stresses openness, union, and cooperation. Agency is regarded as a male pattern by Rossi, as it is in the work of Gilligan, and communion, or affiliation, as characteristic of females—but only until a certain point in life, for Rossi notes shifts in these patterns through the life span, which she attributes to physiological changes. For example, Rossi suggests that the shift noted in Vaillant's and Levinson's studies as well as others (see Rossi, 1980) from the "active, agentic orientation of young males to a more affiliative orientation in later years" and the increase in agentic independence with age among women may be due to "some underlying change in biological functioning." She offers the hypothesis that underlying the mid-life shift in human females is a change in the androgen-estrogen ratio, with a reverse endocrine pattern in the human male. The problems with this hypothesis are illuminated most dramatically by the recent changes we are witnessing in the behavior of certain cohorts of men and women. The assumption that agentic behavior is characteristic of younger men and not of younger women is probably confined to particular periods, settings, and social groups. Stewart and Salt (1983), studying the change in male and female college students' concerns in the period 1964–78, showed that later cohorts of women are more likely to emphasize traditional male objectives such as achievement, whereas men show a lesser,

8. See Gross et al. (1979) for the debate over Rossi's article "A Biosocial Perspective on Parenting," *Signs* 4, no. 4 (1979): 695–717.

but nevertheless increased concern with "expressive preoccupations" (p. 295). Not only do young women today manifest agentic behavior in pursuing careers as lawyers, astronauts, or racing-car drivers and men demonstrate affiliative behavior in sharing child care with their wives or becoming teachers or social workers, but in the past as well women expressed agentic behavior (running family shops) and men affiliative behavior (trading gossip around the cracker barrel). Furthermore, black women and women of the third world have demonstrated agentic behavior through the ages.

Nevertheless, Rossi's perspectives that physical traits are salient in men's and women's view of themselves; that they interact with the social definition of the meaning of physical changes (for example, whether gray hair and facial sagging is considered attractive); and that matters of health related to the aging process are pertinent to social choices should be important to life-span social scientists. Rossi also points out that all men and women do not age in the same way or at the same times, nor do all societies equally note aging or treat it in the same way—some treat it with honor and respect and others as a burden. In fact, she notes that a finding of Srole and Fisher (1978) that, unlike women twenty years before, recent cohorts of middle-aged women showed no elevation of stress compared with men their age might be accounted for by their different access to continuous employment. Women at middle age in the 1980s who were less stressed had had continuous employment with short periods of withdrawal for childbirth and early child rearing and the expectation of continuous employment.

Interest in changes in the life course in adult years is related to theoretical work on adult socialization done in the 1950s and 1960s. Brim and Wheeler (1966) provided an important early statement conceptualizing adult socialization, as did a few psychologists such as Kagan, but the research interest of sociologists in the subject was more or less dormant until Matilda Riley and her associates (1972) began to focus on it in the 1970s. Even then, socialization as a continuing process was not taken up as a major paradigm.[9] A subfield of the sociology of work, however, focused early on professional socialization. A number of scholars examined the process by which neophyte medical students begin to think and act like physicians (Merton et al., 1957; Fox, 1959; Becker et al., 1961). These studies were based on samples of men—medicine was a virtually all-male profession at the time—and did not attempt to determine whether the changes observed during professional socialization were limited to the professional

9. Brim developed the field of age stratification, an inquiry supported by the Russell Sage Foundation.

"self" and whether the attitudes, values, skills and orientations acquired were related to the professional status only or changed the personal completely. No overarching claims were made for developmental theory.

Scholars in different disciplines often develop concepts and theories about the same subject matter without paying attention to each other's work. The concept of adult socialization was largely ignored by psychologists, and sociologists did not work to achieve consensus on its meaning. Some sociologists' enchantment with models of early personality formation (Parsons, 1964) (they might be said to have had cases of psychoanalytic-theory envy) may have also deterred investigation of the perspective.

The appeal of the psychoanalytic model in and outside the scientific community may account for much of the resistance to the notion that change may occur in adult years that is not linked to early development. Although it is true that current psychoanalytic literature still focuses on the consequences of childhood identification, traumas, and relations with parents and siblings as they play out in adult situations and interactions, there has been some movement in psychoanalytic thought toward stressing the current adaptive capacities and functioning of the ego, a position far from radical psychogenetic determination, according to Neil Smelser (personal communication) (see also Person, 1980).

The psychoanalytic model, however, tends to regard the healthy self as an integrated composition of traits with the person having resolved conflicts between the parts (id, ego, superego) of the self, and successfully moved through developmental stages (Oedipal, and so on). This model has been absorbed into the culture and is expressed in themes that press individuals to discover their "real self," the "true *me*." This is a translation of such psychological frameworks as Erik Erikson's (1959), which assert that everyone has a "core identity." This view suggests that sexual identity is an important part of the core and that men and women absorb gender traits as part of early experience. Implicit in this is the view that the self that is discovered is inherited or set early and will unfold predictably through the life sequence. Although people do develop identities as men and women, how they express these identities seems far more bound to social factors than to the unfolding of an early scenario. In conceptualizing sex-role-appropriate behavior, social scientists often ignore the possibility of virtuosity among the several roles gathered along the life course and the accompanying multifaceted identities that can be held by a person when life situations evoke them.

The accompanying view in sociology, that many roles (or statuses) result in "strain" (Goode, 1960a), has been reconceptualized by social scientists who point to the beneficial and energizing effects of multiple roles. Since women in particular have been said to exhibit pathology attributed to role strain, both the reconceptualization and the research that corroborates it have been of theoretical interest. An accumulating body of such work (Sieber, 1974; Marks, 1977; R. Coser, 1982; Crosby, 1982, 1987; Baruch and Barnett, 1979; Epstein, 1984b, 1985) indicates that multiple roles may energize women as well as men, giving them positive self-images and greater freedom. This research is of some ideological interest, since many of those expressing "concern" for women have urged that they reduce their occupationally demanding roles rather than their domestically demanding ones.

The concept of integrated identity or self may be more a preference of social scientists than a reflection of systematic observation. We are beginning to see that an adult's sense of self does change when events and situations are psychologically compelling (Gurin and Brim, 1984; Veroff, 1983). Of course, it is not unreasonable to expect people to be consistent in behavior and to have a consistent personality in the course of playing out several social roles. But the consistency of the roles people exhibit (a social process that we shall describe in more detail later on) seems to depend on the extent to which the norms attached to those roles are enforced. Perhaps the quest for order, which would permit prediction of the progression of the life cycle or of the behavior of a class of persons, such as women, fixes even social scientists in a theoretical myopia.

Orville Brim, Jr., pointed out in his address to the American Psychological Association in 1974 (published in 1976) that the attribution of constancy of personality in the face of experiences and evidence to the contrary is a puzzle, and he asked, "Could it be that society is heavily invested in particular age-sex categories?" Although Brim concentrated on males at mid-life, he noted that the question applied equally to men of all ages and to women as well. He also noted that stability seen in the life sequences of individuals or groups of individuals may depend on an unchanging environment.

One could also say that such stability is a consequence of social expectations and enforcement. The expectations people hold that members of a certain group will behave in a certain manner or according to a certain sequence may lead them to facilitate the expected behavior and inhibit other behavior. Thus, for example, when parents believe that an adolescent will act immaturely, they may put sufficient restrictions on his or her behavior to make mature behavior impossible. Similarly, when parents think adolescence is a "phase" replete with behavior regarded as typical and believe that it passes after the teen years are over, teenagers begin to regard themselves as "adolescents" who are expected to be troublesome, and they act accordingly. Social expectations about the sequencing of events in the lives of men and women determine their occupational profiles. The expectation that women will not be committed to work after they become mothers results in discrimination in many jobs. Women's own expectations about what the appropriate priorities are at various stages in their lives influence their occupational choices. "Socially expected durations" have power in significantly affecting the current behavior of groups and individuals, Robert Merton (1984b) has reminded us.

The expectation that a class of people is destined to play out their lives according to a given sequence because of the traits they inherit or the situations they encounter in their early years is essentially conservative in perspective. If it were based on clearly established truths, then we would, as a society, have to learn to live with it. But the evidence is highly questionable, and indeed there is much support for the alternative view that people are more malleable than we have believed and that, as the destinies of groups change, so can the destinies of individuals. It is a question of the range of possibilities, of course. Men probably will never be able to have babies, but they may be able to mother or teach young children as well as women do. Women may never win a weight-lifting contest competing with men matched for weight and training, but they are fast catching up in marathon running and solving mathematics problems. It seems clear that intellectual capacity and emotional qualities are distributed through humanity without restrictions of sex any more than race or nationality. Believing, however, that men or women cannot develop certain mental and psychological attributes merely because of their sex can result in the patterns that people uncritically observe and believe to be inevitable.

CHAPTER 5

Distinctions of Gender
in the Social System:
The Sociological Approach

lthough biology and psychology may explain differences in the
emotions and capacities of individuals, they do not explain the
social arrangements that divide the sexes, nor do they account
for systematic differences in their behavior and attitudes. How, then, can
we account for these differences?

The social ordering of males and females occurs and is maintained through
the interplay between social constraints and individuals' choices. In this
perspective, individuals and institutions are not equal. Some are more
powerful than others and may have more freedom to make choices and
impose them on others.

Individuals tend to make choices from among socially structured alternatives in patterned ways, with further consequences for social structure.
The sociological perspective, unlike that of classical economic theory or
learning theory, holds that the particular choices of people are socially
established and are part of the institutional order. Individuals make choices,
but institutional patterns shape the alternatives and make one choice more
likely than another. In the process, institutions are molded and remolded,
and people are bound into roles. Robert Merton articulated this in *Social
Theory and Social Structure* ([1949] 1957; see also Stinchcombe, 1975).
In this tradition, Anthony Giddens has formalized a "theory of structura-
tion" in which he specifies how structure emerges from and is constituted
by practice. Thus, some individuals are segregated in space or by station
in the class structure so that they have less information about a variety of
favored choices, whereas others have roles that provide more information
about them. These patterns, and the accompanying social supports for
them, do much to shape the person's social character and personality.

Thus, the structural approach looks at the ways in which factors external to the individual explain even those attributes ordinarily regarded as wholly internal, such as motivation and aspiration.

According to the social structural perspective, one borne out by the research of the past decade, the impact of social structure on the behavior and attitudes of men and women results in most of the perceived differences between them. Connell (1988), commenting on the ambiguity of the concept "social structure"—from the "tight and sophisticated models of Piaget, Lévi-Strauss and Althuser to the much more numerous cases where anything that shows a detectable pattern at all is called 'structure,' suggests it is useful to think of structure as the intractability of the social world." "To describe structure," he writes, "is to specify what it is in the situation that constrains the play of practice." Of course, the variables of social structure include organizational and physical barriers created to control the interaction of people in certain groups or situations, such as schools, prisons, or clubs. They include normative prescriptions for conduct, specifying the proper ways for people to act in their social roles—for example, old or young, upper class or working class, men or women. Social structure thus accounts for the way people are identified according to their statuses by dress and name and then place—for example, at school, at home, at the workplace. The systematic study of the processes involved in setting behavioral norms and physically segregating the sexes is relatively new.

It is important to note that institutions do not merely reflect social patterns and the gradual evolution of patterned behavior. A "new institutionalism" has been characterized by James March and Johan Olsen (1984), who note that "institutions are political actors in their own right" and are not simply reducible to exogenous forces or to the individuals who compose them. They "have linkages with each other and mutual interactions that help to define the terrain in which they operate." Elizabeth Hansot and David Tyack (1988) have proposed, in their analysis of gender distinctions and similarities in the American educational system, that institutions vary considerably in the ways in which gender is made salient; in this way, they account for the variations in the division of labor in different historical periods and places. In this approach, institutions as political actors "allocate money, status and power; they have goals, means, resources, boundaries and systems of control." As Hansot and Tyack suggest, "institutions have explicit rules governing gender relationships but they also have organizational cultures in which many gender practices are implicit, often the more powerful for being taken for granted."

The most powerful sociological approach thus acknowledges the organized settings and directives that form the framework within which people live, including the traditions and customs that form the heritage of a given institution. It also identifies the leading actors in those institutions—those who set its policy, ensure its continuity. Of course, individuals, even those with little power, can have an impact and can make choices. But the powerful, too, are constrained by the patterns of the institutions in their lives and the investments other people have in those patterns. Analyzing how workers are not forced but "choose" to conform to production norms, Michael Burawoy (1979) has shown how "consent" is manufactured in social life, even when it might not be in the worker's self-interest but clearly is to the benefit of institutional goals.

Some years ago, William J. Goode summed up the impact of the social processes affecting behavior. " 'They' can't do much to you," he told his students, "but they don't have to." Sociologists (Parsons, 1967; Davis, 1949) have pointed out that most societies have formal codes and the physical means to enforce them, but that most societies do not depend on coercion. Of course, some informal controls (or choices) come close to physical coercion, but merely the threat of it is enough to persuade many people to conform to rules, and others barely need a hint of it. Informal controls range from harsh social pressures, such as ostracism and shunning, to the subtle disapproval of a raised eyebrow, a warning of "what people might say," and the training and education (socialization) of individuals to believe in the norms of their society and identify with them. Proximity to or distance from the scrutiny of authorities and relative visibility or invisibility of the individual's actions also play a part in the social control process.

Woman's Place Revisited: Sex Typing and Sex Labeling

Culture and social structure interact in the creation of "sex typing," the linking of certain types of behavior with one sex or the other, and sex typing, a core element in the creation of social distinctions, operationalizes dichotomous thinking. Sex typing (Merton, in Epstein, 1970b)[1] or sex labeling (Oppenheimer, 1968) is an important determinant in the acquisition of social roles and statuses. The culture assigns a designation of "male" or "female" to a task, drawing on tradition or ideology. These

1. Robert K. Merton's conceptualization of the dynamics of status-sets was presented in lectures at Columbia University that are as yet unpublished.

cultural assignments may come from the decisions of powerful people or may develop through folk transmissions. Either way, the models become translated into practice in patterned ways. Sex typing structures individuals' choices, and the selections are monitored and controlled by gatekeepers and institutions in a position to permit or deny access to certain statuses, such as surgeon for a woman or nurse for a man. The concept of sex typing has been most thoroughly studied in the division of labor at the workplace, although it applies as well to other institutions, such as the family or polity.

Sex typing leads to the segregation of men and women into spheres, which may be physically separate or symbolically separate through the use of different titles or role assignments. There is a large research literature documenting the extent of such segregation in the workplace.[2] This research has indicated that sex typing involves the setting of social norms; it establishes standardized preferences and a set of expectations, even though some individuals deviate from them and select sex-inappropriate statuses.[3] Nursing, for example, has long been sex typed as a female occupation, although men have demonstrated competence as nurses and have proved willing to become nurses, especially under other labels, when, as in wartime, they are encouraged to do so.

In the late 1960s, researchers began to document the extent and persistence of sex segregation in the workplace, beginning with Gross's important article "Plus ça change . . . ? The Sexual Structure of Occupations over Time" (1968). At the same time, Valerie Oppenheimer (1968) argued that jobs had become sex labeled in ways that reflected employers' beliefs that certain occupations required attributes characteristic of one sex or the other or, in the case of women, represented an extension of domestic non-wage work. She claimed that custom tended to make the sex labels stick and that these labels and their associated norms were learned and perpetuated through childhood and adult socialization. Merton's definition of the sex typing of occupations includes normative as well as numerical elements; he states that "occupations can be described as sex-typed when a very large majority of those in them are of one sex and when there is an associated normative expectation that this is as it should be" (Merton, 1960, in Epstein, 1968, 1970a).

Following this framework, my book *Woman's Place* (Epstein, 1970a)

2. See, for example, Jacobs, 1982; Stevenson, 1977; Bridges, 1980; Beck et al., 1980; Oppenheimer, 1970; Blau, 1977; and Waite, 1981.
3. Merton (in Epstein, 1970a) pointed out that remarkably few jobs are functionally related to sex characteristics; those few include wet nurse and sperm donor.

analyzes the problems women have faced in assuming roles widely regarded as men's. It shows that sex typing is the cultural designation that provides guidelines for the division of labor and maintains gender-specific boundaries and thus is a source of legitimation for gatekeeping. Sex typing also explains the self-selection of men and women in their choice of occupations. It accounts for the discomfort of men and women who constitute a distinct numerical minority in an occupation and are therefore regarded as the "wrong" gender and "deviants" in their work (Epstein, 1970a; Schur, 1984). In my book I assembled documentation showing how sex typing of occupations occurs in all cultures so that some jobs become known as male and others as female, with only a few not assigned to either sex. I found, moreover, that in defining a specific occupational status as properly male or female, societies vary greatly.[4] Further, "because sex typing incurs society's rationalizations about the male nature of some work and the female nature of other work (leading to such irrelevant fears as that women lawyers are masculine and that male home economists are effeminate), many occupations come to be viewed as extensions of a sex role. Cultures demand that one must do masculine work to be considered a man, and *not* do it to be a feminine woman" (Epstein, 1970a: 154).

Merton's concept (1957) of "status-set"—the cluster of statuses that an individual holds at any given time (for example, mother, daughter, beautician, Democrat, PTA member)—and his analysis of the ways in which certain new statuses are acquired and others are not led to the formulation of a new concept of "status-set typing" (Epstein, 1970a).[5] It described how the acquisition of certain new statuses is restricted for persons whose prior statuses are deemed incompatible or inconceivable with them because of social values or norms. Everett Hughes (1945) had much earlier studied the effect of "master statuses"—that is, those that most strongly

4. The consequences of sex typing with regard to gender roles were first (as far as I know) analyzed in my *Woman's Place: Options and Limits in Professional Careers* (1970a). This work built on the conceptual paradigm of the dynamics of status-sets of Robert K. Merton, who elaborated his earlier work on status and role theory in lectures at Columbia University. A fuller statement of the analysis presented here may be found in Epstein (1970a, 1971b). The term *sex typing* has since been widely used, although its authorship has not often been acknowledged. As a result, typically only a partial definition is given; usually the "normative expectation" that behavior will conform to the sex-typed status is neglected.

5. The notion of "status-set typing" met with a resounding silence. However, work paralleling Merton's concept of the dynamics of status-sets was done by the Stanford group of theorists focusing on status characteristics and "expectation states" (Berger et al., 1983). Their experimental studies have shown the perception of people toward incongruent status-sets and how inappropriate behavior would result during interaction with a person whose dominant statuses did not match his or her other statuses (such as a black doctor or a female engineer).

determine what other statuses might or might not follow (for example, priests could not acquire the status of father; women could not acquire the status of priest). Merton, Hughes, and I examined the social outcomes of cases in which individuals' status-sets were inconsistent with the social image of which statuses "belong together." Merton (in Epstein, 1970b) proposed the conditions under which the "wrong" status in a status-set is activated and made "salient"—for example, in the case of a woman truck driver or a black rabbi—when a status-set does not match cultural expectations.[6]

Prevailing notions of properly feminine and masculine statuses lead to sex-typed status-sets in societies. A male-typed status-set might be father–husband–steel worker–veteran; a female status-set, wife–mother–primary school teacher–volunteer community worker. Although women and men share some common statuses, such as U.S. citizen, member of a political party, and high school graduate, these statuses do not carry precise normative expectations regarding behavior (that is, what the associated role is), or they may be defined differently for men and women. A male political party member might run for political office, whereas a female political party member would be expected to work for the male's campaign.

What are the consequences for men and women and the societies of which they are members when they are forced or persuaded to occupy different statuses and play almost entirely different roles? According to some theories of social change (Simmel, 1955; Marx, 1848; Coleman, 1957), they might become polarized and engage in conflict. This happened, after all, to blacks and whites in the United States during the civil rights movement. But although there are similarities between the black experience and that of women, as subordinated groups, there are important differences.

Men and women share common domiciles and class positions and often an array of other statuses. But the barriers to their sharing powerful occupational and political statuses or family roles were strong and eventually contributed to the growing polarization between men and women that was expressed in the women's movement. It led to the growing debate in the social sciences, most notably conceived by Jessie Bernard (1981), who has argued that women and men do not actually share the same world, even while living in the same places. As noted earlier, it also led to a still unresolved discussion about the use of the concept "sex role," since some

6. Patricia Gurin and Hazel Markus (1985) have tested individuals' experiences of high sex-status salience in determining politically relevant gender consciousness.

scholars claimed that the term resulted in a reification that appeared to lodge women (and men) in particular social statuses and justified their playing out of social roles as "natural" when these roles were, in fact, socially assigned and changeable.

Although not many scholars referred to status-sets in their work through the 1970s, they were interested in learning how women and, to a much lesser extent, men acquired and performed social roles. They focused on the problems women or men had in acquiring statuses not viewed as consistent with their sex status and on the consequences this had for role performance. Some also considered culturally determined perceptions of behavior. For example, I distinguished between ideal roles ("ideal" types as archetypical in Max Weber's sense) and the actual roles people played—between notions about what they ought to be doing and what they were actually doing (Epstein [1972] 1976a, 1984b, 1985)—showing how people classified female behavior differently from that of males even when they were doing the same thing.[7] As we saw earlier, a serious source of bias in the social sciences has been the confusion of many researchers themselves about "real" and "ideal" when they are attempting to formulate or analyze studies that specify gender differences.[8]

Selective attention to men's and women's real roles was evident, particularly in the fields of occupational sociology and stratification systems. For example, men's work roles were studied because an occupation was regarded as a virtually universal component of a man's status-set. For the opposite reason, little or no attention was directed to the work roles of women.

To be sure, analysis of women's occupations had received some attention prior to the critiques of feminist scholars in the 1970s. A number of studies conducted under the auspices of the Russell Sage Foundation in the early 1900s investigated artificial flower makers (Van Kleeck, 1913), sales workers (La Dame, 1930), and even munition makers (Hewes, 1917). A few Chicago-school sociologists studied troublesome occupations in the "social problem" tradition, such as taxi-dance girls (Strauss, 1971) and cocktail waitresses (Spradley and Mann, 1974) and analyzed their (downward) mobility. Most studies of women's mobility predictably attributed it to marriage to an upper- or lower-ranking man (Davis, 1949; Strauss, 1971).

7. There is a considerable social-psychological literature on this subject, including reports of a series of experiments done by the Stanford University group working on status-attribution theory (see Berger and Zeldich, 1985).
8. On "real" and "ideal" roles, see Linton's *Study of Man* (1936).

Furthermore, as with men, only the paid work of women was studied in early research. Ann Oakley (1974a) achieved a breakthrough by taking housework as a serious topic for occupational sociologists rather than an incidental focus of researchers on marriage and the family. Later, other unpaid activities such as voluntary work were reconceptualized as research targets for scholars of the work world.[9] If one looked beyond research on mainstream white Americans, untapped fields were emerging, reflecting consciousness about black and white working-class women and third world women.

It was becoming clear that the integration of women's roles and men's roles into sex-typed status-sets had reinforced the social stratification system, propelling, directing, and coercing women and men into spheres believed to be appropriate for them. In the case of women, these largely meant the home and home-based activities, and specific occupations and institutional spheres and positions that were not competitive with those of men, most of them low ranking and subordinate when paired with men's occupations (such as nurse-doctor, secretary-manager).

Until the 1960s, with the exception of the period of the women's suffrage movement, this division of labor was perceived as just. According to Homans (1961), in the exchange system of society, women were not expected to invest much energy or time in high-level occupations and other public activities such as politics. Therefore, the occupations that paid high rewards in return for commitment could not be expected to pay these same wages to presumably low-contributing professional women (Epstein [1972] 1976a).[10] Homans's view is not unlike that of human capital theorists in economics, as we shall see in chapter 7.

Research showed this to be the case; women did in fact tend more than men to be part-time workers in the paid labor force, and at each career level they tended to work fewer hours on average than their male peers and to drop out of their professions to a greater extent than men (Epstein, 1970a; Rossi, 1972). Gary Becker's argument (1985) that a fundamental reason for disparities in socioeconomic attainment is the amount of effort men and women devote to work, even when they work the same number

9. Again, there was a precursor to this: David Sill's *The Volunteers*, published in 1957.

10. This is an example of what Homans explores as "distributive justice": "A man's reward in exchange with others should be proportional to his investments" (1961: 325). Thus, if justice is an equation between investment and reward, and women are believed to make less of an investment (background characteristics such as sex, race, and ethnicity are included along with hard work as "investments"), then, Homans asserts, they should not expect as much reward as a man who has "put in" a *higher* investment (by being male). Homans further suggests that being black or female is an *unchanging* value, unlike "experience" (another investment), which increases with time.

of hours, was reviewed by Bielby and Bielby (1988). Contrary to Becker's hypothesis that women work less hard because of their obligations at home, these researchers found that women allocate *more* effort to work than do men. Furthermore, several studies of women professionals, including my work on lawyers, indicated that where women did have access to opportunity, in many cases their contributions—in terms of publications, professional association committee work, and hours spent at work—equaled or exceeded those of men (Astin and Bayer, 1975; Simon et al., 1967; Epstein, 1970a).

A focus on the opportunity structure as the important variable in determining such qualities as commitment and motivation emerged from this work (Epstein, 1973a, 1974, 1976b). It gained attention with Kanter's book, *Men and Women of the Corporation* (1977a) and was further documented in a review of research by Kaufman and Richardson (1982). Socially structured obstacles to women's full options and participation in society were detailed in the ensuing years. Furthermore, the ambiguity women faced from mixed messages (identified earlier by Komarovsky, 1946) and inappropriate rewards and punishments for work in spheres where they were not supposed to be were seen to undermine their commitment and motivation, the lack of which was seen as their own failing (Epstein, 1974). The concept of opportunity structure was an outgrowth of Merton's analysis ([1938] 1957) of the ways people coped with problems of achieving social goals by socially prescribed means. He identified patterns of anomie stemming from the structural fact that in a culture that proclaims opportunity for all, many have little access to the opportunity structure and adapt either by choosing alternative means or by rejecting or displacing the socially defined goals.

The position of women in high-level jobs, even in spheres defined as female—for example, university professors of home economics who were prevented from becoming deans—was seen to be subject to the same patterned undermining of commitment and other obstacles that kept women out of fields socially defined as male. This suggested that women were prevented from attaining any positions of power because cultural values specified that only men ought to be in charge, whatever the occupational context, male or female.

It was widely recognized that the norms that defined women's roles were those regarded as expressive, nurturant, service-oriented, and ancillary to men's in both personality and behavior, in contrast to the norms for men's roles, which were clustered around instrumental, dominant, and goal-oriented qualities.

Although socially defined roles and actual behavior may not coincide, the belief system serves, of course, to expand or contract the range of behavior (Epstein [1972] 1976a). The research that called into question society's designation of women's roles also challenged the notion of some social scientists that these roles were functional for the societies in which they existed. Many social scientists have explained women's roles within the household, such as cooking and cleaning, and outside it, such as part-time clerical work, as efficient adaptations to childbearing and rearing because "women's tasks" tend to be close to home or suited to their nature. Taking a different perspective, Parsons stated that ascribing women's roles primarily to the family and only secondarily to the workplace was functional because it eliminated "any competition for status . . . between husband and wife which might be disruptive of the solidarity of marriage" (1954: 192). He claimed that the marriage relationship put a premium on "mutuality and equality" and had "no clearly structured superordination-subordination" pattern. Because women did not test or demonstrate their "fundamental equality with husbands in competitive occupational achievement," Parsons saw a "functional equivalent" in women's enactment of "broadly humanistic values such as 'good taste' in personal appearance, house furnishings, cultural things like literature and music." Unwittingly, Parsons was arguing a "separate spheres" approach, which was to be a prominent paradigm among some feminist scholars two decades later.

One of the first attacks on Parsons came from outside the academy and was articulated by Betty Friedan, a writer and later a women's movement leader. In a chapter of her book *The Feminine Mystique* (1963) entitled "The Functionalist Freeze, the Feminine Protest, and Margaret Mead," Friedan argued that Parsons's functional framework did not adequately specify the negative consequences of this arrangement for women, and that narrowing women's horizons by isolating them in the home created psychological problems for women and wasted their talents. Inside the academy Alice Rossi criticized the cultural and historical myopia of Parsons's view and pointed out that the pattern exhibited by middle-class women was unique in American history: "What has not been seen is the more general point that for the first time in the history of any known society, motherhood has become a full-time occupation for [American] adult women" (1964: 615). What Parsons implied to be universally true[11]

11. His discussion appeared in an essay entitled "The Kinship System of the Contemporary United States" ([1943] 1954). Although he noted that preventing women from competing with men in the occupational sphere was functional for the family, he did recognize that traditional

appeared to hold only for middle-class women in the 1940s and 1950s, and even these women deviated from the pattern as they aged. Of course, these patterns did not apply to most women of racial minority groups— blacks, Hispanics, and Orientals (for an overview, see Glenn, 1985).

Thus began a rich inquiry into women's unsung and undocumented roles, particularly those in economic and political life in other times and places.[12] It had been difficult to get data about women in most countries of the world, and data that were available were not translated into other languages.[13] I found that it took months of effort to assemble a table on the proportion of women in professions cross-nationally in the late 1960s for *Woman's Place* (1970). Not until the mid-1970s was there a noticeable change in the data available on the status of women, and even then the information was often incomplete. The greater research interest resulted from women's movement activism. Research was developed by scholars in universities and also by commissions on the status of women created in many countries. Data were also collected under the auspices of the United Nations when 1975 was designated as International Woman's Year, which was later expanded to the Decade of Women. Governments were asked to report on the roles and statuses of women in their countries for three important conferences: the Women's Year Meeting in Mexico City in 1975, which initiated International Woman's Year; a mid-decade conference in Copenhagen in 1980; and an end-of-the-decade conference in Nairobi in 1985 (Tinker, 1982).

The quality of the newly gathered information about women varied greatly. Many governments failed to support research; some probably were reluctant to reveal a dismal account of the status of women in their country, and some countries had few qualified scholars to work on the research. In Eastern Europe as well as China the field of sociology itself was undeveloped or regarded with suspicion, impeding research on gender and other topics regarded as politically sensitive in various periods.[14] Re-

---

women's roles had their drawbacks. Parsons pointed out that women's roles were not clearly defined and that this might produce a high level of insecurity because "the feminine role is a conspicuous focus of the strains inherent in our social structure" (p. 194).

12. For example, Pomeroy (1975, 1984) for the ancient world; Power (1975) on medieval women; Kessler-Harris (1982) on women in the United States; Tilly (1979, 1982) on France and Italy; Lapidus (1978) on the Soviet Union.

13. According to Heitlinger (1985), between 1965 and 1973 only six books and four pamphlets appeared in English in the field of Soviet women's studies. No English-language books were published during this period relating to women in other East European countries. Since about 1975, the literature on women in Eastern Europe has multiplied to some twenty-eight books and booklets. See Heitlinger for the specific bibliography.

14. For example, it was only in the 1960s that sociology was reestablished as an academic discipline in Czechoslovakia and sociologists began to study the "dual roles" of women.

search on women in the third world reflected a general myopia. (Theories abounded, however, about the role mothers played in motivating men to be active in the development of rapidly changing societies. A strong and dominant mother who set high standards of excellence was key, according to Winterbottom [1953] and McClelland [1961], for example.) Theories of development had undervalued and ignored women's economic contributions in traditional and transitional societies, as Irene Tinker has explained (Tinker and Bramsen, 1976). According to Tinker, the concept of an economic activity in the third world, more than elsewhere, was narrowed by development economists to include only modern-sector employment and cash-crop agriculture, in spite of the fact that women are responsible for a great part of agricultural production in these countries. The "women-in-development" field created by Tinker and others found that women typically head one of every three households in this part of the world. Their activity in the home was, ipso facto, also economic activity, but it was not counted as such. Work on time budgets has begun to identify and assign value to such activities as collecting water and firewood (Tinker, personal communication, 1983; Acharya and Bennett, 1981).[15] The studies that have poured out of departments of history and anthropology in universities throughout the world have provided evidence of the limitations imposed on women everywhere forced into sex-role-appropriate tasks. They have also noted the undocumented and little-rewarded performance by women of both "female" tasks such as housework and "male" tasks such as farming and market activity and trading.

Public versus Private Spheres

Why were researchers so neglectful of women in their studies of third world countries? Did they regard them as outside the social, economic, and political systems then being studied and in a separate sphere of their own (the domestic), or were they participants in the public sphere but "invisible" there? Of course, both explanations are true. Women were not considered in studies of power because they did not hold powerful positions. But they were not considered in studies of social stratification either, in which they were surely part of the system, and were neglected

15. Furthermore, sociologists and economists such as Joann Vanek et al. (1985) at the United Nations and Constantina Safilios-Rothschild at the Population Council have been trying to persuade governmental agencies throughout the world to identify and count women's productivity in the economic sector.

in other studies of the occupational world. Public and private spheres were seen as dichotomous domains for men and women by a number of social analysts. The consequences of men's control and occupancy of the public sphere and women's occupancy of the private (social scientists debated whether women controlled the private) received considerable attention in the 1970s.

The meaning and importance of obstacles to women's access to the full range of opportunities in the public sphere were discussed. There were differences between the scholars who documented the scarcity of women in positions of decision making and power and saw this as the source of women's second-class rank in most societies and those who claimed women had a comparable, if different, sphere of power in the home. According to Bourque and Warren (1981), those who argued that women had equal though different roles emphasized the broad range of activities that women organize and administer in the home. This viewpoint pointed to the specialization of women in the care and early training of children and maintenance of the home, and it claimed for women special female powers and qualities: spiritual strength, moral superiority, strong nurturance ability, and emotional sensitivity. It seemed to follow, then, that women would not want to give up their private worlds to compete with men in the public world. This perspective was most specifically articulated in anthropology by a "complementary but equal" argument (Lamphere, 1977), which suggested that women's control over the private sphere compensated for the limitations on their participation elsewhere. Schlegel (1974) claimed, for example, that among the Hopi, the areas in which women exert dominance are no less important than the areas controlled by men. Similarly, Briggs (1975) indicated that male and female roles are interdependent among the Eskimo. Mathiesson (1975: viii), in whose edited volume these works appear, asserts that Eskimo may be classed as "complementary" societies in which women are neither inferior nor superior to men, merely different.

Scholars in other fields such as political science and sociology used the notion of separate spheres to argue that men and women have equivalent power (Jaquette, 1973; Stevens, 1973). Rosaldo, an anthropologist who had earlier (1974) enunciated the separate-spheres idea, later revised her thinking (1980), arguing that women's de facto power in the household cannot be compared with men's power in the public world (Lamphere, 1977); furthermore, even in the household, men can exert authority as they wish, a claim made earlier by Goode ([1963] 1982) in his comparative study of worldwide family systems. The fact that power even in the family is linked to the control of resources outside was first measured in a study by Blood and Wolfe (1960), who found that decision-making power (including decisions about minor things) is related to the wife's earnings outside the home; if she works, she has more to say in the household than if she does not. Anthropologists such as Friedl (1975) reanalyzed data used to support claims of complementary power and concluded that men control the productive resources. Among the Eskimo, Friedl on this basis found male dominance and female submissiveness. Of course, the idea that power depends on the control of valued resources had been suggested long ago by Marx and Lenin as well as John Stuart Mill. These theorists proposed that women could be equal to men only when they shared equally in the industrial system (Lapidus, 1978). This discussion has bearing on the study of women's place in the stratification system and a diagnosis of whether standard categories of class are appropriate to the analysis of their situation.

Where women stand in the class system has been the subject of much debate in sociology. The questions asked by representatives of different schools of thought have centered on whether women share the same social class system as men or are part of another, separate system. Some would have us consider a gender/class system as a way of conceiving social structure.

The study of stratification is one of the major emphases of social science inquiry, and many general theories have been proposed to explain the phenomenon. The reasons for hierarchy, whether in large societies or small subgroups, have been located in everything from the sources of production to the individual psyche, from the instrumentalities of oppression to the consequences of free choice.

Most social analysts studying stratification have concentrated on groups—families and societies—or have focused on men and their acquisition or denial of resources. Most have assumed that a woman's social rank derives from her husband's or father's rank or her role in the reproduction of the family and of the status group. The focus was on the family as a unit, with a male head who determined the family's social position. With few exceptions,[16] class differences between spouses were not especially noted. Only in a handful of studies did scholars search out and find that such indicators of class as differential education of the wife might correlate with children's aspirations.[17] Consequently, women have not received

16. For example, Davis's (1941) and Merton's (1941) studies of intermarriage in the 1940s analyzed caste and class differences between white and black spouses.
17. See Allison Davis and Robert J. Havighurst, "Social Class and Color Differences in Child-Rearing," *American Sociological Review,* December 1946, pp. 698–710, and John E.

much attention as individual actors in the process, nor have women "as a class" commanded attention.

Theory and research of the past decade and a half have been directed toward filling this void. One focus has been control in the various spheres of life, both public and private. This raises the question of women as "other," set forth most dramatically by Simone de Beauvoir (1949).

For much of history, women have held second-class rank when compared to men of their own stratum. Many, of course, have held that "the weaker sex" naturally falls into second place because nature prescribed it that way. Even for women of wealth and privilege, and even where equality has characterized the relationships of their families or groups, wider social norms and practices have contrived to restore and preserve inequality between the sexes. Restraints on movement, voting, credit, education, and employment have resulted in invidious distinctions between men and women.

But there are further questions raised by current scholarship. What can we learn generally about stratification when we introduce gender into the models? What are the consequences for women as a group when equality is so difficult to achieve? What are the consequences of women's greater vulnerability to poverty? What is to be learned by viewing women's and men's ranks separately when they live together but their occupations differ in prestige and in material rewards? How do theories of stratification deal with families in which women are the sole earners? And, more basically, what are the sources and functions of women's inequality in the world?

I do not believe there is yet a systematic theory of stratification that adequately deals with women or with sex stratification. Recent analysis, however, has led to a reevaluation and restructuring of past work in the field and suggests new models.

Debate pervades work focusing on gender issues in theory and methodology. One major question is whether all women may be aggregated for such analysis. Some social researchers assert that women's subordination to men is universal and appears in every stratum of society. Others maintain that there is no commonality of women's experiences since they vary according to class position. According to this view, the problems and potentials of middle-class women differ from those of working-class women, just as those of white women differ from those of black women, and as the concerns of Western women differ from those of women in the third world. Of course, each perspective has merit according to the questions

---

Anderson, *The Young Child in the Home,* White House Conference on Child Health and Protection (New York: Appleton Century, 1936).

asked. Most women hold subordinate positions in all societies, but there are variations among societies in regard to the amount of economic and educational opportunities that are available to women.

It was only in the late 1960s that separate studies of women and stratification began to appear. Before then, with few exceptions (Rossi, 1964; Blake, 1965), it was assumed that women took on the class position of their husbands and fathers, much as the common law had treated women for centuries.

Acker's critique (1973) of most major stratification studies in the United States showed that because they focused on males in analyzing patterns of mobility and social stratification they obscured ''one of the most obvious bases of economic, political and social inequalities''—the division of society by sex. Certainly, limiting women's occupational and political mobility was an important ''holding operation'' by which ruling elites curtailed competition for decision-making places in society. This process of exclusion was crucial to the analysis of who governs (Epstein, 1974).

In the 1970s, a few scholars lifted the missing women in stratification analysis from obscurity and pointed to the consequences of omitting them for an accurate profile of the stratification system and its mechanisms (Haavio-Mannila in Finland, 1969; Holter in Norway, 1970; Oakley in England, 1974a). Randall Collins (1971, 1975) was distinctive among male sociologists in presenting a ''Conflict Theory of Sexual Stratification'' (1971), but, as Oakley pointed out (1974a), he confused gender with sexuality by taking stratification to be based on the sexual market and regarding relationships between men and women primarily as sexual. (Collins later modified this perspective as he became more aware of the bias in his earlier approach.)

The view that women and men are and should be of equal rank in the family but of different (and, for women, inferior) rank in the business community, politics, and all other groups outside the family has guided much of the research on stratification. Steinmetz's early critique of bias in social research (1974) showed how census data reflected such misconceptions in stratification research, as did some highly regarded research on the occupational system. She noted, for example, that the census assigned class position to the family unit on the basis of the occupation of the male head of household. Families in which the husband was a carpenter or autoworker were classified as ''blue-collar'' even if the wife had a college education and was a teacher. (Several years later Valerie Oppenheimer [1977] reconceptualized the socioeconomic status of families by taking wives' occupations into account.) The flawed data were used to create socioeconomic status indices which, when correlated with other variables such as political attitudes and child-care practices, resulted in skewed perspectives about the association between class level (based only on husbands' characteristics) and behavior. Steinmetz pointed out that such discrepant status-sets of husbands and wives were common among some segments of the population, notably blacks and lower working-class groups. For example, she notes that Watson and Barth (1964), using 1960 census data, found that 22 percent of employed women had occupations equal to their husbands' and 42 percent had occupations ranked above those of their husbands. More recently, Heath and Britten (1984), in a British study, have shown that women's jobs are important variables in addition to the husband's occupation in explaining differences in fertility and voting behavior. Blau and Duncan's otherwise distinguished work (1967) on the American occupational system was criticized for its bias in restricting analyses to a survey of twenty thousand males. Other research on mobility has studied women, but questions have been limited to their fathers' and husbands' occupations and the number of their siblings. No questions were asked about the women's occupations or education!

Acker's work on women and stratification (1980) notes that some writers still consider women substantially outside the class system (Giddens, 1973) and continue to think of them as having the same class positions as their husbands (Wright, 1978).[18] In Acker's view, these authors do not discard the old assumptions that female class is determined by the class of male relations and do not deal with sex-based inequality; by implication, that subject must be discussed outside the boundaries of class analysis. Such a practice of separating class and sex stratification is typical of a proliferation of books and articles that deal with sex inequality. Class differences of women and men—as measured by their differing distributions of occupation, for example—are described in a few books (Deckard, 1979; Hacker, 1975), and the relationship between sex and class stratification is given brief treatment by Chafetz (1974) and Walum (1977), with further analysis by Chafetz (1984). But the analyses amount to little more than a declaration that women constitute a caste. Most works on social stratification barely mention sex.

Rae Lesser Blumberg's *Stratification: Socioeconomic and Sexual Inequality* (1978) is acknowledged as a major effort—Acker says the only one—to integrate the class position of women into a larger theoretical framework. The book gives an historical-evolutionary account of socio-

18. As will be clearly seen, much of the reasoning and references to sources in this section on stratification are informed by Joan Acker's comprehensive analysis.

economic and sexual inequalities and develops a theory of sexual inequality under different modes of production, arguing that women's relative lack of economic power is the most important determinant of inequalities, including those of marriage, parenthood, and sexuality. I agree with Acker that Blumberg's work fails to explain women's relatively poor standing in industrial societies where their work is indispensable. Acker points out that to consider sex and class as separate systems obscures class differences among women and also neglects the role of sex status in creating and maintaining power inequities. It is possible, she asserts, that some basic Marxist concepts—such as those invoking exploitation and surplus value—are not useful in explaining sex differences in social standing. The concepts are sex neutral, but they do not account for the complex factors that determine the position of women. Thus, the positing of two separate systems, sex and class, is a more sophisticated form of intellectual sexism than the sexism implicit in theory that accepts the conceptual invisibility of women. The male is still taken to be the prototypical human being and social inequality is viewed essentially as predicated on men's differential attainment of resources. "Women remain standing on the margins, and the subject of sex inequality is something we deal with in a paragraph, or perhaps even a chapter" (Acker, 1980: 27).

Some feminist theorists, inspired by socialist writings from earlier periods, introduced women's reproductive roles into the discussion of class. We shall look at this again in chapter 7; here we need note only their central idea that the family or gender relations reproduced the "relations of production."

Reproduction theory argued a systematic connection between the subordination of women and their economic exploitation in capitalism. But, as stated before, many have argued that the subordination of women started long before capitalism and occurs in states with different political-economic systems. Newer versions see social reproduction and patriarchy as occurring entirely in the realm of ideology, not as part of the sphere of production at all. In other versions, reproduction is connected with a social division of labor.

Connell (1988) has suggested that structural Marxism, developed in the middle and late 1970s provided additional insights. In this perspective, the family, sexuality, or gender was the site of the reproduction of the relations of production. Class relations in industry are perpetuated, according to this view, by family relations, including the raising of children. In reproduction theory, the link between the subordination of women and economic exploitation in capitalism was seen to be embedded in an integrated structure of social organization. The link, however, between capitalism and gender is in fact tenuous. One may argue, as did such early socialists as Engels and Bebel, that in some respects capitalism has broken down patriarchal customs.

Many feminists have turned from this truncated view of reproduction theory to explore women's direct relations in production (that is to say, employment), as well as the impact on employment of their domestic work. This approach has been taken by feminist sociologists generally, some of whom are socialists. At the moment, the school's emerging theory does not embody class and gender in a systematic way.

Only rarely has research located the specific gatekeepers and mechanisms responsible for assigning "sex roles" and thus creating the clustered combinations of statuses that feed the stereotypes of what is regarded as "normal" behavior. These assignments create invidious distinctions between the work of men and that of women. As pointed out earlier, these patterns have been ascribed to custom and tradition, to prior forces, to early socialization, to conditioning of men and women, to natural preferences and desires emanating from their different capacities and interests, and to patriarchy as a general system. Some believed that a search for origins was futile in this case, and that it was sufficient to identify many practices as "institutionalized"—socially embedded.

It is indeed curious that in the field of sociology, although Parsons had posed the two mechanisms maintaining the social order—socialization and social control—he and those who followed his lead gave far more attention and interest to socialization than to social control. Furthermore, economists still give little thought to social control as contributing significantly to the sex division of labor. Some distinct kinds of social control, such as the use of force or discrimination, for example, are accompanied by socialization that persuades women that they are rightly subject to the use of force. So, too, the use of restrictive regulation is accompanied by cultural messages that it is men who ought to be the breadwinners while women are rightly kept out of the competition, or that women should be barred from certain occupations because of society's concern for their health. I shall return to the discussion of gender differentiation in occupations in chapter 7, after first considering the processes of social control that enforce the division of the world by sex.

CHAPTER 6

Social Control: Law, Public Policy, Force, and the Threat of Force

N owhere is the intent of institutions more clearly reflected than in the area of law and its enforcement. Here, the state, through its individual legislatures, makes manifest the will of both the elected officials and those who exert influence on them, such as business, the military, and organizations of citizens. As was pointed out in the preceding chapter, social scientists have returned to their earlier interest in the impact of political institutions (the state) (March and Olsen, 1984; Skocpol, 1980), but few theorists have noted the salience of this approach for the study of gender. In this chapter we will explore the use of law, force, and the threat of force to restrict or encourage women's equality as citizens in business and employment, to control their fertility, and to protect them from assault in the community and in the home.

Sociologists in general have neglected the analysis of how the long arm of the state reaches out to "construct" gender distinctions because they have focused rather on the processes by which society's values and norms are internalized so that they become part of the minds and hearts of its members: women and men not only are taught to play their social roles but are made to feel them as well. But socialization is only one way in which societies encourage their members to stay in line. Another is through the imposition of social controls of various kinds, ranging from mild informal sanctions to the most rigorous formal punishments codified in a body of law and imposed through a criminal justice system.[1]

No society, then, depends solely on the process of socialization to motivate its members to conform to social goals and expectations. Not only

---

1. If sociologists have failed to make the general observation, it has not missed some tough thinkers among working people. A well-known slogan in the labor movement is "If you've got them by the balls, their hearts and minds will follow," which I last observed on a sign prominently displayed at a union hall of the Communication Workers of America.

is it unlikely that there will be consensus on what these values and goals are, but people are socially situated so as to be more or less likely able to conform to the norms (Goode, 1960b). Furthermore, it may well be that the seemingly socialized are not very committed to social values and norms, some of which may rise from the grass roots but most of which are likely to be set by the more powerful members of the society.

Sociologists and anthropologists are trained to focus on customs and "naturally occurring" social patterns. They suggest that laws grow from people's values and customs and are the embodiment of those forces. Correspondingly they tend to agree that laws not based on custom and consensus in time weaken and die. As a result, many social scientists reflect in their work a cultural bias that predisposes them to think of values as passing down informally from generation to generation and growing out of the organic nature of societies. Only some have paid attention to the fact that most policymakers are white men of middle age and older. The consequences for those of different constituencies have received insufficient attention. Yet most societies have a highly defined rule system that informs people how to act and what to believe and what punishments they face if they do not abide by the rules. Rulers prefer to persuade, but, of course, punishment is usually available if persuasion should fail.

In the United States, for example, individuals are taught to be patriotic and love their country—and many do internalize these feelings—but there are also laws that require military service of its men and sanctions for those who refuse conscription or are otherwise seen as traitors. In time of war, government propaganda urges citizens to buy war bonds, instills hatred of the enemy and disdain for dissenters, and persuades parents that it is honorable to risk losing a son in battle.

All societies similarly spell out by rules and laws their preferred organization of the sexes, enunciating the social roles women and men are expected to play. It is interesting that in spite of the cultural belief that allocations of social roles by sex are predetermined by God or by nature, all societies take great care to establish laws, or rules where no formal body of law exists, to ensure that individuals' real roles come close to the culture's ideal roles. Nowhere do a society's watchdogs or its citizens leave this process to chance. (Of course, law is also the instrument of support and legitimation for the class system and other divisions of society—by age and race, for example.) Public policy and laws specify how and where the sexes may and may not mingle and also the conditions of many of men's and women's most intimate interactions (Joffe, 1986). Thus, for example, laws have long required that men and women not engage in sexual activity outside of marriage, they have confined marriage to male-female pairs, and they have banned certain modes of sexual intercourse. Laws require men to support their spouses and children. Other laws prohibit women in military service from engaging in combat but require men to fight when ordered to do so. The laws may not always be enforced, and there may be infringements, but the knowledge that punishments are on the books for those who deviate impels people to conform.

Law has also been an instrument for breaking down barriers and removing distinctions, as we have witnessed in the past two or three decades. But no society leaves women and men entirely free to choose the social roles they prefer or fails to punish them for infringement, although societies differ in their interest in particular infractions and in the harshness of punishment. Some groups, for example, punish adulterers by denying them an invitation to dinner; others stone the person to death.

Social scientists traditionally have assumed that the arrangement of the sexes is more "natural" and "organic" than other social arrangements; they have considered the infringement of norms to be deviance best studied as a social problem or delegated to students of political science, law, and criminality. In fact, law and other aspects of the social control system have rarely been incorporated in the models that attempt to explain the division of the sexes. But the new scholarship on women and the work of some critical social scientists in the recent past have begun to document the use of law and of force or the threat of force in subjugating women and setting men's and women's roles. This research has indicated how vigilant most societies, including our own, are in enforcing gender distinctions and ensuring that they do not wither away.

Law and Public Policy

The ideological character and content of law and its use in promulgating a particular type of social order has been emphasized by a group of legal theorists and sociologists of law in recent years (Hunt, 1985).[2] These critical scholars note that powerful groups use law to achieve their own goals, while insisting that the law serves most people and is an outgrowth of natural phenomena. For example, many groups who object to new laws

2. Hunt (1985) contends that work focusing on the ideological character of law, such as that of scholars in "critical legal studies," has resulted in significant advances over that produced by more orthodox approaches in the sociology of law, such as jurisprudence, which employs normative analysis. Other scholars, however, question whether the work constitutes an "advance."

granting women greater rights do so on the grounds that these laws are
contrary to nature. They fail to understand that the existing laws were no
more "natural," that such matters as the distribution of property and rights
and restrictions in marriage and divorce reflected the choices of those who
devised and passed the laws to suit their benefit and beliefs. But the analysis of political institutions as "intentional" have not been restricted to
members of the critical school. March and Olsen point out that politics
"creates and confirms interpretations of life" and defines the "appropriate" (1984: 741).

Women were—and are—kept in place by laws. Only those women who
have powerful male protectors or independent resources or those who have
banded together in women's movements have had a chance to break away
from the limits imposed on most other women. Of course, law does not
cover every kind of activity: custom and tradition are important, too, either
in supporting law or in undermining it. But law is an important legitimator
of social practice and contributes to establishment of the norms—that is,
it defines what is permitted and what is deviant. For most of legal history,
law restricted women from obtaining both material and human capital resources and prevented their participation in lawmaking and other important establishment institutions.

Furthermore, law is also interpreted by those who possess power—usually men—in the judiciary, in government, in the church. And they determine the punishments of those who violate the law. Research has made
clear that the cultural preferences of gatekeepers determine the way they
mete out justice—whether demonstrated by the variable prosecutions by
lawyers and judges of rapists, wife batterers, and employment discrimi-
nators in the United States or by the lack of enthusiasm for punishing
husbands who murder wives with insufficient dowries in India (Butalia,
1985).

Even in recent decisions of the courts, a different standard of judgment
is applied to women, according to MacKinnon (1979, 1982). There is
considerable disagreement in the judicial system about treating women
equally with men before the law, and rulings still are based on special
considerations for women, which underscore their different status. For
example, evaluating the *Wanrow* decision, which supported the defense
of a woman confined to a wheelchair, who shot and killed an unarmed
child molester, MacKinnon found the court's "special consideration" an
expression of a doctrinal construction such that the sexes are "not similarly situated" with regard to the ability to defend themselves. She also
objected to the court's use of "privacy" rather than women's "rights" as

the basis of Roe v. Wade (1973) which established the legality of abortion. Judge Ruth Bader Ginsburg (1985) also has noted that the Supreme Court has avoided treating abortion statutes as a women's rights issue.

Research has also shown how other kinds of state or religious policies have resulted in inequality between the sexes in the workplace, the family, and the political sphere. Esther Boserup's classic study of women in the third world (1970) showed how the colonizing countries of Europe undermined women's market and political power in East Asia and Africa, so that only men had access to technology and modern education. She reasoned that this enabled men to participate more readily than women in the modernization process, making them even more dominant and leaving women more disadvantaged than they had been. However, as the modernization process proceeds and women gain access to education at later stages (Oboler, 1985), they usually do make gains.

Studies have shown that women are differentially affected by the modernization process in part because of priorities set by government administrators. There is documentation of disparities in the delivery of health care, education, training for employment, and other ways in which resources are made available to men and women, ensuring that they will not be equally prepared to engage in the same activities. Thus, while it is believed that women do not have the same interests as men and will therefore avoid men's activities, care is exercised to make sure they *cannot* prepare for roles considered inappropriate. These disparities are most marked in the third world, but they exist as well in the United States and other societies.[3]

The impact of policy and law affects us all. Of course, many of us would know from personal experience even if historians, political scientists, economists, and lawyers had not brought it to our attention that in the United States and elsewhere the law not so long ago supported practices restricting women's employment in various occupations.[4] For example, it supported prohibitions on their practicing before the bar of certain states, getting credit to transact business or acquire cars and houses,

3. Indian social scientists, for example, note an increasing gap between men and women in literacy, education, and training for employment; a disparity in delivery of health care; and an excessive mortality rate for women (Butalia, 1985). Cynthia Cockburn's British study (1985) of four spheres of work in which new techniques were developed to increase efficiency shows how women are effectively prevented from developing competence in the use of new technology. Women become mere operators while men continue to be the technologists because of managerial directives.

4. Ginsburg (1985) points out that from the 1860s until 1971, the record remained almost unbroken: the Supreme Court rejected virtually every effort to overturn sex-based classification by law.

trading on the floor of stock exchanges, and serving as jurors or judges. Although many restrictions were eliminated during the 1970s, remnants of once pervasive sex-based classifications persist in U.S. law. Ginsburg (1985) has provided a summary of Supreme Court decisions overturning still-remaining sex-based laws:

Men could not be preferred to women for estate administration purposes, the Court declared in the pivotal *Reed v. Reed*[5] decision. Married women in the military could not be denied fringe benefits—family housing and health care allowances—accorded married men in military service, the High Court held in *Frontiero v. Richardson.*[6] Social security benefits, welfare assistance, and workers' compensation secured by a male's employment must be secured, to the same extent, by a female's employment, the Supreme Court ruled in a progression of cases: *Weinberger v. Wiesenfeld,*[7] *Califano v. Goldfarb,*[8] *Califano v. Westcott,*[9] and *Wengler v. Druggists Mutual Insurance Co.*[10] Girls are entitled to the same parental support as boys, the Supreme Court stated in *Stanton v. Stanton.*[11] Evidencing its neutrality, the Court declared in *Craig v. Boren*[12] that boys must be permitted to buy 3.2 percent beer at the same age as girls and, in *Orr v. Orr,*[13] that alimony could not be retained as a one-way street: a state could compel able men to make payments to women in need only if it also held women of means accountable for payments to men unable to fend for themselves. Louisiana's rule, derived from Napoleon's Civil Code, designating husband head and master of the household, was held in *Kirchberg v. Feenstra*[14] to be offensive to the evolving sex equality principle. In its most recent decision, *Mississippi University for Women v. Hogan,*[15] the High Court recognized the right of men to a nursing school education at an institution maintained by the state for women only.

Ginsburg's analysis thus indicates how the Court moved toward enunciating equal rights for women. But she also shows the Court's reluctance to eliminate all distinctions between the sexes in a variety of spheres. For example, she writes that the Court

5. 404 U.S. 71 (1971).
6. 411 U.S. 677 (1973).
7. 420 U.S. 636 (1975) (Social Security).
8. 430 U.S. 199 (1977) (Social Security).
9. 443 U.S. 76 (1979) (Aid to Families with Dependent Children).
10. 446 U.S. 142 (1980) (Workers' Compensation).
11. 421 U.S. 7 (1975).
12. 429 U.S. 190 (1976).
13. 440 U.S. 268 (1979).
14. 450 U.S. 455 (1981). The Louisiana legislation at issue provided specifically that a husband had the unilateral right to dispose of jointly owned property without his wife's consent. Id. at 456.
15. 458 U.S. 718 (1982).

had declined to condemn a state property tax advantage reserved for widows,[16] a state statutory rape law penalizing males but not females,[17] and draft registration limited to males.[18] It has formally reserved judgment on the question whether, absent ratification of an equal rights amendment, sex, like race, should rank as a suspect classification.[19]

The legal scholar Ann Freedman (1983) also argues that although it seemed possible for a time that sex-based laws would generally be struck down, either through judicial interpretation of the equal protection clause or through ratification of the Equal Rights Amendment, it is still the case that equal rights principles have not prevailed in the constitutional process. Even among the liberal-minded justices of the Supreme Court, there has been some ambivalence over interpretation of the meaning of equal rights for women.

This ambivalence has also been reflected in the work of feminist legal scholars. For example, Professors Sylvia Law (1984) of the New York University Law School and Herma Hill Kay (1985) of the Law School of the University of California at Berkeley have argued that the law ought to consider women's biological differences and the different responsibilities they bear for child rearing. Equality of men and women in law creates inequities for women, they claim, because of "the inescapable fact of sexual reproductive difference" (Kay, 1985). Unlike Kay, Sylvia Law also suggests—referring to the work of writers such as Carol Gilligan— that women have psychological differences that ought to be taken into account (a position that has been criticized, as we saw in chapter 4).

Many feminist public interest groups do want the state to intervene to treat women differently from men and to order private persons to do so because of women's special situation. Thus some have sought pregnancy leave for women even when the employer gives no leave for any reason. And some have protested the overturn of protection laws that offer women special benefits before and after childbirth. One such was a federal district court ruling that California's pregnancy laws, which mandate employers to allow women up to four months of maternity leave and guarantee their right to reinstatement in the same or similar jobs, are preempted by Title VII of the Civil Rights Act of 1964. The court maintained that women should be afforded the same benefits and leave time as any temporarily

16. *Kahn* v. *Shevin,* 416 U.S. 351 (1974).
17. *Michael M.* v. *Superior Court,* 450 U.S. 464 (1981).
18. *Rostker* v. *Goldberg,* 453 U.S. 57 (1981).
19. See *Mississippi University for Women* v. *Hogan,* 458 U.S. 718, 724 n.9 (1982); *Frontiero* v. *Richardson,* 411 U.S. 677, 691–92 (1973) (Powell, J., concurring).

disabled employee (a right created by the 1978 Pregnancy Disability Amendment to the Civil Rights Act). But other feminist scholars, such as Wendy Williams of the Georgetown Law School and Ruth Bader Ginsburg of the U.S. Court of Appeals, resist the "new protection" argument, claiming that its ultimate consequences will be deleterious to the course of women's equality—a view that I believe is informed by the lessons of history, as discussed later in this chapter. In this case, the California law was upheld by the Supreme Court.

Outside the Western world, some nations such as Saudi Arabia, Iran, and Yemen prohibit women from driving cars, appearing in certain public places without escorts, swimming together with men, and exposing their faces in public. Men's and women's roles, responsibilities, and privileges in marriage have been regulated in all societies that have a formal legal system, and in those without one, marriage is institutionalized by custom and tradition with controls no less emphatic.

Authoritative works have been published in the last decade documenting differences in U.S. law in the treatment of men and women. The first legal casebook, *Sex-Based Discrimination,* by Davidson, Ginsburg, and Kay, was published in 1974. And in 1978 a book by Sachs and Wilson documented the decades of debate over whether to lift the legal restrictions enacted against women in Britain and the United States before the passage of suffrage in the early 1900s. These debates centered on the philosophical issue of whether women could be considered "persons" with rights to university education, public office, and the vote.[20] At the beginning of the century, when women had managed to acquire appropriate professional qualifications, they often were confronted with a remaining disqualification—they were not considered "persons" under law. This reasoning had been used to restrict their participation in the legal profession (Weisberg, 1977, 1979; Fossum, 1980; Epstein, 1968, 1970a, 1970b, 1981b; Sachs and Wilson, 1978). Even after the "person" issue was resolved, restrictions hampered women's working in medicine (Lopate, 1968; Walsh, 1977; Lorber, 1984 and in teaching (Tyack and Strober, 1981). Restrictions excluded married women from working at all in certain positions, such as that of airline attendant, and in banking and insurance firms until the Civil Rights Act of 1964 made such practices illegal. Gutis (1980) has also shown how occupational segregation has been dealt with in the law.

---

20. According to Sachs and Wilson (1978: 22), British judges wrestled for six decades (up until the turn of the century) with the issue of whether or not a woman could in law be regarded as a "person." A series of statutes provided that access to public office, entry to professions, and entitlement to vote should be granted to any "person" who had the necessary qualifications.

Political scientists, sociologists, jurists, and others have pointed out the restrictions suffered by women because the U.S. Constitution lacks an Equal Rights Amendment which would strike down the remaining state laws affording women and men different rights and privileges and restricting women from certain kinds of employment.[21]

The struggle to end sex discrimination today centers on affirmative action measures intended to compensate for past discrimination rather than attacking acts of legal exclusion, for many of the latter have been overturned by Title VII of the Civil Rights Act of 1964, other legislation such as the Equal Pay Act and the Women's Educational Equity Act of 1974, and today's broadened interpretation of the U.S. Constitution's equal protection clause.

Laws are enacted and changed or withdrawn in step with current ideology in a society. Iran is only the latest of a number of examples indicating that there is no linear progression toward greater equality of the sexes. Usually a correlation exists between democratic (or democratic socialist) political ideology and greater equality (Epstein and Coser, 1981), but other social factors such as tradition, economic insecurity, war, and the rise of charismatic despots can alter the association.

Most socialist regimes, which have come to power with an ideology of equality, have focused on women's equality. In some cases, however, after an initial drive to permit women's full participation in government and employment, these programs are undermined by the resistance of men or the denial of necessary supports such as child care and home services. This was the case in the Soviet Union, as Gail Lapidus has vividly described in *Women in Soviet Society* (1978). Marxist doctrine specified that women should become economically independent of men and equal partners in the economy. After the first decade of implementation, however, concern mounted over declining birth rates, and a renewed emphasis was placed on motherhood as well as the economic participation of women. Government policy on such matters as abortion, child care, housing, delivery of consumer goods, and the integration or segregation of the sexes at school and the workplace has seesawed back and forth, depending on how the Soviet government has viewed the need for women's labor in the economic sphere (as during World War II) and the perceived need for increased procreation. In the United States, the law has also interfered

21. Accounts of the failure of the ERA may be found in Deborah L. Rhode, "Equal Rights in Retrospect," *Law and Inequality: A Journal of Theory and Practice* 1 (June 1983); Mary Frances Berry, *Why ERA Failed: Politics, Women's Rights and the Amending Process of the Constitution* (Bloomington: Indiana University Press, 1986); and Jane J. Mansbridge, *Why We Lost the ERA* (Chicago: University of Chicago Press, 1986).

with men's and women's prerogative not to become parents by prohibiting the use of contraceptives[22] and abortion.[23]

Public policy on the control of fertility has been of great significance in creating opportunity for women. Probably one of the most important factors in women's move toward equality with men has been the decline in their fertility in the developed world, just as their high fertility in the underdeveloped world continues to constrain their opportunities. Size of family is conditional not only on the individual choice of couples but on their access to birth control devices and abortion, which is made easy or difficult depending on the attitudes of government, church authorities, and in some cases the military.[24]

Laws in most countries have controlled women's options to move out of family roles just as rules set by various industries have forced women to spend their lives as servants or prohibited married women with small children or women of reproductive age from working at certain jobs. In some states, court challenges have struck down certain of these prohibitions, but others remain, depending on the area.[25]

The impact of the state may be experienced differently by groups of people within it depending on economic and political institutions and on the public policies affecting state intervention in the various spheres of life. Even in the more equalitarian societies, men and women may be subject to state policies in different ways. In a view of "patriarchy in a welfare state," Hernes (1984) cautions those who would regard the condition of Scandinavian women with admiration that the Norwegian state

22. For example, a Connecticut ban on the use of contraceptives even by married couples was overturned by the Supreme Court only in 1965 (*Griswold* v. *Connecticut* 381 U.S. 479 [1965]).

23. As Ginsburg (1985) has noted, in the United States rights achieved in this sphere are precarious because of continual proposals for overruling *Roe* v. *Wade* by constitutional amendment and a variety of proposals in Congress and state legislatures to contain or curtail the decision. Her examples: "Destro, *Abortion and the Constitution: The Need for Life-Protective Amendment*, 63 CALIF. L. REV. 1250, 1319–25 (1975) (discussing proposed amendments); Hyde, *The Human Life Bill: Some Issues and Answers*, 27 N.Y.L. SCH. L. REV. 1077 (1982) (congressional response); Witherspoon, *The New Pro-Life Legislation: Patterns and Recommendations*, 7 ST. MARY'S L.J. 637 (1976) (state response); Note, *Implications of the Abortion Decisions: Post Roe and Doe Litigation and Legislation*, 74 COLUM. L. REV. 237 (1974) (state response). Furthermore, the Solicitor General, in July 1985 filed a 'friend of the court' (amicus curiae) brief in the pending abortion cases, *Thornburgh* v. *AGOC* and *Diamond* v. *Charles*, specifically asking the Supreme Court to overrule *Roe* v. *Wade*."

24. As Joan Huber (1986) has pointed out (citing Mohr, 1978: 240), abortion was widely used in the United States by middle-class women until the middle of the nineteenth century. By 1880, abortion had become illegal, owing in part to legislators' and physicians' fears that the desertion of motherhood by middle-class white women would permit "foreigners" to swamp the American population.

25. Ginsburg informs me that the Eleventh Circuit has held unlawful under Title VII the exclusion of women from work in places with toxic substances dangerous to procreation (100 U.S. 452).

is gendered and that women are "policy takers" rather than "policymakers." Their relationship to the state as employees and clients in disproportionate numbers means that women's lives are more dependent and regulated by state policies than are men's—first, because women's lives are more closely affected by reproduction, and second, because women, unlike men, do not have organizational buffers between themselves and the authorities to articulate and defend their interests. They remain mired in low-paying part-time work, which imposes low rank and few resources and undermines their ability to consolidate their interests politically. Thus, the state is a new locus of patriarchy. It has, however, been responsive to equality issues. Thus there are countervailing forces even within the state, so that women have also gained some power by mobilizing around gender issues.

Research has shown how attitudes about men's and women's "proper" status-sets (Merton, 1957)—that is, the array of social positions considered appropriate for the two genders—have often been forged into law and into the rules and regulations of professional associations, trade unions, government programs, schools, and business-oriented clubs. The idea that women, married or single, had the right to choose careers of their own, for example, ran counter to common-law tradition in the West. Thus, limitations on women's options to work were supported in 1873 by the U.S. Supreme Court, which upheld the Illinois State Bar's refusal to admit Myra Bradwell as a lawyer. A concurring opinion by Justice Bradley stated that "the natural and proper timidity and delicacy which belongs to the female sex evidently unfit it for many of the occupations of civil life" (Sachs and Wilson, 1978: 98).

Protective labor legislation that covers only women workers also has had the consequence of limiting the kinds of work roles women might acquire in the United States and elsewhere, including Eastern Europe (Heitlinger, 1985). The first protective labor law in the United States was enacted in 1874 with the support of social reformers and feminists (J. Freeman, 1971). This law prohibited women from, for example, lifting more than a certain weight or working at night. Some men, however, supported laws specifying "protected" working conditions for women in order to curb competition from them (Chafe, 1972; J. Freeman, 1971; Andrews and Bliss, 1911, as cited in Farley, 1978).

The issue of protective legislation split the women's movement in the 1920s. The National Women's Party (NWP) proposed an Equal Rights Amendment in 1923 to eliminate special legislation for women. This was opposed by the League of Women Voters (LWV), descendant of the American Women's Suffrage Association. What divided the two groups was the question of whether women's maternal functions took priority over all others, since the argument for protection stemmed from the double burdens borne by employed women. The NWP claimed that protective legislation merely excluded women from high-wage jobs; the LWV, that it eased the burden of women workers (Huber, 1976). The disputes on these issues among feminists today indicate that the debate is still very much alive.

Labor unions have continued to support protective legislation. This was one reason they failed, until 1973, to support the recent attempt to pass the Equal Rights Amendment and are still ambivalent about it—as was so in the California ERA fight.

Some states have specifically barred women from jobs believed to be corrupting (such as bartending) or otherwise inappropriate (mining, smelting, meter reading, pinsetting in bowling alleys, guarding railway crossings, jitney driving, freight handling, trucking) (Clauss, 1982). As Hill (1979) has pointed out, however, protective labor legislation has been directed mainly at women working in factories, laundries, and stores, not as agricultural workers, professionals, or domestic laborers. Laws in California restricting hours and weight lifting were used by railway employers to justify not hiring women as telegraphers (Clauss, 1982). In the past, limitations on weight lifting also barred women from work as postal clerks (Bachrach, 1984).

Today, federal officials have estimated that such protective policies have closed at least 100,000 jobs to women in the United States (Reskin and Hartmann, 1986). Clauss (1982) points out that these policies have usually been limited to workplaces that have historically excluded female employment and that have offered well-paying jobs. Such laws were recently struck down by a federal court of the Eleventh Circuit.[26] But despite policies ostensibly designed to protect women, hazards in predominantly female occupations have been ignored. Women are still exposed to brown-lung disease in cotton mills, and textile and apparel workers, 90 percent of whom are women, are confronted with high noise levels, excessive heat and humidity, poor lighting, and toxic chemicals and dust (O'Farrell and Harlan, 1984). The electrical products industry, which is 30 percent female, ranks third among those industries most likely to expose workers to carcinogens (National Commission on Working Women, 1984).[27]

26. Ginsburg has pointed out (in private communication) that Judge Elbert P. Tuttle held such exclusions to be in violation of Title VII, citing and relying on a law review article (1981) by feminist law professor Wendy Williams of Georgetown University.

27. Newer industries also have been found to expose women (and men) workers to chemicals, radiation, fumes, solvents, acids, and other toxic materials (Green, 1983).

The long-run effect of protective legislation, research has shown (Epstein, 1967, 1969; Baer, 1978), has been not only to exclude women from certain jobs but, where they were tolerated, to make it impossible for them to attain promotions. The legislation also reinforced a view of women as special and not typical members of the work force (A. Hill, 1979). Although in some circumstances men have also been protected by maximum-hours laws, women have usually faced more restrictions. The laws enforcing these limitations were upheld by successive Supreme Courts, which argued that women's physiology and their dependency on men put them in a class by themselves and justified legislation specifying the conditions under which they could work (A. Hill, 1979).[28] Title VII, however, brought about the demise of these laws.

Changing views of the justice of sex typing certain occupations led to legal remedies, among them the reversal of laws, statutes, and regulations preventing women from working as, say, bartenders or men as nurses (Epstein, 1970b) and prohibiting newspapers from classifying jobs as "male" and "female" in their help-wanted advertising. In fact, members of Congress, the Equal Economic Opportunity Commission (EEOC), and the Office of Federal Contract Compliance held hearings at which research findings were presented indicating that such designations were arbitrary and did not rest on any functional relationship between job status and sex status.[29] One such study by Sandra and Daryl Bem (1973) showed the impact of sex-segregated employment advertising.

Although many discriminatory practices were invalidated by the 1964 Civil Rights Act, some have persisted. Bielby and Baron's research (1984) showed that manufacturers using the California State Employment Service in the 1960s and 1970s continued to cite weight-lifting restrictions in order to justify not hiring women. Moreover, although Supreme Court decisions have opened some occupations to women, according to Gates's analysis

28. This refers to the famous "Brandeis Brief" which was incorporated in the Court's decision in *Muller* v. *Oregon* (1908). In it, women were exempted from the freedom-of-contract doctrine because they needed special protection. A "liberal" court thus exempted women from a doctrine detested by everyone sympathetic to labor. Feminists who objected to women's being singled out were accused of antilabor sentiments.

29. Many social scientists, myself included (Epstein, 1967), presented testimony before the EEOC and the Office of Federal Contract Compliance (Epstein, 1969) on the protective laws and help-wanted ads and the general role of sex typing. A leading spokesperson was Betty Friedan, whose book *The Feminine Mystique* was published in 1963. By 1966 she had organized the National Organization for Women (NOW), which mobilized support for implementation of Title VII of the Civil Rights Act of 1964, the subject of the hearings. Friedan's own research was also the basis for striking down official sex typing in many of the spheres under review, much of this in the mid-1960s. The testimony was published in the proceedings of the hearings held by Congresswoman Martha Griffiths (1962).

of occupational segregation and the law (1976), many of the Court's invalidations of non-job-related criteria have not been observed in various localities, according to work done by Martin (1980). Reskin also called attention to an important loophole in the prohibition against using sex as an employment criterion—the Bona Fide Occupational Qualification (BFOQ).[30] This has been used to justify discrimination against women in occupations as diverse as prison chaplain and guard and international oil executive (on the grounds that prejudiced clients would object to their employment).

Wherever a society may lie on the spectrum of distinctions between the sexes, it is improbable (as Dorothy Smith, 1977, has put it) that the state is neutral (Bart and Budinger, unpublished). Whichever is closer to the truth—that "the state is not our friend" (Smith) or that the state is a useful agent of social change—there is no doubt that the state is always mindful of the division of labor by sex.

Whatever the debate between those who believe that recent Court decisions free women and those who believe they create a basis for further distinctions that will ultimately result in maintaining male power (MacKinnon, 1982b), research does more than document changes in the law; it provides an instrument for social change as well. Social science research has been used as the basis for briefs written to reinterpret and change laws that set different standards of justice, education, and employment for men and women (Ginsburg, 1978). And it has resulted on balance in a greater commitment to equality.

Force and the Threat of Force

Enforcement of the law by the courts and police is only one aspect of the social control system that orders gender distinctions. To the force used by agents of government must be added that used by other groups with investments in the social order: elders with social and political power, owners of material resources, or, in some cases, the physically strong. Although force may not always by their first preference and may even be their last resort, it is certainly an important part of their repertoire of strategies.

William J. Goode's presidential address to the American Sociological Association in 1972 criticized the discipline for neglecting the important

---

30. This refers to a situation in which sex can be considered a *valid* requirement for a given job, such as sperm donor.

variables of force and the threat of force. Although critical sociologists identified as Marxists or leftists have, of course, long focused on the oppression and coercion of minorities (and more recently, women), these perspectives did not become part of mainstream sociological analysis until the last decade. Studies of force and violence were largely regarded as properly part of the study of "deviance" or "social problems" rather than of the normal mechanisms by which the social order and the division of labor are kept in place. In part this resulted, as Goode pointed out, from the humanistic bias of many sociologists and from the bias that largely restricted research to contemporary phenomena, to Western democratic societies, and to focuses on male workers, on elite occupations and professions, and on the family as an institution built on love and caring. Although such practices as arranged marriages, the burning of widows on the funeral pyres of their husbands, wife beating, infanticide (primarily of girl babies), and other coercive and violent practices were examined in the study of the family as interesting and different, they did not change the paradigm of the family as a center for socioemotional resolution (Parsons, 1951). In his discussion of the "theoretical importance of love," Goode (1959) noted how potentially inappropriate matings between men and women—those disruptive to the stratification system—are "controlled" by powerful elders.

Other sociologists (Waller, 1938) also observed how groups controlled mate selection and maintained the power of elders, but the more gory aspects of the family system were notably absent from theory, as well as from models of the family as an institution. In the study of the workplace, the concept of "opportunity structure" (Merton [1938] 1957), which ought to have defined all the variables that go into creating opportunities or precluding them, was largely confined to such benign indicators as role models, access to information, the father's (but rarely the mother's) occupation, geographical location, and educational experience. Typically, overt discrimination ("no Irish need apply," "no women wanted here"), sexual and physical harassment, closed shops, and other practices such as strike breaking, slavery, and indenture were confined to historical studies and not included in models of employment.

Sociologists and political scientists vary in their disciplinary attention to force. Even today, social historians (Aries, 1962; Shorter, 1975, 1977; Stone, 1979; Walkowitz, 1982), anthropologists (Collier et al., 1982; Collier and Rosaldo, 1981; Harris, 1978), and lawyers (MacKinnon, 1982) have provided some of the richest insights into the coercive elements in enforcing sex-role obedience. Some political scientists, and sociologists as well (Lapidus, 1978),[31] have identified the use of violence against women as an important feature of social control in the family and have noted the failure of the state to prevent it (Bart, 1981; Russell, 1982). The use of force to restrict women's freedom of movement has also been analyzed by Riger and Gordon (1981) and Bart and O'Brien (1984).

Even sociobiologists, who believe that physical differences between men and women account for such social arrangements as men's roles in politics and women's roles in the home, usually fail to consider that sex segregation and sexual hierarchy may have been initiated or maintained through physical coercion by men. These scholars tend to create a picture of social harmony, in which women willingly take a submissive role, rather than one of conflict, in which they must be subdued.

Chafetz (1984), however, maintains that physical coercion does not explain sex stratification because (among other reasons) the "social nature of our species and enlightened self-interest mitigate against the wholesale use of force to impose domination by one-half of the species over the other half." The use of force by males over females is often viewed as an indicator rather than an explanation of female disadvantage. This reasoning is far from convincing. Research finds, as I have noted, that the wholesale use of force is rarely necessary to keep the subjugated in line. A few examples—even threats—will often suffice.

Since the mid-1970s, the courts as well as periodicals, newspapers, and popular and academic books have focused increasing attention on sexual harassment.[32] According to one 1981 estimate, some 150 scholarly articles on the subject had appeared in print (Blount and Boles, 1981), and since then the number has increased dramatically. Brodsky (1976) found, in interviews with a sample of workers filing for state workman's compensation, that harassment is believed to be an expression of power and control rather than the result of sexual desire or sexuality on the part of most male aggressors. Following Kanter's thesis (1977a) that harassment tac-

31. The Woman's Department of the Soviet Communist party, known as Zhenotdel, formed in 1919 and charged with informing women of their rights and responsibilities under the new regime, faced considerable opposition. This ranged from resistance within the party (especially at lower echelons), which officially sanctioned and encouraged the department's activities but put roadblocks in its way, to much harsher treatment by those who opposed the growing equality of women. According to Lapidus (1978), for example, 203 cases of antifeminist murder were reported in Uzbekistan in 1928 (see also Armstrong, 1983).

32. A recent Supreme Court decision has held that sexual harassment on the job may be considered employment discrimination against women (*Meritor Savings Bank* v. *Vinson*, 106 S.Ct. 2399 [1986] Rehnquist, J.). In an article published in the *National Law Journal*, however, Wyatt (1986: 21), referring to several recent court decisions on alleged sexual harassment, notes, "these lower federal court decisions indicate at best only a grudging acknowledgment of *Meritor*, which did not prevent refusal of relief for all these claimants."

tics involve the inappropriate use of power and serve to affirm the position of male authority in organizations, Loy and Stewart (1984) hypothesize that sexual harassment may be an attempt to express the power differentials associated with gender roles and with organizational position.

In some instances then, sexual harassment is seen as just punishment of women for being in places in which they have no business and as an attempt to force them back into spheres where they are segregated or under the protection of a man—a husband or father, for example. Many complaints brought to the courts, however, stem from harassment of women in traditionally female jobs.[33] Harassment in the form of wife beating has been used ritually in some societies at times of community celebration and drinking (as Harris's 1978 study of a community in Bolivia illustrates) to "ensure that women did not abandon their children or domestic tasks." And the ultimate ritualized use of violence to force women to submit to male authority is found in the maiming of women's genitalia through the practice of clitoridectomy, euphemistically called female circumcision, which continues to be performed in Egypt, Yemen, Ethiopia, Somalia, Sudan, Kenya, and Muslim West Africa.[34] According to a former director of public health in Egypt the practice is designed to ensure that girls and women do not have sexual pleasure and will therefore remain chaste (El Saadawi, 1982). Huber and Spitze (1983) see a relationship between restrictive practices against women, such as clitoridectomy, foot binding, and suttee, and the interests of powerful men in maintaining control over who inherits their land. Restrictions on women's free sexuality reflect men's concern that they not bear illegitimate children, and the incineration of widows, Huber suggests, forestalls the widow's claim on her husband's estate (1985). Women's reproductive function is used to justify their segregation in public and their restriction to the home, as well as their lack of civil and legal rights.[35]

33. For example, *Bundy* v. *Jackson,* 641 Fed. 2nd 934.

34. Huber and Spitze (1983), following El Saadawi (1982: 33), point out that this operation causes both short-term and long-term trauma to women, including hemorrhage, shock, septicemia, chronic infection, and difficulties in childbirth and in coitus.

35. The eye of the journalist recently caught the mood of tension women feel outside the home in contemporary New York City. In a column in the *New York Times* in 1985, Katha Pollitt commented that she counted fifty men in a midtown park one day, "ambling, striding along eating hot dogs, sitting on benches and reading the paper or trading in illegal substances," but she saw only three women, "all walking quickly and grimly . . . as though late for an appointment for the dentist," as she was that afternoon. One of the men "invited me to take off my clothes, and . . . another wanted to know why I wasn't smiling," she wrote. The petty annoyance of the unwanted overtures led her to speculate more generally on men's freedom to use public space and women's restrictions: "Fear of rape and attack, of which low-level aggravation is a reminder, plays a part in keeping women from claiming public space as their own. We are brought up to be wary—of strange men, of dark streets, of underpopulated subway cars." She

The use of physical force against women, or their fear of the use of physical force, is of course modified by legal restraints and social norms. But the specific fears women face, particularly in repressive societies, and the generalized fears women everywhere have of the physical and political strength of men still require careful study by scholars rather than unquestioning acceptance of the belief that women are active agents in their choice of subordinate social roles.

went on to illustrate how societies frame the context within which some men annoy and assault and otherwise keep women from enjoying the public sphere: "In seventeenth-century England, a 'public woman' was a prostitute. In some African countries today (Zimbabwe for an example), unescorted women are periodically rounded up in government morality drives. Too far away? A few years ago, New York City paid a hefty out-of-court settlement to a freelance writer arrested for loitering with intent to solicit. She was standing on a street corner waiting for a friend."

CHAPTER 7

The Structure of Work and the Economic Pyramid

As women have increasingly joined the paid labor force in modern Western societies, scholars interested in issues of gender distinctions and inequality have begun to devote much attention to this phenomenon. Most have focused on the current American context, but a body of knowledge is developing about women's activity in the work force historically as well as across geographic boundaries.

The extent to which the workplace is commonly segregated by sex is striking. In some places the segregation is physical, with men and women separated by buildings or walls within buildings. Sometimes this merely reflects the sex typing of the jobs they do. For example, women performing "women's work" in the textile industry usually work only with other women (under male supervision), and male factory workers working at "men's jobs" in steel plants work in an all-male environment.

Often, however, men and women often are separated not by walls but, as we have seen, by social classifications that define some jobs as male and others as female even though the two sexes occupy much the same physical space. So when male managers work in the same offices with female secretaries, segregation exists in symbolic form. In other cases, men and women may do the same or essentially similar jobs (as janitors and cleaning personnel, for example), but men are assigned one job title and women another. Sex segregation in the workplace also reflects the differential status of men and women, since women's jobs tend to be subordinate to men's and typically offer less prestige and less pay.

Numerous theories have attempted to "explain" the sexual division of labor. When put to the test, some have proven inadequate or questionable in the face of evidence to the contrary, but others have proven to be more reasonable or powerful in explaining the phenomenon.

The explanations generally correspond to cultural perspectives about men's and women's nature. Sociobiologists, as we saw earlier, regard the processes of sex segregation in the work force as a result of "natural" forces stemming from the physiological and psychic characteristics of each sex. They assume a functional relationship between traits they regard as inherited and the gender characteristics of jobs, such as men's aggressiveness and their occupation as "big ticket" salesmen, and women's nurturance and their employment as nurses. But most social scientists offer frameworks that do not rest on a biological model. The major explanations are based on sex-role socialization, human capital, and social structural theories. These explanations are not necessarily mutually exclusive, although some proponents regard them as such.

Socialization

The theory of socialization into sex roles focuses on the process by which the sexes assume different personality characteristics, skills, and preferences. This perspective suggests that cultural views of the proper attitudes and behavior for each sex are communicated to boys and girls through the messages of their parents, the images provided by the media, and the communications of teachers and friends; these messages are then internalized, with consequences for adult life. Socialization contributes to sex segregation by creating in males and females specific orientations, preferences, and competencies for occupations that have been defined as sex-appropriate, while leaving men and women disinclined toward or ignorant of opportunities to pursue other occupations. Thus, socialization is often considered to limit the kinds of occupationally relevant training women acquire and to account for women's and men's choices among kinds of work.

Socialization is usually described as beginning in the cradle, where, depending upon their sex, infants receive different treatment and messages about who they are and what they will become. They are dressed in clothing that provides cues, such as color, so that others will be able to identify their sex readily. Given this information, those who attend the child usually act according to a stereotyped view of the infant boy's or girl's nature—for example, demonstrating more rough-and-tumble play with boys than with girls (Maccoby and Jacklin, 1974). Observers' assessments of a child's behavior have been found to vary according to whether they are told they are watching a female or a male baby (Will et al., 1974; Condry and Condry, 1976). The attitudes regarding appropriate sex-role behavior that are expressed toward the infant extend through childhood and are internalized by the developing males and females. Researchers in the 1950s, for example, noted how similar behavior of girls and boys was differently interpreted and reinforced by middle-class fathers, a relatively equalitarian group. The findings of a study of the fathers of fifty-six children, which was conducted by Aberle and Naegele (1968), reflected the cultural viewpoints of the times. Of those who admitted that they knew that some boys were "holy terrors in their play groups," none expressed any concern that their sons might be bullies. But some of those who proudly guessed that their boys were "a bit of a devil" were troubled by their "bossy" daughters. Socialization is seen as instilling compliance in girls, keeping them closer to home, giving less importance to their education, and orienting them to marriage and motherhood (Komarovsky, 1953).

During the 1960s and 1970s, hundreds of papers published in books and scientific journals reported research that showed the link between cultural messages and practices, such as the depiction of girls and women in picture books (Nilsen, 1977) and in advertising (Goffman, 1976), and their later assumption of roles as housewives and mothers and their choice of "female" occupational roles as teachers and nurses.

Studies indicate that parents hold higher expectations for the adult futures of their sons than their daughters (Maccoby and Jacklin, 1974; Hoffman, 1977; Marini, 1978), and this attitude is believed to be related to men's greater achievement as measured by promotions, honors, and other distinctions. Parents' expectations that their sons will perform better in mathematics than their daughters (Fennema and Sherman, 1977; see Marini and Brinton, 1984 for an extensive review) supposedly account for boys' superior performance in mathematics beyond grade nine.

By the time the child reaches middle to late adolescence, occupational aspirations are almost as sex typed as the workplace itself. Young women aspire to a smaller number of occupations than men (Gottfredson, 1978; Marini and Brinton, 1984), presumably because of the socialization experience.

The focus on early socialization in the belief that it results in distinctive and enduring traits and attitudes in girls and boys has been challenged in many studies (see Reskin and Hartmann, 1986, for a review), including my own (Epstein, 1973a, 1976c). Even in 1970, when I was convinced of the impact of socialization in determining women's sex-typical choices, I wondered if they actually became the people the stereotypes predicted. In *Woman's Place* (1970a) I asked whether the women these girls become, "once attuned to the opinions of parents and family," are actually sensitized to the opinions and preferences of others (other-directed in the sense described by David Riesman in 1953). A speculation current at the time held that women had a propensity to be more people-oriented than object-oriented and that their empathic qualities led many women into social welfare, nursing, and similar work (see Marini and Brinton, 1984, for a review). It seemed to me, however, that "whether this is an innate or an indoctrinated propensity, indeed whether or not women are in fact more compassionate, empathetic, and more interested in people than are men, is yet to be scientifically demonstrated. But there is no doubt that women are thought to be so and this belief has manifold consequences for society's allocation of womanpower" (Epstein, 1970a: 22). I might have added that this also had consequences for social researchers' belief in personality differences between men and women, but bias in methodology was not yet on the agenda.

Knowledge of the relationship between so-called socializing experiences and later behavior is still very limited. Some social researchers have exhibited remarkable selectivity among the indicators they use to predict or explain later behavior. How much is a girl's occupational choice affected by her being given a dress or overalls to wear or a doll or truck to play with?

Reskin and Hartmann (1986) point out in their review of factors leading to sex segregation in the workplace that there is no direct evidence linking sex-role socialization and occupational outcomes. They speculate that the differential socialization of the sexes probably contributes to occupational segregation to some degree, through the formation of both sex-typed preferences in workers and workers' preferences for a particular gender among employers, but there is no established line of causality. They do presume, as do the social scientists Brim, Riley, Kohn, and Schooler, that socialization is a lifelong process, continuing long after childhood and adolescence. Some adult women who have had traditional sex-role socialization have nevertheless gone into nontraditional occupations such as blue-collar crafts (Walshok, 1981) or law (Epstein, 1981b), and there have been successful interventions to reorient or resocialize girls and boys through the use of films and special programs (Atkin, 1975; Flerx et al., 1976; Davidson et al., 1979).[1]

The impact of socialization probably depends not on any single act or set of acts or influences but on their consistency and the absence of other

1. Major problems in reorienting women in nontraditional jobs, however, come from the resistance and opposition they encounter from families, friends and coworkers.

socializing experiences, particularly later in the life cycle. It also depends on the way society defines the links between early experiences and later social roles. For example, boys who become doctors are disproportionately apt to have had fathers who were doctors.[2] An expected assumption of the father's mantle and the father's socializing behavior as a role model are presumed to orient the boy toward medicine, intellectual capacity permitting. This may be true only in a society that permits independent choice or espouses it as a credo. In most societies of the past and in many today, men and women follow in the footsteps of their parents not only because their parents are role models but also because custom, tradition, and social pressure from parents and community make other choices difficult if not impossible.

The need for constant enforcement of social controls on the behavior of men and women through formal and informal punishments and rewards indicates that socialization has only limited impact on the creation of ''natural'' behavior for each sex. When social controls are relaxed, stereotypes may be undermined by people's expression of their individual interests and talents.

Human Capital Theory

Neoclassical economic theory is at the heart of the human capital model, which ascribes occupational segregation and women's assignment to poorer jobs to rational economic choices. The theory stipulates that economic behavior is governed by the free choices of individuals attempting to maximize their utility. According to this view, people also marry to increase their utility, and the resulting division of roles between breadwinner and homemaker is based on their assessment of the benefits likely to accrue to the family from this arrangement.

Mincer and Polachek (1974, 1978) and Polachek (1976, 1978, 1979, 1981a, 1981b) have argued that women's actual or expected family obligations dictate a choice of predominantly female occupations. Following human capital theory, they believe that people invest in training or choose certain occupations with the goal of maximizing their lifetime earnings. Because most women expect to leave work when they become mothers, they do not invest in the specialized training that would lead to careers but

2. According to the American Association of Medical Colleges (AAMC), this is indeed true of the 1985 applicant class, in which 14.2 percent of all the applicants had fathers who were physicians and 1.4 percent had mothers who were physicians.

instead choose occupations that do not penalize intermittent employment, that require only skills that do not depreciate, and that offer relatively high starting wages (although small promise of advancement). As a result of these choices, women are concentrated in predominantly female occupations that characteristically do not reward job experience.

It follows that even those wives who work full time would prefer jobs that do not require overtime or unanticipated work effort, or travel or geographic mobility, and that permit flexibility and time off in domestic emergencies. According to Reskin and Hartmann (1986), these conditions are "all hypothetical characteristics of *some* predominantly female occupations," although they are not actually the case for many others.

The National Academy of Sciences committee that was formed to evaluate the causes of sex segregation in the United States found that human capital theory failed to explain sex segregation in the workplace. Citing theoretical objections, the committee's report asserted that if it were a matter of women seeking jobs requiring less training, there would be no reason to expect them to cluster particularly in female-dominated jobs because many male-dominated jobs also require little skill or training (Blau and Jusenius, 1976) and they pay better than women's jobs. Further, it noted that it was difficult to establish the direction of causation between the patterns of intermittency exhibited by women and their choice of work that is often characterized by little wage growth (Marini and Brinton, 1984). The question is—do women choose such occupations or simply accept what is offered? Posed against a vision of choice and preference is the fact of social constraint.

The concept of human capital has generated considerable research, little of it easily assessed. Economists using the same data often disagree about their interpretation and develop simulation models built on different assumptions. Mincer and Polachek (1974, 1978) attributed the observed relationship of women's work experience, home time, and wages to the decline of their skills while out of the labor force. But the human capital approach has been criticized for failing to take into account the ways in which the attributes of jobs, rather than family responsibilities, affect women's behavior. Low wages and discrimination can affect the choices women or men make in gaining work experience. And both women and men may quit because of undesirable job features (such as distance from home or an oppressive supervisory structure), even if doing so may limit opportunities for promotion (Reskin and Hartmann, 1986).

The human capital approach depends on determining women's assessment of their earning power. They believe that women's expectations that they will interrupt labor-force participation to have children affect their decisions about education, training, and occupation, such as the choice to maximize starting salaries by choosing female-dominated occupations, which hypothetically start at higher wage levels but yield lower long-run returns for experience than do predominately male occupations, which hypothetically offer less to start because they provide on-the-job training and advancement opportunity (Zellner, 1975). In their overview, Reskin and Hartmann (1986) point out that theorists in this tradition make assumptions about women's reasoning without data on the decision-making process. Furthermore, when behavior is subject to such strong structural and cultural constraints as the choice of women's work, there is less reason to expect a theory that assumes economic optimization to hold.

Social Structural Analysis

The assessment of the National Academy of Sciences committee was that job tracks for both men and women are strongly influenced by the opportunities available. Women's opportunities are restricted because of barriers that limit their access to occupations customarily dominated by men. Such barriers include entrance requirements for training and apprenticeship programs. Other barriers are created by employer discrimination, which may stem from prejudices held by both employers and workers based on beliefs about female and male workers' characteristics and the "appropriate" gender for work in particular jobs. Women's positive responses to new job opportunities made available when employers have stopped discriminating or have established affirmative action programs have demonstrated the importance of genuine opportunities for job choice and advancement (Reskin and Hartmann, 1986).

The analysis of the division of labor is complex. We will examine further the social structural approach, but first we must see how the study of social mobility in sociology illustrates the way in which various frameworks have illuminated certain issues regarding men's and women's relative social standing in the occupational world.

Mobility in the United States is achieved primarily by occupational placement. For a long time, the study of mobility was essentially the study of men. As was discussed earlier, women's occupations were not regarded as a source of their social standing; rather, it was their husband's or father's occupation that rooted them in the social structure. Certain sophisticated methodological approaches to the study of social mobility have obscured the role of sex status in mobility processes and socioeconomic states. "Women" and "men" as unitary categories are used as variables, for example, but the use of these categories tends to deflect attention from important differences that emanate from other variables, such as education. The availability of measurement tools became the force driving the study of mobility which began in the 1970s, and sex became a variable along with a vast array of others (Tyree and Hodge, 1978).

Students of stratification have explored the relative social standing or occupational prestige of women and men, the achieved and derived sources of female status, and the mobility rates and processes of men and women. Furthermore, women's occupational status has been taken into account by a number of researchers (Rossi et al., 1974; Felson and Knoke, 1974; Ritter and Hargens, 1975; Hiller and Philliber, 1978; Philliber and Hiller, 1978; Nilson, 1976; Jackman and Jackman, 1983) who concluded that the social standing of women was derived partly from their employment and partly from their mental outlook (although they expressed reservations owing to contradictory findings). Peter Rossi and associates (1974; Sampson and Rossi, 1975; Nock and Rossi, 1978) demonstrated that wives' occupational status can raise the social position of the family, showing the importance of looking at women's social position as well as their husbands' occupations in determining the class position of a family.

In her excellent review of the literature on stratification Acker (1980) points out that some surprising findings about social mobility rates and processes of status attainment say something about the measures used to study stratification.[3] For example, the findings of several prominent social scientists (Treiman and Terrell, 1975b; Featherman and Hauser, 1976; McClendon, 1976) that the process of status attainment—that is, the effect of education and family background on socioeconomic level—is the same for men and women and, even more surprisingly, that their mean occupational status is approximately equal seem doubtful and contrary to experience.

Hauser and Featherman (1977), in their sophisticated analysis of comparative mobility, found similarity of occupational rank after removing the effects of sex differences in the probability of labor-force participation and in occupational distribution. Acker notes:

Thus the destination of women, where they end up in the system of rewards, is very different from that of men even though the distances from fathers' occupation do not differ radically for women and men. It is not

---

3. I have relied on Acker's cogent analysis here as well as in chapter 5.

surprising that few differences remain when most of the sources of difference have been removed from the analysis. The finding of equal average occupational status is also misleading, for while mean status equality may exist at any one time, this is an artifact of the distribution of people in jobs. (1980: 27–28)

As is evident to most observers, researchers have shown that the highest status levels are dominated by men (Bose, 1973) and, perhaps a little less obvious, that men generally experience a rise in status over the life cycle, whereas most women stay at about the same status level from the beginning to the end of their working lives (Wolf and Rosenfeld, 1978). Featherman and Hauser (1976), Suter and Miller (1973), and Treiman and Terrell (1975b) have found that the income disadvantages suffered by most women are persistent and severe; even when they improve their job status, they do not generally benefit from the kind of rewards men receive as they climb a ladder of success.

Some studies measure social standing by comparing the prestige of occupations, measured by scales composed of ranks assigned to various kinds of work. According to these measures, women's jobs rank comparably with men's jobs. But what do prestige scales measure? They do not seem to be congruent with common perceptions, and although common perceptions are often wrong, the discrepancy leads us to question the anomalous finding. On review, we find that women with prestige scores similar to those of men do not have similar incomes, nor do they have similar authority in the workplace (Wolf and Fligstein, 1979). Bose (1980) has found that housewives in the United States were ranked highly on a scale measuring prestige of occupations. Yet, even more than before, women pejoratively characterize themselves as "only" housewives, and certainly men would consider "housewife" a low-ranking position if they were to hold it. Acker (1980) holds that the housewife's prestige score reflects a generalized respect for women (a middling sort of respect) and that one source of the prestige attributed to other predominantly female occupations is the generalized respect women earn as mothers and wives.

Some studies of occupational prestige consider such matters as job authority (Spaeth, 1979), skill and task complexity (Baron and Bielby, 1980), and variation along a continuum ranking jobs from bad to good (Doeringer and Piore, 1971). But whatever the underlying dimensions of occupational prestige scores, it is clear that they do not accurately reflect sex inequality in the domain of paid work. The commitment to these elaborate measures continues, however, in spite of critiques by such sociologists as Wolf and Fligstein (1979) and Rosenfeld (1978). Furthermore, the underlying model, which focuses on a single status rather than a status-set (the array of statuses a person has), cannot capture the nature of sex inequality. Conceptualization of the status-attainment model is rooted in the human capital theory of neoclassical economics, which assumes an open, fully competitive market where individual characteristics are identified and rewarded according to their societal value. It resembles the structural-functional stratification theory of Davis and Moore (1945) in considering the financial sacrifices people make to obtain education—both the cost of education and the income forgone during the training period—as an investment in future higher earnings. Both models regard positional rank as a product of individual inputs such as talent, skills, and motivation and presuppose a uniform and freely competitive labor market.

A structural analysis that does not focus on individual characteristics of workers has been offered by investigators using a theory of a dual economy and labor market segmentation. Bibb and Form (1977) find merit in a model that differentiates between what they term core and peripheral industrial establishments—a differentiation based on material and organizational resources. Core establishments are large, capital-intensive forms that practice economies of scale and earn relatively high and stable profits. Peripheral establishments have few material organizational resources; they are small, labor intensive, and geographically scattered.[4] Some textile manufacturers, restaurants, and hospitals are in this category. Workers in core establishments earn appreciably higher salaries than those in the periphery. Bibb and Form assert that their model explains three times as much variance in blue-collar earnings as a human capital model. Both sexes are at a disadvantage in peripheral industries, but since women tend to work disproportionately in these industries because of lack of access to core industries, their location explains some of the discrepancies between the sexes in gross earnings. But this model also has its limitations. Beck, Horan, and Tolbert (1980) show that compared to men most women with high levels of schooling and experience suffer more wage discrimination in core than in peripheral forms. This may be due to the sex segregation of work that exists there. Their interpretation of the sector-specific occupational distributions suggests that this type of discrimination results from the concentration of highly schooled females in the professions within the peripheral sector but their disproportionate location in clerical occupations within the core sector (p. 122).

Sociologists have become aware of different forms of sex segregation

4. There is some disagreement about whether industries or companies or some other classification is the proper unit of analysis; to some extent they cross-cut each other (see Hodson, 1984).

in the workplace and their consequences for the social standing of men and women. Sex segregation is only one element, however, in new conceptualizations of stratification. Attention is being given to other structural arrangements—economic and organizational characteristics of the workplace, such as occupational sponsorship, job ceilings for women and blacks, the organizational power of unions, and the economic power of the industry (Bibb and Form, 1977), a matter that has consequences for the rank of men as well as women in the stratification system (Villemez, 1977; Treiman and Terrell, 1975b; Wolf and Rosenfeld, 1978; Feuerberg, 1978).

Although much of Marxist theory is devoted to explaining inequality, it fails to account for the subordination of women. The most productive theory on the subject in the Marxist tradition is its view of women as a reserve army of labor in the capitalist economy. Simeral (1978) argues that women have constituted a cyclical reserve, entering the labor force when demand is high and leaving it when demand contracts. She counters those critics who point out that women have never formed a reserve for men's jobs (Milkman, 1976) by claiming that women do not have to substitute directly for men to have an effect on the market and the overall wage rate.

Yet there are problems with attempts to explain female disadvantage solely on the basis of analysis of the processes of capital expansion and capital accumulation. Women's situation in the industrial reserve army is tempered by their unpaid labor in the home and their role in the reproduction of the labor force. Some scholars working within a Marxist perspective consider this by identifying patriarchy as a component of a system that subordinates women. They argue that the two structures, capitalism and patriarchy, are interrelated in complex ways and must be analyzed together in order to understand the position of women. Two currents of thought can be identified among the Marxists. One argues that the material bases of patriarchy are to be found in human reproduction and in sexuality (Firestone, 1972). Male control of both these spheres leads to the subordination of women and is perpetuated because of men's desire to ensure their paternity of their wives' children. Men therefore create a culture (patriarchy) with women universally subjugated even to the interstices of the unconscious (Mitchell, 1971). The other current of thought roots patriarchy in men's objective economic interests, which cut across class interest. Hartmann (1976), for example, argues that capitalism develops out of a preindustrial patriarchal society and preserves patriarchy as part of the system of control. In the process of development male workers gain a privileged position by denying women access to apprenticeships and jobs in male-dominated, unionized fields and by pushing for protective legislation. Thus as the economy develops it does so with a sex-segregated labor force.

Strober (1982) believes that the interests of men in maintaining a system in which women serve them in the home accounts for their resistance to women's access to equal opportunity in the workplace. Although one can agree that it serves any dominant group to keep subordinate those over whom it has power, not all men have done so, and institutions have differed in the extent to which they have insisted on and ensured women's subordination. In some institutions, policies are distinct; in others there may be no policy at all. A good example of this is the American public grade school system, which, as Hansot and Tyack (1988) point out, followed from its inception the norm of coeducation. Institutions at the high school and university level, however, differed considerably more. In Europe and in many countries of the third world, governments have made specific policies segregating both education and occupations. Such policies have not been specified by the U.S. government except in the military, and that is diminishing to some extent. But policymakers in various occupations and workers themselves have made and still make decisions regarding sex integration or exclusion that affect equal opportunity.

Discrimination

Most social science theories about the division of labor by sex discount or ignore discrimination against women. This may result from a belief that basic sex differences account for the division of labor or from the fact that sex segregation in the workplace does not easily fit other models of how the labor market operates.

Because various economic theories operate on the supposition that a free market exists, it is difficult to explain employer preference for men when women workers might be the more economically rational choice in certain job categories. Several scholars have attempted to deal with this issue to explain sex segregation and identify employer prejudice against employing those who otherwise seem capable of performing the jobs available.

Gary Becker's theory of race discrimination ([1957] 1971) suggested that employers might indulge their "taste" for discrimination by hiring higher-priced white male workers when the market offered less expensive black workers. Customers' "tastes" and preferences were also reflected in this selection process. Blau (1982) posited that discriminatory tastes could produce segregation of categories of workers in occupations or establishments. Law firms, for example, attributed their reluctance to hire women attorneys to (among other reasons) the anticipated objection of clients (Epstein, 1968, 1981b). Because of employers' tastes, Bergmann (1971, 1974) pointed out, people in the social categories considered most objectionable were "crowded" into a narrow group of occupations and consequently had to settle for lower wages. Employers have usually objected to hiring women for jobs preferred by men (Strober, 1984) but not to hiring them for jobs in which they are subordinate to men. Some are more specific, claiming that customers or clients will object to women working in certain spheres, especially in positions of authority. Male doctors have opposed women as peers presumably because of patients' objections but are not opposed to having women serve the same patients as nurses.

Both Hartmann (1976) and Strober (1984) assert that discrimination in the workplace results from men's wish to keep women subordinate in their other roles, thus maintaining patriarchy in the society. They claim that men of all social groups and occupations recognize that they derive an advantage from the general exclusion of women from spheres in which they might accumulate resources or that would give them the basis for independence. Hartmann further argues that "job segregation by sex . . . is the primary mechanism [in capitalist society] that maintains the superiority of men over women." [5] Alice Kessler-Harris (1982) claims also that ideological forces have consistently undermined women's attachment to the labor force throughout American history, even when the country was in sore need of their labor. For the dominant ideology has proclaimed—at odds with the theory of free access to the marketplace—that women's first priority is the home.

Although her "ideological forces" seem vague, Kessler-Harris notes that particular governments, employers, and even labor unions have expressed concern that were women to receive unrestricted wages, the balance of power would be upset in the family and ultimately in the whole society. Therefore, she reports, authorities in these sectors tried to make sure it would never happen. Even men who believed it was not in women's nature to perform well at paid work nevertheless believed they could

---

5. Hartmann's claim is that this is the mechanism in capitalist society; but job segregation is also characteristic of communist and socialist societies and is probably as important a factor in maintaining the superiority of men over women in those countries as well.

do a job well enough to displace men.[6] Indeed, some men expressed fears that women's equality constituted not only an economic threat but a threat to the continuation of the race; some turn-of-the-century "scientists" argued that women might create a puny race by siphoning off their energies into intellectual activities.

Those who opposed permitting women access to college education argued that the low fertility of college-educated women threatened the continuity of the upper classes from which they came (for example, Dewey, 1886; Gwynn, 1898; Hall, 1905). Hall argued that coeducation "had resulted in the triumph of women over men," and in women's ousting men from teaching jobs because they were "less expensive" (1906).

Although women had functioned as doctors (without professional training) in the late eighteenth century, particularly in the practice of obstetrics, the field was later taken over almost entirely by men. With the professionalization of medicine and technological innovations in obstetrics (most notably the invention and use of forceps in deliveries) women began to be driven out of the profession. Although the men in the professional associations claimed that their main interest was to improve standards, economic self-interest also motivated their exclusion of women from the profession.

Writing of this history of medicine, Mary Walsh (1977) reports that as early as 1849 the *Boston Medical and Surgical Journal* manifested concern at the preparation of women physicians "for a department of [medical] practice considered quite lucrative," because female patients made up a major part of a doctor's medical practice in the nineteenth century. These physicians worried about what would happen to their practices if women turned to their professionally trained sisters. Walsh quotes John

---

6. These attitudes were prevalent in the labor movement and were a source of women's exclusion from union participation until the 1930s. Chafe (1972) points out that women's lack of participation in the trade union movement resulted *not only* from their clustering in poorly organized industries such as textile mills, laundries, and candy factories but also from the fact that they were not invited into the movement. The American Federation of Labor (AFL) treated women workers with open hostility and did almost nothing to organize them. Both Samuel Gompers and his successor, William Green, denounced the presence of married women in the work force and asserted that women should marry and take care of families. When a group accused the AFL Executive Council of prejudice, Gompers replied that the AFL discriminated against any nonassimilable race. Even when women organized themselves they were denied recognition.

Because the Congress of Industrial Organizations (CIO) organized workers by industry rather than skill, its formation improved the situation of workers excluded by the skill-apprenticeship system of the AFL. Yet inequality continued to pervade organized labor even in the most progressive unions. For example, although half the members of the Amalgamated Clothing Workers were women, the union sanctioned lower wages for women than for men and granted women only token recognition as officers (Chafe, 1972; Huber, 1976).

Ware, a wealthy Massachusetts physician, who cautioned a class of doctors graduating in Boston in 1850 to couch their opposition to women physicians subtly—"in terms other than those that would reflect a mean jealousy of encroachment on a profitable field of labor." Much the same attitude has been expressed by male lawyers who have worried about women "taking bread out of the mouths of their families" in the two decades I have been studying the legal profession (Epstein, 1981b). The discriminatory behavior emanating from such attitudes is well known. Although such prejudiced activity now is illegal, employers prior to the Civil Rights Act of 1964 were often candid in expressing their disdain for women attorneys. A national survey of all types of law practices, conducted by the *Harvard Law Record* and published in 1963, found that women were among the least desirable candidates for firms of all sizes.[7] Dramatic instances of this pattern occur in the biographies of such jurors as Sandra Day O'Connor (the first woman justice on the Supreme Court) and Ruth Bader Ginsburg (the first woman professor at Columbia Law School and a U.S. Appeals Court judge), both of whom were at the top of their law school classes; upon graduation both were promptly offered jobs—as legal secretaries (Epstein, 1981b).

Women with professional credentials in other fields have faced similar treatment. When he compared men and women who matched each other in productivity, university attended, degree attained, and other variables, Jonathan Cole (1979) found that women scientists faced discrimination in promotions. The finding that women scientists were denied jobs for which they were qualified has been documented by Astin (1969), Hornig (1980), Rossiter (1974), Knudson (1974), and Vetter (1975), who found that the unemployment rate for women in science was two to five times higher than for men in the same field with comparable training and experience; moreover, women's salaries in science were lower than men's. Discrimination in promotion was also found at the partnership level in law firms (Epstein, 1968, 1981b), in academia (Bernard, 1964), and in medicine (Lorber, 1984).

The union practices contributing to sex segregation of workers in the United States have been studied by Abbott (1969), Simmons and her colleagues (1975), Hartmann (1976), Wertheimer (1977), Tentler (1979), and Milkman (1980). Their work shows that the exclusion of women from craft trades was firmly established at the turn of the century and that these policies lasted until the early 1970s. Some unions openly excluded women

7. See articles by Abel (1963) and Kucera (1963) in that issue of the *Harvard Law Record* 7 (December 12, 1963).

by policy, by maintaining segregated bargaining units, or by customary nepotistic practices limiting membership to male relatives of union members. The resistance of male union leaders to women's entry into apprenticeship programs in blue-collar craft jobs is documented by Walshok (1981) and others. Kessler-Harris's historical treatise (1982) on women's participation in the U.S. work force uncovered instances in which women were discouraged from organizing and male union members were sanctioned with fines if they taught their crafts to women.

Labor shortages during World War II, however, encouraged changes in government, employer, and union policies, enabling women to enter skilled blue-collar jobs in unprecedented numbers. The government actively recruited women and pressured resistant employers to hire them. As is equally well known, after the war the same government then put pressure on women to leave these jobs. Explorations into the phenomenon of "Rosie the Riveter" have contested the official propaganda, which explained that the thousands of retiring Rosies wished only to get back to housekeeping (Rupp, 1978; Frank, 1980; Kessler-Harris, 1982; Honey, 1984). Chafe (1972), Tobias and Anderson ([1973–74] 1982), and later Milkman (1976) reported that a large proportion of these women did not voluntarily leave craft jobs but were fired to make room for returning male veterans.

Craft unions have been most exclusionary, whereas other unions such as those organizing service workers have been more receptive. Leadership positions, however, even in unions with a high proportion of women members such as the textile workers, are usually held by men. Part of the reason is that leaders of mature unions rarely relinquish power. Thus, only in younger unions do women (and younger men) have much chance to enter the leadership ranks (Milkman, forthcoming).

Employers and union officials often collaborate in maintaining barriers based on gender. Recent field studies of the construction industry, in which hiring quotas are in effect (U.S. Dept. of Labor, Employment Standards Administration, 1981; Westley, 1982), have confirmed that contractors resist hiring women even as they testify that women are competent and under certain circumstances more dependable than men. Some have, of course, attributed their refusal to hire women to the now familiar objections of their working-class male employees (Reskin, 1984).

Sex Typing Reflects Sex Ranking

One fact emerges clearly from sociological research: no matter what logic is used to explain the fit between women's careers and their other duties or attributes, their jobs and specialties have been those accorded least prestige and the lowest remuneration. They have also been the positions least in demand by men, except for men suffering from discrimination or some other disadvantage. It has also worked the other way. Goode (1964) suggested earlier that "whatever the strictly male tasks are, they are defined as more honorific," presaging the research on "comparable worth." This research has found that often when men and women do the same work but their jobs have different titles—for example, when men are called janitors and women, maids—the jobs men hold almost always pay more (Ratner, 1980).

Statistical studies showing differentials in rank between apparently equally qualified female and male workers indicate that discrimination accounts for them. For example, Malkiel and Malkiel (1973) found that women professionals in a large organization were assigned to lower-level jobs than similarly qualified men. Halaby (1979) found this to be true as well for women managerial employees in a California public utility. In these studies as well as many of the others cited in this chapter, at every level of experience and education women are concentrated in lower-level occupations and at lower ranks within occupations, confirming Epstein's hypothesis (1970b) that, whatever stratum they are found in, women tend to cluster at the bottom.

The concentration of women at the bottom of all occupational strata holds for socialist and communist societies as well as Western capitalist societies. Comparing women's occupations in the Soviet Union and the United States, Rose Laub Coser (1981) observed that even though substantial numbers of Russian women worked at jobs sex typed as male in the United States, these were typically jobs at the lowest level; for example, although women constituted 75 percent of the doctors in the USSR, they were unable to achieve entry into the high-ranking academic posts in that profession. Other scholars have found that although women in Eastern-bloc societies hold a wider range of jobs than American women, they are nevertheless consistently situated in the low-skill, low-wage occupations (Scott [1974] 1976; Sacks, 1976; Lapidus, 1978; Jancar, 1978; Heitlinger, 1979; McAuley, 1981). Sex-role stereotyping, occupational segregation, and wage disparities between the sexes have prevailed in these socialist societies since World War II in spite of their avowed ideology of equality.

Informal Barriers in the Workplace

The scholarship of the past two decades or so has revealed how gender distinctions are maintained by a variety of processes more subtle than the old barriers imposed by discriminatory laws and rules. Some of these barriers are erected by informal groups, colleagues, and the community; others are institutionalized in practices regarded as traditions, whose authors are no longer known. As we saw earlier, the sex labeling or typing of roles structures occupational choices for most people. The sex labeling of statuses, although not an absolute barrier, acts as a filter through which only some may pass. And once past the initial set of obstacles, the woman often finds it was merely the first skirmish. As the new lawyer, physician, telephone line worker, or truck driver tries to do her job and enjoy its privileges, she continues to face additional barriers. Male coworkers often try to undermine her performance and make her feel awkward at being in a male world.

The culture sets broad guidelines for what men and women ought to do. These help shape individuals' behavior, the ways in which they educate their children, and the ways they interact with kin, friends, and coworkers in the course of daily life. Culture sets the stage, and when individuals act according to its norms, their behavior becomes part of a pattern. Because the pattern is widespread it seems normal and natural and therefore reinforces the values underlying it. But cultural values and norms do not always match. Culture does not affect all individuals in the same way, and men and women are sometimes exposed differently to change in both the culture and the social structure. For example, immigrants who are unaware of how people of their social class or sex "ought" to act may aspire higher than people more familiar with accepted cultural views. Discrepancies like these lead to the questioning of values and resistance to conformity.

Our knowledge of the barriers to individuals' free choice of occupations suited to their interests and talents has been expanded by recent research. Although some work has concentrated on the difficulties of minorities in choosing certain work roles, much of it has focused on women. Little of the research has explored barriers to male employment in "women's jobs."

For example, there have been few studies of men who take on "deviant" occupational roles such as elementary school teacher or nurse,[8] partly because men encounter fewer problems in such situations and also because social scientists or activists have not been very interested in the question.[9]

It is in the institutional setting that deviant status-sets—those combinations of statuses that are unusual—become most problematic. Some organizations are socially homogeneous in the sense that they are composed of people who share the same status-sets. Members of such organizations regard as outsiders those whose attributes and backgrounds are dissimilar. Homogeneous status-sets are what insider-outsider perspectives are all about. Views about who ought to belong may vary, but because these views have roots in the larger culture, they tend to structure the access of people to jobs that are widely available as well as occupations regarded as communities (such as those of doctors or miners), in which persons interact closely and are governed by professional associations or unions.

The more clublike the sphere, the more restrictions there seem to be on people of the unlike and wrong kind because the culture fails to filter them out and restrictions are imperfect and change over time. So, women now much more often choose "male" jobs such as law and medicine and men choose "female" jobs as nurses and librarians. For both groups, there is a degree of discomfort on the part of role partners because of the "inappropriateness" of their choices. But there seems to be some discrepancy with regard to the pressures each sex experiences. Men, still by and large more powerful, seem to be more active in attempting to force women out of "their" domains than women are in creating discomfort for men in theirs. This impression may merely result from unwitting bias among social scientists who have not studied women's exclusion of men from occupations such as clerical or secretarial work, but it may rest as well on the insights that (1) men are probably more welcome in women's domains than women are in men's (they are believed to bring prestige, for one thing), and (2) women do not usually control the spheres in which they are numerically a majority.

I suspect that women do, in fact, attempt to exclude men from decision-making and other activities in domains where they do have some power—the family, for example. In her study of working-class and middle-class

8. The problem of status crystallization, however, has been considered by a number of social scientists with regard to such behavior as voting (see Lenski, 1966). This research is more geared to the consequences of holding statuses regarded as inconsistent with each other and less to the dynamics by which these inconsistent statuses are acquired and maintained.

9. A few names stand out in the field: Warren Farrell (1974); Joseph Pleck (1976); Deborah David and Robert Bannon (1976); Marc Fasteau (1974); Michael Kimmel (1986).

women who were young adults in the 1970s, Kathleen Gerson found that "domestically oriented" women "who struggled to keep men economically responsible . . . were happy to provide homemaking services . . . and, indeed, excluded men from domestic duties, which they wished to preserve for themselves" (1986: 624).

In the occupational sphere, where men clearly hold power, the exclusion of women has been most clear-cut and severe in cases of jobs that men prize. Here informal processes are often as important as formal processes in maintaining sex segregation. The work of Hall (1946), Hughes (1945), Goode (1957), and others has shown how male-dominated professions act as communities, with shared values, common membership, and rituals that reinforce ties among their members. Like other social groups, they create an insider-outsider perspective that sets a boundary between the profession and the outside world, and also a boundary between practitioners within the profession who are of like kind and preferred and those who are not of like kind and are disdained. Although most occupational communities that have been studied are professions, their behavior is typical also of other communities of workers such as coal miners, crafts people, and industrial workers.

Informal exclusion usually causes the undesirable person's sex or race to become the focus of attention rather than their work status and the talents and competence they bring to it. The focus on the functionally irrelevant status undermines those who hold it by making them feel deviant, and it makes ordinary interaction problematic (Merton, in Epstein, 1970a, 1970b).

Research on this process has shown that male role partners of women professionals—colleagues and clients, for example—tend to treat the women differently from their male colleagues, often expressing their disapproval and disbelief that a woman could assume these roles. My work on the legal establishment (Epstein, 1968, 1981b) showed how in the past the big law firms kept women attorneys from most jobs. For the few women who overcame the obstacles or found rare moments of opportunity—for example, in times of male shortages during World War II—the firms underscored their deviant status by relegating them to a limited set of tasks, keeping them from interacting with clients, and conducting business at social clubs that prohibited women from membership. The distaste for women in large companies was underscored by the fact that many large Wall Street firms gave up male secretarial staffs with great reluctance when so few men entered the occupation that the supply became inadequate. Research has documented the messages to women that they were

wanted in law, medicine, banking, and other high-prestige occupations
only in the lower echelons. It has also shown how a climate was created
that discouraged women from applying for training (S. Cole, 1985). In
this climate, women were persuaded to drop out or to settle for a career
with a shorter track and an earlier plateau than that of men.

One of these processes has been labeled by Judith Lorber (1983) the
"Salieri phenomenon," inspired by Peter Shaffer's play *Amadeus,* in which
Salieri, the court composer and gatekeeper of musical patronage, recom-
mends that the emperor give Mozart a post, but urges that it be of low
rank and pay. Thus, Salieri pretends to be a benefactor of Mozart while
actually blocking the younger man's career. Lorber suggests that women
physicians usually encounter minimal rewards which persuade them that
they are recognized but not worthy of greater honor, a pattern that undermines their ambition. A similar process directs women to, and sometimes
locks them in, ancillary roles. In the academic workplace, for example,
wives often do research for their husbands' books but are rewarded with
only general acknowledgments and thanks rather than specific footnotes
or coauthorship (Epstein, 1970a, 1976). Individual cases of the Salieri
phenomenon have also been documented in the work on scientific achievement. Sayre (1975) noted that the British scientist Rosalind Franklin was
not given appropriate credit by her collaborators, Watson and Crick, for
her work in helping to identify DNA. Watson (1968) diminished her contribution in his account of the Nobel Prize–winning search. Harriet Zuckerman (1977) also documented how few of the "very few" women Nobel
laureates held tenured posts in their universities before the Stockholm judges
awarded them The Prize.

Other sociologists have shown how cultural norms specifying backstage
roles for women in the economic and political spheres and sometimes in
the family reinforced conventions legitimating minimal recognition for
women's occupational performance. Keeping women outsiders, away from
contacts and social networks, through the maintenance of sex distinctions
in the workplace maintains their low rank in the social hierarchy.

Networks

The power dimensions of informal processes in the corporate world that
result in the creation of hierarchies were studied by Kanter (1976), who
wrote "there is a complete system of interacting parties with respect to
larger distributions of opportunity, power, and numerical ratios of social
types. Organizations define a network of power relations outside of the

authority vested in formal positions; the power network defines which
people can be influential beyond the boundaries of their positions.''

In my work on the legal profession (Epstein, 1970a) I found that prior
to the late 1970s and 1980s women's access to the power network en-
shrined in the mainstream male professional associations was severely
limited. Women were either banned from leadership or their representation on committees was limited to those considered appropriate—often the
social activities committee. They seldom were part of the referral network
or asked to contribute to conferences or to special issues of journals. This,
even when they matched their male peers in rank, although they were
usually on other career tracks—parallel for a time, but shorter (Epstein,
1972). Similarly, Nowotny (1981) applied Bourdieu's conceptual framework (1971) to show how women could not accumulate the same kind of
"cultural capital" as men.

An emphasis on networks came out of these and earlier inquiries, cap-
turing the attention of a number of social scientists and popular commen-
tators. This work centered mainly on an understanding of the connections
between "power elites" (Mills, 1956; Domhoff, 1967), which specified
the institutional and family connections among those who became decision makers in society. Neither this work nor the early work of Merton
and Lazarsfeld (1950) explored the ways in which women were isolated
from elite networks, however, although Merton (1957) and Katz and Lazarsfeld (1955) had identified women's roles as "influentials and opinion
leaders" in sex-typed domains (for example, in determining fashion con-
sumption patterns and even in "public affairs").[10] Mark Granovetter (1971)
found how people located professional employment[11] through "loose
ties"—casual acquaintances—rather than through "connections" offered
by good friends. But he did not explore how differently men and women
acquired such ties until later (1980), when he showed that men acquired
loose ties through acquaintances made at professional and business meetings, events women were less likely to attend. According to Rose Laub

10. Bias in respondents' answers to interviewers' questions was perceptively noted in the Katz
and Lazarsfeld study. They reported (in a footnote): "In the study of voting behavior during a
presidential campaign, it was found that while wives frequently referred to discussions with their
husbands, the latter rarely returned the compliment. The husbands apparently did not feel they
were 'discussing' politics with their wives. Rather they were telling their wives what politics was
all about" (1955: 15). Oakley (1974b) then raised the question about the study—"Were the
women influencing the voting choices of their husbands or not?''—noting that Katz and Lazarsfeld found female influence greatest in consumer decisions and weakest in public affairs (although, as in the example of voting choices, these researchers say that this finding may be due
to the men's unwillingness to admit having serious political discussions with women).

11. Granovetter does *not* specify occupations other than to say his sample concentrates on
professional, technical, and managerial workers.

Coser (1975), in her presidential address to the Society for the Study of Social Problems, it often is not within women's power to attend meetings and make connections with others in their fields. Among other things, child-care obligations often make them stay close to home and curtail the time they have for outside activities.

In contrast, strong ties have been helpful to women when prejudice and other restrictions limited their access to an open job market and to the attainment of public office. Until the 1970s, almost all the women elected to Congress and the Senate were widows or daughters of men who had held such office (Epstein, 1981a; Gertzog, 1984). So, too, women who became partners in large Wall Street firms tended to be married to law-yers, some of whom also worked for large firms (Epstein, 1981b). Simi-larly, Kaufman and Richardson (1982) found that successful women pro-fessors also tended to be married to men in academic life, and Zuckerman and Cole (1975) found a similar pattern for scientists. In short, being married to a man with social, political, or organizational connections helped women who might not have been able to make such connections them-selves overcome barriers to domains where they would otherwise have been viewed with suspicion. Particularistic relationships, however, help only women who are well situated; they do little to change the patterns of general exclusion.

Institutional Barriers in the Workplace

Some practices that maintain sex segregation are so embedded in our institutions that we no longer know how they were initiated or who or what is responsible for them now. They are so much a part of our lives that they seem "natural" and "real" (Bourque and Warren, 1981). Some were born of ignorance and some were created with the intention of pre-serving privilege; some were an outgrowth of conditions in a past that no longer exists, and others represent simply persistent resistance to change. Many of these are not embodied in laws or regulations, although some are very formal indeed.

We noted earlier that there are many theories about the root causes of occupational segregation of the sexes. I believe that it is a combination of factors such as employer discrimination, women's choices, family pres-sures, and public policy that has resulted in a high degree of sex segrega-tion in the world of work and that these factors have acted congruently to maintain a system that seems to favor men's preferences, although not all these preferences may be to their advantage. It can be argued, too, that the forces inside work organizations maintaining segregation are usually complemented and justified by forces in other sectors. Imbalance between the major institutions of society—the family and polity, for example—has contributed to changes back and forth, over the years. Informal practices, of course, uphold and reinforce formal organization. Today, as in the past, they reflect more widespread sentiment about "woman's place."

Early social science research on the professions, for example, shed light on the exclusion of women when it found that elite occupations included like-minded people because their shared backgrounds fostered camaraderie and trust (Goode, 1957). Everett Hughes (1962) noted the "social and moral solidarity" of practitioners, which made it difficult for persons not equipped with appropriate statuses to enter the exclusive society, to participate in its informal interactions, to understand the unstated norms, and to be included in the casual exchanges (Epstein, 1970b). Much earlier, Hughes (1945) had pointed to the problems faced by people with unshared statuses (women and blacks) in circles geared to rewarding "their own" and to reinforcing ties of the like-minded with rituals closed to the undesirable. The story is told of the woman engineer who could not join the celebration dinner honoring the flight of the airplane for which she was a chief designer because it was, as it had always been, a stag party.

Today, as public policy has decreed a certain degree of sex integration in some workplaces, resistance has also been manifested in a number of ways. Typically, gender becomes salient for the male occupants, who may subject the women to remarks calculated to "put them in their place." These may take the form of profanity, off-color jokes, anecdotes about male prowess, gossip about the women's personal lives, and unwarranted intimacy toward them (Kanter, 1977a; Martin, 1980). All this does not differ much from the practices of the not-so-distant past. Lorber (1975) describes how in the past female medical students were ignored, left behind, not asked to assist in medical procedures and operations, and subjected to scatological joking about women and to mockery of women's bodies in anatomy classes and laboratories. Male faculty members did not disapprove of such male students' pranks as adding pornographic pictures of women to sets of lecture slides.

Similar degradation of women has gone on in law schools as well. Epstein (1968, 1981b) reports the use of "ladies' days" when only women were called on (but otherwise ignored). Some women law students were made to sit in separate sections of classrooms and to endure insults to their intelligence in their professors' hypothetical cases. The study also showed that judges, clerks, and other lawyers in courtrooms focused on women lawyers' sex status by addressing them disrespectfully, being overly solicitous, or assuming that they were clerks or secretaries.

Kanter (1977a) suggested that men in corporate settings often try to fit women into a small set of stereotyped personalities that are familiar and nonthreatening to the men—for example, "mom" or "kid sister"—stereotypes that prevent the women from participating in the group as full members (Reskin, 1978).

Mentoring

The protégé system is typical of many professions, especially in their upper reaches. It operates both to train personnel in certain specialties and to ensure continuity. The fields in which it exists are marked by interplay between the formal and informal relationships of the practitioners. At certain levels, one must be "in" to learn the job. Thus, experienced senior people act as mentors, informing their protégés of crucial trade secrets and helping them make important contacts. Mentors select promising younger people in whom they take an interest, or a younger person seeks out a senior person with whom he or she hopes to train. Becker and Strauss (1956), Becker et al. (1961), Merton et al. (1957), Hall (1946), and later Mumford (1970), Miller (1970), Bloom (1973), Bucher and Stelling (1977), Coombs (1978), and Scully (1980), in their work on medical students, identified the process by which individuals are socialized and educated to become doctors and mentors' role in the process.

Building on this work, my study (1970a) of women's access to professional careers showed that women were disadvantaged as newcomers in fields in which men predominated because few of the men were willing to teach them crucial trade secrets and help them advance. The study identified the sponsor-protégé (or master-apprentice) system as important both for learning and for placement on an upward track. Women's special problems arose because sponsors in the professions were unwilling to take them on for a number of reasons, including doubts that they could become appropriate disciples who would carry on their work, the belief that they were not committed to work because they were not motivated by financial concerns and might marry, or fears that others might suspect the relationship was sexual as well as professional. Yet, the study proposed that women might actually need mentors more than men if only because of the prejudice against them. The particularistic track had been an important channel of opportunity for women. Remember that most women who rose to positions of high public office had personal ties with their predecessors, and this seemed to be the case for women in many other professional spheres. The only other major track for employment was the highly universalistic realm of government work, where bureaucratically determined criteria were largely enforced.

Kanter (1977a) also identified the importance of sponsors for men and found them "absolutely essential for women" in her study of Indsco, a large corporation.[12] Powerful sponsors provided them with important insider information. Yet she too indicated how sponsors had difficulty in identifying with women subordinates.

The process of sponsorship, known popularly as "mentoring," became a topic of strong interest and speculation—partly as a woman's issue and partly as providing a key to the ways in which men make it to the top. It was popularized by Gail Sheehy in her book *Passages* (1977) in which she indicated the importance of mentors in moving up in a career. As mentoring became a popular topic, however, research on the subject became more difficult. For example, it was hard to compare older and younger lawyers because their identification of factors contributing to professional success followed cultural themes. There was a significant change in the responses of women lawyers I interviewed in 1965 and those interviewed in 1977–78 after Sheehy's book came out. In the 1960s many characterized their careers as "doing it on my own," then still a popular ideology; by the late 1970s, however, when the notion that "mentors" might be of strategic importance in conducting careers, women had become more alert to the fact that the mentoring process was a legitimate part of attaining success. Older women didn't identify mentors since they believed it important to have been without special assistance. Identifying the mentor-protégé relationship as a key element of social structure focused on the institutional setting and the help of strategically placed people in it rather than on only one's personal attributes such as talent and drive. It underscored the fact that one might have these personal qualities and still not be able to negotiate the inner circles of occupational life.

Most discussion of mentoring appeared in the popular media, but some sociologists explored the social circumstances under which women might be selected by either male (Epstein, 1981a; Lorber, 1984) or female mentors (Epstein, 1981b).[13] Mentors explained the success of some women in environments that were otherwise exclusionary, and lack of them ex-

---

12. Harriet Zuckerman (1977) investigated the same process in science, noting the importance of kinship and master-apprentice relationships for Nobel laureates.

13. See Hall and Sandler (1983) for a full analysis of how mentoring affects women's careers; see also Jeanne Speizer's critique (1981) of studies of mentoring.

plained women's inability to gain access to important assignments as interns and residents in medical schools (Lorber, 1984) and as partners in law firms (Epstein, 1968, 1981a).

The work on mentoring grew out of the analysis of professional life and how its structure contributed to women's isolation and diminished performance.[14] Since professions depend on the continual association of their members and their affinity of interest, it could be predicted that "outsiders" would have a difficult time performing at the same level as those regarded as "insiders." Although discrimination was certainly one factor, more important was the general process of professionalization by which the recruit became a full member of the collegial group. Being the protégé of a senior person was one way to become a member; visibility was another. Research showed that women were typically positioned in "male" careers in ways guaranteed to make them invisible, in back-room specialties such as library research or in jobs regarded as uninteresting and unimportant and hence symbolically invisible.

Bernard's study (1964) of women academics revealed that they had less contact with fellow scientists than male academics did, and they were less likely to attend professional meetings or to be on regular mailing lists for reprints of research findings. In short, they were not members of the highly visible "invisible colleges"—the networks of associations that professionals depend on for intellectual and career growth.

Differential placement was noted by Cole (1979) in his analysis of the careers of women and men in science.[15] In describing women's lower rank in the profession he used the *Science Citation Index* to measure the extent to which their published work was used by peers, and found that they did not do as well as men.[16] Thus women's achievement appeared to lag behind that of men. One explanation for the discrepancy appeared to be the greater isolation of women scientists because they failed to win the sponsorship of senior male scientists or to be included in research teams.

My analysis (Epstein, 1970a) of the impediments to women's legal and other professional careers showed that it did not matter whether men made women feel unwanted intentionally, through unawareness or indifference, or out of protectiveness of their own positions—all had the same effect.

14. I have discussed this at greater length in *Woman's Place* (1970a) and in "Encountering the Male Establishment: Sex-Status Limits on Women's Careers in the Professions" (1970b).

15. Cole and Cole (1968) found, for example, that the visibility of physicists is highly correlated with the rank of the department in which they work; a subsequent study found that this continues to be so (Cole and Cole, 1973: 122).

16. The *Science Citation Index*, founded in 1961, is published by the Institute for Scientific Information. It lists citations to scientists who have published or been mentioned in scientific journals around the world.

In response, women often self-selected themselves out of certain firms and specialties and accepted their social isolation at informal but important functions by staying home or finding other women with whom to associate. Finally, they formed their own parallel and less effective women's professional organizations, thus joining in the process of their own exclusion (Epstein, 1970a).

Inadvertent or open hostility to other women also led some of them to exhibit attributes often regarded as peculiarly female. Women might over-conform or underconform in their work and behavior, a process identified by Merton (1957), thus reinforcing male stereotypes about their incapacity to function as professionals. They might exhibit "female" behavior such as flirtatiousness or motherliness in order to gain acceptance, slipping into a "damned if you do, damned if you don't" situation in which much of their behavior was considered inappropriate (Epstein, 1981b).

These processes excluding women were identified in professional career settings (Bernard, 1964; Rossi, 1965; Epstein, 1970a, 1970b; Walsh, 1977; Lorber, 1984), in corporations (Kanter, 1977a), and in other male-dominated occupations (Walshok, 1981). Exclusionary mechanisms and resistance to women's participation were particularly overt and organized where the occupation has a strong subculture, as in the case of police work (Martin, 1980), forestry (Enarson, 1984), and other occupations such as firefighting in which workers spend many hours together, and particularly where they share slack periods.

Outright discrimination against women who managed to acquire specialized training and education was, of course, not uncommon and has been documented. The male-dominated professions, for example, remained relatively closed to women until very recently. The refusal of such institutions as hospitals and universities to hire women physicians (Walsh, 1977) and scientists (Rossiter, 1974; Knudson, 1974) has been recounted in many studies.

Recent studies of women in professional work, however, show a change toward greater acceptance and performance. The study under the auspices of the National Academy of Sciences noted earlier found that women have moved steadily into nontraditional jobs at all levels of the occupational structure, from bartending to lawyering. Although their participation in the professions is still limited and still stereotyped, women have nevertheless done especially well in law and medical schools, increasing their proportion from less than 10 percent only a decade ago to 30 percent or more today. As of 1986, the percentage of women law students (according to the American Bar Association) was almost 40 percent, and for the 1985–

86 academic year 32.5 percent of medical students (according to the American Association of Medical Colleges) were women.

Furthermore, women are doing better in gaining professional partnerships. At last count women made up 19 percent of the new partners appointed during 1987–88 in the largest 250 law firms in the United States (Weisenhaus, 1988). Their share of partnerships has increased at a faster pace than their admission as associates to these same firms. Although the percentage of women partners is low—only 6 percent—this compares with a percentage of 4.9 in 1984, and only 2.8 percent in 1982.

Over the past two decades, women have clearly demonstrated competence in spheres in which it was once believed they had no interest and no qualifications. Their success demonstrates how opening the opportunity structure has developed their interest and ambition. The record of their achievement shows also how important acceptance and training are for the creation of competence and expertise.

CHAPTER 8

Women and the Political Process

That politics is a man's world is a familiar adage; that political science [or social science] tends to keep it that way is less accepted, but perhaps closer to the truth.'' This appraisal by Bourque and Grossholtz in 1974 was a wry comment on social scientists' inattention to women's changing political roles in this society. Because women rarely govern, they have not been regarded as part of the political arena by ordinary citizens or by social scientists. Until recently, politics at every level of participation was considered to be the province of men. The reasons offered were women's disinterest in politics, originating in their early socialization; their assumed incapacity for political leadership roles; and their family responsibilities, which precluded political activity.

People have held to these views although millions of women have participated as voters and as workers in political campaigns and although women formed and led the highly effective political mobilization of the woman's suffrage movement. Perceiving women as "outside" politics is as curious an example of "pluralistic ignorance" or "selective inattention" as can be found in history.

The fact of women's poor representation as political leaders and the fiction that they are not political actors are related issues. Recent political science research shows that women's position in the social structure underplays and undermines their access to decision-making roles; yet, women as a class do not significantly differ from men with regard to their interest in politics. This recent research is at odds with some of the classic studies of the past because it goes to new areas of inquiry and because social scientists today are more careful about letting stereotyped views of women affect their interpretations of data. The number of studies of women in the

An earlier version of this analysis of women and political power appeared in my introductory essay and chapter, "Women and Power: The Roles of Women and Politics in the U.S.A.," in Epstein and Coser (1981).

165

political process has also increased exponentially. Whereas women's political roles were scarcely acknowledged by political scientists before the mid-1970s,[1] their study is a significant area of inquiry within the profession today.

Several lines of research have thrown doubt on the assumptions of the past about women and politics.

Political Activity

Women were in fact far more politically active in the past than was recognized by politicians or students of the political process. Of course, the differences between men and women in the political sphere had been long documented—women's lower voting participation, for example, and the small number of women political candidates. Political socialization studies showed different "awareness" of political issues among women and men. But the common interpretations of why these differences existed were disputed by the scholarship of the 1970s and by the changes in women's political behavior.

The changes were swift and dramatic. The key gender differences in proportions of voters in the United States disappeared after 1968. There was an upsurge in women candidates for political jobs in nearly all parts of the country and at most levels of the political system, and the proportion of offices held by women at the state and local level increased rapidly. By the 1980s, women had become state legislators, county officials, mayors, and agency administrators. A National Women's Political Caucus survey reports that "between 1971 and 1983, there was a dramatic increase in the proportion of female state legislators from 4.7 percent to 13.3 percent; and of female mayors from 1.0 percent to 8.7 percent" (Flamming, 1984). Moreover, between 1975 and 1980, the Center for the American Woman and Politics estimates, "the proportion of female county officials doubled (from 3 percent to 6 percent) and . . . that of municipal officials tripled (from 4 percent to 13 percent)." Women became politically active in many feminist organizations and in antifeminist groups as well. In the 1988 presidential campaigns women were taking major roles

1. In her analysis of the political integration of women, Virginia Sapiro (1983) noted that the journal of the American Political Science Association published only two articles focused on women's political roles between 1906 and 1973. After the women's movement became established, there was a substantial increase in articles (see B. Carroll, 1979, for a precise count of the articles published between 1976 and 1978). But not very many books on the subject were published even during the 1970s.

as campaign managers and press secretaries for major presidential contenders (Toner, 1987).

Until recently, basic differences between women's and men's participation in political activities were explained by mainstream political scientists (Lipset, 1964; Lane, 1964) in terms of their different role obligations; women, they held, were more subject to role conflict because the roles considered primary in their lives as mothers and wives competed with their public roles. Political scientists also claimed that women were reticent and lacked interest in taking responsibility and authority, or that they lacked orientation and preparation for public roles because they were subjected to a different socialization process (Constantini and Craik, 1977; Lee, 1977; Lane, 1964).

All these explanations held germs of truth but also contained a component of myth. For one thing, they were used to explain the "missing political woman" both in societies where women had the vote and no longer faced formal prohibitions on political participation and in societies where formal restrictions still prohibited women from involvement in all aspects of political life. Further, traditional politicians and social scientists focused on women's choices rather than men's restrictiveness as the rationale for men's domination of the political sphere.[2] Feminist political scientists agree with traditional political scientists that women's political roles are apt to be deterred by motherhood (Sapiro, 1983), but they are more alert to the exclusionary behavior of male politicians who undermine women's motivation to participate and who are inhospitable to women with political aspirations. Until the past decade, few social scientists documented the institutionalized bias against women's engaging in visible roles in the public sphere, and the discrimination and prejudice they have faced.

Objections to a view of politics that is largely a description of what men do without regard to women's political activity, election-connected and not, have been voiced by a new crop of feminist political scholars, such as Sapiro (1983) and Klein (1984).[3] Such changes in perspective can be attributed to the contemporary phase of the women's movement in the United States.[4] The movement, which began in the mid-1960s—the Na-

2. For the United States, see Lipset, 1959; Lane, 1964; Campbell et al., 1960.
3. In fact, women's political activity dates back to the American Revolution in such organizations as the Daughters of Liberty and the Anti-Tea Leagues and includes the fifty-year lobbying effort on the part of women suffragists and, more recently, such organizations as the League of Women Voters.
4. As in the United States, concern about the status of women surfaced in other societies in the late 1950s and 1960s. Scandinavia engaged in a wide-ranging debate about sex roles and

tional Organization for Women (NOW) was formed in 1966—activated women politically on many fronts. Activists pressed for women's inclusion in political elites and more generally in the political process.[5] As political scientists, women sought recognition and placement in the academy. Grass-roots organizations and professional researchers who clustered around the centers of public policy in Washington created a climate that encouraged women to go into political science and related academic fields and encouraged the professions to welcome them. That climate also alerted political scientists to the sexism inherent in many of the discipline's explanatory paradigms (Shanley and Schuck, 1974; Goot and Reid, 1975), a process that was also taking place in other social sciences and the humanities.[6]

In political science, as in other academic fields, women's caucuses were formed to set the agenda for study—to challenge ongoing assumptions and to gather data on matters that had received little attention. The "missing woman" of past years became a focus of the new research, and she was soon found. Women had been and were far more active politically than was believed by politicians or by those studying the political process. The effort to uncover such knowledge has been partially successful, as can be seen from the proliferation of books and articles on the subject over the past decade. Still, it is only beginning; many mainstream practitioners have been silent in the face of these criticisms, the new dimensions of political action, and the work of feminist scholars (B. Carroll, 1979; S. Carroll, 1979; Lovenduski, 1981). Some critics point out that merely adding sex as a variable in studies of political behavior is scarcely a sufficient response to the reconceptualization sought. There remain, of course, many gaps in our knowledge about women's political activity, including a lack of attention to the behavior of subsets of women, especially blacks and Hispanics. Changes in women's behavior in both mass and elite politics have called into obvious question many old explanations of women's former lack of participation. As women have become more activated politically, both in seeking equality and in urging a change in public policies, older views about women's lack of interest in politics have been sup-

equality, and official commissions on the status of women were formed (similar to the one set up by President Kennedy in 1961). Unlike those in the United States, political parties in the Nordic countries included programs for women's equality in the 1960s (Haavio-Mannila et al., 1985).

5. For a more specific account of the political activities of women's groups, such as the Women's Equity Action League (WEAL) and the Professional Women's Caucus, formed in the 1960s, see Klein (1984).

6. As outsiders had been important in identifying processes that social scientists were not seeing, Kate Millett's book *Sexual Politics* (1970) proved to be heuristic in expanding the vision of what was "political" and a proper subject for study (Shanley and Schuck, 1974).

planted by interpretations that address factors in the larger social context in which political activity occurs.

Women's political history is another underdeveloped subject. Little attention has been devoted to it, and much of that has centered on the women's suffrage movement (Gurin and Tilly, 1985). Several books have documented aspects of the new women's movement (Evans, 1979; Hole and Levine, 1971), but they only begin to tell the story.

It was not until the 1950s that social scientists, stimulated by a behavioral approach to government and politics, began to study gender similarities and differences as part of their analysis of institutional and public political phenomena. These included political scientists who studied Congress, state legislatures, candidates, voting behavior, and electoral and nonelectoral activities, using survey techniques to gather data in a systematic way. Two models, socialization and role theory, framed the explanations. But, as Kent Jennings pointed out in a presentation on "Gender and Politics" at the Russell Sage Foundation in November 1985, the survey research on political behavior of the 1950s and 1960s tended to be limited because of the social-psychological emphasis reflected in the design of studies and the interpretation of findings.

Differences were consistently found in the participation of men and women in the electoral process and in the seeking and attaining of political office. Smaller proportions of women than men voted from the time of women's suffrage, although the difference steadily decreased and disappeared in 1968 (Klein, 1984). But women's representation in political elites remained insignificant. We will turn to these data later in this chapter. As suggested earlier, explanations for these differences included beliefs that women did not have the early orientation to politics that men did, that their roles as mothers and wives precluded their participation, and that their personality traits made them uninterested in the political sphere.

Socialization and Political Behavior

One set of explanations for women's political behavior drew on the concept of socialization, already familiar in psychology and sociology. This perspective located the roots of adult behavior largely in early experience. Through observation and education, values and other attitudes toward one's role and place in life were believed to be internalized and to become a fixed part of the self. In politics as in occupational and family life, socialization was considered the cause of later behavior.

Thus armed, a number of political scientists and sociologists examined the process by which men and women come to have different political interests. Herbert Hyman, originating the notion of "political socialization," suggested in 1959 that young people become politically socialized early in their lives. "The beginnings of participation must be sought in relatively early childhood years," he wrote, "for already by age 16, the phenomenon appears to be well formed. . . . It is clear that the absorption of political orientation has progressed close to its maximum level by the last year in high school" (1959: 56–57, 58–59). Testing that notion, Greenstein (1961) and others found that boys tended to be more political than girls in that they had more knowledge about political affairs. But later studies did not report findings consistent with this work. Jennings and Niemi (1971) found no differences arising early among young children, and Orum and his associates (1977) found no differences in political attitudes between boys and girls. Further, both sets of researchers objected to the underlying assumptions in the literature on childhood socialization. Jennings and Niemi thought that boys and girls faced many different experiences because of the wide diversity of family situations, and that gender was not a significant differentiating factor. Orum and his associates questioned whether children's "political" views and the sex differences reported in them had any important effect on adult political behavior. Writing at about the same time, Bourque and Grossholtz were also critical of both the methodology and the interpretation of the earlier socialization studies. They claimed that Greenstein's study, for example, used measures that would evoke responses from boys rather than girls—such as being asked whether they identified with outstanding male political leaders. Furthermore, they suggested that Greenstein's interpretation showed bias with such comments as "politics . . . although not of deep interest to children of either sex, is resonant with the 'natural' enthusiasms of boys" (1974: 246).

Other studies examined by Bourque and Grossholtz reflected what they termed a "bias of exception"—that is, a discrepancy between evidence and interpretation. For example, a study by Hess and Torney (1967) claimed: "Girls form a more personal attachment to the political system than boys because experience with their major role model (mother) is a more personal one and because authority figures deal with them in more expressive and personal ways." But no evidence was reported to support this statement. Although some scholars had considered the general effects of adult socialization (Brim and Wheeler, 1966) and its specific effects on professional life (Merton et al., 1957), none had applied the concept to political behavior. Yet the effects of adult socialization as well as the historical changes taking place in society were shown to be important in the development of patterns of political behavior, and attitudes were shown to obscure or supplant childhood learning, according to Sapiro (1983). A formal test of socialization theory by Paul Kleppner (1982) employed comparative data on women's and men's voting behavior in various nations through a recent period of history. Kleppner found that male-female turnout differentials have increased over time in some places and decreased elsewhere. He suggests that historically shaped sociopolitical environments condition voter turnout and that perception of the cost-benefit ratio of voting is an important element in determining voting behavior for both sexes. Thus, the social situation of an individual or group becomes important in influencing relatively active or passive degrees of political participation.

Critical evaluation of past studies of the political socialization of boys and girls and the evidence of change in the political participation of adult women over a short period of time lead to rejection of an early socialization model. It seems clear that early influences, although probably important, may be modified or reversed under changing social circumstances.

Personality and Political Behavior

Personality variables provide another explanation for perceived differences in the political behavior of men and women. Before the 1980s, many studies tended to emphasize social-psychological factors. Their authors interpreted the data showing few women candidates and officeholders as indicating that women did not possess the personality traits of the men who opted for political careers and succeeded in them. One school reasoned that persons chose occupations and careers consonant with their emotional makeup. Since women's personalities were believed to differ radically from men's, it was not considered surprising that they failed to provide a good fit with political life. For example, Constantini and Craik (1972) found male party leaders to be motivated by power more than women were and took this to explain women's poor representation among political officeholders.

Such scholars did not employ the structural orientation and research findings coming out of sociological studies that maintained that personality is flexible, situational, and changing in directions evoked by the role demands lodged in social structures. For women in political life stuck at lower levels of the hierarchy, immobility may be due neither to lack of ambition nor to psychological shortcomings: both factors turned out to be not so great as believed (Sapiro and Farah, 1980). Marilyn Johnson (personal communication, 1981) of the Eagleton Institute found that men and women holding the same public office do not differ substantially with regard to their political ambitions, and Kent Jennings (personal communication, 1985) found heightened political ambitions among women delegates to the national party conventions over a twelve-year span. This finding confirms Gordon Black's thesis (1972) that ambition develops through the career sequence, building as the person achieves each successive advance. Obviously, people experiencing blocked opportunity do not develop the same levels of ambition as those socially defined as promising candidates.[7]

Sapiro and Farah (1980) found that more Democratic than Republican women delegates to the 1972 national nominating conventions wanted to hold public office and sought it with a greater degree of effort. This, they thought, resulted from the greater dedication of Democrats to a reform movement that encouraged the political participation of women. Currently revised perspectives on the formation and workings of ambition question its previous conceptualization. As Sapiro and Farah point out, the concept of "political ambition" continues to evoke in many a highly specific picture of political life—one of power-hungry, achievement-motivated people who plan their political ascent in Machiavellian terms. I have found in my own research on women lawyers that prior to the 1970s women rarely admitted to having such ambitions out of fear that they would be regarded as "masculine" or as assuming socially inappropriate roles (Epstein, 1981b). But not all men interested in public office fit the stereotype either. New research on elite ambitions shows another picture. The work of James Wilson, James Schlesinger, Gordon Black, and Kenneth Prewitt, for example, points up such attributes as civic obligation and duty—qualities that have been seen as more consonant with women's roles and public images of women—as important to the drive toward involvement in political careers.[8] This perspective has led to the assertion that politically tra-

7. A conclusion I had come to as a result of my research in the late 1960s and the early 1970s (Epstein, 1973a). Sapiro and Farah (1980) also show that women delegates to the 1972 presidential nominating conventions aspired to higher offices, but they *expected* to attain lower positions.

8. Gordon Black, "A Theory of Political Ambition: Career Choices and the Role of Structural Incentives," *American Political Science Review* 66 (March 1972): 144–59; Kenneth Prewitt, *The Recruitment of Political Leaders* (Indianapolis: Bobbs-Merrill, 1970); James Schlesinger, *Ambition in Politics* (Chicago: Rand McNally, 1966); James Q. Wilson, *Amateur Democrat* (Chicago: University of Chicago Press, 1966).

ditional women—members of the New Right—as well as nontraditional women may become politically ambitious.[9]

Other objections to conventional studies in political science hold that they have examined only a limited range of relevant traits in making judgments about women's presumed personality. After all, it is obvious that such American political figures as John Kennedy, Harry Truman, Jimmy Carter, Walter Mondale, and Ronald Reagan have scarcely had the same personality types. At the same time, persisting political stereotypes assume a uniform model based on the John Wayne type. Stereotypes also abound about the essential personality traits of women in spite of the transparently different personalities of Geraldine Ferraro and such other women officeholders as Bella Abzug, Elizabeth Dole, and Shirley Chisholm (to say nothing of Margaret Thatcher, Indira Gandhi, and Golda Meir).

Insufficient critical attention to the data and to their interpretation has been a serious impediment to sorting out the truth about the place of alleged gender differences in personality, just as it was for socialization studies. In their critique of the analysis of gender differences in political studies, Bourque and Grossholtz (1974) accused a number of distinguished political scientists of "fudging the footnotes"—making statements about female political characteristics, attitudes, and behavior that were not substantiated in the material cited as the source. Misuse of the data of earlier studies has usually involved removing all the carefully worded qualifications of the original findings to fit a new conclusion. Berenice Carroll (1979), for example, found that Constantini and Craik (1977) failed to use their own data to refute the assumptions about women in a body of political science studies cited in their work on women's political participation. She notes that they provided a concise summary of the conventional wisdom on women's political behavior, asserting that the literature was "replete with evidence that [at] all levels of political action . . . women participate less than men. They appear to be less interested in politics, to belong to fewer organizations, to be less informed politically, and to display a lower sense of political involvement . . . Yet, their own data do not support these assertions" (p. 292).

Bourque and Grossholtz pointed to another kind of distortion—the as-

9. A *New York Times* article, reporting on the results of primaries in nine states and Washington, D.C., said that these primaries "marked the advancement of women who have made a career of elective office," according to politicians and political consultants (September 11, 1986, p. 1). In the same article, Peter D. Hart, a leading Democratic poll taker, was quoted as saying about the candidates, "They're women aged 50 and 60. They're serious and professional candidates. They have their name at the top of the ticket because the party is looking for proven vote-getters." In 1987 for the first time there were a number of races between two women candidates, including one in Maryland for the U.S. Senate.

sumption of male dominance and influence in interpreting women's political behavior. Not only are men commonly assumed to dominate political elites, but women are assumed to defer to their political opinions, a thesis fundamental to some classic studies. The authors of *The American Voter*, for example, do not have data to support their conclusion that "the wife who votes but otherwise pays little attention to politics tends to leave not only the sifting of information up to her husband but abides by his ultimate decision about the direction of the vote as well" (Campbell et al., 1960: 492). This conclusion was challenged by Jennings and Niemi (1971), who, on the basis of real evidence, noted that the division of political labor within the family is less differentiated than many researchers seem to assume. By no means does it consistently result "in the father being the intermediary between and the interpreter of the external world of politics" (p. 82).

Studies of Mass Politics

Survey research of the early 1950s and 1960s was a prime source for the analysis of sex differences in all kinds of political behavior. Yet these studies and the few that preceded them were in large part focused on voting behavior. The study by Campbell and his colleagues, *The American Voter* (1960), is acknowledged to be one of the first systematic efforts to examine the effects of sex status on political behavior. Earlier, Bentley (1908) had considered the women's suffrage movement and Merriam and Gosnell (1924) had considered the political activity of both men and women in their book *Non-voting*. Of course, the field of behavioral political science was not popular until the 1960s; previously, political study was characterized by political philosophy, jurisprudence, and the description of formal rules and principles. Using voting as a measure of political participation, Campbell and his associates found that 10 percent more men than women turned out to vote. They also found that men and women tended to vote at the same rate at higher levels of education and in the same geographical regions, a phenomenon that has held up in more recent studies (Jennings, 1977). Men and women expressed about the same degree of party loyalty, and there was little difference in their expressed sense of civic responsibility. Analysis in *The American Voter*, as mentioned earlier, did reflect stereotypes. It took for granted the restrictiveness of sex-typed roles—dominance in men and passivity in women—and offered the view that men have a conceptual political sophistication that is reflected in their political interest (Bourque and Grossholtz, 1974).

Actually few scholars knew much about the dynamics of women's political participation at all: how and why they vote and whether their awareness of political interests differs substantially from men's. For example, the stereotype of women as uninterested in politics is refuted by their active role in political campaigning; Gruberg (1968) estimates that 6 million women did volunteer work in the Kennedy-Nixon campaign—even before the current women's movement began. In fact, the percentages of women engaging in these kinds of political activities have been and continue to be close to those of men.

In an analysis of several surveys taken in 1972, Maureen Fiedler found that "men and women participate to an equal degree in all major modes of citizen political activity in the United States" (Fiedler, 1975, as cited in Jaquette, 1976)—that is, as voters, campaigners, and communicators.[10] Most of the socioeconomic factors and social-psychological factors that affect male participation affect female participation in the same ways, with slight variations. Kristi Anderson (1975) found that female activism is more constrained than men's by low education, poverty-level income, identification as a housewife only, or "female head of household" status.

Baxter and Lansing (1983) reported in the second edition of their book *Women in Politics* that more women than men have gone to the polls since 1964, when women outvoted men by 1.75 million votes, a difference that more than doubled in the 1972 election. The reason for this difference in absolute numbers was that adult women outnumbered adult men by a more than 52 to 48 percent ratio. By the mid-1970s, the *proportion* of women to men voting was equal. Baxter and Lansing further pointed out that although general voter turnout had decreased in the American population since *The American Voter* appeared, several categories of women—particularly those in the work force and black women—have voted in ever-increasing proportions.

Survey research of the past also tended to neglect the study and analysis of the voting behavior of blacks. Recent research on black women and men not only has uncovered important data but has questioned assumptions for women's motivations to vote or not. The demographic profile of black women in terms of low income, education, social class, and employment, their low levels of trust in the federal government and high sense of discrimination in employment, suggest that black women would

10. Fiedler reexamined data from the 1972 Center for Political Studies (CPS) Election Study, the 1972 CPS Convention Delegate Study, and the 1972 Virginia Slims Poll.

be among the most passive groups in the political process. But, as Baxter and Lansing point out, they are on the move. Since 1952, black women have increased their rate of voting faster than have black men, and faster than either white men or women. Lansing (1977) estimated that in 1952 and 1956 only 25 percent of black women voted compared to about 36 percent of black men. In 1976, 50 percent of eligible black women voted, as compared to 47 percent of black men.

Poor women have voted in a greater proportion than poor men, but the constraints linked to their situation—many are single heads of families— mean that they attend meetings less frequently, do less work for candidates, and, of course, contribute less money than men or women of higher economic status. At the same time, however, they reported engaging in political conversations more frequently than did all women in general and often more frequently than men (Nelson, 1984).

Increased voting on the part of blacks, and black women in particular, can be attributed to the removal of restraints on voting, such as the elimination of the poll tax in some states and other limiting voter registration practices, as well as expectations of opportunity and, for women, their concern about sex discrimination. Black women, like other citizens, select candidates and choose to vote according to the benefits they expect will accrue from that choice. Further participation in the political process depends on their resources of time and money.

Political Participation outside Electoral Politics

In the 1970s another conceptualization of political behavior affected the analysis of American women's political activity. The notion of political participation was expanded to include political work outside electoral politics. It now was taken to include work as volunteers in such organizations as the League of Women Voters (Ware, 1985); as grass-roots community organizers (Gittell, 1980); as political strategists lobbying for passage of the ERA, organizing for or against reproductive freedom, or working on behalf of the elderly with the Gray Panthers; and as activists at women's conferences (Rossi, 1982). In the 1980s, anthropologists' and political scientists' comparative work on women activists and the development of women's political consciousness also began to appear (Bourque and Warren, 1981; Bourque and Divine, 1985).

Much of this work, however, has been limited to studies of women's activities and has not examined men's participation in similar nonelectoral political roles, a matter ripe for further research.

Cross-Cultural Analysis and Elite Studies

Much political science research has centered on political elites and has failed to consider the problem of women's participation in depth. In the arena of political as of occupational behavior, scholars have provided insight through cross-cultural and historical analyses, but the work has been sparse. Such comparisons are difficult under any circumstances; comparability of situations and problems of funding and organization of the research enterprise are questions difficult to resolve.

An early exception was Duverger's study of the political role of women in France, West Germany, Norway, and Yugoslavia (1955), which anticipated many of the issues raised in the 1970s in its consideration of obstacles to women's inclusion in positions of decision making. Harriet Holter's book *Sex Roles and Social Structure* (1970) was an important breakthrough in its analysis and description of women's roles in elites. But the work (written in English) of this Norwegian social scientist was not incorporated into the mainstream and, along with Putnam's analysis of comparative elites (1976), was one of the decade's few studies on this subject that included women. The inattention to women was due partly to the fact that so few were to be found among political elites and there was little interest in the subject.[11] It remained for women scholars to focus on women in the political process.

In the United States, however, scholars at the Eagleton Institute for Women in Politics had begun collecting data on women in politics in and outside the United States in the early 1970s. Several noted European scholars—Elina Haavio-Mannila in Finland, Rita Liljestrom in Sweden, Andréc Michel in France, and Magdalena Sokolowska in Poland[12]—conducted studies on women in their countries which included work on their roles in political life. Some of the interpretive work of these scholars has since been published in Europe and the United States (Epstein and Coser, 1981; Haavio-Mannila et al., 1985). Stacey and Price (1981) have ana-

11. As Bourque and Grossholtz pointed out, an exception was M. Kent Jennings (1968), who did not exclude women from his study of party elites as did Dahl (1956) and Hunter (1953) from their studies of community power.

12. This list is not meant to be comprehensive; these are the names that come to mind of early researchers in the 1960s and 1970s.

lyzed obstacles to women's attainment of political posts in Britain, and Baxter and Lansing (1983) have reviewed the literature on voting behavior, activism, and political attitudes in the United States, disputing prior claims of women's disinterest in politics and showing the forms of political activism in which they have engaged.

Anthropologists were among the first to identify women's leadership roles in small tribes and societies, countering the common belief that women's exclusion from elites was a universal pattern through time and in all societies.[13] Rosaldo and Lamphere's important book *Woman, Culture and Society* (1974) was one of the first collections to include studies showing that women did assume political leadership in some societies.

In the 1970s, a shift in perspective involved a study of both direct and subtle means by which women had been excluded from elite party politics and the judiciary. Susan Carroll (1977) and Epstein (1981b) found that women had less access to contacts and money and were excluded from the inner sanctums of political party caucuses; they were not included in political brokering processes, nor were they named to important committees within professional organizations that were part of the nominating process for state and federal legislative and judicial posts (Tolchin, 1977; Epstein, 1970a, 1981b). Furthermore, fear of sex discrimination inhibited women political activists from running for office, and the attitudes of male activists kept them from accepting women as equals (Lee, 1977). Women also often faced sexual harassment in the political clubhouse unless they were specifically invited to participate in campaign operations (Moran, 1983). Several studies found evidence that party leaders who recruited women as candidates did so for races which they had little chance of winning (Van Hightower, 1977; King, 1977; Gertzog and Simard, 1981). Women are active in school board elections, sometimes surpassing men in participation. In these elections, which are considered suitable for women, marriage and motherhood do not deter their activism. In competitive partisan politics, however, it is another matter.

Intervention has been effective in breaking down barriers to women's participation. Pressure raised the proportion of women delegates to the 1972 Democratic National Convention to 40 percent, for example. Delegates to the convention voted to give women and minorities representation in the national convention in closer proportion to their numbers in the population than they had had in the past, and this policy has been continued. Although the provision did not result in a convention that was 51

13. Sharon Tiffany (1979) argues, however, that women are invisible in the literature of political anthropology, although they are political actors in all societies.

percent female, the Democrats' action brought pressure on the Republicans, and GOP managers raised the proportion of women delegates to their convention to 30 percent (Kirkpatrick, 1976). The National Women's Political Caucus made its appearance on the political scene at this time, speaking for newly mobilized women, raising women's issues, and pressing the campaign in new directions.

Jeane Kirkpatrick (1976) studied convention delegates' behavior and attitudes, building on her earlier (1974) study of the participation of women in state politics. Important assessments also appeared in the work of Shanley and Schuck (1974), Githens and Prestage (1977), Jaquette (1974), Jennings and Farah (1981), and others. These analyses found few basic differences between men and women in political interest and self-concepts, although, as we have noted, men displayed more ambition than women, reflecting their differential chances to attain power. Kirkpatrick found, for example, that most male politicians did not think women were influential—certainly an impediment to their supporting a woman candidate.

Institutional Factors in the Analysis of Elites

It seemed clear from research on elites that women were excluded from the tracks that men typically followed to become members of elites. The tracks included education in male institutions of higher learning (the *grandes écoles* in France; the public schools and Oxford and Cambridge universities in England; exclusively male private boarding schools and Ivy League universities in the United States), membership in professions that were gateways to such elite domains as law, and activities in political clubs and organizations often closed to women.

A Ford Foundation–sponsored Conference on Women in Decision-Making Elites in 1976 brought a number of European and American researchers together to discuss these matters, as reported in *Access to Power: Cross-National Studies on Women and Elites* (Epstein and Coser, 1981). One important finding shared by the conferees was the fact that when women were able to follow the same career lines as men they more often became leaders. For example, participation in guerrilla groups during World War II gave women visibility and legitimation in Yugoslavia (Denitch, 1981); becoming lawyers in the United States (Epstein, 1981b) meant that they were following a status sequence toward political office long adopted by men; equalitarian ideological policies translated into government programs increased women's active roles in politics (Skard and Hernes, 1981;

Sokolowska, 1981; Denitch, 1981). These researchers indicated that few societies have been neutral with regard to the role of women in politics. Either women were guaranteed political opportunities like those of men or, more often, they were hindered. Women who succeeded without intervention on their behalf by a political party or government typically did so either because they traveled an alternate route (through voluntary organizations, for example, rather than through positions in professions or business) (Jennings and Thomas, 1968; S. Carroll, 1977; Johnson, 1978; Epstein, 1981a) or because they were the widows or daughters of men prominent in the political sphere and inherited their positions (Mandel, 1981; Johnson, 1978; Epstein, 1981a; Gertzog, 1984). In the last instance, as in the case of Indira Gandhi, personal linkage to a strong charismatic leader and upper-class position have often superseded sex status as the salient characteristic.

Scholars and activists alike are now devoting much more attention to the role of women in elites. For example, Jean Blondel's comparative work (1985) identifies a general, though modest, increase in the number of women cabinet ministers throughout the world. He shows that the greatest resistance to women in government lies in theocratic states and argues that there is not always "progress" in a linear direction toward greater inclusion of women. Blondel notes that among the countries that were independent before 1970, seventy-two had at least one woman cabinet minister in the 1970s, whereas only forty-three had one or more women ministers before 1970. There were substantial increases in women cabinet members in Black Africa and Latin America but a decrease in women ministers in the communist world (with the exception of Romania and Cuba) and in South and Southeast Asia.[14]

Structural factors rather than the individual characteristics of candidates account for ease or difficulty in women's acquisition of elite positions. These factors include the size of a legislative body (Diamond, 1977), whether members are chosen by proportional elections or by majority votes

14. Blondel found that there has been no movement of women into top government posts in about a third of the world, particularly in countries located in the Islamic area but also including Spain and Switzerland. In Sweden there has been an outstanding breakthrough in the number of women ministers, so that they constitute a fifth to a quarter of the total. Haavio-Mannila et al. (1985) show that all Nordic cabinets are a quarter or more female except for that of Iceland (where the president of the country is a woman). The figures change every day, however. The new prime minister of Norway, a woman, appointed women to half of the posts in her cabinet in 1986. The Norwegian embassy reports that (as of February 5, 1986) 53 of the 155 members of Parliament were women. The United States continues to have one of the lowest proportions of women in office at the national level, although their proportion has been steadily increasing at the city and state levels.

(there is a higher percentage of women in parliaments elected by a proportional system [Haavio-Mannila et al., 1985; Rule, 1981]), and whether
posts are elected or appointed (Epstein and Coser, 1981).[15] President Carter,
for example, appointed more women to the United States judiciary (eleven
to the Federal Appeals Court and twenty-nine to Federal District Courts)
during his term of office than had ever been appointed before.

In their studies of access to elites as well as general participation in the
political process, political scientists have recently found that earlier studies overstated gender differences or failed to understand how tied they
were to specific situations or conditions. Many have become aware that
stereotypes drawn from flawed interpretations of prior studies have tended
to persist.

Political Behavior: Differences and Similarities

During the debates over granting women the vote in the late nineteenth
and early twentieth centuries, participants often expressed the belief that,
once enfranchised, women would behave significantly differently from
men in the political arena. Their views and those of some recent feminist
scholars are remarkably similar—both stressing the presumed greater morality of women.[16] American women did achieve reforms in their first
efforts in the 1920s and 1930s (a bill instituting a merit system for the
Civil Service and a health care education bill for mothers were passed *in
anticipation* of a women's vote before 1920 [Klein, 1984]). But contrary
to suffragist predictions, they voted much like men after 1920. And now,
as in the past, activist political women have organized in groups (such as
the current Congressional Caucus for Women's Issues, formerly the
Congressional Women's Congress) that are devoted to their special interests like pay equity and employment opportunity. Nevertheless, no stable,
predictable women's vote has materialized.

Yet there is a persistent sentiment that women express different values,
focus on different issues, and are motivated by different ambitions than
men. Research on this topic, however, contradicts these perceptions. Once

15. As Alice Rossi (1982) has written, the appointive route, often neglected in the literature
on women in politics, may become increasingly important. She points to the interplay between
women's access to high-paying jobs and acquisition of professional skills and their increasing
attractiveness to those in charge of appointing the staffs of commissions, agencies, and executive
offices at all levels.

16. The work of Carol Gilligan (1982) leads the current discussion. Criticism of her methodology and interpretation may be found in chapter 4.

again, fewer differences are found than are commonly believed to exist, and findings about the structures that produce those differences that do exist are also surprising. For example, folk wisdom pronounces women more altruistic than men. Sometimes researchers have failed to see contradictory evidence in their own studies, perhaps because of their uncritical acceptance of the stereotype. Constantini and Craik (1977) explained the motivation for participation in party activity by arguing that "politics for the male leader is evidently more likely to be a vehicle for personal enhancement and career advancement. But for the woman leader, it is more likely to be a "labor of love." Yet Berenice Carroll (1979) found that Constantini and Craik's own data showed that women's motives for political party activity did not differ from those of men.

Stereotypes have also alternately labeled women as more liberal or more conservative than men and as more moralistic or more responsive to candidates' personal styles. None of these stereotypes is supported by evidence.

Studies of voting in the 1960s and 1970s in the United States and Western Europe show that a greater proportion of women than of men have tended to vote conservatively (Jaquette, 1974), although the more recent "gender gap" studies showed them to be more liberal with regard to such issues as peace. Jack Hammond (1984) argued that there is only slight evidence that women in the United States share a conservative bent shown by European women. In the early years of women's suffrage in Illinois, woman were less likely than men to support Socialists and more likely to vote for Prohibition, but, he pointed out, support for Prohibition did not necessarily mean conservatism; some defined it as part of a program of progressive reform. (Actually Prohibition was passed on the federal level during World War I, before women had the vote across the United States.) Similarly, women's vote for Eisenhower in 1952 may have been motivated by their desire to see an end to the Korean War. The conservative patterns in Europe have been ascribed to the fact that European women are more religious than men (Seymour Martin Lipset, personal communication, 1981). For that reason, in France and Italy, for example, a higher proportion of women than of men have voted for rightist parties. In the United States, religion has not been so salient in determining differences between male and female voting behavior.

Historically in the United States women's voting patterns have been remarkably similar to men's. Polled on issues, a somewhat greater proportion of women have opposed conscription, corruption, the Vietnam War, nuclear weapons, and inflation (Baxter and Lansing, 1983; Verba and Nie, 1972; Epstein, 1981b; Rossi, 1982). But these data document shifts in the political allegiances of only a small percentage of voters. The voting behavior of both women and men is affected principally by their other statuses—as workers or college graduates, for example (Epstein, 1981b; Rossi, 1982). In the matter of morality, women are as rational or irrational as men in voting their own (or others') self-interest; differences that appear to be evidence of greater morality may express self-interest arising from their different position in the social structure (Epstein, 1981b; Rossi, 1982). For example, many women who supported Prohibition did so to protect themselves from the consequences of male alcoholism.

Even the so-called gender gap in voting behavior has proved ephemeral. Since 1964 American women have cast a higher proportion of votes for the Democrats in national elections than have men (except in 1976). This difference was greater in the 1980 election than ever before (Hammond, 1984), to the elation of Democrats who benefited from the difference between women's and men's votes (Abzug and Kelber, 1984; see also Klein, 1984; Sapiro, 1983). Baxter and Lansing (1983) reported that 47 percent of women voters compared with 55 percent of men voted for Ronald Reagan; 42 percent of voting women supported Carter compared to 36 percent of men. In the research reporting the gender gap in voting as in research on sex differences in other spheres, one must bear in mind that the overlaps in voting patterns of women and men far exceed the differences. The differences, however, may be politically significant, for the swing of only a few percent of the electorate can change the result of an election. The support of a significant proportion of women voters whose consciousness had been mobilized about such issues as peace and equal rights is believed by political analysts (Farah, personal communication, 1986) to have clinched the 1984 victories of Democratic candidates in a number of gubernatorial and senatorial elections in Michigan, Massachusetts, and Illinois. But it must also be remembered that in 1984 a majority of women voted for Reagan. Not all women and certainly not even most women voted differently than men did, only a few percent of them. Baxter and Lansing (1983) suggest that gender is not a good determinant of voting behavior and that a multivariate model is necessary. Women and men coming from similar socioeconomic backgrounds tend to vote according to the mood and perspective of their community and workplace. Gender consciousness (Gurin, 1985) is politically salient for a subset of women who are politically alert, but not for most voters.

Surprisingly, women are no more likely than men to support the Equal Rights Amendment or unrestricted abortion (Hammond, 1984). Looking at support for civil liberties, recent scholarship has found that differences reported earlier (Stouffer, 1955) have tended to disappear. The most recent analysis of tolerance of civil liberties in the United States (McClosky and Brill, 1983) found only a few sex differences in attitudes. Analysis of mass public samples showed that males scored slightly more libertarian than did women. Housewives and farmers tended to be less liberal, probably owing to their narrowness of associations and more limited exposure to information. Political scientists have suggested that women's growing educational attainment and participation in the labor force will further reduce differences between them and men with regard to their attitudes about civil liberties. This was borne out by McClosky and Brill's analysis of community and opinion leaders. Among this subgroup, women exhibited higher scores than did men on civil-liberties scales.

This reflects a finding of the Center for the American Woman and Politics (Johnson and Carroll, 1978), which indicated that a greater proportion of women officeholders evaluate themselves as liberal than do their male counterparts. This may be due to their greater opportunity to be elected by the reform wings of parties that are more committed to ideologies of equality—labor parties in Europe and reform Democratic districts in the United States (Epstein, 1981b). McClosky and Brill suggest that women leaders are more finely screened, and "because they have had to traverse a more difficult road, they may have a higher public sensibility and a greater capacity for absorbing the ideas by which the nation is presumably guided" (1983: 385). Jennings and Farah, however, studying Michigan delegates to national party conventions in 1964 and 1976, did not find the political beliefs of men and women elites to be characterized by sharp contrasts, although they found that women are "perhaps a shade more liberal" (1981: 473). Party and general ideology are the crucial variables in their findings. They found further that sex was not a useful predictor of differences, whether in the 1964 or the 1976 study.

Although women as a class display only minor differences from men in their political behavior as voters and citizens (and even these are growing narrower), there is evidence that women leaders have made a difference in the political landscape. They have, for example, been particularly active in support of legislation to improve Social Security, extend credit to women, and provide educational equity (Klein, 1984). Of course, many male legislators as well have been instrumental in promoting legislation on these issues. Groups of activists have been visible in their use of political, legal, and professional influence to further women's equality. Women lawyers and judges have been responsible for changing the administration of justice in dealing with women victims of physical abuse (including rape) and of employment discrimination. They have also been responsible for review of outdated and inequitable views about women in the courts (Williams and Lichtman, 1984; Ginsburg, 1985).

The liberalism of women leaders shows up as a sex difference on female issue–oriented behavior (Epstein, 1981a). Some women in politics are especially alert to women's issues, and they tend also to be sensitive to issues of civil rights, rights of the poor, and other special issues. The Congressional Caucus for Women's Issues has certainly made a difference in congresswomen's introduction of bills designed to give women equality. Although the group is bipartisan, as of 1987, only 16 of a total of 24 congresswomen belonged to it; recently a substantial number of men (101 of a total of 412) joined to express support for these issues. In primaries held in the United States in 1986, women candidates were less identified with feminist causes than with the problems of their parties and communities (Dionne, 1986). Thus women, as a social category, have not demonstrated a different morality, as Carol Gilligan (1982) suggests they have, although some women, like some men, are active in enunciating the interests of women (see Elshtain, 1985).[17]

One study of women judges found that they impose sentences similar to those imposed by male judges (Cook, 1981), although the common wisdom holds otherwise: women judges have been believed to hold diametrically opposed qualities, to be either tougher than male judges or more lenient (Epstein, 1981b). Some women leaders have been active and effective in what are regarded as right-wing activities. Several studies have documented the role of such activists in lobbying for limits on reproductive freedom (Luker, 1984), against the Equal Rights Amendment (Boles, 1979), and in favor of right-wing positions on other issues. In fact, some scholars point out that there has been a greater politicization of women in recent years in all sectors of the political spectrum, from the far right to the far left.

The new scholarship, then, has uncovered the myths about women that have formed the basis for beliefs about their political lives. Further, it has shown that women do not differ substantially from men in their outlook and orientation to political life except insofar as they must work within

---

17. Of course, there is no consensus on what the interests of women are. Traditionalists disagree with those who seek change. Further, evidence indicates that women candidates may activate or minimize their sex status depending on the political context. Merkl (1976) points out that Latin American women politicians are characterized as *supermadres* and appeal at election time to women's interests in "feminine subjects."

the limits set by gatekeepers and must overcome any remaining legal restrictions on their participation.[18] It has shown that social controls (Lynn and Flora, 1977) have kept women out of some spheres and elites but also that positive intervention has the power to bring them in and stimulate higher ambitions (Jennings and Farah, 1981). Like the upper reaches of occupations, position in government is guarded closely, and interlocking networks of economic position, political patronage, informal associations, and entrenched party machinery all act as barriers to outsiders. Women's ability to become insiders depends on the pressures they exert collectively, by political organization through caucuses and the women's movement, for recognition and acceptance by male gatekeepers of their entry onto the track to political careers.

There are no fundamental attitudinal differences in men and women, but there are differences in the opportunity structure and in their social position that affect both their choices and the choices of those who can control women's access to power.

18. Jennings and Farah (1981) found how discouraged women were when a range of political offices they sought appeared to be unobtainable. See also B. Carroll (1979), Flora and Lynn (1974), and King (1977).

CHAPTER 9

Reconceiving the Family

T he family has long been considered the primary domain of women. In the social sciences and in the larger society, women have been defined chiefly by their family roles as men have been defined by their occupational and other public roles. As a result, much of social scientists' research among women has been concentrated in family studies. These studies, influenced by values that affirm the traditional division of labor in the family and outside it, have overemphasized men's roles as breadwinners and women's as homemakers, inadequately considering men's behavior in the family and women's roles as economic providers. Thus, the traditional division of roles in the family conforms to the dichotomous categories that characterize the rest of social life. Indeed, some argue that it has formed the basis for such thinking. According to Huber (forthcoming), it was mainly the social psychology of the family that earlier researchers focused upon, except for a few scholars such as Goode (1963), who provided a structural comparative analysis of families.[1]

But analyses of models of the family increasingly have been subjected to critical evaluation, partly on the basis of new empirical findings and work accomplished in the burgeoning field of social history. "We now possess more accurate information about the family than Marx, Durkheim, or Weber ever knew—we also know more than did the family scholars of the 1950's and 1960's," observed William Goode in the revision of his analysis of family studies (1982b: xiii). A reordering of family patterns over the past decade has also resulted in a reanalysis of the frameworks that guide research.

This chapter will review some of the critiques of the view of the family that has underlain its study, with particular reference to men's and women's roles. It will analyze models of the "normal" family, problems of

1. Joan Huber and Glenna Spitze, "Trends in Family Sociology," in N. Smelser, ed., *Handbook of Sociology* (forthcoming).

methodology, and questions of generalizability. It will also consider perspectives on motherhood and the division of labor in the household. These are some of the issues regarded as most important in the analysis of gender differentiation. Hotly debated, they have torn feminist circles apart. The list is illustrative rather than inclusive, although each issue must be considered of major importance. I shall not treat some timely and important topics, such as problems of female-headed households in poverty, problems of divorce, and new problems that have recently arisen from the use of reproductive technology.

Myth and Reality in the Family

Idealized families and relationships within families have formed the basis of models followed by novelists, theologians, lawmakers, national propagandists, and social service practitioners. Social scientists have also been responsible for selective visions of families and their members, with consequences for the observed behavior and attitudes of the very individuals they have studied. For many people, an orderly family with a clear division of labor, authority, and even emotions between husband and wife and between parents and children—a creation of God, of evolution, or of necessity for the preservation of society—has constituted the core of the ideal.

In his overview of research on families throughout the world more than two decades ago, Goode (1963) cautioned scholars against using stereotyped views of the family as a basis for assessing change. In the United States, for example, he suggested there was a sentimental nostalgic vision of the family living in one large, rambling house, providing warmth, comfort, security, and discipline for its members administered by a strong father and a nurturant mother.[2] Such families were "havens in a heartless world," as characterized by Christopher Lasch more than a decade later (1977). Lasch, like some other social scientists and policymakers, sees in the idealization a model that makes deviations aberrant. Those who be-

2. The vision of an ideal family living in a large household is played out in the fantasies provided by popular prime-time television programs, such as "Dallas," "Dynasty," "The Colbys," and "Falcon Crest." In each, a family composed of parents, children and their spouses, grandchildren, and even estranged spouses live in a grand household. Although relationships are always complicated and filled with the stress necessary for dramatic interest, the family ties are regarded as important and enduring. These programs are also popular in other parts of the world where they are shown—throughout Europe and even in the third world.

lieved their mandate was research and remedy have attempted to restore the "impaired" family to the ideal form. A self-identified feminist political scientist, Jean Bethke Elshtain, has taken a traditional "pro-family" stance that affirms gender differentiation and celebrates qualities such as mothering which are seen as distinctive (Stacey, 1983). Making marriage "work" and finding solutions for other problems of family life have formed a core of concern among many family sociologists, even those who do not succumb to idealization.

Sociologists and psychologists have documented variations in family forms throughout the world for some time. But not all social scientists have applied to their own research the lessons offered by comparative analysis, and many of the critical commentaries have fallen on deaf ears. For one thing, those who have devoted their research to a quest for universals have not paid sufficient attention to variations in the experiences of members of different kinds of family groups. For another, the virtues of stability and order have been stressed without sufficient regard to the costs to women and children when patriarchy and the submission of family members lacking power are the foundations of family order. Once again, the caution of a prescient commentator failed to influence the research agenda. "Order may be based on tyranny," wrote Mirra Komarovsky in 1953. "We shall probably never know, though some writers presume to tell us, just how happy our grandmothers were. There were no Kinseys to record their sexual frustrations, no psychiatrists to unravel their neuroses, no novelists to indict them for momism" (p. 50). There was, rather, the characterization of a harmonious nuclear family in which members played complementary roles, a form that existed universally, according to George Murdock (1949).

In his overview of the world's societies, based on data in the Yale Human Relations Area Files, Murdock claimed that the nuclear family is found "either as the sole prevailing form of the family or as the basic unit from which more complex familial forms are compounded. . . The nuclear family is always recognizable and always has its distinctive and vital functions— sexual, economic, reproductive, and educational. . . . An explanation of the social utility of the nuclear family, and thus of its universality, must . . . be sought not alone in its functions as a collectivity but also in the services and satisfactions of the relationship between its constituent members," he wrote (Murdock, 1949: 2–3). His position was widely adopted, most notably by Parsons and Bales (Parsons, 1954; Parsons and Bales, 1955). Parsons, however, focused on the sexual and socialization functions of the family. He believed these were integrated in such a way as to provide the psychoanalytically optimal structure for the care of children and the ''secure'' adult.

Key aspects of Parsons's work were criticized by, among others, Marion Levy, Jr., and Lloyd Fallers (1959), who refuted his assertion of the ubiquity of the nuclear family on the basis of Levy's study (1949) of the Chinese family and research on other societies that did not conform to the model, such as the Nayar (Gough, 1952) and the Hopi (Eggan, 1950). Parsons, replying to his critics, claimed that the statistical portrait of American family life did document a ''normal American family'' (1965)— 82.7 percent of the population was living in households comprised of a husband, wife, and their children in 1960. The broad picture, he reported, was ''that of an increasingly specialized but structurally intact family.'' He did note, however, an exception to the general pattern in ''the situation of the lowest groups by most of the socio-economic indices'' (p. 38). Parsons insisted firmly that the normal family was best suited to fulfill the functions he had outlined earlier.

Although the form and functions of the family had been widely debated in the field of family sociology, a number of feminist scholars writing in the mid-1970s and 1980s (Thorne and Yalom, 1982; Rubin, 1975; McGrath, 1979) saw their work as discontinuous with the earlier work of family sociologists. The feminist scholars focused their arguments on Parsons's functional approach but ignored or were unaware of the concerns expressed by sociologists as much as four decades earlier about stresses women faced from contradictory expectations in the family and in society (Komarovsky, 1946; Myrdal and Klein, 1956; Bernard, 1968, 1971) or from inequality in the family (Goode, 1963; Rossi, 1964; Epstein, 1970a). The feminists argued that insufficient weight had been given to the stress placed on women in the nuclear family and that as a result scholars did not turn adequate attention to the many alternative family forms in the United States and elsewhere. They were not correct in believing that Parsons's work provided the major orientation for research on the family,[3] as a look at the *Journal of Marriage and the Family* and the many books and articles that appeared in those years indicates.

Betty Friedan's critique of Parsons's work in *The Feminine Mystique* (1963), however, did focus on the functional approach feminist scholars objected to. Within the two or three years following publication of Friedan's book, spirited discussion of women's family roles spread among

3. I am grateful to Mirra Komarovsky for her gentle reminder about this.

feminist activists organizing in groups ranging from the National Organization for Women (NOW), which sought equal partnership with men in the family and society, to radical separatist groups such as Red Stockings and New York Radical Women. The mainstream organization NOW saw itself as the women's counterpart to the black civil rights movement. Radical groups called for destruction of the traditional family in order to restructure society and abolish gender roles (R. Kramer, 1986).[4] Feminists of all political persuasions subscribed to a core of feminist ideology. The 1960s and 1970s focused on a sexual politics that aimed at transforming gender and sexuality both in the public sphere and in the home. Like the activities of the first women's movement in the 1900s, the battle over the family and women's roles in it was fought largely through books, journal articles, position papers, philosophical tracts, and sociological explorations. In the social sciences, and particularly in sociology, scholars began examining women's real roles in the family and the consequences for them of the power structure. Some had new things to say, and some restated the concerns of older scholars, but there was a much greater emphasis in research attention to power relationships within the family, to women's labor within the home, and to motherhood. Of course, they were writing within the context of a demographic portrait very different from the one on which Parsons had based his analysis. By 1977, only 16 percent of families in the United States fit the model he had described in 1960 (Thorne, 1982: 5)—father as sole wage earner, a full-time homemaker-mother, and at least one child living at home. The traditional family was eclipsed, provoking social scientists to consider a new reality, which reflected the increases in dual-earner families, divorce and separation, and female-headed households, and delay in the age of marriage. More and more, women spent considerable time outside the home as they increased their labor force participation in all age categories, and men retired from work to the home at earlier ages.

One of the new wave of social scientists writing on the family, Arlene Skolnick (1979), found fault with those who insisted that the nuclear family embodied a kind of "platonic essence of which real families in the world were only imperfect reflections." Other feminist scholars joined in

4. These writings included the journals *Aphra, Off Our Backs, Up from Under, Notes from the Second Year* (Radical Feminists, 1969); Kate Millet's book *Sexual Politics* (1970) and Shulamith Firestone's *The Dialectic of Sex* (1972); Gayle Rubin's article "The Traffic in Women: Notes on the 'Political Economy' of Sex" (1975), and Jeanne Arrow's "Dangers in the Pro-woman Line and Consciousness-Raising," ideas of the Feminists (1969). Alice Rossi's "Equality among the Sexes" (1964), although not reported as part of the radical literature, was an important theoretical analysis of gender roles and included a prescription for change.

objecting to the assumption that the nuclear family created a common set of experiences that all family members shared. Uniting "women and the family in an apparently unchanging set of biologically given needs" or biologically determined conditions, this perspective appealed to conservative politicians and ideologists and their sociological counterparts, according to Thorne and Yalom (1982) in *Rethinking the Family*. Skolnick's work (1979) had argued earlier for recognition that the other forms of family life found in contemporary society could function well, including single-parent families, households without children, and homosexual and lesbian couples with or without children. The further rethinking offered in the collection of studies edited by Thorne and Henley (1975) denied that the organization of the family is biologically determined in any direct or immutable way. Writing in that volume, anthropologists Collier, Rosaldo, and Yanagisako asserted:

> The Family (thought to be universal by most social scientists today) is a moral and ideological unit that appears, not universally, but in particular social orders. The Family as we know it is not a "natural" group created by the claims of "blood" but a sphere of human relationships shaped by a state that recognized families as units that hold property, provide care and welfare, and attend particularly to the young—a sphere conceptualized as a realm of love and intimacy in opposition to the more "impersonal" norms that dominate modern economies and politics. (1982: 33)

This perspective contributed to a growing body of analysis that led the anthropologist Rayna Rapp (1978) to write: "One of the more valuable achievements of feminist theory has been its effort 'to deconstruct the family as a natural unit, and to reconstruct it as a social unit'—as ideology, as an institutional nexus of social relationships and cultural meanings."

Not all feminist scholars, however, have rejected the claim that universal experiences in family life have far-reaching consequences. There is a feminist school of analysts who propose a "biosocial model of parenting," among whom Alice Rossi (1977) is the major figure. They argue that the mother-child bond is unique and biologically determined, although it should not provide the basis for inequality. Other feminist social scientists have propounded a psychologically oriented view of a distinctive female personality based on women's experience as mothers and as daughters (Chodorow, 1978). And there is a feminist legal perspective that argues that basic biological differences between the sexes with regard to reproduction ought to be recognized in the law (Law, 1984; Kay, 1985).

There is also a school of conservative feminist scholars, including political scientist Jean Elshtain who also regards the family in universal terms.
''The family's status as a moral imperative derives from its universal, pan-
cultural existence in all known societies,'' she wrote in *Private Woman,
Public Man* (1981). Criticizing this work, Judith Stacey (1983) pointed
out that Elshtain obscured the family's authority structure by ''portraying
it as the source of authentic community ties and the source of resistance
to the dehumanizing logic of 'modernity.' '' Although regarded as conservative, these views differ from those of sociobiologists (Goldberg, 1974;
Barash, 1977) who, as we saw in chapter 3, claim that hierarchical family
social arrangements (such as patriarchy) are an outgrowth of biological
evolution and are therefore immutable.

Whatever the differences among the social scientists working today on
the family, there is no doubt that the field itself is characterized by greater
emphasis on the social creation, organization, and consequence of inequality and on the analysis of actual and idealized family gender roles.
Problems of issues and method still plague the field, however.

Bias has affected the perceptions of family researchers as it has the
perceptions of those studying other social institutions. We are so familiar
with our own families that it is difficult to study the family as an institution
with objectivity. Observers are likely to argue about what is *right* rather
than to demonstrate what *is*. And certain other, structural problems associated with the study of the family (in all its forms) have only recently
been recognized. Arlene Skolnick (1979) observes that the tendency to
regard the family as a ''backstage area'' has made research on it more
difficult. (Although behavior in some other institutions may also not be
obvious, at least outside observers do not regard themselves as so knowl-
edgeable about them.) That is one reason that those engaged in public
evaluation of individuals' behavior and roles in families—judges and legislators, clinicians, and many social scientists—tend to measure the family
by an ideal standard.

Furthermore, social scientists must deal with the fact that individuals
may not be accurate informants about their own families and also may
overgeneralize from their families to all families. One problem affecting
people's views of their own families and reports about them is that the
family is partly invisible, and not only to outsiders; in many societies,
segregation of male and female family members may create discrepant
knowledge among insiders (Bernard, 1981). Where women are confined
to the home or reside in different quarters within the household and do
household work with other women, men may be as uninformed about their

behavior as women may be uninformed about the activities and attitudes of the men who congregate separately. Even in modern Western societies, communication between women and men in a family may be proscribed, creating inhibitions about revealing their attitudes and interest in certain topics, such as sex, work, or sports. This kind of symbolic segregation seems to vary by class, generational cohort, and the values of particular subgroups. Mirra Komarovsky, in her study of working-class families (1962), showed that norms defining acceptable topics for conversation differed for couples who had a high school education and those whose educational level was lower. She found, for example, that high school graduates, both male and female, shared their experiences in marriage much more fully than did less-educated persons (65 percent as compared with 16 percent).

One objection to past accounts of family behavior has come from feminist anthropologists and sociologists who note that men have largely been responsible for providing, collecting, and shaping a good deal of the information we have about families and all other spheres of society because they have dominated the social sciences. This has often resulted in a distorted picture, it is charged, because many of the male informants may not have understood the behavior and attitudes of women in their societies, or because the men who dominated the social research agenda may not have been interested in the domains believed to be women's. Lack of recognition of women's economic contributions in the home and failure to appreciate the extent and effect of their participation in the larger economic sphere are regarded as consequences of a traditional conception of women's appropriate roles. As pointed out in earlier chapters, ramifications of the traditional model extended to inadequate data collection about women's economic activity at the site of the home (as farmers and managers of boardinghouses, for example) and the impact of women's changing labor force commitment on their behavior and attitudes inside the home. The charges have some merit, but male social scientists have not been entirely at fault, nor have women social scientists unanimously presented a realistic view. Like all things, this has been a matter of degree, dependent on the insight and sensitivity of the researchers. Several prominent male social scientists have been responsible for outstanding contributions in demythologizing the field of the family, among them William Goode ([1963] 1982), Joseph Pleck (1981), Joseph Pleck and Jack Sawyer (1974), Michael S. Kimmel (1986, forthcoming), Robert Bell (1970); and David W. Tresemer (1977). And some feminists writing on motherhood, such as

Alice Rossi, Dorothy Dinnerstein, and June Flax, have portrayed an idealized version of family life, according to Chodorow and Contratto (1982).

The Division of Labor in the Family

Judgments about the family and about women's and men's roles within it are found in all societies and change from one period to another. For example, social historians (Ariès, 1962; Demos, 1971) and social scientists (Leacock, 1981a) have suggested that a radical change in perception of these roles occurred during the emergence of industrialization, when production moved from the home to the factory. Ideology grew out of the behavior of the majority, so that the spheres of paid work were taken to be men's and those of the home and family were regarded as women's. Men became breadwinners, and wives and children, dependents. According to Skolnick (1979: 304), many notions of femininity and family life were particularly emphasized by industrial capitalism. Popular wisdom downplayed the importance of the home while heralding it as the only place a person might find comfort and security. As a result, the idealized Victorian family of the nineteenth century became the basis for the "normal" family of the twentieth century in much of the world, especially in Western society. This ideology underscored the idea that woman's place is in the home, not in the labor force; the idea that the essence of femininity lies in ministering to the personal and psychological needs of husbands and children; and "the idea that mothers have a Pygmalion-like influence on their children" (p. 304).

Of course, some of these ideas were found in other societies and in other times. The notion that woman's place ideally was in the home was probably as true for the ancient worlds of Rome and Greece as it was and is for women of some unindustrialized third world societies—even though in most of the world, women toil outside the home as well as inside it. Poor women in all societies work at wage labor; in the third world they do much of the agricultural labor, often without pay, and trade in the marketplace. Women and men work in sex-segregated work settings, however. Perhaps the cultural emphasis on women's psychological contributions to the family came about only in complex industrial societies, where the home was seen as a special domain for men to recuperate spiritually from the ordeals of the workplace. Such an emphasis derived from a focus on middle- and upper-class families.[5] The women who toiled on farms or in industry did not easily conform to that idealized picture of an economic and psychological division of labor. The working-class American women who remained at home during the nineteenth century commonly worked hard at physical labor. A third to a half of them took in boarders (Hareven, 1977, 1982; Kessler-Harris, 1981), and housekeeping itself was arduous, dirty, and time-consuming (Strasser, 1978, 1982; Cowan, 1974).

Helena Lopata (1975) has argued that in spite of an ideology that supports confinement of women to the home, all over the world women, like men, leave the home to work because of economic necessity. The ethnocentric and class-bound perspectives of many scholars were probably responsible in part for perceiving as real an ideal of family life rather than actual family behavior.

The translation of this sentimental picture into a concept of male-female role differentiation involving the much discussed and now often rebutted "expressive and instrumental" designation of men's and women's family roles was proposed by Talcott Parsons. He conceived women's roles in the family as expressive and nurturing while men's roles were instrumental, dealing with the "outside" world and tending to the family's material needs. Parsons's depiction of the family as a social support center in which women were the main agents of support reflected widely held views that influenced research and policy agendas. An idealized duo of a nurturant mother and a strong, breadwinning father set the standard, and families were regarded as being in crisis when they deviated from this norm.

The evaluation of the mother's role was particularly stringent in research that looked for causes of family problems, especially those of troublesome or deviant children. The causes of children's problems were usually located in what was defined as "poor mothering"—either "momism," excessive concern for children (Wylie, 1942), or mothering perceived as insufficient because the mother worked outside the home.

5. Talcott Parsons argued that the family's one remaining function for adults was the provision of an emotional refuge in an increasingly rational, bureaucratic society (Parsons and Bales, 1955). He claimed that the family had become the one institution specializing in emotional support (Cherlin, 1983).

Views of Motherhood

The Idealized Mother

The idealized mother and her converse, the neglecting mother, have been at the center of much public and social science attention. The roots of this concept in the United States date to the turn of the century, when mothers were viewed as technical experts whose marketable product was an adjusted and achieving child, according to Ehrenreich and English (1978). The studies that began in the 1940s and continued into the 1970s and beyond embodied the social-problem approach; they focused on improper mothering and ranged from accounts of the overprotective mother who kept the child in a state of arrested development (D. Levy, 1943) to the schizophrenogenic mother whose contradictory behaviors resulted in the mental illness of or neurosis in the child (A. Green, 1946; Lidz, 1973; Bateson and Jackson, 1971). "Mother-blaming" for the mental ills of children appeared in major clinical journals during this period, according to a study by Caplan and Hall-McCorquodale (1985) covering the years 1970, 1976, and 1982.

Some feminist writers shared these cause-and-effect assumptions, focusing attention almost exclusively on the mother as the agent responsible for the mental health and development of the child. Writers such as Dinnerstein (1976) and Flax (1978) created a theme called by Chodorow and Contratto (1982) the "fantasy of the perfect mother." They suggested that idealization and blame of the mother are two sides of the same belief in an all-powerful figure. They proposed that the focus on the mother as principally responsible for the psychological, emotional, and relational state of the child often led to a psychological determinism and reductionism that perceived the mother-infant relationship as the root of all history, society, and culture. They further noted that the perfect mother was perceived not as a person with other tasks, emotions, needs, or history but only as a mother: "This creates the quality of rage we find in the 'blame-the-mother' literature and the unrealistic expectation that perfection would result if only a mother would devote her life completely to her child and all impediments to doing so were removed. Psyche and culture merge here and reflexively create one another" (Chodorow and Contratto, 1982: 65). Research and paradigms thus were oriented toward the presumed necessity for women to assume traditional sex roles lest "failure in mothering do something devastating to children'' (Spiegel, 1982: 95). But, as noted earlier, ''overmothering'' or ''momism'' (Wylie, 1942) brought its own dangers.

Subsequent studies have acknowledged many other factors that may contribute to or independently cause mental illness, homosexuality, or problems in children's adjustment. Some scholars have also noted the therapeutic effects of mothers' working outside the home, effects that vary directly with mothers' feelings about their jobs (Hoffman, 1961; Orden and Bradburn, 1969; Safilios-Rothschild, 1970; Bailyn, 1970; Kanter, 1977b; Crosby, 1987). With the exception of the research of these social scientists, the kinds of jobs mothers had, and their education, economic level, and work experience were not clearly differentiated in the studies that attributed ill effects to mothers' behavior. Here as in countless other studies, insufficient disaggregation colored the researchers' results.

The Biosocial Perspective of Motherhood

The biological fact that women give birth and for most of history have had to nurse children in their first year has set the framework for judging women's roles primarily in terms of their reproductive function. Many scholars and lay people have considered the mothering role an inevitable determinant of female personality.

Conceptions of the centrality of the mothering role for women also have been derived from psychoanalytic writings (Parsons, for one, was influenced by Freud). Many psychoanalysts—particularly classical Freudians—claimed that women were best defined by their mothering role and that a retreat from this role made women neurotic (Deutch et al., 1947).

Alice Rossi's biosocial perspective (1977) claims that a special bond exists between mothers and infants because of women's physiological responses and their experiences in menstruation and childbirth. Nancy Chodorow (1978), a leading advocate for the idea that women's earliest relationships with their own mothers cause them to ''reproduce mothering,'' asserts further that they develop distinctive personalities, in contrast to men's, featuring connectedness, a lack of separation or differentiation, and a lack of orientation toward ''body-ego boundaries.'' Chodorow acknowledges that the division of labor in society, women's inequality in terms of independence and income, and other social-structural factors are important in determining and enforcing women's assumption of the mothering role. Still, she maintains that women have a need for an intensive "interpersonal, diffuse, affective relationship" with a child. More recently, Sylvia Ann Hewlett, an economist, has argued that "modern women—no matter how ambitious—yearn to have children" (1986: 399). Lorber (1981) and others have argued that this perspective is culture- and time-bound; its evidence is usually based on clinical case histories and on personal reflections of the social scientists speculating about motherhood. Jessie Bernard (1972) noted that studies in the mental health field find that married women whose sole identity is that of wife and mother have higher rates of mental illness than do working women, single or married. (See Kanter, 1977b, for a summary of studies.) As discussed earlier, theories ascribing a universal experience to women are more likely to be grounded in ideology or culture than in systematic observation.

We know that women's experiences vary widely in other cultures. Ethnographic evidence indicates that mothers are not the exclusive caretakers of children after infancy in many of the world's societies. Older children or grandparents are assigned the responsibility (Medick and Sabean, 1984), although, of course, most caretakers are women.

Do all women want to be mothers? In the United States as well as elsewhere, there is no evidence to indicate consistent socialization patterns and consistent orientations toward motherhood for all women. In a recent study of middle- and working-class women, Kathleen Gerson (1985b) shows that women's life decisions, including the decision to become mothers, are shaped and influenced by adult experiences rather than by childhood conditioning or predispositions. In *Hard Choices,* she challenges the view that there is one "feminine personality" that all women share and that compels them to prefer a domestic life-style, including children. She asserts that childhood socialization has not produced a universal "mothering need," that not all women wish to mother, and that many women are indifferent to children and some even abuse them (citing Badinter's 1981 study of maternal indifference and other work on maternal abuse). Gerson believes that life circumstances, including the husband's interest in having children, influence women's decisions to become mothers, decisions sometimes involving ambivalence and distress.

Certainly women and men in some other societies have been denied adult recognition until they had children, and sanctions were strong if they were unable to. Even in the United States, women who choose not to have children meet disapproval and concern; clearly motherhood is bolstered by many social controls that stigmatize women who do not have children and reward those who do with social approval.

Few women in any society, however, have wanted to have as many children as they were capable of bearing. People in most societies have desired some limit to family size, accompanied by changing notions of what the ideal should be. Joan Huber and Glenna Spitze (1983) regard the curtailment of fertility as the major turning point in the movement toward equality. They suggest that throughout history, the perceived inevitability of motherhood tethered women to the home, making them unable to engage in the kinds of activities that would result in a wider distribution of wealth or to enter and gain power in the political sphere.

Researchers Paul Glick and Kingsley Davis marked the change in American demographic patterns even though they do not agree in their analysis of it. By the 1960s, the average number of children per family had fallen, and because women were having fewer children, the time span of active mothering had decreased. In the 1970s the typical mother had to care for preschool children for only a little over a decade. Women were having children later in life, and more mothers were working outside the home. But the ability to control the number of children in the family, or the changes that permitted women to delegate child care to others, does not obliterate the strong social emphasis on motherhood as a major social role for women.

Motherhood as Work

New research is uncovering the invisible work that women do as mothers. Whereas traditional studies of mothering focused on structural elements such as whether the mother worked outside the home, more recent work has centered on such elements as the work women do in creating good family relations (DeVault, 1985), in planning, and in helping children prepare for future roles by evaluating alternative educational institutions and the like (D. Smith, 1985). Scholars have become interested in the amount of time women devote to planning for the family and organizing it, as well as "boundary work" with the world outside the family (Rose Coser, 1981) as crucial components of "home work." The pitfalls of mothering and housework, the distractions, the problems of compartmentalization and limitation, are also considered crucial elements in the study of family roles. As yet, however, there have been no actual studies of how much nurturant work women do and how much it varies among women.

Nor has the research been extended to men. Cultural views create a conviction that men abstain from child care and, when called upon to perform mothering roles, do so ineptly. Yet fathers, particularly working-class husbands whose wives work, often take on child-care responsibilities. If much of the work women do within the home is invisible, it is probable that some of the work men do is invisible, too.

The Politics of Motherhood

Today, Americans are keenly aware of the debates in the society about women's rights to fertility control and restrictions on those rights. As Kristen Luker (1985) puts it, the family is contested terrain. The abortion issue, for example, is only the latest in a long history of debates over women's power to select the circumstances and conditions under which they will become mothers and, indeed, whether they will become mothers at all.

Anthropologists agree that there is no society in which women, or men and women together, do not decide on an ideal family size. Birth control has been practiced in all societies with varying degrees of technical competence and knowledge as well as both crude and sophisticated forms of abortion. Although there is a widespread belief that the desire for children is either an inborn or an early acquired trait, the community and the state rarely leave to individuals the right to decide whether to procreate or not— in the same way that the society does not leave gender distinctions or the division of labor to chance.

The state, the community, and the family have always asserted an interest in women's fertility and have expressed that interest through rules and restrictions on sexuality as well as contraception, abortion, and, in some cases, infanticide. Thus, the so-called natural and private consideration of people to become parents, or more particularly, of women to become mothers, has always been intruded upon by persons outside the immediate family.

Gerson's study (1985b) further shows that it is the family situations of women that determine their individual and collective views on family and community roles. Those women who are most economically dependent on men profess the most traditional views. Among women who do not work for pay, or who work outside the home in dead-end jobs but whose husbands are good providers, motherhood is primary. Their positions on such issues as abortion, equal rights for women, affirmative action, or publicly provided day care follow their own choices and situations, a finding that confirms Luker's research on abortion activists on both sides of the issue.

The Homemaker-Worker

The view that it is normal for the typical adult woman to be engaged primarily in family activities may have been an ideal depiction, but it was no longer accurate after the 1950s. In the United States, nearly 70 percent of women aged twenty-five to fifty-four were in the labor force by 1984, including 20 million mothers. (Nearly four out of five women workers were employed full-time.) By that year, most children had a working mother. This included 50 percent of mothers with children under three years of age; 60 percent of those whose children were between three and five; and 70 percent of mothers whose children were between six and thirteen years of age. Thus, 75 percent of all children lived in families in which there were two parents and of these, 61 percent were two-earner families.[6]

This pattern is also the case elsewhere in the world in both capitalist and socialist countries. Not only are women entering and reentering the labor market, but the greatest increases are occurring among married women, including those with preschool children (Lupri and Symons, 1981). Elsewhere in the world, especially in the third world, a majority of women were engaged in the labor market (Boserup, 1970) long before the 1980s. Many analysts, however, defined women's work in agriculture or the marketplace as an extension of their family roles, to be abandoned easily in favor of household work if that was the preference of husbands or elders. A better model of the family would have taken account of the interface between economic work and household roles for both men and women.

The scholarship of the past two decades has been more attuned to the variety of family forms and more conscious of their consequences for family interaction. For example, Rose Coser and Lewis Coser (1974) noted that the traditional family is a "greedy institution" that claims the total allegiance of its members—and that it is especially greedy with respect to women's commitment to family roles, which crowd out other possibilities.

Changes in family composition have also stimulated research. The United States and other Western societies have witnessed a sharp growth in the number of single-parent families, typically headed by the mother, particularly among blacks. As Gerson, Alpert, and Richardson (1984) note in a review of research on mothering, the number of one-parent households with children under eighteen doubled in the United States during the 1970s. By 1984, 10.3 million families drew their principal support from women who were divorced, separated, widowed, or never married (U.S. Dept. of Labor, 1985).[7] During this period as well, alternative structures for mothering have emerged, including households headed by women who never

6. U.S. Department of Labor, Bureau of Statistics, September 19, 1985.
7. In 1984, 44 percent of all black families were headed by women, compared with 23 percent of Hispanic-origin families and 13 percent of white families.

married, unmarried heterosexual couples, and lesbian and gay couples. New forms of the family have also developed as a result of divorce. In the United States, the divorce rate has been rising for the past half century but especially after 1960. Between 1963 and 1976, the divorce rate more than doubled, although the rate of increase has now slowed (Cherlin, 1981). As a result, different forms of custody arrangements, including joint custody (Thomas, 1985), and the growing number of stepfamilies have contributed to the range of variation in family forms.

Although many public pronouncements have decried the negative consequences of such arrangements for children, the effects of alternative family arrangements on both children and adults have not been adequately studied. Blumstein and Schwartz (1983), in their comparison of heterosexual and homosexual couples, found a remarkable similarity between the two in family power structures. Power attribution in both cases was based on each partner's earnings and which partner had the more prestigious job. Comparative work of this type is especially interesting because it shows the fallacy of assuming that power in the family is necessarily attached to sexual attributes (such as maleness) rather than social attributes (such as occupation or income).

The black family probably receives the least attention from the research community. Researchers in the past characterized the black family as a social problem because of the high proportion of mother-headed families (Moynihan, 1965; Pettigrew, 1964). But following claims that an array of family disorders resulted from the absence of fathers in these homes, rebuttals pointed to the surprising strengths of such families (Hill, 1971) and their strategies for survival in a society in which they are regarded as deviant. Carol Stack (1974), for example, has shown how extended kin develop support patterns. Not since E. Franklin Frazier's classic *Black Bourgeoisie* (1957) has there been a comprehensive study of black families who live within the traditional American pattern, although his book was intended as an indictment. Little has been written, for example, about the many roles that black women juggle in working and mothering, and often in grandmothering (but see Valentine, 1980). My own work on black professional women (Epstein, 1973b), for example, shows the impact of mothers in influencing and facilitating the careers of their successful daughters.

Greater attention has been paid recently to the notion that families of different classes and ethnic racial groups experience different life-cycle patterns. J. Allen Williams and Robert Stockton (1973) maintain that the life cycle of the black family is unique, because, for example, families remain intact for a shorter period of time than do whites. Joan Aldous (1978) has shown that the timing of events for divorced women and men differs from that for those who remain in intact families with regard to such behavior as spacing of children. Similarly, Rhona Rapoport, Robert Rapoport, and Ziona Streilitz (1977) have shown that the age at which individuals become parents (whether in their early twenties or late thirties) creates variations in family dynamics because of the generational spans between parents and children.

These kinds of studies have underscored how individuals' roles in the family are interactive with the other circumstances of their lives, such as the historical period and place in which they live.

Force and Power in the Family

Sentimentality and idealization of the family have also obscured the seamy side of family life: its oppression of women and the young (and, as we are learning today, of the old); the problem of incest (surrounded by a powerful taboo which masks its prevalence); and the use of force and violence in the family. Only in the 1970s did sociologists and psychologists begin to notice collectively that if violence was not typical of most families, it was nevertheless widespread. The dirty secrets of family life formerly described by such novelists as Dickens, Zola, Dostoyevski, and Wharton began to surface in the research agendas of social scientists.

Although sociologists had long understood that deviance, even in the form of crime, was as much a part of social life as conformity to norms, they were reluctant to apply this perspective to the family. A few sociological voices did note the "private hell" that describes some marriages (Waller, 1938). Among those who expressed concern over violence in the family, William J. Goode (1971) was almost alone in arguing that family structures were maintained not only by solidarity and love but also by force. He asserted that the power of parents over children and of husbands over wives ultimately was backed by force. Concern expressed by the women's movement about wife beating and maltreatment pressured social scientists to inquire about the prevalence of such activity. The findings were startling; they revealed that family violence occurred not only among the uneducated and poor but also among the middle class, that pregnancy is a likely time for wife-battering to occur, and that violence is not limited to psychopaths but can grow out of the normal stresses of family life (Gelles, 1974, 1977, 1980; Skolnick, 1979; Steinmetz and Strauss, 1974).

As we noted in the earlier discussion of violence and the threat of violence, women's subordination in the family and their vulnerability to the physical consequences of men's anger have been supported by a legal structure that virtually turned its back on family violence.[8] The criminal justice system was not oriented toward family conflict; its officers denied the existence of violence in the family or defined the crimes that occurred in the family as somehow "different" from other crimes. The threat of force by husbands and fathers was often effective enough to control women in the family because they were well aware of the punishments they might face if they failed to perform household tasks or behave deferentially.

Even without the threat of force, the threat of divorce has often served to limit women's power in the household, especially if they were incapable of supporting themselves or if they were unable, through custom and law, to inherit and administer their own wealth. According to Barbara Ehrenreich (1985), many of the women who opposed the Equal Rights Amendment did so because of fear of their vulnerability to divorce.

Of course, women with wealth or education or those living in egalitarian families may not suffer in the way those do who lack these resources. Many women can rely on the love and affection of their husbands or the protection of their fathers. But in most places, for much of recorded history, women ultimately have been subject to the power of their husbands, especially those of means, and the male elders in the family and in the community or state.

Women's Power in the Family

Anthropologists assert that description and analysis of women's subordinate position in the family and the polity must be seen in comparative perspective. Scholars such as Mead (1935), Friedl (1975), Leacock (1978), Hoffer [later MacCormack] (1972, 1974); MacCormack and Strathern (1980), and Rosaldo (1974) have noted that the degree of equality women experience in the family varies. Subordination is not universal, and inequality between spouses based on men's aggression and generally greater ability to enforce their will is not, as sociobiologists claim, an inevitable outgrowth of the human heritage. We have already noted (chapter 3) that observation of other primates and hunter-gatherer societies indicates that equalitarianism rather than hierarchy may have been typical of family groups in small societies.

8. Because of women's movement activity, new legislation has been passed in some states which for the first time requires prosecution of spouses who commit criminal assault.

In evolutionary terms, it seems reasonable to surmise that sociability, cooperation, and equality probably provide better conditions for successful human development than self-absorbed competition and aggression. Leacock (1981b) speculates that women in early human societies occupied public roles—for example, as hunters and gatherers. She hypothesizes that women lost autonomy and were subjected to men's authority as societies became more complex. The subsequent emergence and strengthening of economic classes were accompanied by conflicts over lineality, land rights, and family and kin commitments, all associated with a decline in the status of women. Leacock holds that politics and economics are important factors in setting the structure within which family relations are played out and affect women's power in the family. Although Leacock maintains that women's decline in power started with modern European history, the comparative model she advocates shows that women in various countries suffered or relatively prospered depending on the traditions, religions, and history of the society. Even ancient societies differed in their treatment of women.[9]

Current research has shown that certain universal patterns hold across contemporary societies. In most large societies, Eastern and Western, women and young people of either sex have difficulty achieving or expressing their interests, although in some, as we know, they have engaged in political action to change this pattern. Most typically in these societies, family roles are rigidly prescribed and the controls keeping women in place are stringent and effective. In many societies, control of the wife is explicitly defined, and in some the structure in which she lives restricts her interactions within the family and with people outside the family. Restrictions placed on young couples also affect the process by which young women might develop power. For example, in traditional India, China, and Japan, considerable effort was expended to prevent a young husband and wife from forming a coalition based on affection that was strong enough to undermine the power of their elders. In some societies, women may develop power as they age and learn to manage the system, especially

9. In a recent review of books on ancient Egypt (Pomeroy, 1984) and Rome (Hallet, 1984), Maureen Fant (1985) illustrates the position of women in different parts of the ancient world. She asserts that many accounts that refer to a unitary "ancient world" are based on Athenian society (because records were kept and have survived), which might have been more restrictive than Egyptian society. Pomeroy's work indicates that Egyptian women (and Greek women) who were needy or slaves worked in textile factories. Fant's work on Rome indicates that a structural father-daughter bond gave women somewhat more power than they had in societies where the parental bonds were severed at marriage. "The Roman emphasis on ties of blood and marriage through and to men's female children" was important in giving Roman women greater power than Athenian women.

when they have sons who become a source of legitimation. However, because the daughters-in-law brought into the family by the sons comprise the only group of family adults subordinate to older women, older and younger women are not likely to form alliances. This makes it even harder for the young woman, who initially does not have strong ties with her husband (especially if her marriage has been arranged) and cannot look to the elder women in her new family for comfort.

There is, however, considerable variation in the family practices affecting women depending on the society, class, and age of the individuals. Upper-class families are most likely to set up arrangements for the segregation of men and women; they have a higher stake in maintaining the traditions of the particular family (Goode, 1963). In peasant or working-class families, elders may not share the same household, given its limited accommodations. Husbands and wives tend to work together, developing common experiences and interests that cement the bonds between them.

One structural condition that undermines the power of the woman in the family and contributes to the power of her husband and his family is the widespread practice of patrilocality, in which the new wife moves to the home of the husband. Matrilocality, in which the man comes to live in his wife's domicile, is found in only a few of the world's societies, usually small ones. Men under this system typically have considerably less power, for newcomers are always at a disadvantage. They do not know the rules, they have few social relations, and they must be accepted by their new family if they are to have a pleasant life. This makes the incoming spouse highly dependent. Women have relatively more power in contemporary Western families primarily because couples usually establish households that are independent of both families of origin.

The anthropologist Judith Brown (1982) maintains that in nonindustrial societies the social standing of women tends to improve once they cease to be childbearers. This is manifested in greater personal autonomy, fewer constraints on movement and behavior, and expanded opportunities in the public sphere. In a review of several books on women in the middle years (Baruch et al., 1983; Baruch and Brooks-Gun, 1984; Brown and Kerns, 1985), Beth Hess (1985) concludes that to speak of "the" status of women in the family or society is inaccurate because social power and freedom change with age. For one thing, the degree of social control of younger women by men varies with kinship-based demands intended to certify paternity. Once childbearing is completed and obligations to family and society are discharged, the postmenopausal woman can become a person in her own right or accrue power through manipulation of her adult offspring (although in old age both men and women may find themselves powerless if they lack independent resources).

In family settings, whatever their structure, there is no doubt that attachments develop between people. Thus, the paths of power are not identical even within the same system. The amount of subordination women experience or the power they exert varies to some degree for each person. Women also vary as individuals in their social skills and their ability to adjust within a new system.

As large numbers of women move into the formal economic sector and it becomes less sex-segregated, the balance of power between the sexes in modern societies may shift. The value of women's contributions may be reassessed and the grounds for attaining power altered, affecting the standing of women in family life as their changing roles outside the home contribute to the recalculation of power among family members. For example, Rose Coser (1985) has suggested that for the modern American family, more and more women enter the paid labor market in order to satisfy the family's desire for more material goods or increased educational opportunities for children. When this happens, Coser maintains, men lose power as women gain a measure of financial independence. She points out, however, that men often improve their social standing when the family is enabled to attain a middle-class standard by the wife's earnings. Thus, there can be a trade-off between the husband's loss of power within the home and his gain in the community as family prestige improves.

In the past, the movement of production to the factory and office building made it possible for women to increase their de facto power, according to Coser. In families where men worked away from home and women remained in it, the wife could make most of the decisions concerning the household. Although she was economically dependent upon her husband, he was not at home during the day, which freed her from his supervision. Both men and older women controlled wives' activities in traditional extended families, but in the relatively isolated suburban nuclear family, women could exercise a certain amount of autonomy in the home.

Studies of marital power (Blood and Wolfe, 1960; Scanzoni, 1979; McDonald, 1980) suggest that women's labor-force participation and the economic resources that go with it increase their power in the home. But Huntington (1975) observes that economic contributions alone do not ensure women's power. African women who produce market goods and engage in trade remain under the control of their husbands, who constitute a leisure class because of their wives' work. Furthermore, all over the world, women's incomes are lower than men's, even when occupation, education, number of hours worked, and other factors are controlled (Lupri and Symons, 1981). Some theorists whose work was cited earlier (Hartmann; Strober) believe women's wage inequities are artificially maintained because the intention of male employers is to repress women's power in the home. On balance, however, it is clear that in most societies women's power increases as their ability to be self-supporting increases. As women move into previously male-dominated high-paying occupations, they command more resources.

The reduction of inequity brings its own problems, however. For families undergoing transition from a traditional to a modern pattern, initial disharmonies may result. Tensions are worst where the ideology of the family is based on traditional values of male dominance and least where a concerted effort is made to introduce new values of equality in the culture.

Division of Labor in the Home

The division of labor in the home became a feminist concern in the 1970s, particularly among those scholars and activists who emphasized that the unpaid tasks women perform in the home constituted "work." Ann Oakley's book (1974a) on the sociology of housework, which examined the contemporary Western experience, led to other studies on women's work outside the formal workplace and the industrialized world (Safilios-Rothschild, 1976). The reanalysis of the model of work has recently motivated scholars to press for development of more inclusive statistics on women's participation in the labor force of the third world. Much of the work they perform has been overlooked because it is done in the vicinity of the home (Vanek et al., 1985).

The division of "emotional labor" in the family also became a concern of scholars, who questioned the notion that the family was a haven for its members. They concluded that when men work outside the home, they can retreat to the family and enjoy some leisure there. For women, the home is most frequently a sphere of constant hard work; only a relatively small percentage of privileged women enjoy leisure there. These scholars point out that although the home may provide emotional succor for many, it also generates tension and conflict; some flee it, some tolerate it, and others endure it.

In many parts of the world, anthropologists have observed men sitting in coffeehouses or their equivalent while the women wash and clean, prepare meals, and care for children. In the United States, too, many men enjoy time spent in "hanging around." [10] Women's work and leisure activities tend to be less public and therefore more difficult to assess. Middle-class and working-class women who are full-time homemakers probably have time to socialize with other women when their children are in school. Increasingly, though, mothers are spending school-day hours at work outside the home. And it is important to remember that even women with full-time employment put in an additional twenty to thirty hours a week doing housework.

It is a ubiquitous finding that wives' employment has only a modest effect on the household division of labor in all countries (Lupri and Symons, 1981). They usually retain responsibility for the household's daily organization and for physical chores, including washing, cleaning, and preparing meals. Women who work outside the home, however, receive somewhat more help from husbands than do those who are not employed elsewhere. This is particularly true of child care (Gecas, 1976; Ericksen et al., 1979), which tends to be shared more than routine housekeeping tasks. [11] The father's participation in child care is also related to the age and sex of the child and the number of hours the wife works. It is contingent, too, on whether the wife holds traditional sex-role attitudes, the extent to which she plays a gatekeeper role, and the father's satisfaction or dissatisfaction with his own childhood experience (Barnett and Baruch, 1987). On average, however, the husbands of employed wives do only slightly more housework (between ten and fourteen hours a week) than men whose wives are full-time homemakers (Thorne, 1982). Some feminist social scientists cite these figures when arguing that there is a politics of housework (Mainardi, 1970)—that the sexual division of labor as more women enter the labor force is distorted by male privilege and places an unfair burden on women (Throne, 1982).

The accuracy of data about the division of labor in the home is problematic, however. Because jobs in the home, as in the labor market, are so stereotypically conceived, both the researchers and their subjects may report only the gender-appropriate tasks that are done. I suspect that men may fail to report that they do traditionally "female" tasks such as washing dishes or making beds if they feel this would be regarded as unmanly. There are also perceptual discrepancies (Araji, 1977). Studies have shown that husbands and wives in the United States give different reports about

10. Many men "hang around" at the workplace, socializing with coworkers or engaging in union activities. This is generally regarded as work, however.

11. See Miller and Garrison (1982) for a review of sources on this.

what the other does (Slocum and Nye, 1976; Duncan and Duncan, 1978; Berk and Shih, 1980; Hochschild, 1985), and this is also the case in third world countries. Bourque and Warren (1981) observed that in Peru both women and men are centrally involved in agricultural work, but that although women describe themselves as such, men consider their work peripheral.

These discrepancies may be due partly to genuine unfamiliarity with the total amount of work done and who actually does it, and partly to stereotyped views of who ought to do what. Perception can also be colored by the prestige attached to particular types of work—whether women and men feel proud or ashamed of what they do. It is not only a matter of altering the picture they give to others; they may also truly believe what they report.

Methodological considerations aside, it is no surprise that household tasks are sex typed and that women do most of the housework (Oakley, 1974a; Miller and Garrison, 1982; Hochschild, 1985). Large-scale generalizations, however, tend to obscure class and regional differences. Elizabeth Bott (1955) provided the first analyses of differences between household jobs performed by wives and husbands in working-class and middle-class families.[12] She observed that middle-class British couples who lived far from relatives did not differentiate tasks by sex as much as did working-class couples who lived in closely knit communities where they mingled with extended families and friends from childhood. In the closely knit groups, wives tended to perform women's tasks with other women, and this practice also extended to leisure-time activity. In contrast, middle-class couples in nuclear families tended to share tasks and spend their leisure time together in the same activities. These distinctions held up elsewhere in England (Young and Wilmott, 1957) and in Austria (Szinovacz, 1977), but not in an American study conducted in the 1970s by Ericksen and associates (1979). The latter study found that such factors as education, income, and employment were more important in altering job segregation within the home than was the presence or absence of kin.

There is also disagreement about the impact of education and income on the extent to which the household work is allocated democratically. Young (under thirty-five years of age), educated couples seem to share household responsibilities more than older and less educated ones (Farkas, 1976). However, this also reveals a bias toward equity in other resources, such as income; when husbands' incomes are high, they are less likely to

---

12. This discussion is based on Miller and Garrison (1982).

share in the housework (Ericksen et al., 1979). None of the studies reports on the use of paid household help. In my studies of high-income, highly educated women lawyers, I found that few depend on assistance from husbands; almost all rely on paid housekeepers and child-care workers (Epstein, 1981b).

That equity of resources between the spouses is a basis for sharing household tasks is seen nowhere more clearly than among black couples, who tend to have less income discrepancy. Two studies (Farkas, 1976; Ericksen et al., 1979) found that black husbands do more housework than do white husbands. In the Hispanic community, however, traditional views regarding the division of labor are more strongly held and relatively more so among women than men (Cronkite, 1977).

Women as Daughters, Men as Sons

In exploring the division of labor in the family, emphasis typically is concentrated on the care of children and housekeeping, cooking, and shopping. But because of the increasing elderly population in the Western world, attention has now turned to care for aged parents, a function integrated into the extended family systems of some other societies but regarded as a social problem in the West. An extensive literature on this subject is developing (Riley and Abeles, 1982; Cheal, 1983; Riley, 1971; Stoller, 1983; J. Kramer, 1985; Garms-Homolova et al., 1984; Cicirelli, 1981; Cherlin, 1983). To date, feminist activists have focused on this issue while scholars have not, although interest in the subject is growing.

Care of the elderly raises some important issues for women especially in cross-national and historical terms. In the traditional family, women were usually regarded as caretakers of the elderly. Nursing the elderly sick was seen as an extension of their homemaking roles. But when women's participation in the workplace outside the home increased, this set of obligations became yet another demand on women already overburdened because of the lack of adequate child-care facilities. In the United States 95 percent of the elderly live at home, many of them with or near their adult children, and only 5 percent are in institutions (Sambol, *New York Times*, September 2, 1985). It is likely that women are providing much of their care.

On the other hand, because today's families are small and not all have daughters, many sons are taking on responsibility for elderly parents. We do not know much about this pattern today, but it may be another case in which the changing social structure and the exigencies of life are altering the role prescription that assigned nurturant responsibilities to women only.

Although change has been reported in the attitudes of couples toward sex differentiation of roles over time (Duncan and Duncan, 1978), there has been no *basic* shift in the division of labor by sex in the household. It certainly remains women's domain, and even when women do not actually perform the household work themselves, it is still their responsibility. We can speculate that this is so because society exerts sanctions against women if they do not take on this responsibility and because the reward structure of society is such that women themselves prefer it this way. The household, after all, has been women's only base of prestige and power until recent times, which could explain women's tenacious hold on the domain.

New research has also addressed the dynamic in the family with regard to child care and housework. A study by Baruch and Barnett (1986), for example, points out that high paternal involvement in child care is unlikely to occur without support and approval from others. Thus mothers' sex-role attitudes play a crucial gatekeeping role, either fostering or hindering fathers' participation in family work. This supports the view of sociologist Sarah Fenstermaker Berk (1985), who has conceptualized the family as a "gender factory" which produces not only goods but also gender. In her study of the division of household work she finds that wives expect—and are expected—to assume a vastly greater share of household tasks than other family members, and that wives and husbands are basically satisfied with the division of labor. Her analysis indicates that through housework, husbands and wives affirm their categorical status as male and female.

Other studies show that women receive more prestige in their roles as housewives (Bose, 1980) than in their roles as workers, largely because the kinds of jobs they tend to have are poorly rewarded both absolutely and relative to the rewards men enjoy. For this reason, women often retreat to the home rather than face defeat in the workplace. It would be preposterous to suppose that women who are housewives hold high prestige, but they may receive recognition for being good homemakers and enjoy the vicarious honor of being married to a man who holds a respected position. Today, as in the past, leaving paid work to care for children is an acceptable and often preferred option for a woman, especially if she holds a dead-end job or one that fails to meet her expectations. Of course, some women consider the raising of children an important and rewarding job and do not accept the society's estimate of it as low ranking.

Because the individual first learns about gender distinctions in the family, and because in the family these distinctions are most closely linked to sexuality and reproduction, the reordering of research perspectives on the family has been of particular importance. All families, no matter what their form, specify roles for their members according to gender (as well as age). Families are, of course, influenced by the larger culture and by the political system that proposes and enforces various kinds of gender roles. Families also are affected by sentiments—those that occur through the normal affections and passions of people and those that are stimulated by norms that inform people about the "right" feelings to have. But we have seen how wide the variation can be and to what extent it is dependent on views held by groups and subgroups. Typically, a political system with greater freedom and a healthy economic system create a climate for freedom in the selection and performance of family roles.

CHAPTER 10

Symbolic Segregation: Gender Differences in Everyday Behavior, Communication, and Social Customs

S ymbolic segregation of the sexes is necessary to maintain gender distinctions because physical separation can do only part of the job of differentiation.[1] Men and women always have some contact with each other, so ways must be found to specify that they are different even when they engage in similar activities and exhibit the same behavior in the same social space. Once such device is the different terminology used to describe what men and women do when they do the same thing. Thus men are chefs, women, cooks. Men who work the land are called farmers, but women who do so are usually defined as farmers' wives (Boulding, 1980). English is a relatively sex-free language grammatically, unlike German or French, for example, but male writers of poetry have been called poets while women have been called poetesses; and the same has been so for sculptors (sculptresses), waiters (waitresses), and stewards (stewardesses). These differences have typically incorporated invidious distinctions, with the female version of the noun connoting a lesser commitment or proficiency.

Similarities and Differences in the Language and Nonverbal Communication of Men and Women

The microdynamics of social life—everyday communication between individuals—has been of interest to scholars seeking the sources of gender

---

1. The use of symbolic distinctions to augment physical distinctions accomplishes more than reinforcement of gender differences. Even when there are barriers to contact between races or people of other countries, symbolic means are employed to define one race or country as superior and one as inferior on the basis of presumed differences of intellect or emotional makeup or other reasons. Erik Erikson (1984) calls this pseudo-speciation.

distinctions, the mechanisms perpetuating them, and the myths about them. Both language and nonverbal communication have been analyzed in a tradition stemming from the study of linguistics and the work of anthropologists in kinesics (Birdwhistell, 1970) and proxemics (E. Hall, 1966, 1968).[2] The study of communication has given new depth to the social meanings of language, facial expressions, gestures, and body motion.

Interest in distinct patterns of verbal and nonverbal behavior displayed by women and men increased dramatically in the 1970s and inspired a wide range of experimental and field studies. Many of those who have studied these differences believe they stem from the differential socialization of males and females and from a micropolitics of communication that reflects and reinforces their differential power, status, and positions.

Expressions and gestures are often thought to be outward manifestations of internal states. Some believe they are biologically rooted and others suggest they are learned early through socialization. Girls and boys are believed to move differently, for example, because it is natural to their sexes. Similarly, Westerners and Orientals are believed to exhibit behavior unique to their cultures. The ''inscrutable Orientals,'' for example, are an enigma to the ''expressive Americans.''[3]

In the 1970s feminist scholars became interested in the ways in which language and other forms of communication reflected—and were used to reinforce—gender inequality. They sought to document the gender differences that were perceived and judged to be ''natural'' by the broader culture, to assess whether these perceptions were in fact accurate, and to relate the differences they found to the social positions of men and women, boys and girls.

In spite of a widespread belief that communicative traits such as language and body expression are inborn, most societies invest considerable effort in training the young and monitoring adults in matters of comportment and in manner and content of speech. Of course, language and other forms of communication are part of culture; they both create culture and are an expression of it. As one climbs the socioeconomic ladder, concern with speech and manner becomes more important. Upper-class people adhere to a complex set of rules that govern their expressions, their use of body movement, and their intonation and choice of words. Thus accents

2. Coined by Edward T. Hall, the term *proxemics* is defined as ''the interrelated observations and theories of man's use of space as a specialized elaboration of culture.''

3. Many American women complain that the men they know are as uncommunicative to them as any Oriental. The ''Inexpressive [American] Male'' is the subject of an analysis by Sattel (1982). He maintains that men use inexpressiveness as a power play and are expressive when they wish to attract women.

and speech patterns vary by class as well as by region. These differences are rarely attributed to biology (especially after George Bernard Shaw's character, Henry Higgins, took on the task of changing the language and comportment of Eliza Doolittle in Shaw's play *Pygmalion* and later in the hit musical and film, *My Fair Lady*).

Both verbal and nonverbal communication are related to the creation and maintenance of gender distinctions and are part of the symbolic array that reinforces social arrangements between the sexes, but researchers have found it difficult to describe and explain sex differences in communication as we shall see in the analysis that follows.

Nonverbal Communication

The study of nonverbal communication—"reading the body," for example—as an indicator of both conscious and unconscious intent has become popular as a way to interpret meaning on both the individual and the group level. Scholarly attention to nonverbal variables is a relatively new phenomenon in psychology and sociology, although anthropologists have long been interested in their manifestation in dance and art.

Some feminist scholars interested in the nonverbal aspects of communication and self-presentation have been influenced by the work of Goffman (1967, 1976) and of Birdwhistell (1970). Goffman observed in his essay on "The Nature of Deference and Demeanor" (1967) that in the interaction of superordinates and subordinates nonreciprocal relations are expressed in modes of touching—for example, higher-status people initiate touching more often than lower-status people do. He theorized that nonreciprocal patterns of touching communicate dominance-submission patterns in the relationship and function as the pecking order does in other species. This work led to speculation about differences in touching between men and women and its meaning in social relations. Birdwhistell's work examined a wider spectrum of nonverbal communication, scrutinizing the nature of sex differences in all sorts of expressions. He hypothesized that human beings, as one of a number of weakly dimorphic species, must "organize gender"; that is, humans need to make gender salient for purposes of display and recognition. Thus, individuals learn to hold their heads and hands and move their facial features so as to be recognizably male or female by their position, movement, and expression.

In her review of studies of nonverbal communication, LaFrance (1981) noted that the gist of Birdwhistell's position is that there are many sex cues that are neither anatomical nor physiological but presentational. Acquired cues such as arm-body distances or eye opening and closing for men and women serve the purpose of marking the sex of the person and the social expectations for that sex. These postural and movement cues can be interpreted within the context of other personal-identification signals, as well as within the structure of the situation in which they occur. Gender cues, according to this view, carry social information and serve to regulate much social interaction.

But LaFrance points out that there has been little attempt to follow up on Birdwhistell's insights into the meaning of these differences. The research on the existence of gender differences in gesture and speech shows few differences in some areas of interaction and moderate or strong differences in others. For example, women have been found to show more facial displays of emotion (Buck et al., 1974; Cherulnik, 1979) and to spend more of the interactional time smiling and gazing at a partner than do men (Frances, 1979), whereas males have been found to take more personal space (Baxter, 1970). But differences in linguistic behavior are mixed, as we shall see.

In her widely acclaimed work on "the politics of touch," Nancy Henley (1973, 1977) suggested that men initiate touch with women more than women do with men. She attributed the pattern to the male's greater power and control, a theme that has run consistently through feminist scholarship on gender behavior. A decade later, however, Stier and Hall's empirical and theoretical review (1984) on studies of gender differences in touch found that men did *not* initiate touching more than women. They pointed out that nevertheless touching may have different meanings for women than for men and suggested that even if male-female touch asymmetry is not pervasive and is not entirely due to power differences, as Henley suggested, it is important and interesting that men are *thought* to initiate touch privileges with women. This popular perception may make women more aware of being touched than men are and more likely to define touching as men's attempt to dominate them.

Goffman's early work (1967) on nonverbal communication between superiors and subordinates was important to some researchers in creating a model for interpreting differences between men's gestures toward women and women's toward men. His later work (1976) assessed general cultural attitudes as reflected in advertisements. Goffman collected scores of pictures showing how women's subordination was evidenced by their positions in photographs—sitting or standing below men, encircled by men, or otherwise depicted according to stereotypes, particularly in sexually suggestive poses. Scholars have tried to assess whether the differences in media presentations exist in everyday life. The answer is that some do and some do not.

However gender differences in nonverbal communication may vary, they certainly do exist, and a variety of mechanisms ensures their survival or creates new distinctions. Birdwhistell suggested that gender display increases in frequency and intensity as children grow up and decreases as people age beyond the early adult years. There is, however, no research evidence either to support this or to contradict it.

An important caution must be exercised in evaluating the research on communication patterns. Almost all the studies of sex differences have been based on the behavior of college students, and largely in experimental settings. Of course, in everyday life ordinary people also observe differences, some verifiable by systematic study and some not.

LaFrance (1981) posits three concurrent factors that contribute to differences and to the perception of them. First, following Birdwhistell, she suggests that different styles of behavior may be accentuated to be compatible with the separate functions carried out by men and women in a given society. Second, observed variability between men and women may be due to their segregation in different environments or cultures. For example, general cultural norms in etiquette, some institutionalized, might require women to speak less than men (and listen attentively to them) in some social situations; they will in fact then tend to speak less in these situations. But speaking patterns vary according to the situation and the definition of the situation. In one study (Klein and Willerman, 1979), when women were told they would be assessed on their leadership ability in a discussion group, they spoke up as much as men did. Similarly, displays of "femininity" seem to be context-specific, and some studies confirm commonsense observations. For example, in one study women altered their behavior in the direction of greater sex-stereotypic presentation when told that they would meet attractive male partners who preferred women with those traits (Zanna and Pack, 1975). Other work shows that people are aware of what others expect from them regarding appropriate sex-role behavior and behave accordingly (Deutch and Gilbert, 1976).

Individual differences in self-concept constitute the third factor that contributes to variations in sex display. LaFrance (1981) suggests that some individuals, believing that they are "feminine" or "masculine" (or a combination of both) to a given degree, sex-type themselves and act according to these self-designations. Not surprisingly, studies have found that more traditional men tend to behave less expressively than those who are less traditional in outlook (Ickes and Barnes, 1977). Other studies have shown that androgynous females and males (those who are not wedded to traditional sex-role behaviors) are more nonconforming and exhibit behavior that is the same as that exhibited by the other sex more often than do their sex-typed counterparts (Bem, 1975). As with other evaluations of sex-role identification, it is important to note that people use a variety of gestures and nonverbal behaviors, some of which may be consistent, and others inconsistent, with sex-role stereotyping. For example, a woman may smile a great deal (a "female pattern") but also interrupt (a "male pattern"); a male may hug and demonstrate warmth but also domineer in a discussion.

Research on nonverbal communication must be approached cautiously. LaFrance points out that some studies reify masculinity and femininity into stable, individual traits. She observes that current research has placed us "in a better position from which to view masculine and feminine display as operating in the service of impression management and social maintenance" (1981: 148) and that external and social aspects of structures define gestures associated with gender.

Linguistics

Research on sex differences in language uncovers a conundrum similar to that revealed by research on nonverbal communication. Through language, humans have the capability to set boundaries on phenomena occurring in an unbounded state, to define and classify people and things. Thus humans have the capability to arbitrarily create and shape environments through language.[4] No other animal has this capability, and this is one of the most important characteristics setting humans apart from other species.

Sociolinguists have shown that communication systems are heterogeneous and multilayered. Thus, factors such as social class, religion, ethnicity, age, occupation, and sex all affect speech behavior, as do the specific situation, the topic of conversation, and the roles of the individuals involved. It has been shown, too, that speakers exhibit several repertoires of language in differing settings. Thus, it has been argued, with reliance

4. The Sapir-Whorf hypothesis (see Whorf and Sapir, [1927–41] 1956), states that language itself creates a framework for conceptualization. This analysis recognizes that language may sway people's perspectives and attitudes and that different languages have caused people to think differently. Although few modern sociologists fully accept that people's view of reality is entirely constructed by the language they speak, most agree that there are differences in the way languages represent experiences and that these differences influence how people perceive the world and therefore how they behave.

upon many cross-cultural examples, that there are separate female and
male "languages" (sometimes referred to as dialects) and that the various
features associated with male or female speech in America constitute two
different styles or varieties of English. Kramer (1974) discusses evidence
for there being "systems of co-occurring, sex-linked, linguistic signals in
the United States." For example, she notes that some scholars see the
following sex distinctions in language:

1. Women's speech is more polite, "correct," and "proper" than men's
   speech (Lakoff, 1973).
2. Women's speech is seen as "weaker and less effective than the speech
   of men"; the female style is supposed to be "emotional, vague, euphe-
   mistic, sweetly proper, mindless, endless, high-pitched and silly" (Lakoff, 1973).
3. Women's speech is more emotionally expressive than men's (Wood,
   1966; Barron, 1971).

Kramer claims that some of these perceptions are stereotypical and some
can be confirmed by further analysis. In a review of studies on language,
Kramer, Thorne, and Henley (1978) asserted that many studies have been
rooted in the traditional academic linguistic disciplines, pursuing possible
sex differences in phonology, pitch and intonation, lexicon, and syntax.
The best-documented sex differences among all these possibilities have
been found at the level of phonology (sound changes in language). Female
speakers tend to use a wider range of pitches and more variable intonation
than men (McConnell-Ginet, 1978), and men have been found to speak
louder and with less fluency. No consistent sex differences have been
found in extent of vocabulary or choice of adjectives and adverbs (Thorne
et al., 1983).

Where there are variants in lexicon and syntax, women—compared with
men of the same social class, age, and level of education—more often
choose the more "correct" (that is, grammatical) or prestigious way of
talking. Robin Lakoff (1973), whose work on women's and men's differential use of language has elicited a great deal of attention, suggests that
women are more likely than men to use "tag" questions that convey uncertainty ("George went, *didn't he?*") and intensifiers ("so," "such")
and that they use speech patterns marked by uncertainty, triviality, and
lack of clarity and expressive force. She notes that women also tend to
use "empty" adjectives ("adorable," "divine"), questionlike intonation
patterns, and compound request forms. She asserted that men's language
is typically direct and to the point, whereas women's is centered on inter-

personal exploration. Lakoff has suggested that these patterns are reflections of the marginality and powerlessness of women, their derivative and dependent social roles, and their submerged personal identity.

Lakoff's findings have been criticized by Thorne (1976) and by Kramer, Thorne, and Henley (1978) for being based on anecdotal evidence and for focusing on the person rather than the interactional situation. Since her work was published, tests of her findings have yielded both positive and negative results, which, as these critics claim, result from overgeneralizing from speculative observations and limited studies and from the interviewer's bias in interpreting what is being said.

In the field of language and communication as in other disciplines, some researchers who have hypothesized that specific differences exist have not found them (Kramer, 1974; Hirschman, 1974), but others (such as Kramer et al., 1978) claim that research finding no differences is less often reported and circulated than the findings of studies that point to differences. It may be that researchers tend "to presume and over-report differences rather than similarities between the sexes because our culture is infused with stereotypes which polarize females and males" (Kramer et al., 1978: 640).

Indeed, it has been suggested that many stereotypes about personality traits and behavioral characteristics of men—that they are aggressive, loud, blunt—and of women—that they are emotional, talkative, gentle—may be related to beliefs that the sexes speak in different ways; these beliefs also tend to be reinforced by the popular media (Kramer et al., 1978). Empirical studies of *actual* speech have found relatively few expected sex differences, and in some instances findings have indicated a reverse of the stereotype. One such finding is that with some exceptions women are less talkative than men in mixed-sex groups (Duncan and Fiske, 1977; Soskin and John, 1963; Strodtbeck and Mann, 1956; and Hilpert et al., 1975). This finding has been variously interpreted. Strodtbeck and Mann (1956) suggest that men pro-act and women react to the contributions of others. They also point out that higher-ranking people participate more heavily in group discussion. Feminist scholars see this speaking style as one of the ways in which men control women.

Zimmerman and West's research (1975) indicated that there are definite patterned ways in which the power and dominance held by men in other contexts are exercised in their conversational interaction with women. Basing a study on the model provided by Sacks, Schegloff, and Jefferson (1974), they examined turn-taking and silences in mixed-sex conversations and concluded that men are more likely to interrupt women than the other way around. This pattern between males and females is seen as similar to that of adult-child interactions, in which the child has only restricted rights to speak and to be listened to. Thus they conclude: "at least in our transcripts, men deny equal status to women as conversational partners with respect to rights to the full utilization of their turns and support of the development of topics. Thus we speculate that just as male dominance is exhibited through male control of macro-institutions in society, it is also exhibited through control of at least a part of one micro-institution." (1975: 125).

Kramer, Thorne, and Henley (1978) suggest that the strength and persistence of gender stereotypes call into question the evaluation of speech in the research setting.[5] Similar speech by males and females has been shown to be perceived differentially. For example, in one study an infant's cry was interpreted as angry when subjects were told it was a boy and as fearful when they were told it was a girl (Condry and Condry, 1976).

A study of politeness in language use (Brouwer, 1982) showed no difference between women and men observed buying tickets at an Amsterdam railway station. The researchers hypothesized that the women would be more insecure, more hesitant, and more polite than men. It was found, however, that men and women did not differ; both men and women were more polite when the ticket seller was a man than when the seller was a woman. Studies of forms of address (Ervin-Tripp, 1971) have shown that forms implying respect are directed more often to men than to women. Other sex differences in speech reflect differentials in power; for example, when men are in subordinate positions they tend to use linguistic forms from the "female register" (Crosby and Nyquist, 1977).

In studies of sex differences in speech as in other spheres, findings are often generalized far beyond the population studied. Thus, slight differences in speech have led some to assume that women have their own language. This focus on gender may, as critics observe, deemphasize the effect on language of other factors such as social setting, social class, geographical locale, age, race, and ethnicity.

Sex differences in language may also be explained by the relationship between the speakers and their power positions. For example, a cluster of findings about who interrupts whom in conversations suggests that differ-

5. An anecdote from my experience illustrates this finding. In a research group meeting in which the participants were two women and three men, there was joking commentary on the fact that the women spoke "a lot." Because the session was recorded and later transcribed it was possible to tally the number of words spoken by the men and women. It turned out that the "talkative" women spoke only about a third as much as the men. Yet they had agreed with the men during the joking that they were more verbally active.

ences of power and status are more salient than those of gender alone. Using Fishman's study (1975) of male-female couples' communication patterns in ongoing conversation as a model, Kollock, Blumstein, and Schwartz (1985) found that differences such as women's use of tag questions and males' interruption patterns did not hold for couples when the traditional power relations were reversed. The person with less power in the relationship worked harder to keep the conversation going, and this was not always the woman.

The Context of Language

Sex distinctions in language use and sexism in language structure can be seen as interrelated, although they are sometimes regarded as two separate subjects. Several scholars have shown the importance of language in establishing, reflecting, and maintaining an asymmetrical relationship between women and men. Sexist language has been linked by various authors to sexist behavior (Blaubergs, 1978; Bodine, 1975; Briere and Lanktree, 1983; Association for Women in Psychology, 1975).

In theoretical work analyzing the content of words in the English language, Nilsen (1972, 1973, as discussed in Thorne and Henley, 1975) argues that because men are more highly regarded than women in the culture, male words are "associated with the universal, the general, the subsuming" (including the generic *he,* which will be discussed later); "the female is more often excluded or is the 'special case.' Words associated with males more often have positive connotations—they convey notions of power, prestige and leadership. In contrast, female words are more often negative—conveying weakness, inferiority, immaturity, a sense of the trivial."

Schultz (1975) and Lakoff (1973) found, too, that terms applied to women are narrower in reference than those applied to men, and that women are more likely to assume derogatory sexual connotations that overshadow the other meanings of words. This process of derogation and overgeneralization is related to stereotyping and has the same characteristics as racial and ethnic slurs, implying that women are viewed as proper subjects for ridicule. Language tends to elevate men and deprecate women; for example, seemingly parallel terms for male and female (mister/mistress, bachelor/spinster) have divergent connotations, in most cases derogatory to women.

Part of the repertoire of the powerful is the power to name. This goes

beyond the literal naming of married women with their husbands' sur-
names—a practice backed by law in many states in the United States until
recently—to the labeling and classifying of women and men. Indications
of status are often signaled in exchanges of greeting or in forms of address. It is common knowledge that there is an asymmetrical exchange
between people of different status. Often, for example, the boss is addressed as Mr. or Mrs. (most typically, of course, Mr.), whereas the sec-
retary is addressed by his or her first name. As Henley (1973–74) suggests, there is a general pattern by which "personal information flows
opposite to the flow of authority"; that is, subordinates generally disclose
more personal information than do those over them, information that may
be used for purposes of control. Lakoff (1973) found a tendency for persons to use first names in addressing women sooner than with men, implying that women are more approachable, less threatening than men. Use of
the generic *he* and of terms like *mankind* and *chairman* is seen by a number of social scientists and humanists as well as feminist movement activists as an example of the ways in which women are subsumed under men.
They point out that this is not a mere convention nor a concession to
graceful language as some people have believed (Martyna, 1980). Men
and women do not respond equally to the generic *he*. Studies have shown
that people tend to perceive *he* and the generic *man* as specifically male.[6]
These sorts of gender marking in language influence people's behavior.

Bem and Bem (1973) showed in two studies that sex-biased wording of
"help wanted" newspaper ads decreased both male and female interest in
opposite-sex jobs. The discriminatory consequences of sex-labeling of jobs
are demonstrable and led to the U.S. Equal Economic Opportunities Commission (EEOC) rulings that forced newspapers to discontinue employment
advertising under separate male and female headings. A study by Norma
Shepelak (1978, as cited in Kramer et al., 1978) showed that women had
higher levels of aspiration for tasks labeled female than for those labeled
male and performed them better, that job descriptions marked with masculine or feminine cues were perceived by students from third grade through
college as being limited to the sex specified, and that high school students
responded preferentially to jobs cued to their own sex.

According to Martyna (1980), use of the generic *he* often conveys incorrect information, and Huber (1976) has demonstrated that using *he* and

---

6. Martyna (1980) cites the example of a member of the California State Assembly who
opposed a move to replace *assemblyman* with *assembly member*. "That takes the masculinity out
of it!" he declared (article in the *Los Angeles Times*, January 14, 1977, entitled "Assembly
Moves to De-sex Its Titles").

man in sociology texts creates the wrong impression. One of her illustrations is drawn from a text: "The more education an individual attains, the better his occupation is likely to be, and the more money he is likely to earn." The statement cannot be held to accurately describe the benefits to women of more education. Further, cultural ideology is reflected through and by language-user portrayal. Kramer (1974) has shown that the stereotypes of male and female speech portrayed in cartoons, used in people's daily speech, and recorded in etiquette books assume more sexual differentiation than actually exists. Graham (1975) and Nilsen (1972) show how women are defined in relation to men through the usage of terminology such as *Miss* and *Mrs.* Men who understand vocabulary deemed "female" (that of sewing, cooking, and so on) are often thought of as "experts," according to Conklin (1974), because it is more often expected that experts will be men, regardless of the subject. Thus, if a male is familiar with the jargon of cooking, he will be thought of as a chef more often than as a cook.

The genre of speech has also been found to be important in the analysis of status situations. For example, Coser's study (1960) of staff meetings in a mental hospital found that people in positions of higher rank more often took the initiative to use humor and that the target of a witticism was never higher in authority than the initiator. Coser found that superior status was signaled by making witticisms and inferior status by laughing; but women, even those of high occupational status, more often took the subordinate role. Legman (1968) observed that women are more often than not the butt of humor in dirty jokes, thus reinforcing the notion that "proper" women do not participate in such humor.

Some feminist scholars claim that it is men who create language because they have greater access to the public; although women also may create words and infuse them with meaning, fewer have been newspaper editors, authors, or public speakers (although this is changing). Thus the terms people know and can use to think about their reality are mainly male creations. For example, it is argued that obscene language is used to trivialize women and reduce description of them to their "most mechanical dimension" (Lawrence, 1974). The extensive labeling of women as fruit or animals (for example, "chick," "bird," "peach,") and as mindless or like children ("baby") has no parallels for men (Thorne et al., 1983).

With regard to men's and women's styles of writing or use of words in their written work, findings of no differences have been reported by one analyst (Kramer, 1974), but another (Hiatt, 1977) reports that women writers exhibit some differences in their writing styles when compared with male writers. She concludes that "the way women write reflects a more varied perception of the world than that held by men and their style embraces more varied syntactic structures than that of men. Their style is . . . less fixated and narrow than that of men in terms of perception, fictional subject matter, and sentence structure. . . . They are more moderate, consistent, and even-handed" (pp. 135–36).

Although considerable attention has been devoted to the gender content of language, the use of gender in contexts themselves infused with preconceived ideas about women's worth reinforces such ideas. The persistence of gender stereotypes has led to research specifically on perceptions and evaluations of speech. When women and men use the same words, the same pronunciation, and the same intonation patterns in the same situations, their speech nevertheless may be interpreted differently. Listeners' understandings of what women say and what men say depend in part on the listeners' assumptions about what women and men actually do and should say. Thus, women's speech is heard as different from men's even though they may be saying the same things in the same way.

This kind of research has resulted in social-policy responses in a number of domains. Many professional associations have established guidelines for nonsexist language in their journals. Many publishers now prescribe a nonsexist format in their style manuals for authors (for example, Harper & Row, 1976; Holt, Rinehart and Winston, 1976; Prentice-Hall, 1975) and restrict use of the generic *he*. Many if not most academic and popular writers have now altered their use of pronouns (Miller and Swift, 1972).

The women's movement is probably responsible for the coinage of terms like *sexism* and *Ms.* as a form of address. *Ms.* was coined to identify a female subject without establishing her marital status, as the word *Mr.* does not distinguish marital status for men. Many periodicals now commonly use the title *Ms.* before a woman's name instead of *Miss* or *Mrs.* Long a hold-out, the *New York Times* finally changed its style in 1986. The paper uses *Ms.* for women except where they clearly express a preference for *Miss* or *Mrs.*

There have been other changes in forms of address as more and more women have taken on roles formerly held only by men. The U.S. Supreme Court, for example, changed the form of address from *Mr. Justice* to *Justice* when Sandra Day O'Connor was appointed to the Court, and many organizations have changed the title *chairman* to *chair* or *chairperson.* "People Working" signs have replaced "Men Working" signs in many areas.

Resistance to change remains alive in the differential use of such terms, however. Some people believe that "linguistic sexism" is imaginary, superficial, or trivial and that changes in language forms will result or have resulted in ungainly, inelegant, and uneducated use of language. Efforts at linguistic change are not new, however, and neither is their characterization as inelegant. In 1924 the linguist Otto Jespersen referred to the use of *he or she* instead of the generic *he* as cumbersome and ungainly.

Some resistance may have more to do with general resistance to change in language among those who believe that change ought not be forced nor addressed to feminist concerns about sexism. Critics point out, however, that the switch from *Negro* to *black,* following the preference of black leaders, occurred in a relatively short span of time. Experiments with entirely new neuter terms have been largely unsuccessful, although they have been actually used in experimental communities and in some publications devoted to radical causes and views (C.Miller and Swift, 1975). Alternative forms have also been used in fiction, especially in science fiction. But as Kramer, Thorne, and Henley (1978) point out, they are awkward to the eye and ear and do not have the force of widespread opinion or usage behind them.

Research has pointed out the strategic uses of language. As Kramerae (1981) suggests, when women or men speak, they often do so with an intention to do specific things such as create rapport or assert or resist control, and given the different positions of the sexes in society, speech strategies may vary by sex. The sexes' relative power is reflected in their choice of speech strategies, including the ways in which men exercise power over women, as mentioned earlier, by withholding self-disclosure and response to the topics women raise (Fishman, 1975) and interrupting women more often than women interrupt men (Zimmerman and West, 1975). Women's speech strategies—for example, their "interaction work" (Fishman, 1975) and styles of politeness (Brown and Levinson, 1978; Lakoff, 1975)—may be seen as ways of coping with greater male power. Research on women's and men's use of speech genres such as gossip, joking, chatting, and insults—especially those relating to sexual divisions of labor—offers information about how these are used to create distance or intimacy, to define group values, and to control others or subvert control by others.

According to McConnell-Ginet (1978), traditional linguistics studies have left unanswered many interesting questions about the function of language in people's lives. She objects to linguists' usual practice of abstracting content from social context and focusing on a mythic "ideal" speaker in isolation from other human beings. She points out that they have expanded the horizons of linguistics partly as a result of social and political pressures—originating in the civil rights movement of the 1960s and continuing in the women's movement—to understand how language is used to support ongoing prestige and status systems.

Research on verbal and nonverbal forms of communication rarely refers to the social-control mechanisms that enforce gender distinctions. Anthropologists have paid some attention to the various societies' customs regarding dress and forms of address, but no integrated research literature specifies the punishments for violation of these norms or the enforcements of conformity. Of course, some of the mechanisms that ensure conformity to communication norms are obvious to any man or woman who has served in the armed forces and has had to learn proper address and demeanor. Punishments for violation in the military range from rebuke to incarceration. Serious punishment for violation, less codified but no less severe both verbally and physically, has also been typical in schools and between masters and servants, husbands and wives, and parents and children. Americans, who prize freedom of speech in the West and condemn its control in totalitarian countries, are relatively unaware of the curbs that exist in their everyday lives; violations can exact a high cost. In business, punishment for inappropriate demeanor can result in the loss of a job[7] or failure to be promoted. Deference and demeanor, as Goffman (1967) and Garfinkel (1956) have both observed, are played out in ceremonies and in everyday life; similarly, gender distinctions, often synonymous with deference and authority specification, are also subject to social controls.

Certainly many customs are devoted to reinforcing gender distinctions and creating different behavior by the sexes. The custom of binding women's feet in old China meant they were forced to walk in a mincing manner, distinct from the typical stride of men. Binding the feet broke the bones, making it virtually impossible to walk normally. Of course, women who had their feet bound were nearly all upper class; peasant women who needed to walk in order to work in the fields escaped the practice. Fashion codes through the ages have mandated the use of corsets and bustles, long or short skirts, and veils and draped robes; skirts and pants were mandated for women and men depending on whether they were to do strenuous work

7. A sex discrimination case involving television news anchorwoman Chris Craft was brought to the courts. Craft was fired because the officials at her station claimed she was not deferential enough for a woman, did not wear appropriate makeup, and was also 'too old" and "unattractive." This case was rare only in that it reached the courts (personally, I thought she was quite attractive). Craft won her suit but the decision was reversed on appeal (Williams, 1984; Kerr, 1983, 1984a, 1984b).

or be served by others, and on whether the rulers of society were invested in maintaining distinctions between men and women for ideological, religious, or business purposes.[8] Certainly, the more inequality exists between the sexes, the more emphasis there is on gender-specific dress and demeanor, with punishment for violation that can extend to shunning, stoning, rape, or prison.

In my research on women in male-dominated occupations and professions (Epstein, 1970a, 1981b), I found that gender distinctions differentially controlled women's use of certain kinds of language—for example, foul language, dirty (sexual) jokes, and threatening talk. Such language, regarded as acceptable when used by men in certain contexts and social groups but as objectionable when used by women in mixed company, sometimes becomes an exclusionary mechanism preventing women from informal exchanges with men and embarrassing them, so that they withdraw from professional camaraderie. Lorber (1984) found this to be true for women physicians, noting how some male professors interspersed slides on medical subjects with nude pin-ups in lectures to medical students. Enarson (1984) reported that male forest rangers sometimes urinated in front of women to make them uncomfortable as U.S. Park Service workers; and Walshok (1981) showed how women blue-collar workers faced harassment for stepping out of women's place into men's roles. Women attorneys, who sometimes were ordered to smile by judges, also reported how they had to assess what kind of demeanor to exhibit in the courtroom and at the conference table in order to avoid disapproval from court officers, clients, and other attorneys. They observed that it often was difficult to convey authority and still conform to the norms of "feminine" conduct. Women lawyers whose manner was professional and direct were often faced with disapproval and were perceived and criticized as "stiff"; such behavior was cited sometimes as justification for refusal to admit women to partnership. Having proved themselves professionally competent, they found themselves excluded by judgments that they were interpersonally incompetent.

In a 1971 study of women holding top jobs in Britain, Fogarty, Rapaport, and Rapaport found that there were limits to how high women could expect to rise in the hierarchies of their occupations. No "right" demeanor could be achieved; they were criticized by superiors either for being "nice mice" or for being "dragons" who had trespassed on spheres regarded as inappropriate for women. No studies have documented wom-

8. Roland Barthes (1983) has devoted critical attention to the symbolic meaning of fashion. See also Hollander (1978) and Lurie (1981).

en's verbal and nonverbal styles in female domains, but the popular wisdom is that women may exhibit authoritative demeanor toward their children and toward other women but not toward adult men; depending on the context of social class, women are expected to conform to sex-role-prescribed behavior. Hence has come the term *ladylike,* meaning quiet, softspoken, and demure, with loud talk and boisterous behavior permitted only to lower-class women, and the term *fishwife* or other such epithets to express disapproval of women who exhibit strength in language and behavior—clearly a problem for women in political campaigns.[9]

It has been observed that women's range of permissible "female" behavior is usually narrower than men's range of "masculine" behavior. This generally follows from men's access to a wider range of jobs and of social roles in general (Epstein, 1970a, 1970b, 1984a, 1985). Yet, handbooks—some humorous, others more serious—inform men what they ought and ought not to do to be "real men" (not eat quiche, as a recent bestseller advised [Fierstein, 1982]).

Analyses of research on modes of communication, like research on other behavioral and attitudinal differences between the sexes, indicate that what "everyone knows" to be true may turn out not to be true at all. Differences tend to be superficial, and they are often linked to power differentials—associated with female and male status but not necessarily paired with them—and they are situation-specific. But beyond these findings, the research shows that many widely assumed differences turn out to be mere stereotypes; that there are more similarities in men's and women's behavior than is commonly believed. Whether humans need to create differences between the sexes actively or symbolically (as Birdwhistell hypothesized) or whether the creation and maintenance of distinctions are a self-conscious activity of the powerful whose interests are served by them or whether differences once created by intent or accident become perpetuated through a process of institutionalization, it seems clear that most gender differences are socially created and therefore may be socially altered.

9. The press made much of the fact that Geraldine Ferraro had difficulty creating a public image in her debate with Vice President Bush that would be authoritative but not too "masculine." She, on the other hand, criticized Bush for being patronizing.

CHAPTER 11

Conclusion

This is a book of conclusions, and so I end it by emphasizing some of the general perspectives with which I began, as well as presenting a theoretical view about why gender distinctions remain so intransigent in societies the world over.

As we have seen, no aspect of social life—whether the gathering of crops, the ritual of religion, the formal dinner party, or the organization of government—is free from the dichotomous thinking that casts the world in categories of "male" and "female." All societies, from the most primitive to the most modern, use sex as a convenient and preferred attribute to differentiate members of the human race, dividing work and the pleasures of social life into men's and women's roles. Invariably, this has invited invidious comparisons.

The notion that these basic differences—that is to say, innate qualities or those that arise out of women's exclusive capacity to bear children or men's relatively greater physical strength—inevitably determine social position has been challenged through the ages. But not until the current era has this challenge caught the imagination of a considerable sector of the public and its leadership. A revolution in thinking, created by development of the social sciences and a worldwide shift toward an ideology of equality, has made it possible for the first time in history to seriously question categorical thinking about women and men.

The modern challenge to the notion that basic and immutable differences between men and women determine their values and behavior is also part of the agenda of the women's movement. Feminist scholars have provided much of the new scholarship on this matter, but there is now also a considerable amount of work on it by mainstream social scientists. The findings of this new scholarship are surprising to many since they contradict traditional beliefs that persist in the culture and refute much of the

older ''social-scientific'' findings based on biased methodology and interpretation.

But by no means have the debates been resolved, and many scholars
and policymakers still turn their backs on the evidence. The dichotomous
thinking that fosters superstition and dogma still constitutes a frame of
reference that orders most people's views, including those of great scientific minds. Dichotomous thinking is pervasive in the daily life of all of
us, prescribing our clothing, occupations, and responsibilities. ''Is it a boy
or a girl?'' remains the first question asked of (and by) the parents of a
newborn, setting the stage for role assignments, orientation for life, and
exposure to controls that will order the child's activities. Preference is still
confused with inevitability. Justification accompanies self-interest and group
interest.

Dichotomous thinking is not limited to those whose mind-sets make
them enemies of justice and equality, however. Educated and liberal friends
also relax into the easy, efficient organization that dichotomous thinking
provides. Today, as we have seen, scholars who are feminists join with
scholars who are traditionalists in declaring that basic differences between
the sexes guide their responses to the world, that men and women live in
two cultures, two domains, that they are, in effect, two species. In the
past, most of those who held women to be different judged them to be
inferior. Today some theorists maintain they are different and superior.
Others hold to a separate-but-equal notion, stressing the complementary
quality of many conceptual differences.

We have explored how the two-culture approach perpetuates gender
inequality. Dichotomous distinctions rarely avoid creating ranked comparisons, and, in the case of female-male, whatever characteristics are
ascribed to each gender, those associated with men rank higher. How does
this happen? We shall never know. When classification occurs in human
society some win out because they are more intelligent; some because they
are bullies; and many because they got there first and set up the rules.
Small advantages make winners in sports and art, and also in society; and
winners are in a better position to hold on to their advantage than those
who would usurp it.

Dichotomous categories are especially effective as an ideological mechanism to preserve advantage. Dichotomous systems of thought serve the
existing power structures and organization of society by reinforcing the
notion of the ''we'' and the ''not-we,'' the deserving and the undeserving.
Gatekeepers of ideas and of resources have always affixed values to distinctions and, in their absence, create inequalities conceptually. Having

documented the process throughout this study, a question remains. It is not surprising that men who hold power in the various institutions—government, education, industry, or the family—believe that the sexes have basically different capacities, should do certain kinds of work and not others, and should have different rights and rewards. This is the "agenda-setting" factor in power, as Steven Lukes has put it. But as women have been largely convinced of their "place," so have men convinced themselves. The privileged do not seem to require much persuasion to be convinced that their gifts are inevitable or deserved.

But how do we account for the fact that so many women subscribe to their comparatively lower position and accept the notion that they are not only "other" and different, but lesser? That they should take on the devalued work of society? I suspect that it is human, no matter what one's station in life, to seek a rationale for it. Theology, tradition, and folk wisdom all provide rationales. Arguments of the common culture persuade women to accept and accommodate to their position. But also, as we have seen, enforcement accompanies persuasion. For those who have a choice, women also grasp or are lured by secondary gains that alternately put them on moral pedestals or lower their levels of enterprise, both of which remove them from the risks as well as the rewards of competition in the world of affairs in which men labor. Most women enjoy the prospect or dream of being protected, unaware of or insecure about their own ability to protect themselves and other dependents.

Without de jure power in most societies, women seek to maximize their power in those domains in which they find opportunities to exert control. Typically, these are the spheres relinquished by men. But the benefits of such strategies are limited. Moving into occupations that men disdain or that they are leaving or have deserted, women are caught in the workplace equivalent of an endless household routine. On the whole, "woman's work" is repetitious and poorly valued and rejected by men for good reason when they are able to assign it to others. The skills attached to women's work are rarely transferable or are regarded as so. Much of their work out of the marketplace—mothering, performing household chores and farm work, for example—is not characterized by discrete boundaries, leaving little time for activities that might serve them politically. Within any social class, women do more work of lower status than men. Women's work outside the home is more routine and more supervised than is men's, further reducing their opportunities to accumulate power. By their labor, they generate (as some neo-Marxists put it) less surplus value which may be traded or used as leverage for power. It is not women's desires and preferences but their location in the market that structures their opportunities and rewards.

Unless they are especially privileged, women as a group have more work to do than men, moving between paid and unpaid labor in the workplace and home, caring for children, or producing food and clothing. Yet even women who work at relatively prestigious jobs have primary and sometimes absolute responsibilities for the household. They work two shifts, as sociologist Arlie Hochschild has said. Women's labor in the home, we now realize, suffers from not being *called* work; it is not tallied and accumulated as human capital which then becomes marketable as a resource. Women who work exclusively in the home are not, indeed, considered to be working at all. And although their activities (such as education of children, preparation of food, and house care and management in Western societies) are, paradoxically, less supervised and potentially offer opportunities for more creative activities than those afforded women in the official labor force, achievements in the home are rarely recognized and are outside the reward system of society.

Keeping women working hard at their routine sex-typed jobs prevents them from amassing power. Yet women's work is essential—what would societies do without their participation in reproduction and economic production? The problem may extend beyond the specific situation of women. No society rewards or honors the people assigned to do its most essential work—the mundane labor that keeps it going on a day-to-day basis, providing food and shelter, cleansing the wastes, burying the dead. It gives them *some* reward (so they will keep at their tasks) and, as this book has detailed, it may coerce them to continue. But it is the high-flyers who do the dramatic things that get the honors and the privileges and the time to engage in politics, to make decisions, to set the rules, at all levels. Women, like the poor of the earth, have been kept busy and uninformed, their contacts and networks limited. Behind barriers, closed doors, in secret meetings, behind masks, men have parlayed insider information to create institutions that disproportionately generate for them windfall profits of opportunity and advantage. As we know today insiders are not necessarily smarter than their colleagues, but having information others do not gives them competence that others respect as long as its source remains shrouded in mystery.

The symbolic and actual segregation of women looms large as mechanisms to reduce women's visibility, supporting the myth that they do not perform adequately in spheres normally associated with men. Women are not generally perceived as working seriously in the economically produc-

tive marketplace. Those who do acknowledge women's labor force participation view their work (disproportionately in the service sector) as less
productive than that of male workers and do not believe they work very
hard. Women's personality traits, learning capacities, wish and ability to
control, their needs to compete and excel—all are seen as less vigorous
than those of men.

The maintenance of separate spheres at work or in the home perpetuates
myths of difference in another way. It leads women themselves to believe
that they are worth less than men because they are less committed to work
and exert less effort at it. Laboratory research indicates that on average
women pay themselves less than men performing the same tasks, women
undervalue their efforts relative to men's, and women have lower standards of personal entitlements.[1] In fact, women may work harder than
men in the workplace as well as at home. Working in segregated spheres
keeps women from knowing that the work men do is not harder or more
difficult and that men as a class are not smarter, more courageous, less
emotional, or, at many times in the life cycle, even physically stronger
than women. Exclusive clubs, special schools, and segregated workplaces
not only function to keep women out of interesting and important areas of
activity; they also prevent women from seeing that what men do in these
places is nothing women cannot do and might prefer to do.[2] Indeed, the
male colleagues of women lawyers, doctors, prime ministers, and techni-
cians have been repeatedly surprised to find women performing credibly.

In the past, men have made policies permitting women limited access
to knowledge about male spheres as long as the women did not aspire to
male prerogatives within them; secretaries and nurses, for instance, did
not expect to become executives or physicians. Such women were not
only instructed to stand by (and behind) the men as helpmates but were
subject to a reward system that tied their own social rank or employment
to their participation in the conspiracy. Women whose social standing is
dependent upon the reflected glory of their men (''my son, the doctor'')
can also be counted on to assist in mystifying their occupational roles,
making it seem that their accomplishments are unique and unattainable by
others.

Women's cynicism today about these sycophantic activities indicates

1. See Bielby and Bielby (1988) for a review and evaluation of studies about this phenomenon.

2. Separate schools and public institutions for men also have been instruments for communi-
cating an ethos of ''maleness.'' Because, as Michael Kimmel has pointed out, concepts of masculine and feminine are relational, separate spheres permitted polarization of traits associated
with these concepts. As far back as the turn of the century, ''pro-male'' programs were developed
to combat a perceived feminization of American culture (Douglas, 1977) ''through institutions
to train young men in a virile hardiness appropriate to their gender'' (Kimmel, 1986).

that the agenda has been more than latent. There has always been a theme in women's folklore, at least in the Western world, that women know best what men need, that men are often childlike and incompetent, that their egos need bolstering because they are unsure of themselves and easily threatened at work, that they are vulnerable weak reeds depending on a woman's strength in matters of emotion, and that they cannot cope with children, the home, and other aspects of life in the female domain. This is expressed visibly through the media most egregiously in articles in women's magazines and in television comedies, and experientially in the jokes and conversation of women beyond the earshot of men. This cynicism occurs worldwide. I have heard it expressed by colleagues and journalists in the north of Europe, in the Mediterranean countries, in India, and right at home.

Women participate in the conspiracy; they protect men and help maintain the myths. For example, they argue that men do not exhibit feelings and will not cry. But men do cry and express emotion, usually in the presence of women who remain mute about it for fear of damaging the male self-image.[3] On the other hand, men also perpetuate myths about women. They are often cautious about reporting the strengths and abilities of their wives and secretaries; they accept at face value women who "play dumb" or are deferential. Accepting their mandate to "protect," they are reserved in asking women to share equally in providing income for the home; many willingly pay the full cost of dominance, assuming the burden of sole responsibility for economic support of the family and of isolation from their children.

Ambivalence hangs over all these cases. Women who "prop up" men and at the same time view them as superior also protect their own sphere (the home) from male control by arguing that they have special competence for their domain as men do for theirs—asserting that women manage the home better and are naturally suited to it. Women prevent men from becoming competent in the home, holding that men's personality traits are not suitable for women's roles and that men's biological makeup impedes their acquisition of the required attributes such as nurturance or home management. Men also conspire to remain incompetent, as women suspect, because such skills are poorly rewarded. But then, too, women maintain incompetence for work they regard as unpleasant or unsuitable, such as work that makes them dirty.

Yet changes in ideology have persuaded some men that their priorities

3. But there are exceptions, and norms are changing. A recent example was the behavior of the Boston Red Sox baseball team after they lost the World Series to the New York Mets. They shed tears in the dugout, observed by tens of millions of television viewers.

are misplaced and they have neglected important experiences by distancing themselves from activities such as child care. Others have had little choice but to fill in at some of the tasks relinquished by employed wives now committed to the demands of other roles. Men, however, still get maximum rewards for minimal activity in these areas and have little incentive to improve their performance or to work harder or longer at them than do women. And women, still unsure of their new gains, often hesitate to relinquish control of this sphere to men.

But women too have been exposed to ideological changes that make it acceptable to take on ''men's work'' and find it satisfying and materially rewarding. Because of social change, great numbers of women are working outside the home. In a few countries, almost as many women as men now go to work. Inevitably, this means that a sizable proportion of women will be less and less satisfied with secondary gains and limited power in segregrated spheres. Although women initially entered a narrow range of familiar traditional jobs, the next decade is going to see more of them emerge as CEOs, employers entrepreneurs, bankers, and politicians. Even so cautious a media voice as the London *Economist* predicts: ''Women have long found it easy to pick up work when economies boom. They are now doing so fast even in hard times. . . . In the next ten years . . . women [will] move into a wider variety of jobs where 'equal pay for equal work' will be an unquestioned truth'' (August 23, 1986). This has done much and will do more to transform the way men regard women and the way women regard themselves, even those least receptive to feminist ideology. As more and more women demonstrate competence in once-proscribed areas, reality will make it more difficult for both men and women to retain old and inaccurate conceptions.

Women will continue to meet resistance, however, and gatekeepers will continue to repackage old prejudices until the very end. Some historical analyses have pointed out that after women's challenge to traditional roles at the turn of the century, various cultural and organizational responses emphasized differences between men and women. Kimmel, for example, points to the ''remasculinization'' of Christ through texts such as Thomas Hughes's *The Manliness of Christ* (1880) and Carl Case's *The Masculine in Religion* (1906). In politics rhetoric called on ''real men'' not to approve women's suffrage by referring to those who supported it as ''miss-Nancys, 'man-milliners,' and political hermaphrodites'' (Trachtenberg, 1982: 163; cited in Kimmel, 1987). The organization of the Boy Scouts was seen as countering the forces of feminization and aimed at creating ''real *men* in every sense of the word'' (Anthony Baden-Powell, founder of the Boy Scouts in England, in Kimmel, 1986b).

Feminist and egalitarian challenges today similarly have met with a renewed emphasis on segregation of the sexes in the increasingly popular fundamentalist Christian churches, Orthodox Judaism, and Islam fundamentalism. The hypermacho film image of Rambo, the American fighter winning the battle for democracy, is a cultural theme attractive to a majority of Americans. Even among the more secular and rational Americans, women's demonstration of abilities equaling those of men in business, the professions, and skilled blue-collar work has often resulted in a backlash directed not at their technical abilities but at their interpersonal skills. Women lawyers, for example, as we saw earlier, find that male colleagues regard them as socially awkward, stiff, and inflexible (as opposed to the men's view of themselves as warm and relaxed). Women working in blue-collar jobs often face hazards put in their way by resistant men, such as assignment to broken-down equipment or poor schedules, but the courts are forcing employers to monitor such activities, and even the Supreme Court has held that sexual harassment at the workplace is clearly against the law.

Gender-linked preconceptions and prejudices cut both ways (Walshok, 1983; see also Esptein, 1981b). In a current study of employees in a giant corporation, I am finding that women operators regard men who work at the same jobs as unsuited to their "woman's work" and expect them to be transferred to better jobs faster than women. And the men complain that customers show surprise and anger at encountering a man when they expect a woman, sometimes taunting them as homosexual. These attitudes are changing, however, as colleagues and customers get used to desegregation at the job site.

Other changes in society also have meant that many women can no longer benefit from the secondary gains of gender inequality because they lack an appropriate man (husband, father, brother, son) to offer them the possibility of security, or "vicarious achievement" (to use Jean Lipman-Blumen's term, in Spence, 1983). Current research shows that women most likely to take on nontraditional blue-collar work are older women, those divorced, and black women with dependents; they all require primary rewards and are less subject to the guilt that women with employed spouses are made to feel about entering the male work world.

Yet many women still keep alive old beliefs and doubts about their competence. They deny their common cause with women as an underclass and cling to a definition, complimentary to men, of women as "other" and different. Some continue to claim the secondary benefits of femininity even while assuming roles regarded as belonging to the male sex. Some expression of this ambivalent response can be found in a 1983 *New York*

Times/CBS Poll, which showed that one-fourth of a sample of Americans, both men and women, felt that their lives had been improved by the women's movement. Responding to another question, however, two-thirds were not convinced that women had changed for the better, and many—even among those men and women who said their work lives had improved in the last fifteen years—felt that the movement had "led women astray."

One important theme of this book has been change. It has emphasized the capacity of human beings to be guided, manipulated, and coerced into assuming social roles, demonstrating behavior, and expressing thoughts that conform to socially accepted values. But the individual has the capacity for change and the ability to seize opportunities when they are available. People, after all, do have judgment and will. If it were not for these characteristics, we could not have the social changes that are expressed both by social movements and in the instances of deviance and creativity that mark human society. Yet, where social investment in continuity is strong, one sees fewer demonstrations of individual will and less appreciation in society of individual capacity. Since the investment in gender differentiation is high, we see about us much resistance to the notion of change in sex-associated social roles.

The mounting evidence cited and collected in this book, however, makes it increasingly difficult to obscure the overwhelming similarities between men and women. The studies gathered here bring to light the processes by which the powerful contrive to create, emphasize, and maintain gender differences. From the knowledge generated by such research we can expect the realities of men's and women's lives to emerge, superseding the stereotyped perceptions of the past. Although people manage reality and make imagined things real, scholars and activists are discovering a non-dichotomous reality that may one day put an end to the self-fulfilling prophecy of differences between men and women. This may be the time when we discover—to paraphrase a sociological grandfather—that "what [we thought] was solid, melts into air . . . and men [and women] at last are forced to face with sober senses the real conditions of their lives and their relations with their fellow men [and women]."[4]

---

4. Originally from Karl Marx, *Communist Manifesto*, trans. Samuel Moore (London, 1888).

References

Abbott, Edith. *Women in Industry* (New York: Arno Press, 1969).

Abel, Bruce. "The Firms—What Do They Want?" *Harvard Law Record* 37 (December 12, 1963): 1.

Aberle, David F., and Kaspar Naegele. "Middle-Class Fathers' Occupational Role and Attitudes toward Children." In Bell and Vogel, eds., *A Modern Introduction to the Family*, rev. ed. (New York: Free Press, 1968): 188–198.

Abzug, Bella, and Mimi Kelber. *Gender Gap, 1984: How Women Will Decide the Next Election* (Boston: Houghton Mifflin, 1984).

Acharya, Meena, and Lynn Bennett. *The Rural Women of Nepal: An Aggregate Analysis and Summary of Eight Village Studies*. vol. 2, pt. 9. (CEDA/Status on Women Project, 1981).

Acker, Joan. "Women and Social Stratification: A Case of Intellectual Sexism." *American Journal of Sociology* 78(4) (January 1973). Reprinted in Huber, ed., *Changing Women in a Changing Society* (Chicago: University of Chicago Press, 1973): 174–183.

———. "Women and Stratification: A Review of Recent Literature."*Contemporary Sociology* 9 (January 1980): 25–39.

Aldous, Joan. *Family Careers: Developmental Changes in Families* (New York: John Wiley, 1978).

Alexander, Richard D. *Darwinism and Human Affairs* (Seattle: University of Washington Press, 1979).

Anderson, John E. *The Young Child in the Home*. White House Conference on Child Health and Protection (New York: Appleton Century, 1936).

Anderson, Kristi. "Working Women and Political Participation, 1952–1972." *American Journal of Political Science* 19 (August 1975): 439–453.

Andrews, John B., and W. D. P. Bliss. "History of Women in Trade Unions." In *Report on Condition of Woman and Child Wage-Earners in the United States*, vol. 10 (Washington, D.C.: U.S. Government Printing Office, 1911). Reprinted as *History of Women in the Trade Unions* (New York: Arno Press, 1974).

Apfelbaum, Erika. "Relations of Domination and Movements for Liberation: An Analysis of Power between Groups." In W. Austin and S. Worchel, eds., *The Social Psychology of Intergroup Relations* (Monterey, Calif.: Brooks/Cole, 1978): 188–204.

Araji, S. K. "Husbands' and Wives' Attitude-Behavior Congruence on Family Roles." *Journal of Marriage and the Family* 39 (1977): 309–322.

Ardiner, Edwin. "Belief and the Problem of Women." In La Fontaine, ed., *Interpretation of Ritual* (London: Tavistock, 1972): 135–158.

Ardrey, Robert. *African Genesis: A Personal Investigation into the Animal Origins and Nature of Man* (New York: Atheneum, 1963).

———. *The Territorial Imperative: A Personal Inquiry into the Animal Origins of Property and Nations* (New York: Atheneum, 1966).

———. *The Hunting Hypothesis: A Personal Conclusion concerning the Evolutionary Nature of Man* (New York: Atheneum, 1976).

Ariès, Philippe. *Centuries of Childhood: A Social History of Family Life.* Trans. Robert Baldick (New York: Alfred A. Knopf, 1962).

Armstrong, Louise. *The Home Front: Notes from the Family War Zone* (New York: McGraw-Hill, 1983).

Arrow, Jeanne. "Dangers in the Pro-woman Line and Consciousness-Raising," ideas of the Feminists, mimeo, November 1969. Reprinted in C. Epstein and W. Goode, eds., *The Other Half: Roads to Women's Equality* (Englewood Cliffs, N.J.: Prentice-Hall, 1971): 203–207.

Association for Women in Psychology, Ad Hoc Committee on Sexist Language. "Eliminating Sexist Language: The Can, Should and How To." Paper presented at the Open Forum meeting of the A.P.A., Chicago, August 1975.

Astin, Helen S. *The Woman Doctorate in America* (New York: Russell Sage Foundation, 1969).

Astin, Helen S., and Alan E. Bayer. "Sex Discrimination in Academe." In Medrick, Tangri, and Hoffman, eds., *Women and Achievement: Social and Motivational Analysis* (New York: John Wiley, 1975): 372–395. Originally published in *Educational Record,* Spring 1972.

Atkin, Charles K. "Effects of Television Advertising on Children: Second Year Experimental Evidence." Manuscript, 1975, cited in Reskin and Hartmann, eds., *Women's Work, Men's Work: Sex Segregation on the Job* (Washington, D.C.: National Academy Press, 1986).

Bachrach, Susan. *Dames Employées: The Feminization of Postal Workers in Nineteenth Century France* (New York: Haworth Press, 1984).

Badinter, Elizabeth. *Mother Love: Myth and Reality* (New York: Macmillan, 1981).

Baer, Judith A. *The Chains of Protection: The Judicial Response to Women's Labor Legislation* (Westport, Conn.: Greenwood Press, 1978).

Bahr, Robert. *The Virility Factor: Masculinity through Testosterone, the Male Sex Hormone* (New York: G. P. Putnam's Sons, 1976).

Bailyn, Lotte. "Career and Family Orientation of Husbands and Wives in Relation to Marital Happiness." *Human Relations* 22 (1970): 97–113.

Bakan, David. *The Duality of Human Existence: An Essay on Psychology and Religion* (Chicago: Rand McNally, 1966).

Barash, David P. *Sociobiology and Behavior* (New York: Elsevier, 1977).

———. *The Whisperings Within* (New York: Harper & Row, 1979).

Barber, Bernard. *Science and the Social Order* (New York: Free Press, 1952).

Barchas, Patricia R., and Hamit Fisek. "Hierarchical Differentiation in Newly Formed Groups of Rhesus and Humans." In Barchas, ed., *Social Hierarchies: Essays toward a Sociophysiological Perspective.* Contributions in Sociology Series no. 47 (Westport, Conn.: Greenwood Press, 1984): 23–44.

Barchas, Patricia R., and Sally P. Mendoza, eds. *Social Cohesion: Essays toward a Sociophysiological Perspective.* Contributions in Sociology Series no. 49 (Westport, Conn.: Greenwood Press, 1984).

Barnett, Rosalind C., and Grace K. Baruch. "Determinants of Fathers' Participation in Family Work." *Journal of Marriage and the Family* 49 (February 1987): 29–40.

Baron, J. N., and W. T. Bielby. "Workers and Machines: A Missing Link in Current Stratification Research." Paper presented at the Annual Meeting of the American Sociological Association, New York, 1980.

Barron, N. "Sex-typed Language: The Production of Grammatical Cases." *Acta Sociologica* 14 (1971): 24–72.

Bart, Pauline, "Sexism and Social Science: From the Gilded Cage to the Iron Cage; Or, The Perils of Pauline." *Journal of Marriage and the Family* 33(4) (November 1971): 742–745.

———. "Although We Are Angry, We Are No Longer Mad." Review of *Women and Madness,* by Phyllis Chesler. *Society* 11(2) (January-February 1974): 95–98.

———. "A Study of Women Who Were Both Raped and Avoided Rape." *Journal of Social Issues* 37(4) (1981): 123–37.

Bart, Pauline, and Patricia H. O'Brien. "Stopping Rape: Effective Avoidance Strategies." *Signs* 10(11) (1984): 83–101.

Barthes, Roland. *The Fashion System,* Trans. Matthew Ward and Richard Howard. (1967. New York: Hill and Wang, 1983).

Baruch, Grace K., and Rosalind C. Barnett. "Multiple Roles and Well-Being: A Study of Mother of Preschool Age Children." Working Paper no. 3, Wellesley College, 1979.

———. "Consequences of Fathers' Participation in Family Work: Parents' Role Strain and Well-being." *Journal of Personality and Social Psychology* 51 (1986): 983–992.

Baruch, Grace K., Rosalind Barnett, and Caryl Rivers. *Lifeprints: New Patterns of Love and Work for Today's Women* (New York: McGraw-Hill, 1983).

Baruch, Grace K., and Jeanne Brooks-Gun, eds. *Women in Midlife* (New York: Plenum, 1984).

Bateson, G., and D. Jackson. "Toward a Theory of Schizophrenia." In J. G. Howells, ed. *Theory and Practice of Family Psychiatry* (New York: Brunner/Mazel, 1971): 745–764.

Bateson, Gregory. *Steps toward an Ecology of Mind* (New York: Ballantine Books, 1975).

Baxter, J. C. "Interpersonal Spacing in Natural Settings." *Sociometry* 33 (1970): 444–456.

Baxter, Sandra, and Marjorie Lansing. *Women and Politics: The Visible Majority,* 2d ed. (Ann Arbor: University of Michigan Press, 1983).

Beauvoir, Simone de. *The Second Sex* (Paris: Gallimard, 1949). Trans. H. M. Parshley (New York: Vintage Books, 1952).

Beck, E. M., Patrick M. Horan, and Charles M. Tolbert II. "Industrial Segmentation and Labor Market Discrimination." *Social Problems* 28 (2) (December 1980): 113–130.

Becker, Gary S. *The Economics of Discrimination*. 2d ed. (1957. Chicago: University of Chicago Press, 1971).

———. "A Theory of Marriage." In Schultz, ed. *Economics of the Family: Marriage, Children and Human Capital*. Conference Report of the National Bureau of Economic Research (Chicago: University of Chicago Press, 1974): 299–344.

———. *A Treatise on the Family* (Cambridge: Harvard University Press, 1981).

———. "Human Capital, Effort and the Sexual Division of Labor." *Journal of Labor Economics* 3, supp. (1985): s33–58.

Becker, Howard S., Blanche Geer, Everett C. Hughes, and Anselm L. Strauss. *Boys in White: Student Culture in Medical School* (Chicago: University of Chicago Press, 1961).

Becker, Howard S., and Anselm L. Strauss. "Careers, Personality and Adult Socialization." *American Journal of Sociology* 62 (1956): 253–263.

Bell, Robert. "Marriage and Family Differences among Lower-Class Negro and East Indian Women in Trinidad." *Race* (July 1970): 59–73.

Bem, Sandra L. "Sex-Role Adaptability: One Consequence of Psychological Androgyny." *Journal of Personality and Social Psychology* 31 (1975): 634–643.

———. "Probing the Promise of Androgyny." In Kaplan and Bean, eds. *Beyond Sex-Role Stereotypes: Readings toward a Psychology of Androgyny* (Boston: Little, Brown, 1976): 47–62.

Bem, Sandra L., and Daryl Bem. "Does Sex-Biased Job Advertising Aid and Abet Sex Discrimination?" *Journal of Applied Social Psychology* 3(1) (1973): 6–18.

Bentley, Arthur. *The Process of Government* (Chicago: University of Chicago Press, 1908).

Berger, J., B. P. Cohen, and M. Zelditch, Jr. "Status Characteristics and Expectation States." In Berger, Zelditch, and Anderson, eds., *Sociological Theories in Progress*, vol. 1 (Boston: Houghton Mifflin, 1966).

———. "Status Characteristics and Social Interaction." *American Sociological Review* 37 (1972): 241–255.

Berger, Joseph, David C. Wagner, and Morris Zelditch, Jr. *Expectation States Theory: The Status of a Research Program*. Technical Report no. 90 (Stanford: Stanford University, June 1983).

Berger, Joseph, and Morris Zelditch, Jr., eds. *Status Rewards and Influence* (San Francisco: Jossey-Bass, 1985).

Bergmann, Barbara R. "The Effect on White Incomes of Discrimination in Employment." *Journal of Political Economy* 79 (March-April 1971): 294–313.

———. "Occupational Segregation, Wages and Profits When Employers Discriminate by Race or Sex." *Eastern Economic Journal* 74 (April-July 1974): 103–110.

Berk, S. F., and A. Shih. "Contributions to Household Labor: Comparing Wives and Husbands' Reports." In S. F. Berk, ed. *Women and Household Labor* (Beverly Hills: Sage, 1980): 191–227.

Berk, Sarah Fenstermaker. *The Gender Factory* (New York: Plenum Press, 1985).

Berman, Edgar. *The Complete Chauvinist: A Survival Guide for the Bedeviled Man* (New York: Macmillan, 1982).

Bernard, Jessie. *Academic Women* (University Park: Pennsylvania State University Press, 1964).

————. "The Status of Women in Modern Patterns of Culture." *Annals of the American Academy of Political and Social Science* 375 (January 1968): 3–14.

————. *Women and the Public Interest* (Chicago and New York: Aldine, Atherton, 1971).

————. *The Future of Marriage* (New York: World, 1972).

————. "Adolescence and Socialization for Motherhood." In S. Dragastin and G. Elder, eds. *Adolescence in the Life Cycle, Psychological Change, and Social Context* (Washington, D.C.: Hemisphere Publishing, 1975): 227–252.

————. *The Female World* (Glencoe, Ill.: Free Press, 1981).

Berndt, Catherine H. "Interpretations and 'Facts' in Aboriginal Australia." In Dahlberg, ed., *Woman the Gatherer* (New Haven: Yale University Press, 1981): 153–204.

Berry, Mary Francis. *Why ERA Failed: Politics, Women's Rights and the Amending Process of the Constitution* (Bloomington: Indiana University Press, 1986).

Bibb, Robert, and William H. Form. "The Effects of Industrial, Occupational and Sex Stratification on Wages in Blue Collar Markets." *Social Forces* 55(4) (1977): 974–996.

Bielby, Denise D., and William T. Bielby. "She Works Hard for the Money: Household Responsibilities and the Allocation of Work Effort." *American Journal of Sociology* 5(9) (March 1988): 1031–1059.

Bielby, William T., and James N. Baron. "A Woman's Place Is with Other Women: Sex Segregation within Organizations." In Reskin, ed., *Sex Segregation in the Workplace: Trends, Explanations, Remedies* (Washington, D.C.: National Academy Press, 1984): 27–55. Originally a paper presented at the Workshop on Job Segregation by Sex, National Academy of Sciences Committee on Women's Employment and Related Social Issues, Washington, D.C., May 24–25, 1982.

Bieri, J., Wendy M. Bradburn, and M. David Galinsky. "Sex Differences in Perceptual Behavior." *Journal of Personality* 26(1) (1958): 1–12.

Birdwhistell, Ray L. *Kinesics and Context: Essays on Body Motion Communication* (Philadelphia: University of Pennsylvania Press, 1970).

Black, Gordon. "A Theory of Political Ambition: Career Choices and the Role of Structural Incentives." *American Political Science Review* 66 (March 1972): 144–59.

Blake, Judith. "Demographic Science and the Redirection of Population Policy." In Mendel Sheps and Jeanne Clare Ridley, eds., *Public Health and Population Change* (Pittsburgh: University of Pittsburgh Press, 1965).

Blau, Francine D. *Equal Pay in the Office* (Lexington, Mass.: Lexington Books, 1977).

————. "Discrimination against Women: Theory and Evidence." In Darity, ed., *Labor Economics: Modern Views* (Boston: Martinus Nijhoff, 1982): 53–90.

Blau, Francine D., and Carol L. Jusenius. "Economists' Approaches to Sex Segregation in the Labor Market: An Appraisal." In Blaxall and Reagan, eds., *Women in the Workplace* (Chicago: University of Chicago Press, 1976): 181–99.

Blau, Peter M., and Otis D. Duncan. *The American Occupational Structure* (New York: John Wiley, 1967).

Blaubergs, Maija S. "Changing the Sexist Language: The Theory behind the Practice." *Psychology of Women Quarterly* 2 (1978): 244–261.

Bleier, Ruth. "Bias in Biological and Human Sciences—Some Comments." *Signs* 4(1) (1978): 159–162.

———. *Science and Gender: A Critique of Biology and Its Theories on Women* (New York: Pergamon Press, 1984).

———. "Biology and Women's Policy: A View from the Biological Sciences." In Sapiro, ed., *Women, Biology and Public Policy.* Sage Yearbooks in Women's Studies, vol. 10 (Beverly Hills: Sage, 1985): 19–40.

Block, Jeanne H. "Debatable Conclusions about Sex Differences." *Contemporary Psychology* 21 (1976): 517–522.

Blondel, Jean. *Government Ministers in the Contemporary World* (Beverly Hills: Sage, 1985).

Blood, Robert O., Jr., and Donald M. Wolfe. *Husbands and Wives: The Dynamics of Married Living* (New York: Free Press, 1968).

Bloom, B. *Stability and Change in Human Characteristics* (New York: John Wiley, 1964).

Bloom, S. W. *Power and Dissent in Medical School* (New York: Free Press, 1973).

Blotnick, Srully. *The Corporate Steeplechase: Predictable Crises in a Business Career* (New York: Facts on File, 1984).

Blount, John, and Jacqueline Boles. "Structural Determinants of Sexual Harassment and Its Psychological Consequences." Paper presented at the Annual Meeting of the Eastern Economic Association, Philadelphia, Pa., 1981.

Blumberg, Rae Lesser. *Stratification: Socioeconomic and Sexual Inequality* (Dubuque, Iowa: William C. Brown, 1978).

Blumstein, Philip, and Pepper Schwartz. *The American Couple: Money, Work and Sex* (New York: Morrow, 1983).

Bodine, Ann. "Sex Differentiation in Language." In Thorne and Henley, eds., *Language and Sex: Difference and Dominance* (Rowley, Mass.: Newbury House, 1975a): 130–151.

———. "Androcentrism in Prescriptive Grammar: Singular 'They,' Sex Indefinite 'He,' and 'He or She.' " *Language in Society* 4 (1975b): 129–146.

Bogess, Jane. "Troop Male Membership Changes and Infant Killing in Langurs *(Presbytis entellus)." Folia Primatologica* 32 (1979): 65–107.

Boles, Janet K. *The Politics of the Equal Rights Amendment: Conflict and the Decision Process* (New York: Longman, 1979).

Boring, Edwin G. *A History of Experimental Psychology,* 2d ed. (New York: Appleton-Century-Crofts, 1950).

Bose, Christine. *Jobs and Gender: Sex and Occupational Prestige* (Baltimore: Johns Hopkins University, Center for Metropolitan Planning and Research, 1973).

———. "Social Status of the Homemaker." In Berk, ed., *Women and Household Labor* (Beverly Hills: Sage, 1980): 69–87.

Boserup, Esther. *Women's Role in Economic Development* (London: George Allen and Unwin, 1970).

Bott, Elizabeth. "Urban Families, Conjugal Roles and Social Networks." *Human Relations* 8 (1955): 345–384.

Boulding, Elise. *The Underside of History: A View of Women through Time* (Boulder, Colo.: Westview Press, 1976).

————. "The Labor of United States Farm Women: A Knowledge Gap." *Sociology of Work and Occupations* 7 (August 1980): 261–290.

Bourdieu, Pierre. "Reproduction culturelle et reproduction sociale" (Social Science Information). *Information sur les sciences sociales* 10(2) (1971): 45–79.

————. "Outline of a Theory of Practice (London, New York, and Melbourne: Cambridge University Press, 1977).

Bourque, Susan C., and Donna Robinson Divine, eds. *Women Living Change* (Philadelphia: Temple University Press, 1985).

Bourque, Susan, and Jean Grossholtz. "Politics and Unnatural Practice: Political Science Looks at Female Participation." *Politics and Society* 4 (Winter 1974): 225–266.

Bourque, Susan C., and Kay B. Warren. *Women of the Andes: Patriarchy and Social Change in Two Peruvian Towns* (Ann Arbor: University of Michigan Press, 1981).

Brady, Ivan, ed. "Speaking in the Name of the Real: Freeman and Mead on Samoa." *American Anthropologist* 85(4) (December 1983): 908–947.

Bridges, William P. "Industry Marginality and Female Employment: A New Appraisal." *American Sociological Review* 45 (February 1980): 58–75.

————. "The Sexual Stratification of Occupations: Theories of Labor Stratification in Industry." *American Journal of Sociology* 88(2) (1982): 270–294.

Briere, John, and Cheryl Lanktree. "Sex-Role Related Effects of Sex Bias in Language." *Sex Roles* 9 (1983): 625–632.

Briggs, Jean. "Eskimo Women: Makers of Men." In Matthiasson, ed., *Many Sisters* (New York: Free Press, 1975): 261–304.

Brim, Orville G., Jr. "Socialization through the Life Cycle." In Brim and Wheeler, eds. *Socialization after Childhood: Two Essays* (New York: John Wiley, 1966): 1–49.

————. "Theories of the Male Mid-Life Crisis." *Counseling Psychologist* 6(1) (1976): 2–9.

————. "Social and Personal Management of Ambition." Paper presented at the Russell Sage Foundation, December 4, 1985.

————. "Gender Similarities and Differences in Goal Sectors." Manuscript.

Brim, Orville G., Jr., and Jerome Kagan. "Constancy and Change: A View of the Issues." In Brim and Kagan, eds., *Constancy and Change in Human Development* (Cambridge: Harvard University Press, 1980): 1–25.

Brim, Orville G., Jr., and Stanton Wheeler. *Socialization after Childhood: Two Essays* (New York: John Wiley, 1966).

Brinkerhoff, David B., and Alan Booth. "Gender, Dominance and Stress." *Journal of Social Biological Structure* 7(2) (1984): 159–177.

Brodsky, Carol. *The Harassed Worker* (Lexington, Mass.: D. C. Heath, 1976).

Brouwer, D., and M. Gerritsen. *Sociolinguistiek en de tweede sekse.* In G. G. Geerts and A. Hagen, eds., *Sociolinguistische studies 1: Bijdragen uit het Nederlandse taalgebied* (Groningen: Wolters-Noordhoff, 1980): 50–61.

Brouwer, Dede. "The Influence of the Addressee's Sex on Politeness in Language Use." *Linguistics* 20 (1982): 697–711.

Broverman, I. K., S. R. Vogel, D. M. Broverman, F. E. Clarkson, and P. S. Rosenkrantz. "Sex Role Stereotypes: A Current Appraisal." *Journal of Social Issues* 28 (1972): 59–78.

Brown, Judith K. "Cross-Cultural Perspectives on Middle-Aged Women." *Current Anthropology* 23 (1982): 143–156.

Brown, Judith K., and Virginia Kerns, eds. *In Her Prime: A New View of Middle-Aged Women* (South Hadley, Mass.: Bergin and Garvey, 1985).

Brown, P. and S. Levinson. "Universals in Language Usage: Politeness Phenomena." In E. N. Goody, ed., *Questions and Politeness* (Cambridge: Cambridge University Press, 1978): 56–289.

Bucher, R., and J. G. Stelling. *Becoming Professional* (Beverly Hills: Sage, 1977).

Buck, R., R. E. Miller, and W. F. Caul. "Sex, Personality and Physiological Variables in the Communication of Emotion via Facial Expression." *Journal of Personality and Social Psychology* 30 (1974): 587–596.

Burawoy, Michael. *Manufacturing Consent: Changes in the Labor Process under Monopoly Capitalism* (Chicago: University of Chicago Press, 1979).

Burke, Deborah, Gayle Burnett, and Peggy Levenstein. "Menstrual Symptoms: New Data from a Double-Blind Study." Paper presented at the Annual Meeting of the Western Psychological Association, San Francisco, 1978.

Burke, Kenneth. *Permanence and Change* (New York: New Republic, 1935).

Butalia, Urvashi. "Indian Women and the New Movement." *Women's Studies International Forum* 8(2) (1985): 131–133.

Campbell, Angus, Philip E. Converse, Warren E. Millar, and Donald E. Stokes. *The American Voter* (Chicago: University of Chicago Press, 1960).

Cantor, N., and J. Kihlstrom. *Social Intelligence: The Cognitive Basis of Personality.* Technical Report no. 60, Cognitive Science Center (Ann Arbor: University of Michigan, 1983).

Caplan, N. "The New Ghetto Man: A Review of Recent Empirical Studies." *Journal of Social Issues* 26 (1970): 59–73.

Caplan, Paula, and Ian Hall-McCorquodale. "Mother-Blaming in Major Clinical Journals." *American Journal of Orthopsychiatry* 55(3) (July 1985): 345–613.

Caplow, Theodore. *The Sociology of Work* (Minneapolis: University of Minnesota Press, 1954).

Carlson, Rae. "Sex Differences in Ego Functioning: Exploratory Studies of Agency and Communion." *Journal of Consulting and Clinical Psychology* 37 (1971): 267–277.

Carroll, Berenice A. "Political Science, Part One: American Politics and Political Behavior." *Signs* 5(2) (1979): 289–306.

Carroll, Susan. "Woman Candidates and State Legislative Elections, 1976: Limitations in the Political Opportunity Structure and Their Effects on Electoral Participation and Success." Paper presented at the Annual Meeting of the American Political Science Association, Washington, D.C., 1977.

———. "Feminist Scholarship or Political Leadership." In Kellerman, ed., *Leadership: Multidisciplinary Perspectives* (Engelwood Cliffs, N.J.: Prentice-Hall, 1979): 139–156.

Case, Carl. *The Masculine in Religion* (1906), as cited in Kimmel, 1987.

Cassell, Frank H., and Samuel L. Doctors. *A Three Company Study of the Intra-firm Mobility of Blue Collar and Lower Level White Collar Workers* (Chicago: Northwestern University Press, 1972).

Chafe, William H. *The American Woman: Her Changing Social, Economic and Political Roles: 1920–1970* (Oxford: Oxford University Press, 1972).

Chafetz, Janet Saltzman. *Masculine/Feminine or Human?* (Itasca, Ill.: F. E. Peacock, 1974).

———. *Sex and Advantage: A Comparative Macro-Structural Theory of Sex Stratification* (Totowa, N.J.: Rowman & Allanheld, 1984).

Chagnon, Napolean. *Evolutionary Biology and Human Social Behavior: An Anthropological Perspective* (Boston: Duxbury Press, 1979).

Cheal, David J. "Intergenerational Family Transfers." *Journal of Marriage and the Family* 45(4) (November 1983): 805–813.

Cherlin, Andrew. *Marriage, Divorce, Remarriage: Changing Patterns in the Postwar United States* (Cambridge: Harvard University Press, 1981).

———. "Changing Family and Household: Contemporary Lessons from Historical Research." *Annual Review of Sociology* 9 (1983): 51–150.

Cherulnik, P. D. "Sex Differences in the Expression of Emotion in a Structured Social Encounter." *Sex Roles* 5 (1979): 413–424.

Chodorow, Nancy. *The Reproduction of Mothering: Psychoanalysis and the Sociology of Gender* (Berkeley: University of California Press, 1978).

———. "Is There a Feminist Methodology?" Paper presented at the Annual Meeting of the American Sociological Society, Washington, D.C., August 1985.

Chodorow, Nancy, and Susan Contratto. "The Fantasy of the Perfect Mother." In Thorne and Yalom, eds., *Rethinking the Family* (New York: Longman, 1982): 34–75.

Chomsky, Noam. *Syntactic Structures* (The Hague: Mouton, 1957).

Cicirelli, Victor G. *Helping Elderly Parents: The Role of Adult Children* (Boston: Auburn House, 1981).

Clauss, Carin. "Legal Factors Affecting Job Segregation by Sex: An Assessment of the Impact on Job Segregation of Barriers Imposed or Permitted by Law." Paper presented at the Workshop on Job Segregation by Sex, National Academy of Science, Washington, D.C., May 24–25, 1982.

Cockburn, Cynthia. *Machinery of Dominance: Women, Men and Technical Know-How* (London: Pluto Press, 1985).

Cole, Jonathan. *Fair Science: Women in the Scientific Community* (New York: Free Press, 1979).

Cole, Jonathan, and Stephen Cole. "Visibility and the Structural Basis of Awareness in Science." *American Sociological Review* 33(3) (June 1968): 397–413.

———. *Social Stratification in Science* (Chicago: University of Chicago Press, 1973).

Cole, Stephen. "Sex Discrimination and Admission to Medical School: 1929–1984." Manuscript, Center for the Social Sciences at Columbia University, 1985.

Coleman, James. *Community Conflict* (Glencoe, Ill.: Free Press, 1957).

Coleman, James, Elihu Katz, and Herbert Menzel. "The Diffusion of an Innovation among Physicians." *Sociometry* 4(20) (December 1957): 253–270. Reprinted in Lienhardt, ed., *Social Networks: A Developing Paradigm* (New York: Academic Press, 1977).

Collier, Jane F., and Michelle Z. Rosaldo. "Politics and Gender in Simple Societies." In Ortner and Whitehead, eds., *Sexual Meanings: The Cultural Construction of Gender and Sexuality* (Cambridge: Cambridge University Press, 1981): 275–329.

Collier, Jane F., Michelle Z. Rosaldo, and Sylvia Yanagisako "Is There a Family? New Anthropological Views." In Thorne and Yalom, eds., *Rethinking the Family: Some Feminist Questions* (New York: Longman, 1982): 25–39.

Collins, Randall. "A Conflict Theory of Sexual Stratification." *Social Problems* 19 (1971): 3–21.

———. *Conflict Sociology: Toward an Explanatory Science* (New York: Academic Press, 1975).

Condry, John, and Sandra Condry. "Sex Differences: A Study of the Eye of the Beholder." *Child Development* 47 (1976): 812–819.

Condry, John, and Sharon Dyer. "Fear of Success: Attribution of Cause to the Victim." *Journal of Social Issues* 32(3) (1976): 63–83.

Conklin, N. F. "Toward a Feminist Analysis of Linguistic Behavior." *University of Michigan Papers in Women's Studies* 1(1) (1974): 51–73.

Connell, R. W. "Theorizing Gender." *Sociology* 19(2) (May 1985): 260–272.

———. *The Social Basis of Sexual Politics* (Palo Alto: Stanford University Press, 1988).

Constantini, Edward, and Kenneth H. Craik. "The Social Background, Personality and Political Careers of Female Party Leaders." *Journal of Social Issues* 28(2) (1972): 217–236.

———. "Women as Politicians: The Social Background, Personality and Political Careers of Female Party Leaders." In Githens and Prestage, eds., *A Portrait of Marginality: The Political Behavior of the American Woman* ((New York: David McKay, 1977): 222–240.

Cook, Beverly B. "Will Women Judges Make a Difference in Women's Legal Rights? A Prediction from Attitudes and Simulated Behavior." In Rendel, ed., *Women, Power and Political Systems* (London and New York: St. Martin's Press, 1981): 216–239.

Coombs, R. H. *Mastering Medicine: Professional Socialization in Medical School* (New York: Free Press, 1978).

Coser, Lewis, and Rose Laub Coser. "The Housewife and Her 'Greedy Family.' " In Coser and Coser, eds., *Greedy Institutions: Patterns of Undivided Commitment* (New York: Free Press, 1974): 89–100.

Coser, Rose Laub. "Laughter Among Colleagues." *Psychiatry* 23 (1960): 81–95.

———. "Stay Home, Little Sheba: On Placement, Displacement and Social Change." In Kahn-hut, Daniels, and Colvard, eds., *Women and Work: Problems and Perspectives* (New York: Oxford University Press, 1982): 153–59. Presidential address, Society for the Study of Social Problems, 1975. Originally published in *Social Problems* 22(4) (April 1975): 470–480.

———. "Where Have All the Women Gone? Like the Sediment of a Good Wine, They Have Sunk to the Bottom." In Epstein and Coser, eds., *Access to Power* (London: George Allen and Unwin, 1981): 16–36.

———. "Women at Work: Power and Exchange in the Family." Paper presented at the Annual Meeting of the American Sociological Association, Washington, D.C., August 29, 1985.

Coveney, Lal, Margaret Jackson, Sheila Jeffries, Leslie Kay, and Pat Mahony. *The Sexuality Papers: Male Sexuality and the Social Control of Women* (London: Hutchinson, 1984).

Cowan, Ruth Schwartz. "A Case Study of Technical and Social Change: The Washing Machine and the Working Woman." In Hartman and Banner, eds., *Clio's Consciousness Raised* (New York: Harper Torchbooks, 1974): 245–253.

Cronkite, R. C. "The Determinants of Spouses' Normative Preferences for Family Roles." *Journal of Marriage and Family* 39 (1977): 575–585.

Crosby, Faye J. *Relative Deprivation and Working Women* (New York: Oxford University Press, 1982).

―――. "Work and Domestic Life." Paper presented at the Symposium on the Effective Management of Work and Personal Life, Faculty of Management, McGill University, April 28, 1983.

Crosby, Faye J., ed. *Spouse, Parent, Worker: On Gender and Multiple Roles* (New Haven: Yale University Press, 1987).

Crosby, Faye J., and Linda Nyquist. "The Female Register: An Empirical Study of Lakoff's Hypothesis." *Language in Society* 6(3) (December 1977): 313–322.

Crowley, J. T., T. Levitan, and R. Quinn. "The Seven Deadly Half-Truths about Women." *Psychology Today,* March 1973, p. 94.

Dahl, Robert A. *Who Governs?* (New Haven: Yale University Press, 1956).

Dahlberg, Frances, ed. *Woman the Gatherer* (New Haven: Yale University Press, 1981).

Dalton, Katherina. *The Premenstrual Syndrome* (Springfield, Ill.: Charles C. Thomas, 1964).

Daniels, Arlene K. "Feminist Perspectives in Sociological Research." In Kanter and Millman, eds., *Another Voice* (New York: Anchor Press, 1975): 340–380.

David, Deborah, and Robert Bannon, eds. *The Forty-nine Percent Majority: The Male Sex Role* (Reading, Mass.: Addison-Wesley, 1976).

Davidoff, Leonore. "Class and Gender in Victorian England: The Diaries of Arthur J. Munby and Hannah Cullwick." *Feminist Studies* 5(1) (Spring 1979): 87–141.

Davidson, Emily S., Amy Yasuna, and Alan Tower. "The Effects of Television Cartoons on Sex-Role Stereotyping in Young Girls." *Child Development* 50 (1979): 597–600.

Davidson, Kenneth, Ruth Ginsburg, and Herma Kay. *Sex-Based Discrimination: Text, Cases and Materials* (St. Paul, Minn.: West, 1979).

Davis, Allison, and Robert J. Havighurst. "Social Class and Color Differences in Child-Rearing." *American Sociological Review* 11(6) (December 1946): 698–710.

Davis Kingsley. "Intermarriage in Caste Societies." *American Anthropologist* 43 (July-September 1941): 376–395.

―――. *Human Society* (New York: Macmillan, 1949).

Davis, Kingsley, and Wilbert E. Moore. "Some Principles of Stratification." *American Sociological Review* 10 (April 1945): 242–249.

Dawkins, Richard. *The Selfish Gene* (Oxford: Oxford University Press, 1976).

Deaux, Kay. "Sex: A Perspective on the Attribution Process." In Harvey, Ickes, and Kidd, eds., *New Directions in Attribution Research* (Hillsdale, N.J.: Erlbaum, 1976): 335–352.

―――. "From Individual Differences to Social Categories: Analysis of a Decade's Research on Gender." *American Psychology* 39(2) (February 1984): 105–116.

Deaux, Kay, and T. Emswiller. "Explanations for Successful Performance on Sex-Linked Tasks: What Is Skill for the Male Is Luck for the Female." *Journal of Personality and Social Psychology* 29 (1974): 80–85.

Deckard, Barbara. *The Women's Movement* (New York: Harper & Row, 1979).

Demos, John. "Developmental Perspectives on the History of Childhood." In Robb, ed., *The Family in History: Interdisciplinary Essays* (New York: Harper Torch-books, 1971): 127–140.

Denitch, Bogdan. "Women and Political Power in a Revolutionary Society: The Yugoslav Case." In Epstein and Coser, eds., *Access to Power* (London: George Allen and Unwin, 1981): 115–123.

Deutch, C. J., and L. Gilbert. "Sex-Role Stereotypes: Effect of Perception of Self and Others on Personal Adjustment." *Journal of Consulting Psychology* 23 (1976): 373–379.

Deutch, Helene. *The Psychology of Women: A Psychoanalytical Interpretation* (London: Research Books, 1947).

DeVault, Marjorie. "Housework: Keeping in Mind What's Out of Sight." Paper presented at Annual Meeting of the American Sociological Association, Washington, D.C., August 28, 1985.

Dewey, J. "Health and Sex in Higher Education." *Popular Science Monthly* 28 (1886): 606–614.

Diamond, Irene. *Sex Roles and the State House* (New Haven: Yale University Press, 1977).

Dinnerstein, Dorothy. *The Mermaid and the Minotaur: Sexual Arrangements and Human Malaise* (New York: Harper & Row, 1976).

Dionne, E. J., Jr. "Primaries Show Women Emerging as Seasonal Political Contenders." *New York Times,* September 11, 1986, pp. A1, B13.

Doeringer, Peter B., and Michael J. Piore. *Internal Labor Markets and Manpower Analysis* (Lexington, Mass.: D. C. Heath, 1971).

Dolhinow, Phyllis Jay. "The North Indian Langur." In Dolhinow, ed., *Primate Patterns* (New York: Holt, Rinehart and Winston, 1972): 181–238.

Domhoff, William G. *Who Rules America?* (Englewood Cliffs, N.J.: Prentice-Hall, 1967).

Douglas, Ann. *The Feminization of American Culture* (New York: Alfred A. Knopf, 1977).

Douglas, Mary. *Implicit Meanings: Essays in Anthropology* (London: Routledge, 1975).
———. "A Backdoor Approach to Thinking about the Social Order." Paper presented at the Annual Meeting of the American Sociological Association, San Antonio, Texas, August 29, 1984.

Doyal, Leslie, and Imogen Pennell. *The Political Economy of Health* (Boston: South End Press, 1981).

Draper, Patricia. Communication, cited in Dahlberg, 1981.

Duberman, Lucille. *Gender and Sex in Society* (New York: Praeger, 1975).

Dunbar, Roxanne. "Female Liberation and the Basis for Social Revolution." *Journal of Female Liberation* 1(2) (February 1969): 103–115.

Duncan, Otis D. "Social Stratification and Mobility: Problems in the Measurement of Trend." In Sheldon and Moore, eds., *Indicators of Social Changes* (New York: Russell Sage Foundation, 1968): 675–719.

Duncan, Otis Dudley, and Beverly Duncan. *Sex Typing and Social Roles: A Research Report* (New York: Academic Press, 1978).

Duncan, S., and Fiske, D. *Face-to-Face Interaction: Research, Method and Theory* (Hillsdale, N.J.: Erlbaum, 1977).

Durkheim, Emile. *The Elementary Forms of the Religious Life,* trans. Joseph W. Swain (1915. New York: Free Press, 1947).

Duverger, Maurice. *The Political Role of Women* (New York: UNESCO, 1955).

Eagly, A. H. "Gender and Social Influence: A Social Psychological Analysis." *American Psychologist* 38 (1983): 971–981.

———. *Sex Differences in Social Behavior: A Social-Role Interpretation* (Hillsdale, N.J.: Erlbaum, 1987).

Eagly, A. H., and L. L. Carli. "Sex of Researchers and Sex-Typed Communication as Determinants of Sex Differences in Influenceability: A Meta-analysis of Social Influence Studies." *Pyschological Bulletin* 90 (1981): 1–20.

Eckholm, Erik. "New View of Female Primates Assails Stereotypes." *New York Times,* September 18, 1984, p. C1.

Eggan, Fred. *Social Organization of the Western Pueblos* (Chicago: University of Chicago Press, 1950).

Ehrenreich, Barbara. "The Work Women Do to Stay Married." Paper presented at the Annual Meeting of the American Sociological Association, Washington, D.C., August 27, 1985.

Ehrenreich, Barbara, and Deirdre English. *For Her Own Good: 150 Years of Experts' Advice to Women* (New York: Doubleday, 1978).

Eisenstein, Hester. "Is 'Objectivity' a Code-Word for Male Domination?" Paper presented at "The Second Sex—Thirty Years Later" Conference, New York Institute for the Humanities, September 28, 1979.

———. *Contemporary Feminist Thought* (Boston: G. K. Hall, 1983).

Elshtain, Jean Bethke. "Politics and the Battered Woman." *Dissent* 32(1) (Winter 1985): 55–61.

Enarson, Elaine. *Woods-Working Women: Sexual Integration in the U.S. Forest Service* (University: University of Alabama Press, 1984).

England, Paula. "The Failure of the Human Capital Theory to Explain Occupational Sex Segregation." *Journal of Human Resources* 17 (Summer 1982): 358–370.

Epstein, Cynthia Fuchs. Testimony presented to the Equal Economic Opportunity Commission on Sex-Segregated Classified Advertising, Washington, D.C., May 2, 1967.

———. "Women in Professional Life." *Psychiatric Spectator,* November 1968.

———. Testimony presented to the Department of Labor, Office of Federal Contract Compliance, Washington, D.C., August 4, 1969.

———. *Woman's Place: Options and Limits in Professional Careers* (Berkeley: University of California Press, 1970a).

———. "Encountering the Male Establishment: Sex-Status Limits on Women's Careers in the Professions." *American Journal of Sociology* 75 (May 1970b): 965–983.

———. Review of *The Woman Doctorate in America,* by Helen S. Astin. *American Journal of Sociology* 77(2) (September 1971a): 359–361.

———. "Law Partners and Marital Partners: Strains and Solutions in the Dual-Career Family Enterprise." *Human Relations* 24(6) (1971b): 549–564.

———. "Bringing Women In: Rewards, Punishments and the Structure of Achievement." *Annals of the New York Academy of Sciences* 108 (March 1973a): 62–70.

————. "Positive Effects of the Multiple Negative: Explaining the Success of Black Professional Women." *American Journal of Sociology* 78 (January 1973b): 912–935.

————. "A Different Angle of Vision: Notes on the Selective Eye of Sociology." *Social Science Quarterly* 55(3) (December 1974): 645–656.

————. "Tracking and Careers: The Case of Women in American Society." In E. L. Zuckerman, ed., *Women and Men: Roles, Attitudes and Power Relationships* (New York: Radcliffe Club, 1975): 26–33.

————. "Sex Role Stereotyping, Occupations and Social Exchange." Paper presented at Radcliffe Institute Conference, "Women: Resource for a Changing World." Radcliffe College, April 18, 1972. Reprinted in *Women's Studies* 3 (1976a): 183–194.

————. "Separate and Unequal: Notes on Women's Achievement." *Social Policy* 6(5) (1976b): 17–23.

————. "Sex Roles." In R. K. Merton and R. Nisbet, eds., *Social Problems,* 4th ed. (New York: Harcourt Brace Jovanovich, 1976c).

————. "A Discourse on Method: Sex Typing and Social Roles: A Research Report." *Contemporary Sociology* 9(4) (July 1980): 515–517.

————. "Women and Power: The Roles of Women in Politics in the United States." In Epstein and Coser, eds., *Access to Power* (London: George Allen and Unwin, 1981a): 124–146.

————. *Women in Law* (New York: Basic Books, 1981b).

————. "Changing Perspectives and Opportunities and Their Impact on Careers and Aspirations: The Case of Women Lawyers." Paper presented at the session on "Work and the Life Course: Sociological Perspectives," at the Annual Scientific Meeting of the Gerontological Society of America, Boston, November 20, 1982.

————. "Paradigms and Politics: Continuities in the Functions of Social Conflict." In Powell and Robbins, eds., *Conflict and Consensus: A Festschrift in Honor of Lewis A. Coser* (New York: Free Press, 1984a).

————. "Ideal Images and Real Roles: The Perpetuation of Gender Inequality." *Dissent* 31(4) (Fall 1984b): 441–447.

————. "Ideal Roles and Real Roles or the Fallacy of the Misplaced Dichotomy." *Research in Social Stratification and Mobility* 4 (1985): 29–51.

Epstein, Cynthia Fuchs, and Rose Laub Coser, eds. *Access to Power: Cross-National Studies of Women and Elites* (London: George Allen and Unwin, 1981).

Epstein, Cynthia Fuchs, and Kai T. Erikson. *The Culture of the Workplace* (New York: Russell Sage Foundation, forthcoming).

Ericksen, J. A., W. L. Yancey, and E. P. Ericksen. "The Division of Family Roles." *Journal of Marriage and the Family* 41 (1979): 307–314.

Erikson, Erik H. "Identity and the Life Cycle." Monograph. *Psychological Issues* 1 (New York: International Universities Press, 1959).

————. *Childhood and Society* (1950. New York: W. W. Norton, 1963).

————. "Reflections on Ethos and War." *Yale Review* 73(4) (Summer 1984): 481–490.

Ervin-Tripp, S. "Sociolinguistics." In J. A. Fishman, ed., *Advances in the Sociology of Language* (The Hague: Mouton, 1971): 15–151.

Estioko-Griffin, Agnes, and P. Bion Griffin. "Woman the Hunter: The Agta." In

Dahlberg, ed., *Woman the Gatherer* (New Haven: Yale University Press, 1981): 121–152.

Evans, Sara. *Personal Politics: The Roots of Women's Liberation in the Civil Rights Movement and the New Left* (New York: Vintage Press, 1979).

Evans-Pritchard, Edward E. *The Nuer: A Description of the Modes of Livelihood and Political Institutions of a Nilotic People* (New York: Oxford University Press, 1940).

Fant, Maureen B. "Egyptian Riddles and Roman Remains." *Women's Review of Books* 2(9) (June 1985): 8–9.

Farkas, G. "Education, Wage Rates and the Division of Labor between Husband and Wife." *Journal of Marriage and the Family* 38 (1976): 473–484.

Farley, Lin. *Sexual Harassment of Women on the Job* (New York: McGraw-Hill, 1978).

Farrell, Warren. *The Liberated Man: Freeing Men and Their Relationships with Women* (New York: Random House, 1974).

Fasteau, Marc. *The Male Machine* (New York: McGraw Hill, 1974).

Fausto-Sterling, Anne. *Myths of Gender: Biological Theories about Women and Men* (New York: Basic Books, 1985).

Feather, N. T. "Attribution of Responsibility and Valence of Success and Failure in Relation to Initial Confidence and Perceived Locus of Control." *Journal of Personality and Social Psychology* 13 (1969): 129–144.

Featherman, David L., and Robert M. Hauser. "Sexual Inequalities and Socioeconomic Achievement in the United States, 1962–1973." *American Sociological Review* 41(3) (June 1976): 462–483.

Felson, Marcus, and David Knoke. "Social Status and the Married Woman." *Journal of Marriage and the Family* 36 (1974): 116–121.

Fennema, Elizabeth, and Julia Sherman. "Sex-Related Differences in Mathematics Achievements, Spatial Visualization and Affective Factors." *American Educational Research Journal* 14 (1977): 51–71.

Festinger, Leon, Derwin Cartwright, Kathleen Barber, Juliet Fleischi, Josephine Gottsdanker, Annette Keyson, and Gloria Leavitt. "A Study of Humor: Its Origin and Spread." *Human Relations* 1(4) (1948): 464–486.

Feuerberg, Marvin. "Sexual Inequality: A Theoretical and Empirical Exploration." (Ph.D. diss., University of Oregon, 1978, cited in Acker, 1980).

Fielder, Maureen. "The Participation of Women in American Politics." Paper presented at the Annual Meeting of the American Political Science Association, San Francisco, 1975.

Fierstein, Bruce. *Real Men Don't Eat Quiche* (New York: Pocket Books, 1982).

Firestone, Shulamith. *The Dialectic of Sex* (New York: Bantam Books, 1972).

Fishman, Pamela. "Interaction: The Work Women Do." Paper presented at the Annual Meeting of the American Sociological Association, San Francisco, August 1975. Published in *Social Problems* 25 (1978): 397–406.

Flammang, Janet A. *Political Women: Current Roles in State and Local Government* (Beverly Hills: Sage, 1984).

Flax, Jane. "The Conflict between Nurturance and Autonomy in Mother-Daughter Relationships and within Feminism." *Feminist Studies* 4(2) (June 2, 1978): 171–189.

Flerx, Vicki C., Dorothy S. Fidler, and Ronald W. Rogers. "Sex Role Stereotypes:

Developmental Aspects and Early Intervention." *Child Development* 47 (1976): 998–1007.

Flint, Marcha. "Male and Female Menopause: A Cultural Put-on." In A. M. Voda, M. Dinnerstein, and S. O'Donnell, eds., *Changing Perspectives on Menopause* (Austin: University of Texas Press, 1982): 363–375.

Flora, Cornelia, and Naomi B. Lynn. "Women and Political Socialization: Considerations of the Impact of Motherhood." In Jaquette, ed., *Women in Politics* (New York: Wiley, 1974): 37–53.

Fogarty, Michael, A. J. Allen, Isobel Allen, and Patricia Walters. *Women in Top Jobs: Four Studies in Achievement* (London: George Allen and Unwin, 1971).

Fogarty, Michael P., Rhona Rapoport, and Robert N. Rapoport. *Sex, Career and Family*. Prepared jointly by Political and Economic Planning and the Tavistock Institute (London: George Allen and Unwin, 1971).

Fossum, Donna. "Women Law Professors." *American Bar Foundation Research Journal* 4 (Fall 1980): 906–914.

Fox, Renee. *Experiment Perilous* (Glencoe, Ill.: Free Press, 1959).

Fox, Robin. *The Imperial Animal* (New York: Dell, 1971).

Frances, S. J. "Sex Differences in Non-verbal Behavior." *Sex Roles* 5 (1979): 519–535.

Frank, Marian. *The Life and Times of "Rosie the Riveter."* A study guide for the video *Rosie the Riveter,* Connie Field, director (Los Angeles: Direct Cinema, 1980).

Frazier, Edward Franklin. *Black Bourgeoisie* (Glenco, Ill.: Free Press, 1957).

Freedman, Ann E. "Sex Equality, Sex Differences and the Supreme Court." *Yale Law Journal* 92(6) (May 1983): 913–968.

Freeman, Derek. *Margaret Mead and Samoa: The Making and Unmaking of an Anthropological Myth* (Cambridge: Harvard University Press, 1983).

Freeman, Jo. "Growing up Girlish." *Trans-Action* 8 (November-December 1970): 36–43.

———. "The Legal Basis of the Sexual Case System." *Valparaiso Law Review* 5 (1971): 203–256.

Freud, Sigmund. "Three Essays on the Theory of Sexuality." In *Standard Edition of the Complete Psychological Works of Sigmund Freud,* vol. 7 (London: Hogarth Press and the Institute of Psychoanalysis, 1905).

———. "The Dissolution of the Oedipus Complex." In *Standard Edition of the Complete Psychological Works of Sigmund Freud,* vol. 19 (London: Hogarth Press and the Institute of Psychoanalysis, 1924).

Friedan, Betty. *The Feminine Mystique* (New York: W. W. Norton, 1963).

Friedl, Ernestine. *Women and Men: An Anthropologist's View* (New York: Holt, Rinehart and Winston, 1975).

Frodi, Ann, Jacqueline Macaulay, and Pauline Robert Thome. "Are Women Always Less Aggressive than Men? A Review of the Experimental Literature." *Psychological Bulletin* 84(4) (1977): 634–660.

Furstenberg, Frank F., Jr. "Remarriage and Intergenerational Relations." Paper presented at the Workshop on Stability and Change in the Family, National Academy of Sciences, Annapolis, Md., March 1979.

Gallup, Gordon G. "Self-Recognition in Primates: A Comparative Approach to the

Bidirectional Properties of Consciousness.'' *American Psychologist* 32 (1977): 329–338.

Garai, Josef E., and Amram Scheinfield. ''Sex Differences in Mental and Behavioral Traits.'' *Genetic Psychology Monographs* 77 (1968): 169–299.

Garfinkel, Harold. ''Conditions of Successful Degradation Ceremonies.'' *American Journal of Sociology* 61 (March 1956): 420–424.

Garms-Homolova, Vjenka, Erika M. Hoerning, and Doris Schaffer, eds. *Intergenerational Relationships* (Lewiston, N.Y.: Hogrefe International, 1984).

Gates, Margaret. ''Occupational Segregation and the Law.'' *Signs* 1(3) (pt. 2) (Spring 1976): 335–341.

Gazzaniga, Michael S. *The Social Brain: Discovering the Networks of the Mind* (New York: Basic Books, 1985).

Gecas, V. ''The Socialization and Childcare Roles.'' In F. I. Nye, ed., *Role Structure and Analysis of the Family* (Beverly Hills: Sage, 1976): 35–59.

Geertz, Clifford. *Local Knowledge: Further Essays in Interpretive Anthropology* (New York: Basic Books, 1984).

Gelles, R. J. *The Violent Home: A Study of Physical Aggression between Husbands and Wives* (Beverly Hills: Sage, 1974).

———. ''Violence in the American Family.'' In J. P. Martin, ed., *Violence and the Family* (New York: John Wiley, 1977): 169–182.

———. ''Violence in the Family: A Review of Research in the Seventies.'' *Journal of Marriage and the Family* 42(4) (November 1980): 873–885.

Gerson, Kathleen. ''Emerging Social Divisions among Women: Implications for Welfare State Politics.'' Paper presented at the Annual Meeting of the American Sociological Association, Washington, D.C., August 29, 1985a.

———. *Hard Choices: How Women Decide about Work, Career and Motherhood* (Berkeley: University of California Press, 1985b).

———. ''What Do Women Want from Men?'' *American Behavioral Scientist* 29(5) (May-June 1986): 619–634.

Gerson, Kathleen, Judith L. Alpert, and Mary Sue Richardson. ''Mothering: The View from Psychological Research.'' *Signs* 9(31) (Spring 1984): 434–453.

Gertzog, Irwin N. *Congressional Women: Their Recruitment, Treatment and Behavior* (New York: Praeger, 1984).

Gertzog, Irwin, and M. Michelle Simard. ''Women and 'Hopeless' Congressional Candidacies.'' *American Politics Quarterly* 9 (October 1981): 449–466.

Geschwind, Norman. ''Language and the Brain.'' *Scientific American* 226(4) (1972): 76–83.

———. ''The Anatomical Basis of Hemispheric Differentiation.'' In Dimond and Beaumont, eds., *Hemispheric Function in the Human Brain* (New York: John Wiley, 1974).

———. ''Specializations of the Human Brain.'' *Scientific American* 241(3) (1979): 180–199.

Giddens, Anthony. *The Class Structure of the Advanced Societies* (London: Hutchinson University Library, 1973).

Gilligan, Carol. *In a Different Voice: Psychological Theory and Women's Development* (Cambridge: Harvard University Press, 1982).

Gilman, Sander. *Difference and Pathology: Stereotypes of Sexuality, Race and Madness* (Ithaca: Cornell University Press, 1985).

Ginsburg, Ruth Bader. "Sex Equality and the Constitution." *Tulane Law Review* 52(3) (April 1978): 451–475.

———. "Some Thoughts on Autonomy and Equality in Relation to Roe v. Wade." William T. Joyner Lecture, University of North Carolina School of Law, delivered April 6, 1984. Published in *North Carolina Law Review* 63(2) (January 1985): 375–386.

Githens, Marianne, and Jewel Prestage, eds. *A Portrait of Marginality: The Political Behavior of Women* (New York: David McKay, 1977).

Gittell, Marilyn. *Limits to Citizen Participation: The Decline of Community Organizations* (Beverly Hills: Sage, 1980).

Gittins, Diana. *The Family in Question: Changing Households and Familiar Ideologies* (Atlantic Highlands, N.J.: Humanities Press International, 1985).

Glenn, Evelyn Nakano. "Racial Ethnic Women's Labor: The Intersection of Race, Gender and Class Oppression." *Review of Radical Political Economy* 17(3) (Fall 1985): 86–108.

Gluck, Sherna Berger. *Rosie the Riveter Revisited: Women, the War, and Social Change* (Boston: Twayne, 1987).

Goffman, Erving. "On the Nature of Difference and Demeanor." In *Interaction Ritual: Essays on Face to Face Behavior* (Garden City, N.Y.: Anchor Books, 1967).

———. *Gender Advertisements* (London: Macmillan, 1976).

———. "Arrangement between Sexes." *Theory and Society* 4 (1977): 301–331.

Goldberg, Steven. *The Inevitability of Patriarchy*, 2d ed. (New York: Morrow, 1974).

Goleman, Daniel. "Not the Father of the Man." Review of *The Nature of the Child*, by Jerome Kagan. *New York Times Book Review*, November 18, 1984, p. 15.

———. *Vital Lies, Simple Truths: The Psychology of Self-Deception* (New York: Simon and Schuster, 1985).

Golub, Sharon. "The Effect of Premenstrual Anxiety and Depression on Cognitive Function." Paper presented at the Annual Convention of the American Psychological Association, Chicago, 1975.

Goode, William J. "Community within a Community: The Professions." *American Sociological Review* 22 (1957): 194–200.

———. "The Theoretical Importance of Love." *American Sociological Review* 24 (February 1959): 38–47.

———. "A Theory of Role Strain." *American Sociological Review* 25 (1960a): 483–496.

———. "Norm Commitment and Conformity to Role-Status Obligations." *American Journal of Sociology* 66 (November 1960b): 248–258.

———. *World Revolution and Family Patterns* (New York: Free Press of Glencoe, 1963) (2d ed., 1982).

———. "Force and Violence in the Family." *Journal of Marriage and the Family* 33 (1971): 624–636.

———. "The Place of Force in Human Society." *American Sociological Review* 37 (October 1972): 507–519.

———. *Explorations in Social Theory* (New York: Oxford University Press, 1973).

―――. "Why Men Resist." In Thorne and Yalom, eds., *Rethinking the Family: Some Feminist Questions* (New York: Longman, 1982a): 131–150.

―――. *The Family*, 2d ed. (1964. Englewood Cliffs, N.J.: Prentice-Hall, 1982b).

Goode, William J., ed. *The Contemporary American Family* (New York: Quadrangle Books, 1964).

Goot, M., and E. Reid. "Women and Voting Studies: Mindless Matrons or Sexist Scientism." *Political Science* 27(1–2) (1975): 143–145.

Gorski, R. A. "Long-Term Hormonal Modulation of Neuronal Structure and Function." In Schmidt and Worden, eds., *The Neurosciences: 4th Study Program* (Cambridge: MIT Press, 1979): 969–982.

Gottfredson, Linda S. *Race and Class Differences in Occupational Aspirations: Their Development and Consequences for Occupational Segregation.* Center for Social Organization of Schools Report no. 254 (Baltimore: Johns Hopkins University Press, 1978).

Gough, E. Kathleen. "Changing Kinship Usages in the Setting of Political and Economic Change among the Nayars of Malabar." *Journal of the Royal Anthropological Institute* 82, pt. 1 (1952): 71–88.

Gould, Roger. *Transformations: Growth and Change in Adult Life* (New York: Simon and Schuster, 1978).

Gould, Stephen J. *The Mismeasure of Man* (New York: Norton, 1981).

―――. "Triumph of a Naturalist." Review of *A Feeling for the Organism: The Life and Work of Barbara McClintock,* by Evelyn Fox Keller. *New York Review of Books,* March 29, 1984a: 58–71.

―――. "Similarities between the Sexes." Review of *A Critique of Biology and Its Theories on Women,* by Ruth Bleier. *New York Times Book Review* (August 12, 1984b): 7.

Graham, A. "The Making of a Non-sexist Dictionary." *Ms.* (December 1973): 12–14, 16. Reprinted in Thorne and Henley, eds., *Language and Sex* (Rowley, Mass.: Newbury House, 1975): 57–63.

Granovetter, Mark. "The Strength of Weak Ties." *American Sociological Review* 65 (March 1971): 69–82.

―――. *Getting a Job: A Study of Contracts and Careers* (Cambridge: Harvard University Press, 1974).

Green, Arnold W. "The Middle-class Male Child and Neurosis." *American Sociological Review* 11 (February 1946): 31–41.

Green, Richard. *Sexual Identity and Conflict in Children and Adults* (New York: Basic Books, 1975).

Green, Susan S. "Silicone Valley's Women's Work: A Theoretical Analysis of Sex Segregation in the Economics Industry Labor Market." In Nash and Fernandez-Kelly, eds., *Women, Men, and the International Division of Labor* (Albany: State University of New York Press, 1983).

Greeno, Catherine, and Eleanor Maccoby. "How Different Is the Different Voice?" *Signs* 11(2) (Winter 1986): 310–316.

Greenstein, Fred. "Sex-Related Political Differences in Childhood." *Journal of Politics* 23 (1961): 353–371.

Gregory, Michael, Anita Silvers, and Diane Sutch, eds. *Sociobiology and Human*

Nature: An Interdisciplinary Critique and Defense (San Francisco: Jossey-Bass, 1979).

Griffiths, Martha. Equal Pay for Equal Worth, Pt. 1: Hearings on H.R. 8898 and H.R. 10226 before the House Select Subcommittee on Labor, House Committee on Education and Labor, 87th Cong., 2d sess., 1962.

Gross, Edward. "Plus ça change . . . ? The Sexual Structure of Occupations over Time." *Social Problems* 16 (1968): 198–208.

Gross, Harriet E., Jessie Bernard, Alice J. Dan, Nona Glazer, Judith Lorber, Martha McClintock, Niles Newton, and Alice Rossi. "Considering a Biosocial Perspective on Parenting." *Signs* 4(4) (Summer 1979): 695–717.

Gruber, James, and Lars Bjorn. "Automobile Workers and the American Dream: The Case of Women on the Line." Paper presented at the Annual Meeting of the North Central Sociological Association, Detroit, May 1982.

Gruberg, Martin. *Women in American Politics* (Oshkosh, Wis.: Academia, 1968).

Gurin, Patricia. "Women's Gender Consciousness." *Public Opinion Quarterly* 49 (1985): 143–163.

Gurin, Patricia, and Orville G. Brim, Jr. "Change of Self in Adulthood: The Example of Sense of Control." *Life-span Development and Behavior* 6 (1984): 281–334.

Gurin, P., G. Gurin, and B. M. Morrison. "Personal and Ideological Aspects of Internal and External Control." *Social Psychology Quarterly* 41 (1978): 275–296.

Gurin, Patricia, and Hazel Markus. "Cognitive Consequences of Gender Identity." Manuscript, Russell Sage Foundation, 1985.

Gurin, Patricia, and Louise Tilly. "Women in Twentieth Century Politics." Proposal to Russell Sage Foundation, 1985.

Gwynn, Stephen. "Bachelor Women." *Contemporary Review* 73 (1898): 866–875.

Haavio-Mannila, Elina. "The Position of Finnish Women: Regional and Cross-National Comparisons." *Journal of Marriage and the Family* 31(2) (1969): 339–347.

———. "Women in the Economic, Political and Cultural Elites in Finland." In Epstein and Coser, eds., *Access to Power* (London: George Allen and Unwin, 1981): 53–75.

Haavio-Mannila, Elina, Drude Dahlerup, Maud Eduards, Esther Gudmudsdóttir, Beatrice Halsaa, Helga Maria Hernes, Eva Hänninen-Salmelin, Bergthora Sigmundsdóttir, Sirkka Sinkkonen, and Torild Skard, eds. *Unfinished Democracy: Women in Nordic Politics*. Trans. Christine Badcock. (Oxford: Pergamon Press, 1985).

Haberman, Clyde. Review of *Shadows of the Rising Sun: A Critical View of the "Japanese Miracle,"* by Jared Taylor. *New York Times,* January 16, 1984, p. C16.

Hacker, Helen Mayer. "Class and Race Differences in Gender Roles." In Duberman, ed., *Gender and Sex in Society* (New York: Praeger, 1975).

Hagen, Everett E. *The Economics of Development,* 3d ed. (1968. Homewood, Ill.: R. D. Irwin, 1980).

Halaby, Charles N. "Job-Specific Sex Differences in Organizational Reward Attainment: Wage Discrimination vs. Rank Segregation." *Social Forces* 58 (September 1979): 108–127.

Hall, Edward T. *The Hidden Dimension* (New York: Random House, 1966).

———. "Proxemics." *Current Anthropology* 9 (1968): 83–108.

Hall, G. S. *Adolescence: Its Psychology and Its Relations to Physiology, Anthropol-*

ogy, Sociology, Sex, Crime, Religion and Education, vol. 3. (New York: Appleton, 1905).

———. "Question of Coeducation." *Munsey's Magazine* 34 (1906): 588–592.

Hall, Oswald. "The Stages of a Medical Career." *American Journal of Sociology* 53 (March 1946): 327–336.

Hall, Roberta M., and Bernice R. Sandler. "Academic Mentoring for Women, Students and Faculty: A New Look at an Old Way to Get Ahead." Paper written for Project on the Status and Education of Women at the Association of American Colleges, 1983.

Hallett, Judith. *Fathers and Daughters in Roman Society* (Princeton: Princeton University Press, 1984).

Hammond, Jack. "The Gender Gap: Social Bases and Political Consequences." Manuscript, 1984.

Hansot, E., and D. Tyack. "Gender in American Public Schools: Thinking Institutionally." *Signs* 13(4) (Summer 1988).

Haraway, Donna. "In the Beginning Was the Word: The Genesis of Biological Theory." *Signs* 6(3) (1981): 469–481.

———. "We Think, Therefore We Are." Review of *Discovering Reality: Feminist Perspectives on Epistemology, Metaphysics, Methodology and Philosophy of Science*, ed. Sandra Harding and Merrill B. Hintikka. *Women's Review of Books* 1(2) (November 1983a): 3–5.

———. "The Contest for Primate Nature: Daughters of Man-the-Hunter in the Field, 1960–1980." In Kann, ed., *The Future of American Democracy: Views from the Left* (Philadelphia: Temple University Press, 1983b): 175–207.

Harding, Sandra, and Merrill B. Hintikka, eds. *Discovering Reality: Feminist Perspectives on Epistemology, Metaphysics, Methodology and Philosophy of Science* (Amsterdam: Reidel, 1983).

Hareven, Tamara. "Family Time and Historical Time." *Daedalus* 106 (Spring 1977): 57–70.

———. *Family Time and Industrial Time* (Cambridge: Cambridge University Press, 1982).

Harlow, Harry F. *Learning to Love* (San Francisco: Albion, 1971).

Harper & Row. *Harper & Row Guidelines on Equal Treatment of the Sexes in Textbooks* (New York: Harper & Row, 1976).

Harris, Olivia. "Complementarity and Conflict: An Andean View of Women and Men." In La Fontaine, ed., *Sex and Age as Principles of Social Differentiation* (New York: Academic Press, 1978), 21–40.

Hartmann, Heidi. "Capitalism, Patriarchy and Job Segregation by Sex." *Signs* 1(pt. 2) (Spring 1976): 137–169.

———. "The Family as the Locus of Gender, Class and Political Struggle: The Example of Housework." *Signs* 6 (1981): 360–394.

Hartsock, Nancy. "The Feminist Standpoint: Developing the Ground for a Specifically Historical Materialism." In Harding and Hintikka, eds., *Discovering Reality* (Amsterdam: Reidel, 1983): 283–310.

Hauser, Robert M., and David L. Featherman. *The Process of Stratification: Trends and Analyses* (New York: Academic Press, 1977).

Heath, Anthony, and Nicky Britten. "Women's Jobs Do Make a Difference: A Reply to Goldthorpe." *Sociology* 18(4) (1984): 475–490.

Heitlinger, Alena. *Women and State Socialism: Sex Inequality in the Soviet Union and Czechoslovakia* (London: Macmillan, 1979).

———. "Women in Eastern Europe: Survey of Literature." *Women's Studies International Forum* 8(2) (1985): 147–152.

Henley, Nancy. "Status and Sex: Some Touching Observations." *Bulletin of the Psychonomic Society* 17 (1973): 79–81.

———. "Power, Sex and Nonverbal Communication." *Berkeley Journal of Sociology* 18 (1973-74): 1–26. Reprinted in Thorne and Henley, eds., *Language and Sex* (Rowley, Mass.: Newbury House, 1975): 184–202.

———. *Body Politics: Power, Sex and Nonverbal Communication* (Englewood Cliffs, N.J.: Prentice-Hall, 1977).

Hernes, Helga Maria. "Women and the Welfare State: The Transition from Private to Public Dependence." In Holter, ed., *Patriarchy in a Welfare State* (Oslo-Bergen, Stavanger, and Tromso: Universitetsforlaget, 1984): 26–45.

Hess, Beth. "Prime Time." *Women's Review of Books* 2(9) (June 1985): 6–7.

Hess, Robert, and Judith Torney. *The Development of Political Attitudes of Children* (Chicago: Aldine, 1967).

Hewes, Amy. *Women as Munition Makers: A Study of Conditions in Bridgeport, Conn.* (New York: Russell Sage, 1917).

Hewlett, Sylvia Ann. *A Lesser Life: The Myth of Women's Liberation in America* (New York: Morrow, 1986).

Hiatt, Mary P. *The Way Women Write* (New York: Teachers College Press, 1977).

Hill, Ann Corinne. "Protection of Women Workers and the Courts: A Legal Case History." *Feminist Studies* 5(2) (Summer 1979): 247–273.

Hill, Robert B. *The Strengths of Families* (New York: Emerson Hall, 1971).

Hiller, D. V., and W. W. Philliber. "Derivation of Status Benefits from Occupational Attainments of Working Wives." *Journal of Marriage and the Family* 40 (1978): 63–69.

Hilpert, Fred, Cheris Kramer, and Ruth Ann Clark. "Participants' Perceptions of Self and Partner in Mixed-Sex Dyads." *Central States Speech Journal* 26(1) (Spring 1975): 52–56.

Hirschman, Lynette. "Analysis of Supportive and Assertive Behavior in Conversation." Paper presented at the Annual Meeting of the Linguistic Society of America, Amherst, Mass., July 1974.

Hochschild, Arlie. "A Review of Sex Role Research." In Huber, ed., *Changing Women in a Changing Society* (Chicago: University of Chicago Press, 1973): 249–267.

———. "The Sociology of Feeling and Emotion: Selected Possibilities." In Millman and Kanter, eds., *Another Voice* (New York: Doubleday/Anchor, 1975): 280–307.

———. "Emotion Work, Feeling Rules and Social Structure." *American Journal of Sociology* 85(2) (November 1979): 551–595.

———. *The Managed Heart: Commercialization of Human Feeling* (Berkeley: University of California Press, 1983).

———. "Housework and Gender Strategies for Getting Out of It." Paper presented at the Annual Meeting of the American Sociological Association, Washington, D.C., August 27, 1985.

Hodson, Randy. "Companies, Industries, and the Measurement of Economic Segmentation." *American Sociological Review* 49 (June 1984): 335–348.

Hoffer, Carol P. [later MacCormack]. "Mende and Sherbro Women in High Office." *Canadian Journal of African Studies* 6 (1972): 151–164.

———. "Madame Yoko: Ruler of the Kpa Mende Confederacy." In Rosaldo and Lamphere, eds., *Woman, Culture, and Society* (Stanford, Calif.: Stanford University Press, 1974): 173–187.

Hoffman, Joan C. "Biorhythms in Human Reproduction: The Not So Steady States." *Signs* 7(4) (1982): 829–844.

Hoffman, Lois Wladis. "Mothers' Enjoyment of Work and Effects on the Child." *Child Development* 32 (March 1961): 187–197.

Hoffman, Lois Wladis, and Martin Hoffman. "The Value of Children to Parents." In Fawcett, ed., *Psychological Perspectives on Population* (New York: Basic Books, 1973): 19–76.

Hoffman, S. "Marital Instability and the Economic Status of Women." *Demography* 14 (1977): 67–76.

Hole, Judith, and Ellen Levine. *Rebirth of Feminism* (New York: Quadrangle Books, 1971).

Hollander, Anne. *Seeing through Clothes* (New York: Viking Books, 1978).

Holloway, Ralph, and Christine de Lacoste-Utamsing. "Sexual Dimorphism in the Human *Corpus Callosum.*" *Science* 216 (June 25, 1982): 1431.

Holt, Rinehart and Winston, College Division. *The Treatment of Sex Roles and Minorities* (New York: Harper & Row, 1976).

Holter, Harriet. *Sex Roles and Social Structure* (Oslo: Universitetsforlaget, 1970).

Holter, Harriet, ed. *Patriarchy in a Welfare State* (Oslo-Bergen, Stavanger, and Tromso: Universitetsforlaget, 1984).

Homans, George C. "Social Behavior as Exchange." *American Journal of Sociology* 62 (May 1961): 595–606.

Honey, Maureen. *Creating Rosie the Riveter: Class, Gender and Propaganda during World War 2* (Boston: University of Massachusetts Press, 1984).

Horan, Patrick M. "Is Status Attainment Research Atheoretical?" *American Sociological Review* 43(4) (1978): 534–540.

Horner, Matina. "Sex Differences in Achievement Motivation and Performance in Competitive and Non-Competitive Situations" (Ph.D. diss. University of Michigan, 1968).

———. "Femininity and Successful Achievement: A Basic Inconsistency." In J. Bardwick, E. M. Douvan, M. S. Horner, and D. Gutmann, eds., *Feminine Personality and Conflict* (Belmont, Calif.: Brooks-Cole, 1970).

———. "Toward an Understanding of Achievement-Related Conflicts in Women." *Journal of Social Issues* 28(2) (1972): 157–175.

Horney, Karen. *Feminine Psychology*. Ed. H. Kelman (1924. New York: W. W. Norton, 1967).

Hornig, Lilli S. "The Missing Scientists: Women in Science and Engineering." Unpublished National Academy of Science document, March 1980.

Hrdy, Sara Blaffer. *The Langurs of Abu: Female and Male Strategies of Reproduction* (Cambridge: Harvard University Press, 1977).

———. *The Woman That Never Evolved* (Cambridge: Harvard University Press, 1981).

Hubbard, Ruth, Mary S. Henefin, and Barbara Fried, eds. *Women Look at Biology Looking at Women: A Collection of Feminist Critiques* (Cambridge: Schenkman, 1979).

Hubbard, Ruth, and Marian Lowe, eds. *Pitfalls in Research on Sex and Gender,* vol. 2 of *Genes and Gender* (Staten Island, N.Y.: Gordian Press, 1979).

Huber, Joan. "Sociology." *Signs* 1(pt. 1) (Spring 1976): 685–698.

———. "Trends in Gender Stratification." Paper presented at the Conference on Trends in Sociology, sponsored by the National Academy of Science Committee on Scholarly Communication with the People's Republic of China, Warrenton, Va., August 23–25, 1985. Published as "Trends in Gender Stratification, 1970–1985." *Sociological Forum* 1 (1986): 476–495.

Huber, Joan, and Glenna Spitze. *Sex Stratification: Children, Housework and Jobs* (New York: Academic Press, 1983).

Hughes, Everett C. "Dilemmas and Contradictions of Status." *American Journal of Sociology* 50 (March 1945): 353–359.

———. "Good People and Dirty Work." *Social Problems* 9 (1962). Reprinted in H. Becker, ed., *The Other Side* (New York: Free Press, 1964).

Hughes, Thomas. *The Manliness of Christ* (London: Macmillan, c.1880).

Hunt, Alan. "The Ideology of Law: Advances and Problems in Recent Applications of the Concept of Ideology to the Analysis of Law." *Law and Society Review* 19(1) (1985): 11–37.

Hunter, Floyd. *Community Power Structure* (Chapel Hill: University of North Carolina Press, 1953).

Huntington, Suellen. "Issues in Women's Role in Economic Development: Critique and Alternatives." *Journal of Marriage and the Family* 37 (November 1975): 1001–1012.

Hyde, Janet Shibley. "How Large Are Gender Differences in Aggression?: A Developmental Meta-analysis." *Developmental Psychology* 20 (1984): 722–736.

Hyman, Herbert. *Political Socialization* (Glencoe, Ill.: Free Press, 1959).

Ickes, W., and R. D. Barnes. "The Role of Sex and Self-Monitoring in Unstructured Dyadic Interactions." *Journal of Personality and Social Psychology* 35 (1977): 315–330.

Iltis, Carolyn Merchant. "Bacon and Harvey: Views of Nature and the Female in the Scientific Revolution." Paper, Center for Advanced Study in the Behavioral Sciences, 1978.

Jacobs, Jerry. "On Comparing the Social Standing of Men and Women." Working paper, University of Pennsylvania, March 1982.

Jacobs, P. A., M. Brunton, M. M. Melville, R. P. Brittan, and W. F. McClamont. "Aggressive Behavior, Mental Subnormality and XYY Male." *Nature* 208 (1970): 1351–1352.

Jacklin, Carol N., Eleanor E. Maccoby, Charles H. Doering, and David R. King. "Neonatal Sex-steroid Hormones and Muscular Strength of Boys and Girls in the First Three Years." *Developmental Psychobiology* 20(3) (May 1984): 459–472.

Jackman, Mary, and Robert Jackman. *Class Awareness in the United States* (Berkeley: University of California Press, 1983).

Jancar, Barbara. *Women under Communism* (Baltimore: Johns Hopkins University Press, 1978).

Jaquette, Jane S. "Review Essay: Political Science." *Signs* 2(1) (1976): 147–164.

Jaquette, Jane S., ed. *Women in Politics* (New York: John Wiley, 1974).

Jennings, M. Kent. *Another Look at the Life Cycle and Political Participation* (Ann Arbor, University of Michigan Press, 1977).

Jennings, M. Kent, and Barbara G. Farah. "Social Roles and Political Resources: An Over-time Study of Men and Women in Party Elites." *American Journal of Political Science* 25(3) (August 1981): 462–482.

Jennings, M. Kent, and Richard G. Niemi. "The Division of Political Labor between Mothers and Fathers." *American Political Science Review* 65 (March 1971): 69–82.

———. "Continuity and Change in Political Orientations: A Longitudinal Study of Two Generations." *American Political Science Review* 69 (December 1975): 1316–1335.

Jennings, M. Kent, and Norman Thomas. "Men and Women in Party Elites: Social Roles and Political Resources." *Midwest Journal of Political Science* 12(12) (November 1968): 469–492.

Jespersen, Otto. *Language: Its Nature, Development and Origin* (New York: Henry Holt, 1924).

Joffe, Carole. *The Regulation of Sexuality: Experiences of Family Planning Workers* (Philadelphia: Temple University Press, 1986).

Johnson, Marilyn. "Broadening Elective and Appointive Political Participation." In Cahn, ed., *Women in Midlife: Security and Fulfillment*, pt. 1 (Washington, D.C.: U.S. Government Printing Office, 1978): 299–319.

Johnson, Marilyn, and Susan Carroll. "Profile of Women Holding Office, 1977." In *Women in Public Office: A Biographical Dictionary and Statistical Analysis*, comp. Center for the American Woman and Politics (New York: R. R. Bowker, 1978).

Jolly, Alison. *Lemur Behavior: A Madagascar Field Study* (Chicago: University of Chicago Press, 1966).

"Judge Upholds Award to TV Anchorwoman." *New York Times*, September 1, 1983, p. 18.

Kaberry, Phylis M. *Aboriginal Woman: Sacred and Profane* (Philadelphia: Blakiston, 1939; London: Routledge and Kegan Paul, 1970).

Kagan, Jerome, "Perspectives on Continuity." In Brim and Kagan, eds., *Constancy and Change in Human Development* (Cambridge: Harvard University Press, 1980): 26–74.

———. *The Nature of the Child* (New York: Basic Books, 1984).

Kagan, Jerome, and Howard Moss. *Birth to Maturity: A Study in Psychological Development* (New York: John Wiley, 1962).

Kamin, L. "Heredity, Intelligence, Politics and Psychology: I." In Block and Dworkin, eds., *The I.Q. Controversy* (New York: Pantheon, 1976): 242–264.

Kanter, Rosabeth Moss. "The Impact of Hierarchical Structures on the Work Behavior of Women and Men." *Social Problems* 23 (1976): 415–430.

————. *Men and Women of the Corporation* (New York: Basic Books, 1977a).

————. *Work and Family in the United States: A Critical Review and Agenda for Research and Policy* (New York: Russell Sage Foundation, 1977b).

Katz, Elihu, and Paul F. Lazarsfeld. *Personal Influence* (Glencoe, Ill.: Free Press, 1955).

Kaufman, Debra R., and Barbara L. Richardson. *Achievement and Women: Challenging the Assumptions* (New York: Free Press, 1982).

Kay, Herma Hill. "Models of Equality." *University of Illinois Law Review* 1 (1985): 39–88.

Keller, Evelyn Fox. "Feminism and Science." *Signs* 7 (1982): 589–602.

————. "Feminism as an Analytic Tool for the Study of Science." *Academe* 69(5) (1983): 15–21.

————. *Reflections on Gender and Science* (New Haven: Yale University Press, 1985).

Kelly, Lowell. "Consistency of the Adult Personality." *American Psychologist* 10 (1955): 659–681.

Kelly-Gadol, Joan. "Did Women Have a Renaissance?" In Bridenthal and Koonz, eds., *Becoming Visible: Women in European History* (Boston: Houghton Mifflin, 1977): 139–163.

Kemper, Theodore D. "Social Constructionist and Positivist Approaches to the Sociology of Emotions." *American Journal of Sociology* 87(2) (September 1981): 336–362.

Kerber, Linda K.; Catherine G. Greeno and Eleanor E. Maccoby; Zella Luria; Carol B. Stack; and Carol Gilligan. "On *In a Different Voice*: An Interdisciplinary Forum" *Signs* 11(2) (Winter 1986): 304–333.

Kerr, Peter. "Judge Overturns Finding by Jury of Sex Bias in Newscaster's Suit." *New York Times,* November 1, 1983, pp. 1, A1.

————. "Jury Selection Begins in Retrial of Craft Case." *New York Times,* January 5, 1984a, pp. 18, C27.

————. "Jury Awards Chris Craft $325,000." *New York Times,* January 14, 1984b, pp. 13, 43.

Kessler-Harris, Alice. *Women Have Always Worked: A Historical Overview* (Old Westbury, Conn.: Feminist Press, 1981).

————. *Out to Work: A History of Wage-Earning Women in the United States* (New York: Oxford University Press, 1982).

Kimmel, Michael S., ed. "Researching Male Roles." *American Behavioral Scientist* 29(5) (May-June 1986); whole issue.

Kimmel, Michael S. "From Separate Spheres to Sexual Equality: Male Responses to Feminism at the Turn of the Century." Published in an edited version as "Men's Responses to Feminism at the Turn of the Century." *Gender & Society* 1(3) (September 1987): 261–283.

————. *Changing Men: New Directions in the Study of Men and Masculinity* (Beverly Hills: Sage, forthcoming).

King, Elizabeth G. "Women in Iowa Legislative Politics." In Githens and Prestage, eds., *A Portrait of Marginality* (New York: David McKay, 1977): 284–303.

Kirkpatrick, Jeane. *Political Women* (New York: Basic Books, 1974).

————. *The New Presidential Elite* (New York: Russell Sage Foundation, 1976).

Kitcher, Philip. *Vaulting Ambition: Sociobiology and the Quest for Human Nature* (Cambridge: MIT Press, 1985).

Klein, Ethel. *Gender Politics* (Cambridge: Harvard University Press, 1984).

Klein, H. M., and L. Willerman. "Psychological Masculinity and Femininity and Typical and Maximal Dominance Expression in Women." *Journal of Personality and Social Psychology* 37(11) (November 1979): 2059–2070.

Kleppner, Paul. "Were Women to Blame? Female Suffrage and Voter Turnout." *Journal of Interdisciplinary History* 7(4) (Spring 1982): 621–643.

Knorr-Cetina, Karis D., and Michael Mulkay, eds. *Science Observed: Perspectives on the Social Study of Science* (Beverly Hills: Sage, 1983).

Knudson, Ruth B., ed. *Women and Success* (New York: William Morrow, 1974).

Koeski, R. K., and G. F. Koeski. "An Attributional Approach to Moods and the Menstrual Cycle." *Journal of Personality and Social Psychology* 31 (1975): 473–478.

Kohn, Melvin L. *Class and Conformity: A Study on Values*, 2d ed. (Chicago: University of Chicago Press, 1977).

Kohn, Melvin, and Carmi Schooler. "Occupational Experience and Psychological Functioning: An Assessment of Reciprocal Effects." *American Sociological Review* 38 (February 1973): 97–118.

———. "The Reciprocal Effects of the Substantive Complexity of Work and Intellectual Flexibility: A Longitudinal Assessment." *American Journal of Sociology* 84 (July 1978): 24–52.

———. "Job Conditions and Personality: A Longitudinal Assessment of Their Reciprocal Effects." *American Journal of Sociology* 87(6) (May 1982): 1257–1286.

Kollock, Peter, Philip Blumstein, and Pepper Schwartz. "Sex and Power in Interaction: Conversational Privileges and Duties." *American Sociological Review* 50 (1985): 34–46.

Komarovsky, Mirra. "Cultural Contradictions and Sex Roles." *American Journal of Sociology* 52 (1946): 184–189.

———. *Blue-Collar Marriage* (New York: Random House, 1962).

———. *Women in the Modern World* (Boston: Little, Brown, 1953; New York: Irvington Books, 1971).

Kosa, John, and Robert E. Coker, Jr. "The Female Physician in Public Health: Conflict and Reconciliation of the Professional and Sex Roles." *Sociology and Social Research* 49 (April 1965): 295.

Kramarae, Cheris. *Women and Men Speaking: Frameworks for Analysis* (Rowley, Mass.: Newbury House, 1981).

Kramer, Cheris. "Folklinguistics." *Psychology Today* 8 (1974): 82–85.

———. "Women's Speech: Separate But Unequal?" *Quarterly Journal of Speech* 60 (February 1974): 14–24. Reprinted in Thorne and Henley, eds., *Language and Sex: Difference and Dominance* (Rowley, Mass.: Newbury House, 1975): 43–56.

Kramer, Cheris, Barrie Thorne, and Nancy Henley. "Review Essay: Perspectives on Language and Communication." *Signs* 3(3) (Spring 1978): 638–651.

Kramer, Jeanette R. *Family Interfaces: Transgenerational Patterns* (New York: Brunner/Mazel, 1985).

Kramer, Rita. "The Third Wave." *Wilson Quarterly* 10(4) (Autumn 1986): 110–129.

Kroeber, Alfred. *The Nature of Culture* (Chicago: University of Chicago Press, 1952).

Kucera, Daniel J. "Women Unwanted." *Harvard Law Record* 37 (December 12, 1963): 1.

Kuhn, Thomas S. *The Structure of Scientific Revolutions* (Chicago: University of Chicago Press, 1962).

La Dame, Mary. *The Filene Store: A Study of Employees' Relation to Management in a Retail Store* (New York: Russell Sage, 1930).

LaFrance, Marianne. "Gender Gestures: Sex, Sex-Role, and Nonverbal Communication." In Mayot and Henley, eds., *Gender and Non-verbal Behavior* (New York: Springer-Verlag, 1981).

Lakoff, Robin. "Language and Woman's Place." *Language and Society* 2 (1973): 45–80.

———. *Language and Women's Place* (New York: Harper & Row, 1975).

Lamphere, Louise. "Anthropology." *Signs* 2(3) (Spring 1977): 612–628.

Lancaster, Jane. "In Praise of the Achieving Female Monkey." *Psychology Today* 7 (September 1973): 30.

———. "Introduction." In Small, ed., *Female Primates: Studies by Women Primatologists* (New York: Alan R. Liss, 1984).

Lane, Robert. *Political Life: Why People Get Involved in Politics* (1959. Glencoe, Ill.: Free Press, 1964).

Lange, Lynda. "Woman Is Not a Rational Animal: On Aristotle's Biology of Reproduction." In Harding and Hintikka, eds., *Discovering Reality* (Amsterdam: Reidel, 1983): 1–16.

Langland, Elizabeth, and Walter Gove, eds., "A Feminist Perspective in the Academy: The Difference It Makes."*Soundings: An Interdisciplinary Journal* 64(4) (Winter 1981).

Lansing, Marjorie. "The Voting Patterns of American Black Women." In Githens and Prestage, eds., *A Portrait of Marginality* (New York: David McKay, 1977): 379–394.

Lapidus, Gail Warshofsky. *Women in Soviet Society: Equality, Development and Social Change* (Berkeley: University of California Press, 1978).

Lasch, Christopher. *Haven in a Heartless World: The Family Besieged* (New York: Basic Books, 1977).

Latane, Bibb, and John Darley. *The Unresponsive Bystander: Why Doesn't He Help?* (Englewood Cliffs, N.J.: Prentice-Hall, 1970).

Law, Sylvia. "Rethinking Sex and the Constitution." *University of Pennsylvania Law Review* 132 (1984): 955–1040.

Lawrence, Barbara. "Dirty Words *Can* Harm You." *Redbook* 143 (May 1974): 33.

Laws, Judith Long. "Work Aspirations of Women: False Leads and New Starts." *Signs* 1 (Spring 1976): 33–49.

Lazarsfeld, Paul, F., and Morris Rosenberg, eds. *Language of Social Research: A Reader in the Methodology of Social Research* (Glencoe, Ill.: Free Press, 1955).

Leacock, Eleanor. "Women's Status in Equalitarian Society: Implications for Social Evolution." *Current Anthropology* 19 (1978): 247–275.

———. "History, Development and the Division of Labor by Sex: Implications for Organizations." *Signs* (Winter 1981a): 474–491.

————. *Myths of Male Dominance: Collected Articles on Women Cross-Culturally* (New York: Monthly Review Press, 1981b).

Lee, Marcia Manning. "Toward Understanding Why So Few Women Hold Public Office: Factors Affecting the Participation of Women in Local Politics." In Githens and Prestage, eds., *A Portrait of Marginality* (New York: David McKay, 1977): 118–138.

Lee, Richard B. "What Hunters Do for a Living, or, How to Make Out on Scarce Resources." In Lee and DeVore, eds., *Man the Hunter* (Chicago: Aldine, 1968): 30–48.

Lee, Richard B., and Irven DeVore, eds. *Man the Hunter* (Chicago: Aldine, 1968).

Legman, D. *Rationale of the Dirty Joke: An Analysis of Sexual Humor* (Memphis, Tenn.: Castle Books, 1968).

Lenski, Gerhard E. *Power and Privilege* (New York: McGraw-Hill, 1966).

Lerner, Richard M. *Concepts and Theories of Human Development* (1976. Reading, Mass.: Addison-Wesley, 1986).

Levine, Adeline, and Janice Crumrine. "Women and the Fear of Success: A Problem in Replication." *American Journal of Sociology* 80(4) (1975): 964–974.

Levinson, Daniel J., C. N. Darrow, E. B. Klein, M. H. Levinson, and B. McKee. *The Seasons of a Man's Life* (New York: Alfred A. Knopf, 1978).

Levi-Strauss, Claude. *Elementary Structures in Kinship* (1949. Boston: Beacon Press, 1969).

————. *Myth and Meaning* (London: Routledge and Kegan Paul, 1978).

Levitan, Teresa, Robert P. Quinn, and Graham L. Staines. "Sex Discrimination against the American Working Woman." *American Behavioral Scientist* 15(2) (1971): 237–254.

Levy, David. *Maternal Overprotection* (New York: Columbia University Press, 1943).

Levy, Marion Joseph, Jr., *The Family Revolution in Modern China* (Cambridge: Harvard University Press, 1949).

Levy, Marion Joseph, Jr., and Lloyd Fallers. "The Family: Some Comparative Considerations." *American Anthropologist* 61(4) (August 1959): 647–651.

Levy, Robert I. "The Attack on Mead." *Science* 220 (1983): 829–832.

Lewontin, R. C., Steven Rose, and Leon Kamin. *Not in Our Genes* (New York: Pantheon Books, 1984).

Lidz, T. *The Origin and Treatment of Schizophrenic Disorders* (New York: Basic Books, 1973).

Linden, Eugene. *Apes, Men and Language* (New York: Penguin, 1974).

Linton, Ralph. *The Study of Man.* (New York: Appleton-Century, 1936).

————. *The Cultural Background of Personality* (Englewood Cliffs, N.J.: Prentice-Hall, 1945).

Linton, Sally. "Woman the Gatherer: Male Bias in Anthropology." In Jacobs, ed., *Women in Cross-Cultural Perspective* (Champaign-Urbana: University of Illinois Press, 1971).

Lipman-Blumen, Jean, Alice Handley-Isaksen, and Harold J. Leavitt. "Achieving Styles in Men and Women: A Model and Instrument and Some Findings." In Spence, ed., *Achievement and Achievement Motives* (San Francisco: W. H. Freeman, 1983).

Lipset, Seymour Martin. "Democracy and the Working Class Authoritarian." *American Sociological Review* 24(4) (August 1959): 482–501.

————. *Political Man: The Social Basis of Politics* (Baltimore: Johns Hopkins University Press, 1960).

————. "Sociology and Political Science: A Bibliographical Note." *American Sociological Review* 29(5) (October 1964): 730–734.

Litwak, Eugene. "The Use of Extended Family Groups in the Achievement of Social Goals: Some Policy Implications." *Social Problems* 7 (1959–60): 177–187.

Lopata, Helena Z. Review of *The Myth of Golden Years—Socioenvironmental Theory of Aging,* by J. F. Gubrium. *Contemporary Sociology* 4(3) (1975): 232–234.

————. "Sociology." *Signs* 2(1) (Autumn 1976): 165–176.

Lopate, Carol. *Women in Medicine* (Baltimore: Johns Hopkins University Press, 1968).

Lorber, Judith. "Women and Medical Sociology: Invisible Professionals and Ubiquitous Patients." In Millman and Kanter, eds., *Another Voice* (Garden City, N.Y.: Doubleday/Anchor, 1975): 75–105.

————. "The Limits of Sponsorship of Women Physicians." *Journal of the American Medical Women's Association* 36 (1981): 11.

————. "Women as Colleagues: The Matthew Effect and the Salieri Phenomenon." Paper presented at the Annual Meeting of the American Sociological Association, Detroit, August 1983.

————. *Women Physicians: Careers, Status and Power* (New York: Methuen, 1984).

Lovenduski, Joni. "Toward the Emasculation of Political Science: The Impact of Feminism." In Spender, ed., *Men's Studies Modified: The Impact of Feminization on the American Disciplines* (Oxford: Pergamon Press, 1981): 83–98.

Lowe, Marian. "Sex Differences, Science and Society." In Zimmerman, ed., *The Technological Woman* (New York: Praeger, 1983a): 7–17.

————. "The Dialectic of Biology and Culture." In Lowe and Hubbard, eds., *Women's Nature: Rationalizations of Inequality* (New York: Pergamon Press, 1983b): 39–62.

Lowe, Marian, and Ruth Hubbard, eds. *Women's Nature: Rationalizations of Inequality* (New York: Pergamon Press, 1983).

Loy, Pamela Hewitt, and Lea P. Stewart. "The Extent and Effects of the Sexual Harassment of Working Women." *Sociological Focus* 17(1) (January 1984): 31–43.

Luker, Kristen. *Abortion and the Politics of Motherhood.* (Berkeley: University of California Press, 1984).

————. *Taking Chances: Abortion and the Decision Not to Contracept* (Berkeley: University of California Press, 1985).

Lupri, Eugene, and Gladys Symons. "The Emerging Symmetrical Family: Fact or Fiction." *International Journal of Comparative Sociology* 23(3–4) (September-November 1981): 166–189.

Luria, Zella. "A Methodological Critique." *Signs* 11(2) (Winter 1986): 316–321.

Lurie, Allison. *The Language of Clothes* (New York: Random House, 1981).

Lynd, Robert. *Knowledge for What?* (Princeton: Princeton University Press, 1939).

Lynn, Naomi, and Cornelia B. Flora. "Societal Punishment and Aspects of Female Political Participation: 1972 National Convention Delegates." In Githens and Prestage, eds., *A Portrait of Marginality: The Political Behavior of the American Woman* (New York: David McKay, 1977): 139–149.

MacBrayer, C. T. "Differences in Perception of the Opposite Sex by Males and Females." *Journal of Social Psychology* 52 (1960): 309–314.

Maccoby, Eleanor, ed. *The Development of Sex Differences* (Stanford, Calif.: Stanford University Press, 1966).

Maccoby, Eleanor E., and Carol N. Jacklin. *The Psychology of Sex Differences* (Stanford, Calif.: Stanford University Press, 1974).

MacCormack, Carol, and Marilyn Strathern. *Nature, Culture and Gender* (New York: Cambridge University Press, 1980).

MacKinnon, Catherine A. *Sexual Harassment of Working Women* (New Haven: Yale Universitty Press, 1979).

———. "Toward a Feminist Jurisprudence." *Stanford Law Review* 34(3) (1982a): 703–737.

———. "Feminism, Marxism, Method and the State: An Agenda for Theory." *Signs* 7 (Spring 1982b): 514–544.

Mainardi, Pat. "The Politics of Housework." In Morgan, ed., *Sisterhood Is Powerful* (New York: Vintage, 1970): 447–455.

Malkiel, B. G., and J. A. Malkiel. "Male-Female Pay Differentials in Professional Employment." *American Economic Review* 63 (1973): 693–705.

Mandel, Ruth B. *In the Running: The New Woman Candidate* (New Haven: Ticknor and Fields, 1981).

Mansbridge, Jane J. *Why We Lost the ERA* (Chicago: University of Chicago Press, 1986).

March, James, and Johan P. Olsen. "The New Institutionalism: Organizational Factors in Political Life." *American Political Science Review* 78 (1984): 734–749.

Marcus, George. "One Man's Mead." *New York Times Book Review*, March 28, 1983, pp. 3, 22, 24.

Marini, Margaret Mooney. "Sex Differences in the Determination of Adolescent Aspirations: A Review of Research." *Sex Roles* 4(5) (1978): 723–753.

Marini, Margaret Mooney, and Mary Brinton. "Sex Typing in Occupational Socialization." In Reskin, ed., *Sex Segregation in the Workplace* (Washington, D.C.: National Academy Press, 1984): 192–232.

Marks, Stephen R. "Multiple Roles and Role Strain: Some Notes on Human Energy, Time and Commitment." *American Sociological Review* 42(6) (December 1977): 921–936.

Martin, Susan E. *Breaking and Entering: Policewoman on Patrol* (Berkeley: University of California Press, 1980).

Martyna, Wendy. "Beyond the 'He-Man' Approach: The Case for Nonsexist Language." *Signs* 5 (1980): 482–493.

Marx, Karl, and Frederick Engels. *The Communist Manifesto*. Trans. Samuel Moore. Ed. Joseph Katz (1848. New York: Washington Square Press, 1964).

Masters, William H., and Virginia Johnson. *Human Sexual Reponse* (Boston: Little, Brown, 1966).

———. *Human Sexual Inadequacy* (Boston: Little, Brown, 1970).

Mathiesson, Carolyn J., ed. *Many Sisters* (New York: Free Press, 1975).

Mazur, A., and T. A. Lamb. "Testosterone, Status and Mood in Human Males." *Hormones and Behavior* 14 (1980). 236–246.

McAuley, Alastair. *Women's Work and Wages in the Soviet Union* (London: George Allen and Unwin, 1981).

McClelland, David C. *The Achieving Society* (New York: Free Press, 1961).

McClendon, McKee J. "The Occupational Status Attainment Process of Males and Females." *American Sociological Review* 41(1) (1976): 52–64.

McClosky, Herbert, and Alida Brill. *Dimensions of Tolerance: What Americans Believe about Civil Liberties* (New York: Russell Sage Foundation, 1983).

McConnell-Ginet, Sally. "Intonation in a Man's World." *Signs* 3(3) (1978): 541–559.

———. "Linguistics and the Feminist Challenge." In McConnell-Ginet, Borker, and Furman, eds., *Women and Language in Literature and Society* (New York: Praeger, 1980): 3–25.

McCormack, Thelma. "Toward a Non-Sexist Perspective on Social and Political Change." In Millman and Kanter, eds., *Another Voice* (Garden City, N.Y.: Anchor Books, 1975): 1–33.

McDonald, Gerald W. "Family Power: The Assessment of a Decade of Theory and Research, 1970–79." *Journal of Marriage and the Family* 42(4) (November 1980): 841–854.

McGrew, W. C. "The Female Chimpanzee as a Human Evolutionary Prototype." In Dahlberg, ed., *Woman the Gatherer* (New Haven: Yale University Press, 1981): 35–74.

McKee, J., and A. Sheriffs. "The Differential Evaluation of Males and Females." *Journal of Personality* 25(2) (1956): 357–371.

McKenna, Wendy, and Suzanne Kessler. "Experimental Design as a Source of Sex Bias in Social Psychology." Paper presented at the Annual Meeting of the American Psychological Association, New Orleans, August 1974.

———. *Gender: An Ethnomethodological Approach* (New York: John Wiley, 1978).

McLuhan, Marshall. *Understanding Media: The Extensions of Man* (New York: Signet, 1964).

Mead, Margaret. *Sex and Temperament in Three Primitive Societies* (New York: William Morrow, 1935).

Medick, Hans, and David Warren Sabean, eds. *Interest and Emotion: Essays on the Study of Family and Kinship* (Cambridge, London, and New York: Cambridge University Press, 1984).

Merkl, Peter H. "The Study of Women in Comparative Politics: Reflections on a Conference." *Signs* 1(3) (1976): 749–756.

Merriam, Charles, and H. F. Gosnell. *Non-voting: Causes and Methods of Control* (Chicago: University of Chicago Press, 1924).

Merton, Robert K. "Science and the Social Order." *Philosophy and Science* 5 (1938). Reprinted as "Science and the Social Order." In Merton, *Social Theory and Social Structure* (Glencoe, Ill.: Free Press, 1957): 537–549.

———. "Intermarriage and the Social Structure: Fact and Theory." *Psychiatry* 4 (August 1941): 361–374.

———. "The Self-Fulfilling Prophecy." *Antioch Review* 8(2) (Summer 1948): 193–210.

———. "Foreword." In B. Barber, *Science and the Social Order* (New York: Free Press, 1952).

————. *Social Theory and Social Structure: Toward the Codification of Theory and Research* (1949. Glencoe, Ill.: Free Press, 1957).

————. "Insiders and Outsiders: A Chapter in the Sociology of Knowledge." *American Journal of Sociology* 78(1) (1972): 9–47.

————. *The Sociology of Science: Theoretical and Empirical Investigations* (Chicago: University of Chicago Press, 1973).

————. "The Fallacy of the Latest Word: The Case of 'Pietism and Science.' " *American Journal of Sociology* 89(5) (March 1984a): 1091–1121.

————. "Socially Expected Durations: A Case of Concept Formation in Sociology." In W. W. Powell and R. Robbins, eds., *Conflict and Consensus: A Festschrift in Honor of Lewis A. Coser* (New York: Free Press, 1984b): 262–283.

Merton, Robert K., and Paul F. Lazarsfeld, eds. *Continuities in Social Research* (Glencoe, Ill.: Free Press, 1950).

Merton, Robert K., and Robert Nisbet. *Contemporary Social Problems*, 4th ed. (New York: Harcourt Brace Jovanovich, 1976).

Merton, Robert K., George Reader, and Patricia Kendall, eds. *Student-Physician: Introductory Studies in the Sociology of Medical Education* (Cambridge: Harvard University Press, 1957).

Milkman, Ruth. "Women's Work and Economic Crisis—Some Lessons of the Great Depression." *Review of Radical Politics* 8(1) (1976): 73–97.

————. "Organizing the Sexual Division of Labor: Historical Perspective on Women's Work and the American Labor Movement." *Socialist Review* 10(1) (January-February 1980). 95–150.

————. "Women and Labor Unions in the Twentieth Century United States." In Gurin and Tilly, eds., *Women and Twentieth Century American Politics* (New York: Russell Sage Foundation, forthcoming).

Mill, John Stuart. "Periodical Literature: 'Edinburgh Review.' " *Westminster Review* 1(2) (April 1824): 505–541.

————. *The Subjection of Women* (Philadelphia: J. B. Lippincott, 1869).

Miller, Casey, and Kate Swift. *Words and Women: New Language in New Times* (New York: Doubleday, 1975).

Miller, Joanne, and Howard H. Garrison. "Sex Roles: The Division of Labor at Home and in the Workplace." *Annual Review of Sociology* 8 (1982): 237–262.

Miller, Joanne, Carmi Schooler, Melvin Kohn, and Karen Miller. "Women and Work: The Psychological Effects of Occupational Conditions." *American Journal of Sociology* 85(1) (July 1979): 66–94.

Miller, S. J. *Prescription for Leadership: Training for the Medical Elite* (Chicago: Aldine, 1970).

Millett, Kate. *Sexual Politics* (Garden City, N.Y.: Doubleday, 1970).

Millman, Marcia, and Rosabeth Kanter, eds. *Another Voice, Feminist Perspectives on Social Life and Social Sciences* (Garden City, N.Y.: Anchor Books, 1975).

Mills, C. Wright. *The Power Elite* (New York: Oxford University Press, 1956).

Mincer, Jacob, and Solomon Polachek. "Family Investments in Human Capital: Earnings of Women." *Journal of Political Economy* 82(pt. 2) (March-April 1974): S76–S108.

————. "Women's Earnings Reexamined." *Journal of Human Resources* 13 (Winter 1978): 118–134.

Mischel, W. "Change and Continuity in Personality." *American Psychologist* 24 (1969): 1012–1018.

———. "Convergence and Challenges in the Search for Consistency." *American Psychologist* 39 (1984): 351–364.

Mitchell, Gary, William K. Redican, and Judy Gomber. "Lesson from a Primate: Males Can Raise Babies." *Psychology Today* 7(11) (April 1974): 63–68.

Mitchell, Juliet. *Psychoanalysis and Feminism* (New York: Pantheon, 1971).

Mohr, James. *Abortion in America: The Origins and Evolution of National Policy, 1800–1900* (New York: Oxford University Press, 1978).

Moore, Kristin A., and Isabel V. Sawhill. "Implications of Occupational Segregation." In Stromberg and Harkess, eds., *Women Working: Theories and Facts in Perspective* (Palo Alto, Calif.: Mayfield, 1978): 201–225.

Moran, Eileen G. "Gender Tracking in a County Democratic Party Organization: An Issue in Social Stratification" (Ph.D. diss., City University of New York, 1983).

Morris, Desmond. *The Naked Ape* (New York: MacGraw-Hill, 1967).

Moss, Howard A., and Elizabeth J. Susman. "Longitudinal Study of Personality Development." In Brim and Kagan, eds., *Constancy and Change in Human Development* (Cambridge: Harvard University Press, 1980): 530–595.

Moynihan, Daniel P. *The Negro Family: The Case for National Action* (Washington, D.C.: U.S. Department of Labor, Office of Policy Planning and Research, 1965).

Mumford, Emily. *Interns: From Students to Physicians* (Cambridge: Harvard University Press, 1970).

Murdock, George Peter. *Social Structure* (New York: Macmillan, 1949).

Murray, Henry A., and Clyde Kluckhohn. "Outline of a Conception of Personality." In Kluckhohn and Murray, eds., *Personality in Nature, Society and Culture* (1948. New York: Alfred A. Knopf, 1950): 3–32.

Myrdal, Alva, and Viola Klein. *Women's Two Roles* (London: Routledge and Kegan Paul, 1956).

National Commission on Working Women. "Caution, Your Work May Be Hazardous to Your Health." *Women at Work,* Summer 1984, pp. 3–4.

Nebraska Feminist Collective. "A Feminist Ethic for Social Science Research." *Women's Studies International Forum* 6(5) (1983): 535–543.

Nelson, Barbara J. "Women's Poverty and Women's Citizenship: Some Political Consequences of Economic Marginality." *Signs* 10(2) (1984): 209–231.

Nesselroade, J. R., and P. B. Baltes. *Adolescent Personality Development and Historical Change: 1970–1972.* Monographs of the Society for Research in Child Development no. 39 (1, ser. no. 154, 1974).

Neugarten, Bernice. "Adaptation and Life-Cycle." *Counseling Psychologist* 6(1) (1976): 16–20.

———. "Time, Age and the Life-Cycle." *American Journal of Psychiatry* 136(7) (1979): 887–894.

Neugarten, Bernice, and David L. Gutman. "Age, Sex Roles, and Personality in Middle Age: A Thematic Apperception Study." In Neugarten, ed., *Middle Age and Aging* (Chicago: University of Chicago Press, 1968): 58–71.

Nicholson, John. *Men and Women: How Different Are They?* (Oxford: Oxford University Press, 1984).

Nilsen, Alleen Pace. "The Correlation between Gender and Other Semantic Features in American English." Paper presented at the Annual Meeting of the Linguistic Society of America, San Diego, December 1973.

———. *Sexism and Language* (Urbana, Ill.: National Council of Teachers of English, 1977).

Nilson, Linda Burzotta. "The Social Standing of a Married Woman." *Social Problems* 23 (1976): 582–591.

Nock, Steven L., and Peter H. Rossi. "Ascription versus Achievement in the Attribution of Family Social Status." *American Journal of Sociology* 84 (1978): 565–590.

Nowotny, Helga. "Women in Public Life in Austria." In Epstein and Coser, eds., *Access to Power* (London: George Allen and Unwin, 1981): 146–156.

Oakley, Ann. *Sex, Gender and Society* (London: Temple Smith, 1972).

———. *The Sociology of Housework* (New York: Pantheon, 1974a).

———. *Women's Work: The Housewife Past and Present* (New York: Pantheon, 1974b).

Oboler, Regina S. *Women, Power and Economic Change: The Nandi of Kenya* (Palo Alto, Calif.: Stanford University Press, 1985).

O'Farrell, Brigid. "Women in Blue Collar Occupations: Traditional and Non-Traditional." In Stromberg and Harkess, eds., *Women Working: Theories and Facts in Perspective* (Palo Alto, Calif.: Mayfield, 1978).

O'Farrell, Brigid, and Sharon L. Harlan. "Job Integration Strategies: Today's Programs and Tomorrow's Needs." In Barbara F. Reskin, ed., *Sex Segregation in the Workplace: Trends, Explanations, Remedies* (Washington, D.C.: National Academy Press, 1984): 267–291.

Okin, Susan Moller. *Women in Western Political Thought* (Princeton: Princeton University Press, 1979).

Oppenheimer, Valerie Kincaid. "The Sex-Labeling of Jobs." *Industrial Relations* 7 (1968): 219–234.

———. *The Female Labor Force in the United States: Demographic and Economic Factors Governing Its Growth and Changing Composition.* Population Monograph Series no. 5 (Westport, Conn.: Greenwood Press, 1970).

———. "The Sociology of Women's Economic Role in the Family." *American Sociological Review* 42 (June 1977): 387–406.

Orden, S. R., and N. N. Bradburn. "Working Wives and Marriage Happiness." *American Journal of Sociology* 78 (January 1969): 853–872.

Ortner, Sherry B. "Is Female to Male as Nature Is to Culture?" In Rosaldo and Lamphere, eds., *Woman, Culture and Society* (Stanford, Calif.: Stanford University Press, 1974): 67–88.

Orum, Anthony, Roberta S. Cohen, Sheri Grasmuck, and Amy W. Orum. "The Problem of Being a Minority: Sex, Socialization and Politics." In Githens and Prestage, eds., *A Portrait of Marginality* (New York: David McKay, 1977): 17–37.

Parlee, Mary Brown. "The Premenstrual Syndrome." *Psychological Bulletin* 80(6) (1973): 454–465.

———. "Changes in Moods and Activation Levels during the Menstrual Cycle in Experimentally Naive Subjects." *Psychology of Women Quarterly* 7(2) (1982): 119–131.

Parsons, Talcott. "The Social Structure of the Family." In Anshen, ed., *The Family: Its Function and Destiny* (New York: Harper & Row, 1949): 173–201.

———. *The Social System* (Glencoe, Ill.: Free Press, 1951).

———. "The Kinship System of the Contemporary United States." In Parsons, ed., *Essays in Sociological Theory,* rev. ed. (1943. Glencoe, Ill.: Free Press, 1954): 177–196.

———. *Social Structure and Personality* (New York: Free Press, 1965).

———. "Some Reflections on the Place of Force in the Social Process." In Parsons, ed., *Sociological Theory and Modern Society* (New York: Free Press, 1967): 264–296.

Parsons, Talcott, and Robert Bales, eds. *Family, Socialization and Inter-action Process* (Glencoe, Ill.: Free Press, 1955).

Persky, Harold. "Reproductive Hormones, Moods and the Menstrual Cycle." In Friedman, Richart, and Vande Wiele, eds., *Sex Differences in Behavior* (New York: John Wiley, 1974): 455–466.

Person, Ethel Spector. "Sexuality as the Mainstay of Identity: Psychoanalytic Perspectives." *Signs* 5(4) (1980): 605–630.

Pettigrew, Thomas. *A Profile of the Negro American* (Princeton: D. Van Nostrand, 1964).

Philliber, William H., and Dana V. Hiller. "The Implication of a Wife's Occupational Attainment for Husband's Class Identification." *Sociological Quarterly* 19(3) (1978): 450–458.

Pleck, Joseph H. "The Psychology of Sex Roles: Traditional and New Views." In Cater and Scott, eds., *Women and Men: Changing Roles, Relationships and Perceptions* (New York: Aspen Institute for Humanistic Studies, 1976).

———. *The Myth of Masculinity* (Cambridge: MIT Press, 1981).

Pleck, Joseph H., and Jack Sawyer, eds. *Men and Masculinity* (New York: Prentice-Hall, 1974).

Poewe, Karla O. "Universal Male Dominance: An Ethnological Illusion." *Dialectical Anthropology* 5 (1980): 111–125.

Polachek, Solomon. "Occupational Segregation: An Alternative Hypothesis." *Journal of Contemporary Business* 5 (Winter 1976): 1–12.

———. "Sex Differences in Education: An Analysis of the Determinants of College Major." *Industrial and Labor Relations Review* 31 (1978): 498–508.

———. "Occupational Segregation among Women: Theory, Evidence and a Prognosis." In Lloyd, Andrews, and Gilroy, eds., *Women in the Labor Market* (New York: Columbia University Press, 1979).

———. "Occupational Self-Selection: A Human Capital Approach to Sex Differences in Occupational Structure." *Review of Economics and Statistics* 63(1) (February 1981a): 60–69.

———. "A Supply Side Approach to Occupational Segregation." Paper presented at the Annual Meeting of the American Sociological Association, Toronto, August 1981b.

Pollitt, Katha. "Hers." *New York Times,* December 12, 1985, p. C2.

Pomeroy, Sarah B. *Goddesses, Whores, Wives and Slaves: Women in Classical Antiquity* (New York: Schocken Books, 1975).

————. *Women in Hellenistic Egypt from Alexander to Cleopatra* (New York: Schocken Books, 1984).

Popper, Karl. *The Logic of Scientific Discovery* (London: Hutchinson, 1959). Originally published as *Logik der Forschung* (Vienna 1935).

Power, Eileen. *Medieval Women* (New York: Cambridge University Press, 1975).

Prentice-Hall. *Prentice-Hall Author's Guide* (Englewood Cliffs, N.J.: Prentice-Hall, 1975).

Prewitt, Kenneth. *The Recruitment of Political Leaders* (Indianapolis: Bobbs-Merrill, 1970).

Putnam, Robert D. *The Comparative Study of Political Elites* (Englewood Cliffs, N.J.: Prentice-Hall, 1976).

Pyeritz, R., H. Schrier, C. Madovsky, L. Miller, and J. Beckwith. "The XYY Male: The Making of a Myth." In Ann Arbor Science for the People Editorial Collective, *Biology as a Social Weapon* (Minneapolis, Minn.: Burgess, 1977): 86–100.

Ramey, E. R. "Sex Hormones and Executive Ability." *Annals of the New York Academy of Science* 308 (1973): 237–245.

Randall, V., and J. Short. "Women in Toxic Environments." *Social Problems* 30(4) (1983): 410–424.

Rapoport, Rhona, Robert Rapoport, and Ziona Streilitz. *Fathers, Mothers and Society* (New York: Basic Books, 1977).

Rapp, Rayna. "Family and Class in Contemporary America: Notes toward an Understanding of Ideology." *Science and Society* 42 (Fall 1978): 278–300. Reprinted in Thorne and Henley, eds., *Rethinking the Family: Some Feminist Questions* (New York: Longman, 1982): 168–187.

Reiter, Rayna, ed. *Toward an Anthropology of Women* (New York: Monthly Review Press, 1975).

Rensberger, Boyce. "What Made Humans Human?" *New York Times Magazine*, April 8, 1984, pp. 80–95.

Reskin, Barbara F. "Sex Differentiation and the Social Organization of Science." In Gaston, ed., *Sociology of Science* (San Francisco: Jossey-Bass, 1978): 6–37.

Reskin, Barbara F., ed. *Sex Segregation in the Workplace: Trends, Explanations and Remedies* (Washington, D.C.: National Academy Press, 1984).

Reskin, Barbara F., and Heidi Hartmann. *Women's Work, Men's Work: Sex Segregation in the Job* (Washington, D.C.: National Academy Press, 1986).

Rhode, Deborah L. "Equal Rights in Retrospect." *Law and Inequality: A Journal of Theory and Practice* 1 (June 1983): 1–72.

Riesman, David. *The Lonely Crowd: A Study of the Changing American Character*. Studies in National Policy Series no. 3 (New Haven: Yale University Press, 1950).

Riger, Stephanie, and Margaret T. Gordon. "The Fear of Rape: A Study in Social Control." *Journal of Social Issues* 37(4) (1981): 71–92.

Riley, Matilda W. "Social Gerontology and the Age Stratification of Society." *Gerontologist* 11 (1971): 79–87.

Riley, Matilda W., and Ronald P. Abeles, eds. *Aging from Birth to Death: Sociotemporal Perspectives*, vol. 2 (Boulder, Colo.: Westview Press, 1982).

Riley, Matilda W., Marilyn Johnson, and Anne Foner, in association with Mary E.

Moore, Beth Hess, and Barbara K. Roth, eds. *A Sociology of Age Stratification*, vol. 3 of *Aging and Society* (New York: Russell Sage Foundation, 1972).

Ripley, Suzanne. "Infanticide in Langurs and Man: Adaptive Advantages or Social Pathology." In M. N. Cohen, R. S. Malpass, and H. G. Klein, eds., *Biosocial Mechanisms of Population Regulation* (New Haven: Yale University Press, 1980): 349–390.

Ritter, K. V., and L. L. Hargens. "Occupational Positions and Class Identifications: A Test of the Asymmetry Hypothesis." *American Journal of Sociology* 80 (1975): 934–948.

Roos, Patricia. "Marriage and Women's Occupational Attainment in Cross-Cultural Perspective." *American Sociological Review* 48 (December 1983): 852–864.

Rosaldo, Michelle Z. "Women, Culture and Society: A Theoretical Overview." In Rosaldo and Lamphere, eds., *Woman, Culture and Society* (Stanford, Calif.: Stanford University Press, 1974): 17–42.

———. "The Use and Abuse of Anthropology: Reflections on Feminism and Cross-Cultural Understanding." *Signs* 5(3) (Spring 1980): 389–417.

Rosaldo, Michelle Z., and Louise Lamphere. *Woman, Culture and Society* (Stanford, Calif.: Stanford University Press, 1974).

Rose, Robert, Thomas Gordon, and Irwin Bernstein. "Plasma Testosterone Levels in the Male Rhesus Monkeys: Influences of Sexual and Social Stimuli." *Science* 178 (1972): 634–645.

Rosenberg, Rosalind. *Beyond Separate Spheres: Intellectual Roots of Feminism* (New Haven: Yale University Press, 1982).

Rosenfeld, Rachel A. "Women's Intergenerational Occupational Mobility." *American Sociological Review* 43(1) (1978): 36–46.

Rosenkrantz, P. S., S. R. Vogel, H. Bee, I. K. Broverman, and D. M. Broverman. "Sex-Role Stereotypes and Self-Concepts in College Students." *Journal of Consulting and Clinical Psychology* 32 (1968): 287–295.

Rossi, Alice. "Equally between the Sexes: An Immodest Proposal." *Daedalus* 93(2) (Spring 1964): 607–652.

———. "Barriers to the Career Choice of Engineering, Medicine, or Science among American Women." In Jacquelyn A. Mattfield and Carol G. Van Allen, eds., *Women and the Scientific Professions* (Cambridge: MIT Press, 1965).

———. "Women in Science—Why So Few?" In C. Safilios-Rothschild, ed., *Toward a Sociology of Women* (Lexington, Mass.: Xerox College Publishers, 1972): 141–153.

———. *The Feminist Papers: From Adams to Beauvoir* (New York: Columbia University Press, 1973).

———. "The Biosocial Basis of Parenting." *Daedalus* 106 (1977): 1–31.

———. "Life-Span Theories and Women's Lives." *Signs* 6(1) (1980): 4–32.

———. *Feminists in Politics: A Panel Analysis of the First National Women's Conference* (New York: Academic Press, 1982).

———. "Gender and Parenthood." *American Sociological Review* 49 (February 1984): 1–19. Presidential address presented at the Annual Meeting of the American Sociological Association, Detroit, Michigan, 1983.

Rossi, Alice, ed. *Essays on Sex Equality by John Stuart Mill and Harriet Taylor Mill* (Chicago: University of Chicago Press, 1970).

Rossi, Peter H., William A. Sampson, Christine E. Bose, Guillermina Jasso, and Jeff Passel. "Measuring Household Social Standing." *Social Science Research* 3(3) (1974): 169–190.

Rossiter, Margaret W. "Women Scientists in America before 1920." *American Scientist* 62 (1974): 312–323.

Rousseau, Jean-Jacques. *Émile et Sophie,* vol. 4 of *Oeuvres complètes.* Ed. B. Gagnebin and M. Raymond (Paris: Gallimard 1969).

Rubin, Gayle. "The Traffic in Women: Notes on the 'Political Economy' of Sex." In Reiter, ed., *Toward an Anthropology of Women* (New York: Monthly Review Press, 1975): 157–210.

Ruble, Diane N. "Premenstrual Symptoms: A Reinterpretation." *Science* 197 (1977): 291–292.

Rule, Wilma. "Why Women Don't Run: The Critical Contextual Factors in Women's Legislative Recruitment." *Western Political Quarterly* 34 (1981): 60–77.

Rupp, Leila J. *Mobilizing Women for War: German and American Propaganda, 1939– 1945* (Princeton: Princeton University Press, 1978).

Russell, Diana. *Rape in Marriage* (New York: Macmillan, 1982).

Russo, Nancy. *The Motherhood Mandate: Special Issue of Psychology of Women Quarterly* (New York: Human Sciences Press, 1978).

El Saadawi, Nawal. *The Hidden Face of Eve: Women in the Arab World* (Boston: Beacon Press, 1982).

Sachs, Albie, and Joan Hoff Wilson. *Sexism and the Law: Male Beliefs and Legal Bias In Britain and the United States* (New York: Free Press, 1978).

Sacks, Harvey, Emanuel Schegloff, and Gail Jefferson. "A Simplest Systematics for the Organization of Turn-Taking for Conversation." *Language* 50 (1974): 696– 735.

Sacks, Michael Paul. *Women's Work in Soviet Russia: Continuity in the Midst of Change* (New York: Praeger, 1976).

Safilios-Rothschild, Constantina. "Toward a Cross-Cultural Conceptualization of Modernity." *Journal of Comparative Family Studies* 1(1) (Fall 1970): 17– 25.

———. "Dual Linkages between the Occupational and Family Systems: A Macrosociological Analysis." *Signs* 1 (1976): 51–60.

Sambol, Daniel. Letter to the Editor. *New York Times,* September 2, 1985, p. 20.

Sampson, William A., and Peter H. Rossi. "Race and Family Standing." *American Sociological Review* 40(2) (1975): 201–214.

Sanday, Peggy R. "Female Status in the Public Domain." In Rosaldo and Lamphere, eds., *Woman, Culture and Society* (Stanford, Calif.: Stanford University Press, 1974): 189–207.

———. *Female Power and Male Dominance: On the Origins of Sexual Inequality* (New York: Cambridge University Press, 1981).

Sapiro, Virginia. *The Political Integration of Women: Roles, Socialization and Politics* (Urbana: University of Illinois Press, 1983).

Sapiro, Virginia, and Barbara Farah. "New Pride and Old Prejudice: Political Ambitions and Role Orientations among Female Partisan Elites." *Women in Politics* 1 (Spring 1980): 13–36.

Sattel, Jack W. "The Inexpressive Male: Tragedy or Sexual Politics?" In Kahn-hut,

Daniels, and Colvard, eds., *Women and Work* (New York: Oxford University Press, 1982): 160–169.

Sayers, Janet. *Biological Politics: Feminist and Anti-Feminist Perspectives* (New York: Tavistock, 1982).

Sayre, A. *Rosalind Franklin and DNA* (New York: W. W. Norton, 1975).

Scanzoni, John. "Sexual Processes and Power in Families." In W. R. Burr, R. Hill, F. I. Nye, and I. L. Reiss, eds., *Contemporary Theories about the Family,* vol. 1 (New York: Free Press, 1979).

Schlegel, Alice. "Women Anthropologists Looking at Women." *Reviews in Anthropology* 1(6) (November-December 1974): 553–560.

Schlegel, Alice, ed. *Sexual Stratification: A Cross-Cultural View* (New York: Columbia University Press, 1977).

Schlesinger, James. *Ambition in Politics* (Chicago: Rand McNally, 1966).

Schuck, Victoria, and Judy Corder Tully, eds. "A Symposium: Masculine Blinders in the Social Sciences." *Social Science Quarterly* 55(3) (December 1974); whole issue.

Schulz, Muriel R. "The Semantic Derogation of Women." In Thorne and Henley, eds., *Language and Sex: Difference and Dominance* (Rowley, Mass.: Newbury House, 1975): 64–75.

Schur, Edwin M. *Labeling Women Deviant: Gender Based Stigma and Social Control* (New York: Random House, 1984).

Schwartz, Barry. *Vertical Classification: A Study in Structuralism and the Sociology of Knowledge* (Chicago: University of Chicago, 1981).

Scott, Hilda. *Does Socialism Liberate Women? Experiences from Eastern Europe.* (Boston: Beacon Press, 1974). Second ed. (1976) retitled *Women and Socialism.*

Scully, D. *Men Who Control Women's Health: The Miseducation of Obstetrician-Gynecologists* (Boston: Houghton Mifflin, 1980).

"Sexism Is Alive." *Time,* December 31, 1984, p. 14.

Shanley, Mary, and Victoria Schuck. "In Search of Political Woman." *Social Science Quarterly* 55(3) (December 1974): 632–644.

Shaver, Phillip. "Questions concerning Fear of Success and Its Conceptual Relatives." *Sex Roles* 2(3) (September 1976): 305–320.

Sheehy, Gail. *Passages: Predictable Crises of Adult Life* (New York: Bantam Books, 1977).

Shepelak, Norma. "Does 'He' Mean 'She' Too? The Case of the Generic Anomaly." Manuscript, 1978.

Sherif, Carolyn Wood. "Women's Role in the Human Relations of a Changing World." In C. M. Class, ed., *The Role of the Educated Woman* (Houston: Rice University Press, 1964): 29–41.

———. "Bias in Psychology." In Sherman and Beck, eds., *The Prism of Sex* (Madison: University of Wisconsin Press, 1979): 93–133.

Sherman, Julia A. *On the Psychology of Women: A Survey of Empirical Studies* (Springfield, Ill.: Charles C. Thomas, 1971).

———. Review of *Psychology of Sex Differences,* by Eleanor E. Maccoby and Carol N. Jacklin. *Sex Roles* 1(3) (1975): 297–301.

Sherman, Julia A., and Evelyn T. Beck, eds. *The Prism of Sex: Essays in the Sociology of Knowledge* (Madison: University of Wisconsin Press, 1979).

Shields, Stephanie A. "Functionalism, Darwinism and the Psychology of Women." *American Psychologist* 30 (1975): 739–754.

Shorter, Edward. *The Making of the Modern Family* (New York: Basic Books, 1975).

———. "On Writing the History of Rape." *Signs* 3(2) (Winter 1977): 471–482.

Shott, Susan. "Emotional and Social Life: A Symbolic Interactionalist Analysis." *American Journal of Sociology* 84 (May 1979): 1317–1334.

Sieber, Sam. "Toward a Theory of Role Accumulation." *American Sociological Review* 39 (August 1974): 567–578.

Sills, David L. *The Volunteers: Means and Ends in a National Organization* (Glencoe, Ill.: Free Press, 1957).

Silveira, Jeanette. "Generic Masculine Words and Thinking." *Women's Studies International Quarterly* 3(2–3) (1980): 165–178.

Simeral, Margaret H. "Women and the Reserve Army of Labor." *Insurgent Sociology* 8(2–3) (1978): 164–179.

Simmel, Georg. "Conflict." In *Conflict and the Web of Group Affiliation*, trans. Kurt H. Wolff (Glencoe, Ill.: Free Press, 1955): 11–123.

Simmons, Adele, Ann Freedman, Margaret Dunkle, and Francine Blau. *Exploitation from 9 to 5: Report of the 20th Century Fund Task Force on Women and Employment* (Lexington, Mass.: Lexington Books, 1975).

Simon, Rita J., Shirley Merritt Clark, and Kathleen Galway. "The Woman Ph.D.: A Recent Profile." *Social Problems* 15 (Fall 1967): 221–236.

Singer, Jerome. "The Importance of Daydreaming." *Psychology Today* 1 (April 1968): 18–27.

Sinicle, D. "Two Anxiety Scales Correlated and Examined for Sex Differences." *Journal of Clinical Psychology* 12(4) (1956): 394–395.

Skard, Torild (with the assistance of Helga Hernes). "Progress for Women: Increased Female Representation in Political Elites in Norway." In Epstein and Coser, eds., *Access to Power* (London: George Allen and Unwin, 1981): 76–89.

Skocpol, Theda. "Political Response to Capitalist Crises: Neo-Marxist Theories of the State and the Case of the New Deal." *Politics and Society* 10(2) (1980): 155–201.

Skolnick, Arlene. "Public Images, Private Realities: The American Family in Popular Culture and Social Science." In Myerhoff and Tufte, eds., *Changing Images of the Family* (New Haven: Yale University Press, 1979): 297–318.

Slocum, W. L., and F. I. Nye. "Provider and Housekeeper Roles." In Nye, ed., *Role Structure and Analysis of the Family* (Beverly Hills: Sage, 1976): 81–99.

Small, Meredith F., ed. *Female Primates: Studies by Women Primatologists* (New York: Alan R. Liss, 1984).

Smelser, Neil. *Social Change in the Industrial Revolution.* (Chicago: University of Chicago Press, 1965).

Smith, Dorothy E. "Women's Perspective as a Radical Critique of Sociology." *Sociological Inquiry* 44(1) (1974): 7–13.

———. *Feminism and Marxism: A Place to Begin, a Way to Go.* (Vancouver: New Star Books, 1977).

———. "A Peculiar Eclipsing: Women's Exclusion from Man's Culture." *Women's Studies International Quarterly* 1(4) (1978): 281–295

———. "A Sociology for Women." In Sherman and Beck, eds., *The Prism of Sex:*

Essays in the Sociology of Knowledge (Madison: University of Wisconsin Press, 1979): 135–187.

―――. "Mothering as Work." Paper presented at the Annual Meeting of the American Sociological Association, Washington, D.C., August 28, 1985.

Smith, Ralph. *The Subtle Revolution: Women at Work* (Washington, D.C.: Urban Institute, 1979).

Snyder, M., E. D. Tanke, and E. Berscheid. "Social Perception and Interpersonal Behavior: On the Self-Fulfilling Nature of Social Stereotypes." *Journal of Personality and Social Psychology* 35 (1977): 656–666.

Sober, Elliott. *The Nature of Selection: Evolutionary Theory in Philosophical Focus* (Cambridge: MIT Press, 1984).

Sokolowska, Magdalena. "Women in Decision-Making Elites: The Case of Poland." In Epstein and Coser, eds., *Access to Power* (London: George Allen and Unwin, 1981): 90–114.

Soskin, W. F., and V. P. John. "The Study of Spontaneous Talk." In Barker, ed., *The Stream of Behavior* (New York: Appleton-Century-Crofts, 1963): 228–281.

Soule, John W., and Wilma E. McGrath. "A Comparative Study of Male-Female Political Attitudes at Citizen and Elite Levels." In Githens and Prestage, eds., *A Portrait of Marginality* (New York: David McKay, 1977): 178–195.

Spaeth, J. L. "Vertical Differentiation among Occupations." *American Sociological Review* 44 (October 1979): 746–762.

Speizer, Jeanne J. "Role Models, Mentors and Sponsors: The Elusive Concepts." *Signs* 6(4) (Summer 1981): 692–712.

Spence, Janet T., ed. *Achievement and Achievement Motives* (San Francisco: W. H. Freeman, 1983).

Spence, Janet T., and Robert L. Heimreich. *Masculinity and Femininity: Their Psychological Dimensions, Correlates and Antecedents* (Austin: University of Texas Press, 1978).

Spender, Dale, ed. *Men's Studies Modified: The Impact of Feminism on the Academic Disciplines* (Oxford: Pergamon Press, 1981).

Sperry, Roger. "Some Effects of Disconnecting the Cerebral Hemispheres." *Science* 217 (1982): 1223–1226.

Spiegel, David. "Mothering, Fathering and Mental Illness." In Thorne and Yalom, eds., *Rethinking the Family* (New York: Longman, 1982): 95–110.

Spradley, James P., and Brenda J. Mann. *The Cocktail Waitress: Woman's Work in a Man's World* (New York: John Wiley, 1974).

Springer, S. P., and G. Deutsch. *Left Brain, Right Brain* (San Francisco: Freeman, 1981).

Srole, Leo, and Anita K. Fisher, eds. *Mental Health in the Metropolis: The Midtown Manhattan Study* (New York: New York University Press, 1978).

Stacey, Judith. "The New Conservative Feminism." *Feminist Studies* 9(3) (Fall 1983): 559–583.

Stacey, Judith, and Barrie Thorne. "The Missing Feminist Revolution in Sociology." Paper presented at the Annual Meeting of the American Sociological Association, San Antonio, Texas, August 27–31, 1984. Published in *Social Problems* 32(4) (April 1985): 301–316.

Stacey, Margaret, and Marion Price. *Women, Power and Politics* (London: Tavistock, 1981).

Stack, Carol B. *All Our Kin* (New York: Harper & Row, 1974).

———. "The Culture of Gender: Women and Men of Color." *Signs* 11(2) (Winter 1986): 321–324.

Stanley, Liz, and Sue Wise. *Breaking Out: Feminist Consciousness and Feminist Research* (New York: Routledge and Kegan Paul, 1983).

Steinberg-Ratner, Ronnie. "Labor Market Inequality and Equal Opportunity Policy for Women: A Cross-National Comparison." Manuscript, 1979.

———. "Research: Wage Discrimination and Pay Equity." In *Preliminary Memorandum on Pay Equity: Achieving Equal Pay for Work of Comparable Value* (Washington, D.C.: Conference on Alternative State and Local Policies, April 1980).

Steinmetz, Suzanne K. "The Sexual Context of Social Research." *American Sociologist* 9 (August 1974): 111–116.

Steinmetz, S., and M. Strauss, eds. *Violence in the Family* (New York: Dodd-Mead, 1974).

Stevens, Robert. "Law Schools and Law Students." *Virginia Law Review* 59(4) (April 1973): 551–707.

Stevenson, Mary H. "Internal Labor Markets and the Employment of Women in Complex Organizations." Working paper, Center for Research on Women, Wellesley College, 1977.

Steward, Ulian H. "Causal Factors and Processes in the Evolution of Pre-farming Societies." In Lee and DeVore, eds., *Man the Hunter* (Chicago: Aldine, 1968): 321–334.

Stewart, Abigail, and Patricia Salt, "Changing Sex Roles: College Graduates of the 1960s and 1970s." In Matina Horner, Carol C. Nadelson, and Malkah T. Notman, eds., *The Challenge of Change: Perspectives on Family, Work and Education* (New York: Plenum Press, 1983).

Stiehm, Judith H. *Bring Me Men and Women: Mandated Change at the United States Air Force Academy* (Berkeley: University of California Press, 1981).

———. "The Unit of Political Analysis: Our Aristotelian Hangup." In Harding and Hintikka, eds., *Discovering Reality* (Amsterdam: Reidel, 1983): 31–44.

Stier, Deborah S., and Judith A. Hall. "Gender Differences in Touch: An Empirical and Theoretical Review." *Journal of Personality and Social Psychology* 47(2) (1984): 440–459.

Stimpson, Catherine H. "Contemporary Women's Studies." Paper prepared for the Ford Foundation, September 1983.

Stinchcombe, Arthur L. "Evaluating Changes in Occupational Distribution and Occupational System." *American Behavioral Scientist* 18 (January 1975): 401–432.

Stoll, Clarice Stasz. *Female and Male* (Dubuque, Iowa: William C. Brown, 1974).

Stoller, Eleanor Palo. "Parental Caregiving by Adult Children." *Journal of Marriage and the Family* 45(4) (November 1983): 851–858.

Stone, Lawrence. *The Family, Sex and Marriage: In England 1500–1800*. (New York: Harper, 1979).

Stouffer, Samuel. *Communism, Conformity and Civil Liberties* (New York: Doubleday, 1955).

Strasser, Susan M. "Mistress and Maid, Employer and Employee: Domestic Service Reform in the United States, 1897–1920." *Marxist Perspectives* 1(4) (Winter 1978): 52–67.

———. *Never Done: A History of American Housework* (New York: Pantheon, 1982).

Strauss, Anselm L. *The Context of Social Mobility* (Chicago: Aldine, 1971).

Strober, Myra. "The M.B.A.: Same Passport to Success for Women and Men?" In Wallace, ed., *Women in the Workplace* (Boston: Auburn House, 1982): 25–44.

———. "Toward a General Theory of Occupational Sex Segregation: The Case of Public School Teaching." In B. Reskin, ed., *Sex Segregation in the Workplace: Trends, Explanations, Remedies* (Washington, D.C.: National Academy Press, 1984).

Strober, Myra H., and David Tyack. "Why Do Women Teach and Men Manage? A Report on Research on Schools." *Signs* 5(3) (Spring 1980): 494–503.

Strodtbeck, F. L., and R. D. Mann. "Sex Role Differentiation in Jury Deliberations." *Sociometry* 19 (1956): 3–11.

Sussman, Marvin. "The Isolated Nuclear Family: Fact or Fiction?" *Social Problems* 6 (Spring 1959): 333–340.

Suter, Barbara A. "Masculinity-Femininity in Creative Women" (Ph.D. diss., Fordham University, 1971).

Suter, Larry E., and Herman P. Miller. "Income Differences between Men and Career Women." *American Journal of Sociology* 78(4) (1973): 200–212.

Sutton, Connie. "Tired of Arguing about Biological Inferiority." *Ms.,* November 1982, pp. 41–47.

Szinovacz, M. "Role Allocation, Family Structure and Female Employment." *Journal of Marriage and the Family* 39 (1977): 781–792.

Tanner, Nancy. *On Becoming Human* (New York: Cambridge University Press, 1981).

Tanner, Nancy, and Adrienne Zihlman. "Women in Evolution, Part I: Innovation and Selection in Human Origins." *Signs* 1(3, pt. 1) (1976): 585–608.

Tavris, Carol, and Carole Wade. *The Longest War: Sex Differences in Perspective,* 2d ed. (1977. New York: Harcourt Brace Jovanovich, 1984).

Tentler, Leslie. *Wage Earning Women: Industrial Work and Family Life in the United States, 1900–1930* (New York: Oxford University Press, 1979).

Thomas, A., and S. Chess. *Temperament and Development* (New York: Brunner/Mazel, 1977).

Thomas, A., S. Chess, H. G. Birch, M. E. Hertzig, and S. Korn. *Behavioral Individuality in Early Childhood* (New York: New York University Press, 1963).

Thomas, Judith. "Parenting by the Clock: Child Care Schedules among Divorced Co-Parents." Paper presented at the Annual Meeting of the American Sociological Association, Washington, D.C., August 26, 1985.

Thompson, Richard A. "Language, the Brain, and the Question of Dichotomies." *American Anthropologist* 86(1) (March 1984): 98–102.

Thorne, Barrie. Review of *Language and Woman's Place,* by Robin Lakoff. *Signs* 1 (pt. 1) (Spring 1976): 744–745.

———. "Feminist Rethinking of the Family: An Overview." In Thorne and Yalom, eds., *Rethinking the Family: Some Feminist Questions* (New York: Longman, 1982): 1–24.

Thorne, Barrie, and Nancy Henley, eds. *Language and Sex: Difference and Dominance* (Rowley, Mass.: Newbury House, 1975): 5–42.

Thorne, Barrie, Cheris Kramerae, and Nancy Henley. "Language, Gender and Society: Opening a Second Decade of Research." In *Language, Gender and Society* (Rowley, Mass.: Newbury House, 1983): 7–24.

Thorne, Barrie, and Marilyn Yalom, eds. *Rethinking the Family: Some Feminist Questions* (New York: Longman, 1982).

Thornhill, Randy. "Rape in *Panorpa scorpionflies* and General Rape Hypothesis." *Animal Behavior* 28 (1980): 52–59.

Thornhill, Randy, and N. Thornhill. "Human Rape: An Evolutionary Analysis." *Ethology and Sociobiology* 4(3) (1983): 137–173.

Tiffany, Sharon. "Women, Power and the Anthropology of Politics: A Review." *International Journal of Women's Studies* 2(5) (September-October 1979): 430–442.

Tiger, Lionel. *Men in Groups* (New York: Vintage Books, 1969).

Tilly, Louise A. "The Family Wage Economy of a French Textile City, Roubaix, 1872–1906." *Journal of Family History* 4 (1979): 381–394.

———. "Rich and Poor in a French Textile City." Walter Prescott Webb Lecture presented at the University of Texas at Arlington, 1982.

Tinker, Irene. "Gender Equity in Development: A Policy Perspective." Paper prepared for the Workshop on Women, Households and Human Capital Development in Low-Income Countries, convened by the Rockefeller Foundation, Mount Kisco, New York, July 12–14, 1982.

———. Personal communication, 1983.

Tinker, Irene, and Michelle Bo Bramsen, eds. *Women and World Development*, vol. 1 (Washington, D.C.: Overseas Development Council, 1976).

Tobias, Sheila, and L. Anderson. "What Really Happened to Rosie the Riveter? Demobilization and the Female Labor Force 1944–47." In Kerber and Matthews, eds., *Women's America* (New York: Oxford University Press, 1982): 354–373.

Tocqueville, Alexis de. *Democracy in America*. Edited and abridged with an introduction by Andrew Hacker. (1835–40. New York: Washington Square Press, 1964).

Tolchin, Susan. "The Exclusion of Women from the Judicial Process." *Signs* 2(4) (1977): 877–887.

Toner, Robin. "Women Taking Major Roles in '88 Presidential Campaigns." *New York Times,* December 29, 1987, p. 1.

Touhey, John C. "Effects of Additional Women Professionals on Ratings of Occupational Prestige and Desirability." *Journal of Personality and Social Psychology* 29 (1974): 86–89.

Trachtenberg, Alan. *The Incorporation of America: Culture and Society in the Gilded Age* (New York: Hill and Wang, 1982).

Treiman, D. J., and K. Terrell. "Sex and the Process of Status Attainment: A Comparison of Working Men and Women." *American Sociological Review* 40(2) (1975a): 174–200.

———. "Women, Work and Wages: Trends in the Female Occupational Structure since 1940." In Land and Spilerman, eds., *Social Indicator Models* (New York: Russell Sage Foundation, 1975b): 157–200.

Tresemer, David W. *Fear of Success* (New York: Plenum, 1977).

Trivers, Robert L. "The Evolution of Reciprocal Altruism." *Quarterly Review of Biology* 46 (1971): 35–57.

———. "Parental Investment and Sexual Selection." In Campbell, ed., *Sexual Selection and the Descent of Man, 1871–1971* (Chicago: Aldine, 1972): 136–179.

———. "Parent-Offspring Conflict." *American Zoologist* 14 (1974): 249–269.

Turnbull, Colin. "Trouble in Paradise." *New Republic,* March 28, 1983, pp. 32–34.

Turner, Ralph. "Some Aspects of Women's Ambitions." *American Journal of Sociology* 70 (November 1964): 271–285.

Tyack, David. "Ways of Seeing: An Essay on the History of Compulsory Schooling." *Harvard Educational Review* 46 (August 1976): 355–389.

Tyack, David, and Myra Strober. "Jobs and Gender: A History of the Structuring of Educational Employment by Sex." In Schmuck and Charters, eds., *Educational Policy and Management: Sex Differentials* (New York: Academic Press, 1981): 131–152.

Tyree, Andrea, and Robert W. Hodge. "Editorial Foreword: Five Empirical Landmarks." *Social Forces* 56(3) (1978): 761–769.

Uesugi, T. K., and W. E. Viachke. "Strategy in a Feminine Game." *Sociometry* 26(1) (1963): 75–88.

U.S. Department of Labor, Employment Standards Administration. "Participation of Females in the Construction Trades." Prepared by the Office of Federal Contract Compliance Programs, September 4, 1981.

U.S. Department of Labor, Women's Bureau. Fact Sheet, 85-1/85-2, July 1985.

Vaillant, George E. *Adaptation to Life* (Boston: Little, Brown, 1977).

Valadez, Joseph J., and Remi Clignet. "Household Work as an Ordeal: Culture of Standards versus Standardization of Culture." *American Journal of Sociology* 89(4) (January 1984): 812–835.

Valentine, Bettylou. *Hustling and Other Hard Work: Life Styles of the Ghetto* (New York: Free Press, 1980).

Van den Berghe, Pierre. *Man in Society: A Biosocial View,* 2d ed. (1975. New York: Elsevier, 1978).

———. "Bridging the Paradigms: Biology and the Social Sciences." In Gregory, Silvers, and Sutch, eds., *Sociobiology and Human Nature* (San Francisco: Jossey-Bass, 1979): 33–52.

Vanek, Joann, Robert Johnston, and William Seltzer. "Improving Statistics on Women." *Populi* 12(2) (1985): 57–66.

Van Hightower, Nikki R. "The Recruitment of Women for Public Office." *American Politics Quarterly* 5 (July 1977): 301–314.

Van Kleeck, Mary. *Artificial Flower Makers* (New York: Russell Sage, 1913).

Vaughter, Reesa M. "Psychology." *Signs* 2(1) (Autumn 1976): 120–146.

Verba, S., and N. H. Nie. *Participation in America* (New York: Harper & Row, 1972).

Veroff, Joseph. "Contextual Determinants of Personality." *Personality and Social Psychology Bulletin* 9(3) (1983): 331–343.

Veroff, J., E. Douvan, and R. Kulka. *The Inner American* (New York: Basic Books, 1981).

Vetter, Betty M. "Women and Minority Scientists." *Science* 189(4205) (1975): 751.

Villemez, Wayne J. "Male Economic Gain from Female Subordination: A Caveat and Reanalysis." *Social Forces* 56(2) (1977): 626–636.

Waite, Linda J. "U.S. Women at Work" *Population Bulletin* 36 (May 1981): 1–44.

Walker, Lawrence. "Sex Differences in the Development of Moral Reasoning: A Critical Review." *Child Development* 55(3) (June 1984): 667–691.

Walkowitz, Judith R. "Jack the Ripper and the Myth of Male Violence." *Feminist Studies* 8(5) (Fall 1982): 543–574.

Waller, Willard. *The Family: A Dynamic Interpretation* (New York: Dryden, 1938).

Walsh, Mary Roth. *Doctors Wanted—No Women Need Apply: Sexual Barriers in the Medical Profession* (New Haven: Yale University Press, 1977).

Walshok, Mary L. *Blue Collar Women* (New York: Doubleday, 1981; Anchor Books, 1983).

Walum, Laurel Richardson. *The Dynamics of Sex and Gender: A Sociological Perspective* (Chicago: Rand McNally, 1977).

Ware, Susan. "Introduction." In *Research Collections in Women's Studies: Papers of the League of Women Voters, 1918–1974* (Frederick, Md.: University Publications of America, 1985).

Washburn, S. L. "Animal Behavior and Social Anthropology." In Gregory, Silvers, and Sutch, eds., *Sociobiology and Human Behavior* (San Francisco: Jossey-Bass, 1979): 53–74.

Washburn, Sherwood L., and Irven DeVore. "Social Behavior of Baboons and Early Man." In Washburn, ed., *Social Life of Early Man*. Viking Fund Publications in Anthropology no. 31 (New York: Wenner-Gren Foundation for Anthropological Research, 1961): 91–105.

Washburn, Sherwood L., and C. S. Lancaster. "The Evolution of Hunting." In R. B. Lee and I. DeVore, eds., *Man the Hunter* (Chicago: Aldine, 1968): 293–303.

Watson, J. D. *The Double Helix* (New York: Atheneum, 1968).

Watson, W. B., and E. A. T. Barth. "Questionable Assumptions in the Theory of Social Stratification." *Pacific Sociological Review* 7 (Spring 1964): 10–16.

Weber, Max. "Religious Ethics and the World: Sexuality and Art." In *Economy and Society*, trans. Guenther Roth and Claus Wittich (1922. Glencoe, Ill.: Free Press, 1968).

Weisberg, D. Kelly. "Barred from the Bar: Women and Legal Education in the United States, 1870–1890." *Journal of Legal Education* 28(4) (1977): 485–507.

———. "Women in Law School Teaching: Problems and Progress." *Journal of Legal Education* 30 (1979): 226–248.

Weisenhaus, Doreen. "Still a Long Way To Go for Women, Minorities." *National Law Journal* 10 (22) (Feb. 8, 1988): 1, 48.

Weisstein, Naomi. "Psychology Constructs the Female, or the Fantasy Life of the Male Psychologist." In Garskof, ed., *Roles Women Play: Readings toward Women's Liberation* (Belmont, N.Y.: Wadsworth, 1971): 68–83.

———. "Tired of Arguing about Biological Inferiority?" *Ms.*, November 1982, pp. 41–47.

Wertheimer, Barbara. *We Were There: The Story of Working Women in America* (New York: Pantheon, 1977).

Westley, Laurie A. *A Territorial Issue: A Study of Women in the Construction Trades* (Washington, D.C.: Wider Opportunities for Women, 1982).

White, Harrison. *Chains of Opportunity: System Models of Mobility in Organizations* (Cambridge: Harvard University Press, 1970).

Whorf, Benjamin, and Edward Sapir. *Language, Thought and Reality*. Ed. John B. Carroll (1927–41. Cambridge: MIT Press, 1956).

Whyte, William H. *The Organization Man* (Garden City, N.Y.: Doubleday, 1957).

Will, Jerrie, Patricia Self, and Nancy Datan. "Maternal Behavior and Sex of Infant." Paper presented at the Annual Meeting of the American Psychological Association, New Orleans, 1974.

Williams, Brenda. "Second Co-anchor Charges Bias." *New York Times,* September 21, 1984, pp. 23, C30.

Williams, Gregory. "Trends in Occupational Differentiation by Sex." *Sociology of Work and Occupations* 3 (February 1976): 38–62.

Williams, J. Allen, and Robert Stockton. "Black Family Structure and Functions: An Empirical Examination of Some Suggestions Made by Billingsley." *Journal of Marriage and the Family* 35(1) (February 1973): 39–51.

Williams, Wendy. "Firing the Woman to Protect the Fetus: The Reconciliation of Fetal Protection with Employment Opportunity Goals under Title VII." *Georgetown Law Journal* 69 (1981): 641–704.

Williams, Wendy, and Judith T. Lichtman. "Closing the Law's Gender Gap." *Nation,* September 29, 1984, pp. 280–285.

Wilson, Edward O. *Sociobiology: The New Synthesis* (Cambridge: Belknap Press of Harvard University Press, 1975a).

———. "Human Decency Is Animal." *New York Times Magazine,* October 12, 1975b, pp. 38–50.

———. *On Human Nature* (Cambridge: Harvard University Press, 1978).

Wilson, James Q. *Amateur Democrat* (Chicago: University of Chicago Press, 1966).

Winterbottom, Mirian R. "The Relation of Childhood Training in Independence to Achievement Motivation." (Ph.D. diss., University of Michigan, 1953).

Wolf, Wendy, and Neil Fligstein. "Sexual Stratification: Differences in Power in the Work Setting." *Social Forces* 58 (1979): 94–107.

Wolf, Wendy, and Rachel Rosenfeld. "Sex Structure of Occupations and Job Mobility." *Social Forces* 56(3) (1978): 823–844.

Wood, Marion M. "The Influence of Sex and Knowledge of Communication Effectiveness on Spontaneous Speech." *Word* 22 (1966): 112–137.

Wooley, Helen Bradford Thompson. *The Mental Traits of Sex: An Experimental Investigation of the Normal Mind in Men and Women* (Chicago: University of Chicago Press, 1903).

———. "A Review of Recent Literature on the Psychology of Sex." *Pychological Bulletin* 7 (October 1910).

Wright, Erik Olin. *Class, Crisis and the State* (London: New Left Books, 1978).

Wyatt, Michael K. "Avoiding Sexual Abuse Claims after *Meritor.*" *National Law Journal* 9(7) (October 27, 1986): 15, 19, 21.

Wylie, Phillip. *Generation of Vipers* (New York: Farrar, Rinehart, 1942).

Yengoyan, Aram A. Review of *In the Active Voice,* by Mary Douglas. In *Knowledge: Creation, Diffusion, Utilization* 6(2) (December 1984): 187–192.

Young, M., and P. Wilmott. *Family and Kinship in East London* (London: Routledge and Kegan Paul, 1957).

Zanna, M. P., and S. J. Pack. "On the Self-fulfilling Nature of Apparent Sex Differences in Behavior." *Journal of Experimental Social Psychology* 11 (1975): 583–591.

Zelditch, Morris. "Role Differentiation in the Nuclear Family: A Comparative Story."

In Parsons and Bales, eds., *Family, Socialization and Inter-action Process* (Glencoe, Ill.: Free Press, 1955): 307–349.

Zellner, Harriet. "The Determinants of Occupational Segregation." In Cynthia Lloyd, ed., *Sex Discrimination and the Division of Labor* (New York: Columbia University Press, 1975): 125–145.

Zihlman, Adrienne L. "Women as Shapers of Human Adaptation." In Dahlberg, ed., *Woman the Gatherer* (New Haven: Yale University Press, 1981): 75–120.

Zimmerman, D. H., and C. West. "Sex Roles, Interpretations and Silences in Conversation." In Thorne and Henley, eds., *Language and Sex* (Rowley, Mass.: Newbury House, 1975): 105–129.

Zuckerman, Harriet. *The Scientific Elite: Nobel Laureates in the United States* (New York: Free Press, 1977).

Zuckerman, Harriet, and Jonathan Cole. "Women in American Science." *Minerva* 13(1) (January 1975): 82–102.

Zuckerman, Harriet, and Robert K. Merton. "Age, Aging and Age Structure in Science." In M. W. Riley, M. Johnson, and A. Foner, eds., *A Sociology of Age Stratification*, vol. 3 of *Aging and Society* (New York: Russell Sage Foundation, 1972): 292–356.

Zuckerman, M. "Attribution of Success and Failure Revisited, or: The Motivational Bias Is Alive and Well in Attribution Theory." *Journal of Personality* 47 (1979): 245–287.

Index